'In a world of increased conflict, mass atrocities and political turmoil – and at a time when many academic writers have retreated into despair – Ramesh Thakur always writes with impressive passion, power and clarity of vision. His words are much-needed intellectual ammunition for those of us who are trying to prevent mass atrocities and build a better world at the United Nations and beyond.'

Simon Adams, Executive Director, Global Centre for the Responsibility to Protect, New York

'Starting with his service as a commissioner and a principal author of the original ICISS report, and continuing afterwards as an analyst and advocate, no one has been more insightful than Ramesh Thakur about R2P's normative and operational impacts.'

Thomas G. Weiss, Presidential Professor of Political Science and Director Emeritus, Ralph Bunche Institute for International Studies, The Graduate Center, City University of New York

'Over two decades, Ramesh Thakur has made an immense contribution to the development, implementation, and analysis of the Responsibility to Protect principle. In this volume, he brings his keen analytical eye to the most important questions surrounding the global campaign to prevent and end atrocity crimes. Combining the unique insights of one of the principle's key progenitors with wisdom derived from years of practical experience and painstaking research, this volume sheds important light on the campaign to end atrocities thus far and the lessons that must be learned for the future.'

Alex J. Bellamy, The University of Queensland, Australia

Reviewing the Responsibility to Protect

This volume is a collection of some of the key essays by Ramesh Thakur on the origins, implementation and future prospects of the Responsibility to Protect (R2P) norm.

The book offers a comprehensive yet accessible review of the origins, evolution, advances and shortcomings of the R2P principle. A literature review is followed by an overview of the background, meaning and development of R2P. With a focus on the International Commission on Intervention and State Sovereignty (ICISS), Part I analyses the features of, and explains the factors that make for success and failure of commission diplomacy. Part II discusses the controversies surrounding efforts to implement R2P, including the role and importance of emerging powers. Part III describes the remaining protection gaps and explains why R2P will remain relevant because it is essentially demand driven. Finally, the book concludes with a look back at the origins of R2P and looks ahead to possible future directions.

This book will be essential for students of the Responsibility to Protect, and of much interest to students of global governance, human rights, international law and international relations.

Ramesh Thakur is Emeritus Professor at the Australian National University, Canberra. He is a former United Nations Assistant Secretary-General and was a Responsibility to Protect Commissioner. He is the author of numerous books and articles on the UN, R2P and global governance.

Global Politics and the Responsibility to Protect

Series Editors: Alex J. Bellamy
Griffith University
Sara E. Davies
Griffith University
and
Monica Serrano
The City University of New York.

The aim of this book series is to gather the best new thinking about the Responsibility to Protect into a core set of volumes that provides a definitive account of the principle, its implementation and its role in crises, that reflects a plurality of views and regional perspectives.

Moral Responsibility, Statecraft, and Humanitarian Intervention
The US Response to Rwanda, Darfur, and Libya
Cathinka Vik

Reassessing the Responsibility to Protect
Conceptual and Operational Challenges
Edited by Brett R. O'Bannon

The Responsibility to Protect and the International Criminal Court
Protection and Prosecution in Kenya
Serena K. Sharma

Evaluating the Responsibility to Protect
Mass Atrocity Prevention as a Consolidating Norm in International Society
Noële Crossley

International Organizations and the Rise of ISIL
Global Responses to Human Security Threats
Edited by Daniel Silander, Don Wallace and John Janzekovic

Reviewing the Responsibility to Protect
Origins, Implementation and Controversies
Ramesh Thakur

For more information about this series, please visit: www.routledge.com/Global-Politics-and-the-Responsibility-to-Protect/book-series/GPRP

Reviewing the Responsibility to Protect

Origins, Implementation and Controversies

Ramesh Thakur

Routledge
Taylor & Francis Group
LONDON AND NEW YORK

First published 2019
by Routledge

2 Park Square, Milton Park, Abingdon, Oxfordshire OX14 4RN
52 Vanderbilt Avenue, New York, NY 10017

Routledge is an imprint of the Taylor & Francis Group, an informa business

First issued in paperback 2020

British Library Cataloguing-in-Publication Data
A catalogue record for this book is available from the British Library

Library of Congress Cataloging-in-Publication Data
Names: Thakur, Ramesh Chandra, 1948–author.
Title: Reviewing the responsibility to protect : origins, implementation and controversies / Ramesh Thakur.
Description: Abingdon, Oxon ; New York, NY : Routledge, 2019. |
Series: Global politics and the responsibility to protect | Includes bibliographical references and index.
Identifiers: LCCN 2018042233 (print) | LCCN 2018042577 (ebook) | ISBN 9781351016780 (Web PDF) | ISBN 9781351016773 (ePub) | ISBN 9781351016766 (Mobi) | ISBN 9781138498174 (hardback) | ISBN 9781351016797 (e-book)
Subjects: LCSH: Responsibility to protect (International law)
Classification: LCC KZ4082 (ebook) | LCC KZ4082 .T48 2091 (print) | DDC 341.4/8–dc23
LC record available at https://lccn.loc.gov/2018042233v

ISBN: 978-1-138-49817-4 (hbk)
ISBN: 978-0-367-49887-0 (pbk)

Typeset in Times New Roman
by Wearset Ltd, Boldon, Tyne and Wear

Dedicated to the memory of Mohamed Sahnoun (1931–2018), co-chair of the International Commission on Intervention and State Sovereignty. His humility, gentleness, wisdom, patience, and capacity to conciliate different viewpoints and personalities, along with an inexhaustible store of apposite African folktales involving a diverse range of animals, were greatly treasured by all who knew him and will be sorely missed by a world in disarray.

Contents

Acknowledgements

I would like to express my warmest appreciation to Andrew Humphrys and his team at Routledge. Their help, assistance and encouragement throughout, from conception to completion, was exemplary in their professionalism and it has been a pleasure working with them.

I am also grateful to the publishers of the following articles and book chapters for permission to re-use earlier articles and book chapters:

Chapter 2: Ramesh Thakur, 'The Responsibility to Protect at 15', *International Affairs* 92:2 (March 2016), 415–34

Chapter 3: Ramesh Thakur, 'High-level Panels', in Jacob Cogan, Ian Hurd and Ian Johnstone, eds., *The Oxford Handbook of International Organizations* (Oxford: Oxford University Press, 2016), 859–80

Chapter 4: Ramesh Thakur, 'Rwanda, Kosovo and the International Commission on Intervention and State Sovereignty', in Alex J. Bellamy and Tim Dunne, eds., *The Oxford Handbook of the Responsibility to Protect* (Oxford: Oxford University Press, 2016), 94–113

Chapter 5: Charles Sampford and Ramesh Thakur, 'From the Right to Persecute to the Responsibility to Protect: Feuerbachian Inversions of Rights and Responsibilities in State–Citizen Relations', in Ramesh Thakur and William Maley, eds., *Theorising the Responsibility to Protect* (Cambridge: Cambridge University Press, 2015), 38–58

Chapter 6: Ramesh Thakur, 'From Humanitarian Intervention to R2P: Cosmetic or Consequential?', in *The United Nations, Peace and Security: From Collective Security to the Responsibility to Protect*, 2nd ed. (Cambridge: Cambridge University Press, 2017), 272–300

Chapter 7: Ramesh Thakur, 'R2P after Libya and Syria: Engaging Emerging Powers', *The Washington Quarterly* 36:2 (Spring 2013), 61–76

Chapter 8: Ramesh Thakur, 'R2P's "Structural" Problems: A Response to Roland Paris', *International Peacekeeping* 22:1 (2015), 11–25

Chapter 9: Srinjoy Bose and Ramesh Thakur, 'The UN Secretary-General and the Forgotten Third R2P Responsibility', *Global Responsibility to Protect* 8:4 (2016), 343–65

Chapter 10: Ramesh Thakur, 'Protection Gaps for Civilian Victims of Political Violence', *South African Journal of International Affairs* 20:3 (December 2013), 321–33

Chapter 11: Ramesh Thakur, 'Atrocity Crimes and Global Governance', in Amitav Acharya, ed., *Why Govern: Rethinking Demand and Progress in Global Governance* (Cambridge: Cambridge University Press, 2016), 138–56

As a general rule, I have edited the articles and book chapters only very lightly from the versions originally published, mainly to standardise usage and style. A more important criterion has been to avoid repetition and duplication, except where the material is judged to have been important to the integrity of the chapter as a self-contained essay.

1 Introduction

Tyranny is not restricted to any particular religion, culture, civilisation or gender. Political rule based in terror rather than citizen's welfare, safety and security is a universal moral failing. Because the ability of tyrants to rule by terror free from external restraints and counter-measures was seen as having been sanctified by the Westphalian system of sovereign states, the need arose for a matching universal norm to ban and stop atrocities. One of the most important developments in world politics in the last two decades has been the spread of the twin ideas that state sovereignty comes with responsibilities – both domestic and international – as well as privileges, and that there exists a global responsibility to protect people threatened by mass atrocity crimes. The 2001 report of the International Commission on Intervention and State Sovereignty (ICISS) entitled *The Responsibility to Protect* put these ideas into active circulation, and United Nations resolutions in 2005, on the 60th anniversary of the establishment of the organisation, gave the ideas further substance.

More recently, the justification of action by the North Atlantic Treaty Organization (NATO) in Libya, on the strength of Security Council Resolutions 1970 and 1973, made explicit reference to the principle of the Responsibility to Protect (R2P), and put this particular notion at the centre of discussion of some of the most challenging political dilemmas of our times. As international leaders struggled in vain to find ways to deal with mounting political violence in Syria, and then again with the emergence of the 'Islamic State in Iraq and Syria', the idea of R2P was never far below the surface. For advocates, R2P is a poster child of liberal internationalism, summoning forth the better angels of human nature to save strangers in distant lands within a rules-based global order. But for critics, it is the enabler of choice for powerful countries to appropriate the language of humanitarianism in which to cloak base geopolitical motives when violating the sovereignty of weak nations.

These concrete political developments have helped to generate a substantial scholarly literature concerned with the genesis of the idea of R2P and with the ways in which it has been refined through multilateral deliberation. Through mainstream as well as dedicated journals, such as *Global Responsibility to Protect*, researchers have sought to explore the ambit of the R2P doctrine, discussing, for example, whether it can properly be applied in circumstances where a population is threatened by the ravages of natural disaster or is living under the rule of a foreign occupying power.

One key element of the context within which the idea of a responsibility to protect took shape was a critical weakness in the normative framework determining how sovereign states should relate to one another and to international organisations. This weakness arose because of the unsatisfactory nature of ideas about 'humanitarian intervention' that had resurfaced. Another key element was a sequence of events in which ordinary people were brutalised in ghastly ways in various parts of the world. Whilst the Holocaust had already provided an unprecedentedly horrific example of mass murder on an industrial scale, there had been hopes in the aftermath of the Second World War that the new architecture of the United Nations, the development and anathematisation of the idea of genocide and the capacity of media to expose horrendous acts of cruelty would put a stop to such events. Yet they persisted, and in the post-Cold War period, developments such as ethnic cleansing in the Balkans, and above all the Rwanda genocide of 1994, made it a matter of urgency to find a better way of 'saving strangers' and protecting the vulnerable.

The use of the vocabulary of humanitarianism to justify political and coercive measures – up to and including the use of force – is not a novel development. Unfortunately, the claim to be acting on humanitarian grounds was open to being abused to camouflage other self-interested geopolitical and commercial motives. Many developing countries were intimately familiar with this as part of their historical encounter with European colonial powers. A grim example of this was provided in Europe itself by Germany in the 1930s, where Berlin frequently sought to justify the expansionism of Nazi Germany by reference to the need to protect the alleged infractions of the rights and freedoms of ethnic Germans living in other countries such as Czechoslovakia and Poland. At the same time, the phenomenon of Nazism is an enduring reminder that the Universal Declaration of Human Rights and the Genocide Convention have their roots in the recognition of the capacity for evil of Western civilisation and the desire to ban it through universal norms. Similarly, the instinct to brutality over subjects by some rulers found its greatest enabler in Westphalian sovereignty that too originated in Europe. Because the instinct is universal it needs a universal norm to ban it. To that extent R2P is a global response to a distinctly Western-origin problem, not a Western response to a third world problem.

While earlier conflicts had certainly attracted attention in terms of their humanitarian implications, and statesmen in the 1920s had sought to outlaw war as an instrument of policy, in the aftermath of the Second World War, a new framework of norms and rules was developed to deal with the use of force in international relations, a framework centred on the Charter of the new United Nations. At one level, the framework was a simple one:

> *Article 2.4* provided that 'All Members shall refrain in their international relations from the threat or use of force against the territorial integrity or political independence of any state, or in any other manner inconsistent with the Purposes of the United Nations'.

> *Article 39* sought to head off unilateral impulses by stating that 'The Security Council shall determine the existence of any threat to the peace, breach of the peace, or act of aggression and shall make recommendations, or decide what measures shall be taken in accordance with Articles 41 and 42, to maintain or restore international peace and security'.
>
> *Article 41* provided that 'The Security Council may decide what measures not involving the use of armed force are to be employed to give effect to its decisions'.
>
> *Article 42* provided that 'Should the Security Council consider that measures provided for in Article 41 would be inadequate or have proved to be inadequate, it may take such action by air, sea, or land forces as may be necessary to maintain or restore international peace and security. Such action may include demonstrations, blockade, and other operations by air, sea, or land forces of Members of the United Nations'.
>
> *Article 51* provided that 'Nothing in the present Charter shall impair the inherent right of individual or collective self-defence if an armed attack occurs against a Member of the United Nations, until the Security Council has taken measures necessary to maintain international peace and security'.

Thus, the United Nations Charter codified both the law and the new normative consensus. One crucial problem, however, remained. The Charter granted permanent membership of the Security Council to five states – the United States, the United Kingdom, the Soviet Union, France and China – and with it, the power to veto any non-procedural resolution. The possibility, if not the virtual certainty, that the Council could prove impotent – either because of a stand-off between the superpowers, or by virtue of a simple lack of interest in some remote part of the world on the margins of global interest and attention – raised the question of what should be done when some horror seemed to require action, but action could not be justified either by reference to self-defence, or alternatively to explicit Security Council authorisation. An answer came with the idea of 'humanitarian intervention', which might be morally justifiable even if not defensible legally. Various examples of state behaviour were from time to time cited as examples of humanitarian intervention, including the Indian intervention in East Pakistan in 1971 that created Bangladesh as an independent state, the Vietnamese invasion of Cambodia in 1978 that resulted in the displacement of the genocidal Khmer Rouge regime, and the Tanzanian overthrow of Idi Amin in Uganda in 1979.

While a number of observers welcomed the consequences of these specific actions, many others voiced unease about the principles involved and the future risk to the multilateral rules-based global order from the precedent being set of unilateral interventions. A wide range of criticisms surfaced. One related to sincerity of purpose. Did Vietnam *really* invade Cambodia on the basis of humanitarian motives, or did such claimed motives simply provide convenient cover for an intervention carried out for quite different purposes? Another related to consistency and to the fear that the doctrine of humanitarian intervention would simply magnify asymmetries of power in the international system, with states that had long seen themselves as meeting some standard of 'civilisation' becoming moral policemen for younger states only recently freed from colonial domination, and acting with considerable hypocrisy to boot. Yet another criticism drew on the ethics of consequences to suggest that humanitarian intervention provided no guarantee that the 'beneficiaries' would ultimately be better off than if no intervention had occurred. None of these objections was trivial and, in large parts of the world, they undermined claims to legitimacy that humanitarian intervention might have sought.

Despite these inadequacies in the concept of humanitarian intervention, it did seem in some ways to fill a need. The first half of the decade of the 'new' post-Cold War era was dominated by a number of developments that seemed to create anew the need for some morally defensible form of international action to shelter the vulnerable. With the attention of the wider world focussed on the holding of the first multiracial elections in South Africa, extremists in Rwanda embarked on the genocidal slaughter of those whom they conceived to be enemies. And as Yugoslavia disintegrated, Bosnia-Herzegovina became the theatre for hideous exercises in 'ethnic cleansing' and the United Nations itself was comprehensively humiliated by the massacre of men and boys in Srebrenica in 1995 sheltering in UN 'Safe Areas' under the protection of UN blue helmets. The killing of Africans seemed to weigh very differently in the moral calculus of key Western leaders than did the killing or displacement of people in Europe who looked rather like them. NATO's intervention in Kosovo in 1999 without Security Council authorisation added to this impression.

ICISS and R2P

The combination of problems crying out for attention, and a doctrinal response, the weaknesses of which seemed to undermine its legitimacy, set the scene for conceptual innovation and normative entrepreneurship. Lloyd Axworthy, Canada's foreign minister (1996–2000), launched ICISS in September 2000. Its report, *The Responsibility to Protect*, was published in late 2001. The principle was endorsed unanimously by world leaders meeting at the United Nations summit in 2005. Since then, R2P has progressed along three parallel tracks in the UN system: in numerous UN Security Council resolutions and presidential statements, starting with Resolution 1674 (28 April 2006); in successive reports of the Secretary-General since 2009; and in annual debates in the General Assembly on these reports. In addition, it has been progressively institutionalised in the UN system and in some national governments and widely disseminated and promoted by civil society organisations.

The 2005 UN world summit outcome resolution clarified, narrowed and sharpened the scope of R2P by limiting it to four crimes – genocide, ethnic

cleansing, other crimes against humanity and war crimes. The nature of the new principle-cum-norm was further refined in the Secretary-General's inaugural report on R2P in 2009, drafted by his special adviser on R2P Edward Luck, which reformulated R2P in the language of three distinct 'pillars': a state's responsibility not to commit such mass atrocity crimes or allow them to occur ('Pillar One'); the responsibility of other states to assist those lacking the capacity to so protect ('Pillar Two'); and the responsibility of the international community to respond with 'timely and decisive action' – including ultimately with coercive military force, but only if authorised by the UN Security Council – if a state is 'manifestly failing' to meet its protection responsibilities ('Pillar Three').

With these clarifications and refinements, R2P became the normative instrument of choice for converting a shocked international conscience into decisive collective action – for channelling selective moral indignation into collective policy remedies – to prevent and stop atrocities. In the vacuum of responsibility for the safety of the marginalised, stigmatised and dehumanised out-group subject to mass atrocities, R2P provided an entry point for the international community to step in and take up the moral and military slack. The essence of R2P is that those of us fortunate enough to live in zones of safety, accept first, a duty of care towards the unfortunate strangers trapped in zones of danger, and second an obligation not to unilaterally violate international community norms. In reconciling the two often contradictory imperatives, R2P attempts to strike a delicate balance between institutionalised indifference and unilateral interference. The success of the balance arrived at is shown by the fact that, despite continuing controversy over implementation and contention regarding its normative status, R2P is no longer seriously contested in the policy community as a principle.

Yet the controversy over R2P does indeed continue on two broad fronts, that it offers too little protection: first, against self-interested abuses by powerful countries of the non-intervention norm; and second, against gross abuses by powerful national leaders of the human rights norm. On the one side, the Security Council-authorised and NATO-led military intervention in Libya in 2011 seemed to have borne out the fears of many critics about the potential for abuse of R2P, just like the previous humanitarian intervention doctrine. The post-intervention instability, volatility, lawlessness and killings in Libya only strengthened the criticism. On the other side, R2P remains even more vulnerable to criticisms that in failing to alter state practice, it has failed to deliver on the promise of protection. That is, the greater criticism directed at R2P is not too much and too soon, but too little and too late.

Thus, R2P remains conceptually contested in academic discourse, and its implementation and non-implementation remains politically controversial in the policy community, as demonstrated most vividly in the still unresolved Syrian tragedy and the failure to protect its civilian population caught in the murderous cross-fire between the regime troops and the rebel fighters. The broader criticism is: where is the sense in sanctioning an expansive international use of force in order to enforce restrictive norms against the domestic use of force by states? R2P created intellectual and political excitement in 2001 and 2005 because it was fresh and challenging with the potential to help save strangers' lives in mass numbers. But the hard edge of its implementation involved the use of force inside sovereign jurisdictions and this proved controversial and confronting in practice.

Nevertheless, it is equally noteworthy that there has been no effort made to rescind R2P as the UN's organising principle for responding to the threat or outbreak of mass atrocity crimes. There have been scores of Security Council and Human Rights Council resolutions (of which the vast majority were adopted post-Libya Resolution 1973 of 17 March 2011). There are more than 50 each of national focal points in UN member states and Group of Friends of R2P in New York and Geneva. The Global Centre for the Responsibility to Protect, established in 2008, has offices in New York and Geneva, acts as the secretariat for the Global Network of R2P Focal Points and the UN Group of Friends of R2P, publishes regular R2P Monitor and Atrocity Alerts and engages in training programs as well as policy advocacy. The International Coalition for RtoP was formed a year later and has over 92 non-governmental organisations (NGOs) as members. The Asia Pacific Centre for R2P, established at the University of Queensland in 2008 in partnership with Australia's Department of Foreign Affairs and Trade, promotes the principle in Asia and the Pacific through research and policy dialogue. On the academic side, there have been handbooks, numerous books, innumerable articles and a dedicated and well-regarded journal – *The Global Responsibility to Protect* – devoted to R2P.

In summary, the Responsibility to Protect is very much part of the contemporary international normative and policy debate on the lawfulness and legitimacy of using force to protect at-risk populations inside sovereign jurisdictions. This book brings together a collection of articles by an insider/outsider who has been part of that debate for the past two decades. It supplements the earlier collection of essays on the topic published by Routledge in 2011, without reprinting any of the essays already published in the first volume.

Structure of the book

The book begins with a literature review published in *International Affairs* to mark 15 years of the original ICISS report. I have received uniformly positive feedback on the usefulness of this review. This will introduce the reader to the main contours of the responsibility to protect scholarship and debate.

In Part I, the four chapters cover the origins, meaning and development of R2P from 2001 to 2016. Chapter 3 discusses international commissions as instruments of entrepreneurial diplomacy. Drawing on but not limited to the ICISS experience, it analyses the features of, and explains the attributes and factors that make for success and failure of, commission diplomacy. Chapter 4 traces the role that the Rwanda genocide in 1994 and the NATO intervention in Kosovo in 1999 played in influencing debates in and the report of ICISS. Chapters 5 and 6 explain the reasons for and meaning of the shift from 'humanitarian intervention' to the 'responsibility to protect', and the importance of the shift.

Part II discusses the controversies surrounding efforts to implement R2P. It begins with a landmark article on the role and importance of emerging powers in the world of international politics against the crises in Libya and Syria. The next chapter is a response to a major article in *International Peacekeeping*, not challenging the critique but locating it more broadly in the context of the structural problems that dog any use of international force in contemporary conditions. This is followed by a plea to return to the original third responsibility, to rebuild and reconstruct after a protective intervention.

Part III begins with an overview of remaining protection gaps, whether normatively or operationally; discusses why R2P will remain relevant because it is essentially demand driven; and concludes with a look back at the origins and development of R2P and then looks ahead at likely, possible and desirable future directions.

2 The Responsibility to Protect at 15*

Anniversaries are occasions to take stock: reflect on progress, celebrate successes, acknowledge setbacks and outline a vision and roadmap for doing better. This year [2016] marks the fifteenth anniversary of the publication of the landmark report by ICISS that first introduced the innovative principle of the Responsibility to Protect. Within four years, R2P was endorsed unanimously at a UN summit of world leaders as the central organising principle for responding to mass atrocity crimes of genocide, crimes against humanity, war crimes and ethnic cleansing.

The 'original' documents comprise the initial report of the international commission, its supporting supplementary volume, the 2005 UN summit's Outcome Document which adopted R2P as official UN policy,[1] the special reports of the Secretary-General issued annually since 2009, the debates in the General Assembly around his annual reports,[2] resolutions adopted by the Security Council and statements issued by its president, and statements and speeches by the Secretary-General and his special advisers on R2P and Genocide Prevention. To this we might add the series of speeches and reports by Kofi Annan from his time as Secretary-General.[3] In the secondary literature, it is worth highlighting the central role of *Global Responsibility to Protect* (*GR2P*), a journal dedicated to this topic. Occasionally special issues of other journals have focussed on R2P, for example *Ethics & International Affairs* 25:3 (2011). ICISS co-chair Gareth Evans and Commissioner Ramesh Thakur have provided their accounts,[4] and ICISS research director Tom Weiss has written an elegant account of R2P in the longer and broader context of humanitarian intervention.[5] Ed Luck, the Secretary-General's first special adviser on R2P, has written several accounts of the development and evolution of R2P during his term in office.[6] There are hundreds of research projects, books, articles and competing handbooks.[7]

In the pre-R2P era, the two paradigmatic cases that highlighted the flaws of the then-existing normative architecture were Rwanda in 1994, where there was international inaction to prevent or halt the genocide, and Kosovo, where NATO intervened without UN authorisation to bring an end to alleged Serbian atrocities. In the post-R2P era, the two paradigmatic cases to date that highlight its mobilising power but also underline its problems might well comprise Libya in 2011 when NATO led a UN-authorised R2P intervention, and Syria since 2011 where despite large numbers of civilian deaths and the confirmed use of chemical weapons, the United Nations has failed to take any robust and effective action.[8] Other recent examples of ineffectual UN response to mass atrocities include South Sudan and the Central African Republic.[9] Given the massive and still burgeoning literature on all aspects of R2P, this chapter focuses on five issues: the displacement of 'humanitarian intervention', atrocity prevention, unsatisfactory implementation, the main R2P actors and continuing scepticism about R2P.

From humanitarian intervention to R2P[10]

The key innovation in 2001 was the reconceptualisation of 'humanitarian intervention' as R2P; everything else in this discourse flows from that distinction. As the author of the initial draft of the relevant sections of the ICISS report, I believe the differences between them are real and consequential.[11] Even people associated with ICISS, including Weiss and I,[12] have used 'humanitarian intervention' when discussing the historical record. Intervention has a long lineage in the history of political thinking, including, most notably, just war theory.[13] Several European powers engaged in humanitarian intervention throughout the nineteenth century.[14] Taking a major British political philosopher as the point of departure, *The Question of Intervention: John Stuart Mill and the Responsibility to Protect*[15] by Michael Doyle, unpacks the thorny issue of when a state's sovereignty should be respected and when overridden by other states in the name of humanitarian protection, national self-determination or national security. Drawing on the ideas of Rousseau, Kant and Hegel, Bjorn Gomes shows that intervention on humanitarian grounds is not just permissible, but may indeed be obligatory.[16] Luke Glanville's *Sovereignty and the Responsibility to Protect: A New History*[17] traces the notion of sovereignty as protective responsibility to the sixteenth–seventeenth centuries, noting that the right to wage a just war to punish tyranny and rescue the oppressed predates non-intervention as an *attribute* of sovereignty.[18] Jennifer Welsh goes back to assess Vincent's scepticism about humanitarian intervention and concludes that his fears were exaggerated.[19]

During the Cold War, state practice reflected the unwillingness of many countries – not just the two power blocs, but also some former colonies like India and Tanzania – to give up intervention as an instrument of policy. But where previously interveners had justified their action as exceptional, in Kosovo in 1999 Western leaders for the first time challenged the non-intervention norm itself. NATO claims of an emerging new norm of 'humanitarian intervention' were emphatically rejected by a majority of the world's countries. The ensuing controversy highlighted a lacuna in the existing legal regime governing the international use of force.[20] R2P was the ICISS answer to reconciling the neuralgic rejection of humanitarian intervention by the global South with the determination by the North to end atrocities.

Politically, the visceral hostility of a large number of former colonised countries to 'humanitarian intervention' is explained by the historical baggage of rapacious exploitation and cynical hypocrisy. Insistence on the discredited and discarded discourse by self-referencing Western scholars amounts to an in-your-face disrespect to them, ICISS and all the various groups of actors who have embraced R2P as an acceptable replacement. *Conceptually*, while R2P upends state–citizen relations internally and defines the distribution of authority and jurisdiction between states on the one side and the international community on the other, 'humanitarian intervention' does so with respect to different states. *Normatively*, 'humanitarian intervention' rejects non-intervention and privileges the perspectives and rights of the intervening states. R2P reformulates sovereignty as responsibility, links it to the human protection norm, sidesteps without rejecting non-intervention and addresses the issue from the perspective of the victims. *Procedurally*, R2P can only be authorised by the UN whereas 'humanitarian intervention' is agnostic between UN and unilateral interventions. *Operationally*, protection of victims from mass atrocities requires distinctive guidelines and rules of engagement and different relationships to civil authorities and humanitarian actors, always prioritising the protection of civilians over the safety and security of the intervening troops.

Given that all three of the Holzgrefe-Keohane,[21] Welsh[22] and Scheid volumes deal with humanitarian intervention, the fact that there is a 100 per cent Western cast of authors rather confirms the point about humanitarian intervention approaching the topic from the point of view of the rights and privileges of the intervening countries. *Humanitarian Intervention: Ethical, Legal and Political Dilemmas* and *Humanitarian Intervention and International Relations* reflect the language of their time. *The Ethics of Armed Humanitarian Intervention*, edited by Don E. Scheid,[23] makes an important contribution to the *ethics of humanitarian intervention* from the perspective of Western countries who have engaged in or might contemplate such ventures. But its contribution to the *politics of the responsibility to protect* is negligible. It seems bad enough to persist with the 'humanitarian intervention' terminology in general. The use of that language with respect to UN operations in Norrie MacQueen's *Humanitarian Intervention and the United Nations*[24] is particularly disconcerting.

Prevention: work in progress

R2P emerged against the backdrop of a growing awareness among peoples and policymakers of mass atrocities in various parts of the world. What is the state of our knowledge with respect to the causes of atrocities, the institutional vulnerabilities and points of resilience, the pathways from simmering animosities to mass killings, the most effective preventive and response mechanisms, the indicators and precursors, for example incitement by radio and leaflets?[25] Armed conflict is neither a necessary nor a sufficient condition of atrocities: most (although not all) atrocities occur against the backdrop of armed conflict, but most armed conflicts do not also lead to mass atrocities. In *Massacres and Morality: Mass Atrocities in an Age of Civilian Immunity*,[26] Alex Bellamy argues the world has made impressive progress in legislating against the intentional

killing of civilians and constructing institutions to give meaning to that prohibition. It has become more difficult, but not impossible, for states to get away with mass murder. *Reconstructing Atrocity Prevention*[27] attempts to address the topic of the prevention of mass atrocities from the theoretical, policy and practising standpoints simultaneously. But with 21 of 24 contributors being Westerners, its utility is greatly limited.[28] The 'white man's burden' continues to be evident in Western scholarship, broadening Kishore Mahbubani's question – can Asians think?[29] – to people from the developing countries generally, and answering in the negative.

Atrocity prevention remains challenging and requires using early warning information and analyses,[30] and a range of legal instruments and regimes, including the International Criminal Court (ICC).[31] The best early warnings include reports from the Brussels-based International Crisis Group[32] and the 'R2P Monitor' published by the New York-based Global Centre for R2P.[33] Civil society can organise to mobilise public and political will of peoples and governments to intervene to prevent atrocities.[34] Often, however, the focus is mistakenly on the *need* to respond when the real challenge is inadequate *means* to respond, in particular a lack of capacity on the part of regional organisations to undertake upstream preventive activities.[35] *The Responsibility to Prevent: Overcoming the Challenges of Atrocity Prevention*, edited by Serena Sharma and Jennifer Welsh,[36] is devoted exclusively to the preventive dimension of R2P. Sharma and Welsh have assembled an international group of academics and practitioners to investigate how to operationalise the responsibility to prevent through the conceptual lens of crimes prevention, using tools and approaches like sanctions, mediation, international criminal justice and military force.

The Latin American Network for Genocide and Mass Atrocity Prevention was launched in March 2012 as the first initiative of its kind. On 29 May 2015 it adopted a Declaration affirming the group as 'a regional tool that contributes to the continued mainstreaming of atrocity prevention in national agendas', and that it would develop and consolidate a common curriculum on atrocity prevention and support the work of the UN Office of the Special Adviser on the Prevention of Genocide.[37] The formation of the Asia Pacific Partnership for Atrocity Prevention followed in October 2015.[38]

Implementation gaps

In the 60-year period from the UN's creation in 1945 to the adoption of R2P in 2005, the peace and security agenda of the world body was significantly recalibrated as the norm of non-intervention steadily softened and the cluster of human rights and humanitarian norms progressively hardened,[39] as manifested across a wide range of agenda items, culminating in R2P. In the Feuerbachian reframing of state–citizen relations,[40] R2P makes sovereign rights conditional upon the state delivering on the protection rights of people. In his first report on R2P, Secretary-General Ban Ki-moon articulated an agenda to convert R2P from promise to practice, 'turning the authoritative and enduring words of the 2005 World Summit Outcome into doctrine, policy and, most importantly, deeds'.[41] Action to prevent or halt atrocities requires the adoption of R2P as national policy by key state actors, and as international policy by the UN community collectively.[42]

R2P initiated a debate in policy and academic circles on its precise status. Is it a powerful new 'moral compact'[43] or does it compromise the existing moral primacy of peace by extending permissible military action;[44] does it have legal force;[45] should we describe it as a principle; has it attained the status of a global norm through some process of circulation?[46] Our understanding in 2001 was that the call to protect people from atrocity crimes had a strong basis in UN Charter and customary international law in that it 'epitomises the humanitarian character and central purpose of international human rights, humanitarian law, refugee law and international criminal law'.[47] Despite R2P's uncertain legal character, 'there is a responsibility under international law to protect populations from genocide, war crimes, ethnic cleansing, and crimes against humanity'. At the very least, therefore, R2P 'does challenge states to meet their *existing* responsibilities'.[48] Even though it may well rest on an unarticulated theory of international obligation,[49] in *The Responsibility to Protect (R2P): A New Paradigm of International Law?*[50] Peter Hilpold argues that the likelihood of R2P 'hardening' into a norm of customary international law is slim. The shared understandings on it to date are not deep enough and its practice remains too inconsistent.[51] Heather Roff's *Global Justice, Kant and the Responsibility to Protect: A Provisional Duty*[52] develops the intriguing argument that the route to institutionalising R2P as a peremptory norm in contemporary global politics is to root it in eighteenth century European philosophy.

Global norms lie at the intersection of ethics, law and international affairs. Normative shifts take place when the law-ethics equation is recomputed. Ines-Jacqueline Werkner and Dirk Rademacher's (eds) *Protecting People – and Losing Just Peace? Debates on the Responsibility to Protect in the Context of Christian Peace Ethics*[53] and Semegnish Asfaw, Guillermo Kerber and Peter Weiderud's (eds) *Responsibility to Protect: Ethical and Theological Reflections*,[54] discuss ethical challenges, dilemmas and imperatives in relation to religious and philosophical principles. However, an intervention can neither be explained nor judged by purely ethical criteria: political factors are integral both to the explanation of the initial intervention and its outcome.[55] Theresa Reinold's *Sovereignty and the Responsibility to Protect: The Power of Norms and the Norms of the Powerful*[56] is one of the more interesting books on the disproportionate capacity of powerful actors to frame global norms. Reinold dissects the complex interactions between power and norms and is especially illuminating in demonstrating how normative frames can be imported across discourses like protection, counter-terrorism and non-proliferation. In *Humanitarian Intervention and the Responsibility to Protect: Security and Human Rights*,[57] Cristina Badescu interrogates the intersection of R2P, security and human rights. ICISS itself located R2P within the broader normative umbrella of human security, the subject of Hannes Peltonen's

International Responsibility and Grave Humanitarian Crises: Collective Provision for Human Security[58] which explores its links with collective responsibility and international community. Hilpold ascribes R2P's rapid adoption to the conviction that in an age of mass atrocities, international law was in urgent need of being 'humanized'.[59]

Although R2P (along with its sibling norms protection of civilians and international criminal justice[60]) is an important innovation, many gaps remain in the protection agenda's normative architecture[61] with respect to civilians in occupied territories (Gaza[62]), internally displaced persons,[63] refugees,[64] natural disasters (Cyclone Nargis in Myanmar), kin states (overseas Chinese, Indians, Russians),[65] armed civil wars and insurgencies (Sri Lanka, Syria), victims of anarchic violence unleashed in the aftermath of illegal invasions and chaotic occupations as of Iraq in 2003 (a war appropriately described as humanitarian imperialism[66]), etc. R2P is subject, like all policy-significant norms, to inconsistency (the uneven application of a norm) and incoherence (tensions between different cognate norms, the best example being non-intervention and R2P). Its applicability to any particular crisis, and the manner of its implementation, can also generate normative contestation.[67] On the last point, importantly, Welsh distinguishes between procedural contestation over who should 'own' its development as a norm and substantive contestation over its content.[68]

Can R2P help us to take the small but important steps 'towards a world free of mass atrocities'?[69] Given the demand-driven origins of R2P and its bias towards action, a fruitful approach is to try and combine philosophical and theoretical reflections with empirical case studies, to bring together scholars and practitioners in one collection, and to assemble a global cast of authors to speak to the relevance and limits of a putatively global norm. Jared Genser and Irwin Cotler's (eds) *The Responsibility to Protect: The Promise of Stopping Mass Atrocities in Our Time*,[70] does all this unusually well. Charles Sampford and Ramesh Thakur's (eds) *Responsibility to Protect and Sovereignty*[71] examines both the theoretical tensions between sovereignty and R2P and also how they played out in the cases of East Timor, Sri Lanka, Sudan and Kosovo. Bellamy's *Global Politics and the Responsibility to Protect* is a substantial account of the issues relating to the implementation challenges confronting R2P. Julia Hoffman and Andre Nollkaemper's (eds) *Responsibility to Protect: From Principle to Practice*[72] similarly explores the transitional issues in moving from principle to practice, and Part IV of Kuwali and Viljoen's (eds) *Africa and the Responsibility to Protect* examines the operationalisation possibilities under Article 4(h) of the African Union (AU) Charter.

The best study of R2P's 'track record' as actionable principle-cum-norm in the first five years is by Bellamy. It had become mainstreamed in international diplomatic discourse, served as a lens through which to evaluate events and frame responses and sharpened calls to implement existing obligations and policies. But it was not yet a reliable catalyst for robust international action.[73] The poster children of the critics of the ways in which R2P has been conceptualised and implemented are Darfur and Syria,[74] where strangers in peril were not saved. While de

Waal located the failure to intervene in Darfur in the unrealistic expectations raised by R2P,[75] to Badescu and Berghorn, Darfur highlighted political limitations inherent in the R2P framework, moral dilemmas emerging from military action and tactical challenges operationally.[76] To some, inaction on Darfur reflected heightened scepticism about interventionism after the 2003 Iraq war,[77] Western strategic interests in Sudan and the complex linkages with Sudan's other wars.[78] Others tried to show how media framing of the crisis could mobilise public opinion.[79] Given the logistical and other practical difficulties of using force against the Sudanese government, and the likely damaging consequences for humanitarian relief operations and the fragile peace process, Evans argues, 'the failure has been in the application of other measures, not the non-application of coercive force'.[80]

Part of the implementation difficulty lies in the danger of R2P being hijacked by conflict partisans and yoked to their agendas. In Sri Lanka, for example, based on a heavily biased reading of R2P (like Russia in South Ossetia),[81] Damien Kingsbury's *Sri Lanka and the Responsibility to Protect: Politics, Ethnicity and Genocide*[82] bemoans the failure to invoke R2P against the government as it crushed the Tamil Tigers in 2009. Yet, given the nature of the conflict as a civil war and the particular brutality of the Tigers, the government would have been just as entitled to seek international help under R2P in order to discharge its responsibility to protect all people in its territorial jurisdiction.[83] As Gallagher correctly notes, international assistance is 'the most overlooked and under-researched of the three pillars' of R2P.[84] Westerners innocent of the complexities and nuances of the fog of war in third world conditions where insurgency and terrorism had fused in a 'liberation movement' are not best placed to judge the morality of government actions in desperately trying to defend the authority of the state and the integrity of its borders. Any more than the rest have the right to determine the best balance between safety and freedoms in the anti-terrorism policies of Western governments. None of this exempts any of the conflict parties from criminal accountability under international humanitarian and human rights laws. With the report of the Commission of Inquiry set up by the UN Human Rights Council under the distinguished Australian jurist Michael Kirby as chair,[85] the idea of holding North Korea to account under R2P was placed on the international agenda. There are problems, however, with treating this as primarily a legal violation rather than a political challenge.[86]

Moreover, while the coercive end of R2P is to be found only in Pillar Three, the latter is not restricted solely to coercive tools (military and non-military). Rather, as Bellamy highlights, even in Pillar Three, the default first response is peaceful means, and forceful means is the option of last resort.[87] The correct distinctions between the three pillars, therefore, are not based on the element of coercion but on the 'horizontal' distribution of responsibility: of the state (One) not precluding the use of force on its own to deal with perpetrators, of the international community to assist the state concerned, and of the international community to act on its own.

Unsurprisingly, as the only such actual case study to date, Libya figures prominently in the discourse on the potential and limits of R2P-type military intervention and Aidan Hehir and Robert Murray's (eds) *Libya, the Responsibility to Protect and the Future of Humanitarian Intervention*[88] is part of a growing list.[89] According to Kuperman, the 2011 intervention prolonged the war's duration about sixfold, increased the death toll up to tenfold, worsened human rights abuses and humanitarian suffering, fed Islamic radicalism and led to weapons proliferation in Libya and its neighbours.[90] In arguing that the intervention highlighted four inescapable 'structural' dilemmas intrinsic to R2P,[91] Paris conflates the structural dilemmas inherent in any contemporary use of force into a central dilemma of R2P.[92] How many instances of the international use of force on a significant scale in the last 100 years have been free of major controversy?

Hehir uses the Libya intervention to develop the unexceptionable thesis that Security Council decisions flow from 'politics and pragmatism' more than principles. Mostly the Council demonstrates inertia, with occasional flourishes of activism when the interests of the P5 coincide with humanitarian needs of the crisis du jour.[93] For ICISS, the dual hope and expectation was that first, R2P would enhance the prospect of protective action by the Council, without in any way guaranteeing such an outcome; and second, it would reduce but not eliminate the element of inconsistency in decision-making. The very existence of R2P becomes a factor in the construction of state interests and identities and conditions the politics of interaction in the Council.[94] The other noteworthy feature of the Libya intervention was the key role of regional organisations – the Arab League and Organisation of Islamic Conference (OIC) (but not AU)[95] – as gatekeepers for R2P implementation.[96]

While some have focussed on 'responsibility',[97] others have examined 'protection'. Sara Davies, Zim Nwokora, Eli Stamnes and Sarah Teitt's (eds) *Responsibility to Protect and Women, Peace, and Security: Aligning the Protection Agendas*[98] is one of many works to explore the relationship between R2P and women as potential victims but also empowered agents of structural change for preventing and mitigating the effects of gendered mass atrocity crimes.[99] The operationalisation of R2P in peacekeeping missions[100] inevitably raises the complexity of the relationship between R2P and protection of civilians.[101] Vesselin Popovski, Charles Sampford and Angus Francis (eds), in *Norms of Protection: Responsibility to Protect, Protection of Civilians, and Their Interaction*,[102] show that the sibling norms have many overlaps and similarities, but also important differences and tensions. A special issue of *Global R2P*, while taking as its point of departure that humanitarian action contributes to the attainment of R2P goals, explored the complex and fraught relationship between the two agendas that pose practical, ethical and strategic challenges.[103]

The evolution of peacekeeping doctrine and practice has closely tracked the development of R2P policy.[104] Reference to R2P has become a staple of many UN Security Council resolutions and presidential statements, while civilian protection has become an integral component of many UN peacekeeping mandates, now issued as often as not under the coercive Chapter VII of the UN Charter.[105] This reached its zenith with Resolution 2098 (28 March 2013) authorising the creation of a 'Force Intervention Brigade' in the Democratic Republic of Congo. The protection of victims from mass atrocities requires distinctive guidelines and rules of engagement.[106] There is a need to examine the respective roles of military and civilian actors and how they should collaborate with and reinforce one another.[107]

Annie Herro, in *UN Emergency Peace and the Responsibility to Protect*,[108] advocates the creation of an emergency UN peace service as key to rapid response capability by the UN. Daniel Fiott and Joachim Koops's (eds) *The Responsibility to Protect and the Third Pillar: Legitimacy and Operationalization*[109] is one of the very few to take up the issue of operationalising the military intervention dimension of R2P, highlighting the processes, opportunities and risks involved and the timeliness, legitimacy, proportionality and effectiveness of Pillar Three responses through international law, economic sanctions, military intervention and alternative actions. A noteworthy feature of the book is self-contained chapters on China, India (by Chinese and Indian authors) and Russia, and on the role of business and informational technology.

Actors: multilevel responsibility vacuum

International organisations

For any collective responsibility, which identifiable actors have moral agency? Can formal organisations bear duties and be ascribed blame in the same way that we understand individual human beings to be morally responsible for actions? According to the Organisation of African Unity (OAU) inquiry panel on Rwanda's 'preventable genocide', 'the silence of the OAU … constituted a shocking moral failure'.[110] The idea of the 'institutional moral agent' is critically examined in Toni Erskine's (ed.) *Can Institutions Have Responsibilities? Collective Moral Agency and International Relations*[111] with respect to states, transnational corporations, the UN, NATO and international society in the context of some of the most contested issues and events in international relations, including Kosovo and Rwanda.

Many analysts continue to draw on the distinction, established by the independent commission on Kosovo, between the legality and legitimacy of interventions,[112] insisting that even where an intervention may be illegal, the authority of moral law trumps that of international law.[113] The legality of intervention must be assessed within the broader context of the use of force in international law.[114] The morality of intervention draws on the well established tradition of just war theory.[115] In fact the two are deeply intertwined.[116] They converge most effectively when interventions are UN-authorised and so considerable attention has been devoted to enhancing the prospects of authorisation and improving the efficacy of such interventions.[117] While refinement and development of R2P as principle are the responsibility of the General Assembly, responsibility for its implementation rests with the Security Council.

Daniel Silander and Don Wallace's (eds) *International Organizations and the Implementation of the Responsibility to Protect: The Humanitarian Crisis in Syria*[118] examines the roles, formal responsibility and actual capabilities of the UN, the ICC, OIC, Arab League, Gulf Cooperation Council, NATO, G8 and the Organisation of Security and Cooperation in Europe to protect civilians from systematic mass atrocities. Zyberi's (ed) *Institutional Approach to the Responsibility to Protect* covers the main political organs of the UN, important regional and security organisations, international judicial institutions and the regional human rights protection systems – with care taken on the regional chapters to include authors from the regions. In *The Responsibility to Protect: Rhetoric, Reality and the Future of Humanitarian Intervention,*[119] Aidan Hehir's solution to the problem of R2P having failed to respond effectively and in time to humanitarian crises requires major structural UN reform. Given the decades of futile efforts on this point so far, it is difficult to see just how this 'solution' advances timely and effective international response capacity. In *Humanitarian Intervention and the Responsibility to Protect*, Pattison broadens the question to ask: which particular agents should undertake 'humanitarian intervention' from among the UN, NATO, regional organisations, and individual or groups of states? Inevitably, he has his own menu of reforms to the mechanism as well as agents of intervention. However, his exploration of 'the ethics and politics of humanitarian intervention' (p. 245) is flawed with the persistence of the old conceptual framework that is all the more surprising for his interest in the importance of legitimacy as a key attribute of agency.

Major and emerging powers

Because the US is by far the most influential UN member state, Washington more than any other national capital still sets its agenda,[120] and its policy on R2P will continue to be the most decisive in conditioning the UN's record of R2P implementation.[121] The analysis in Cathinka Vik's *Moral Responsibility, Statecraft and Humanitarian Intervention: The US Response to Rwanda, Darfur, and Libya*[122] makes it unintentionally clear that the answer to her concluding question – responsibility to whom? (Chapter 5) – differs when we change lens from humanitarian intervention (to your own soldiers and citizens first) to R2P (to the victims and the international community). The right or duty of intervention under 'humanitarian intervention' falls within a long tradition of the special responsibilities that major powers have for underwriting the stability of the existing international order.[123] In *Responsibility to Protect*, Hehir argues that R2P has raised international consciousness but not significantly improved the international response to humanitarian crises. He proposes strengthening international law based on obligations rather than discretionary rights. This is problematic. R2P, like any law, norm, rule or code of behaviour, has both an enabling and a constraining function. Major powers were bound to resist it on both counts. In 2005 John Bolton argued, correctly, that the responsibility of host states to protect their populations was a legal obligation but the UN was not legally obligated to protect endangered civilians.[124] Washington rejected the idea of criteria for the use of force: it would not offer pre-commitments to engage military forces where it had no national interests, nor bind itself to criteria that would constrain its right to decide when and where to use force.[125] But 'the majority of states shared the view that if the responsibility to protect was to *constrain* Western interventionism – a core component of the argument in favor of the concept – then the absolute primacy of the Security Council had to be reaffirmed'[126] – as it was.

As relative US power declines, the future of R2P will depend on how the big emerging powers engage with it,[127] and on conversations among them and between them and the relatively declining Western powers.[128] An especially noteworthy effort to foster a North–South dialogue is Serrano and Weiss's (eds) *International Politics of Human Rights*, with several fine contributions from Adekeye Adebajo (Nigeria, South Africa), Monica Herz (Brazil), Liu Tiewa (China), and Kudrat Virk (India). BRICS (Brazil, Russia, India, China and South Africa)[129] have endorsed R2P as principle, support Pillars One and Two, but diverge occasionally from Western countries on Pillar Three regarding when and how to apply it.[130] Asia is particularly interesting because during the ICISS outreach in 2001, its opposition to intervention was the most hardline of all continents.[131] The Asia Pacific Centre for R2P has led efforts to socialise the region on the 2005 version of R2P.[132] India remains conflicted and hesitant rather than either supportive or opposed,[133] notwithstanding the fact that key antecedents of R2P can be traced directly to its own constitution.[134] In Kai Michael Kenkel and Philip Cunliffe's (eds) *Brazil as a Rising Power: Intervention Norms and the Contestation of Global Order*,[135] debates around intervention serve as a locus for examining the clash of norms that accompanies emergence as a global player. This is not to suggest, however, that Western countries can be exempted from their protection responsibilities.[136]

Russia has tried to misuse R2P against Georgia in the past, tolerated Security Council authorisation of a NATO-led R2P operation in Libya, but stoutly resisted efforts to authorise any robust resolution for dealing with the Syrian crisis.[137] Given its rising global profile and growing regional assertiveness, China's views on global rules,[138] intervention and R2P are drawing particular attention.[139] Notions of responsibility and the corollary concept of responsible governance have deep roots in Chinese traditions of statecraft and corresponding visions of world order,[140] suggesting that 'responsible protection'[141] speaks to Chinese political thought and could anchor its growing engagement with global governance. One of the more interesting books, Rama Mani and Thomas Weiss's (eds) *Responsibility to Protect: Cultural Perspectives in the Global South*,[142] addresses the question of whether the R2P norm and its constitutive values have resonance and grounding within diverse cultures and the experiences of societies torn apart by mass atrocity crimes: a richly rewarding set of perspectives because of the breadth of disciplines, the diversity of authors (with some located in countries that experienced violent political upheaval), and the geographical and cultural spread of the coverage.

By the end of the last century, Africa was home to the overwhelming proportion of violent armed conflicts and associated civilian casualties.[143] If scholars, students and practitioners wish to understand the complexities, nuances, limits and potential of coercive policy tools in challenging transnational conflicts that are concentrated in Africa, they should make a conscious effort to listen mostly to African voices. A second reason for doing so with respect to R2P is that the AU is the only intergovernmental organisation that has explicitly made the right to intervene in a member state part of its foundational text in Article 4(h) of its Constitutive Act. Dan Kuwali, in *The Responsibility to Protect: Implementation of Article 4(h) Intervention*,[144] explores the scope and limits of Article 4(h) and investigates if the clause provides sufficient legal basis for forcible military intervention to prevent serious crimes under international law in Africa. Kuwali and Viljoen's (eds) *Africa and the Responsibility to Protect* explores the many legal and policy challenges to the implementation of Article 4(h). Because the authors across many disciplines are primarily from but not limited to Africa, the book provides a comprehensive and systematic examination of the parallel experiences and evolution of Article 4(h) in Africa and R2P globally.

In the first Gulf War, Colin Powell, then the Chairman of the Joint Chiefs of Staff, refused to expand the war from the limited objective of expelling Iraq from Kuwait to the broader goal of regime change in Baghdad through invasion and occupation. Wisely and very presciently, he warned of the risks of breaking Iraq and if you break it, you own it. In 2015 the world reacted with horror to the savagery and brutality of the Islamic State that rapidly occupied large swathes of territory in Syria and Iraq and proceeded to inflict unspeakable atrocities on sectarian groups, like the Yazidis, who came under its control. Many of us called for their protection under the R2P principle. But a more targeted question is the extent to which the intensity and brutality of the violence in the region in 2015 had its roots in the waves of destabilisation of the autocratic regimes unleashed with the invasion of Iraq and the overthrow of Saddam Hussein in 2003. In turn, if today's violence can be traced back to Iraq in 2003 and proxy interventions by external powers in Syria since 2011, do those who invaded Iraq and have armed and backed the different conflict parties in Syria with weapons and training bear a particular R2P burden for protecting the civilian victims? Jason Ralph and James Souter explore this challenging question with respect to Australia and the UK.[145] They answer in the affirmative to 'a significant degree' (p. 723), 'based on the widely held principle of reparation' (p. 710).

At the end of the day, individuals make and implement decisions, whether it is to commit or stop/halt atrocities. Thus, US President George W. Bush and British Prime Minister Tony Blair will forever be identified with the folly of the 2003 Iraq War.[146] The Lucks identify several categories of individual actors including the vulnerable populations and survivors, perpetrators, bystanders, leaders and international officials.[147]

R2P scepticism

In addition to political controversy on implementation, R2P remains contested among scholars. Bellamy's writings[148] show an interesting journey from a somewhat sceptical and critical analyst to a staunch defender. In an early article he argued the search for consensus had prompted ICISS advocates to 'bargain away' and abandon most of its key central tenets.[149] Now, in *Responsibility to Protect: A Defense*,[150] while not blind to its imperfections, he believes R2P offers the best chance to prevent mass atrocity crimes and protect vulnerable populations. In part, his intellectual journey reflects a growing awareness of distinctions between R2P as an analytic concept with a requirement for philosophical rigour and conceptual coherence, a normative enterprise seeking to entrench the principle as the new norm, and a political project operating in the messy and untidy real world of international politics.[151]

Philip Cunliffe's (ed) *Critical Perspectives on the Responsibility to Protect: Interrogating Theory and Practice*[152] is a 'critical interrogation' of the principles underpinning and the policy consequences flowing from R2P. It concludes that R2P does not embody progressive values but may instead undermine political accountability within states and international peace among them. Suspicions persist among some, including Yang Razali Kassim, in *The Geopolitics of Intervention: Asia and the Responsibility to Protect*,[153] that R2P merely provides a more respectable cloak to geopolitical drivers of major power action. Cunliffe argues that with no mechanism for enacting the 'duty of care', powerful states will continue to determine the conditions under which the 'responsibility to protect' is discharged.[154] Similarly Theresa Reinold argues that lacking intersubjective consensus on its meaning, R2P is merely a duty to *consider* intervention.[155] Sometimes the criticisms are frankly bizarre. R2P was demand driven, responding to a gap in the normative architecture regulating state behaviour with respect to their use of force both internally and internationally in the interstate system. Yet to some, the statist discourse of intervention is a 'critical gap'.[156]

R2P does have a built-in moral hazard: it can create perverse incentives for rebels and dissidents to provoke state retaliation to armed challenges in order to intensify and internationalise a local conflict.[157] The risk was recognised by Annan.[158]

Conclusion

R2P is an improvement on humanitarian intervention on almost all dimensions that most of the international community found objectionable. Consequently, military intervention under R2P has much better prospects of a convergence of legality and legitimacy in the use of force. R2P was meant to compel an analysis of – and policy response to – atrocities from the point of view of those in need of urgent protection, not the rights, privileges and interests of the intervening powers. My one lament about the flourishing literature on R2P is the unhealthy dominance of Western analysts and the neglect and silencing of voices from the global South. On this topic more than most, our responsibility as scholars extends to making that extra effort to seek out and heed the worldviews, insights and wisdom, if not the deep scholarship, of intellectuals and analysts from the distant other.

Notes

* Originally published in *International Affairs* 92:2 (March 2016), 415–34. Reprinted by permission of Wiley Blackwell Publishing on behalf of the Royal Institute of International Affairs.

1 For a discussion of what constitutes UN policy, see Ramesh Thakur and Thomas G. Weiss, 'United Nations "Policy": An Argument with Three Illustrations', *International Studies Perspectives* 10:1 (2009), 18–35.

2 Summaries available at: www.globalr2p.org.

3 These have been helpfully reprinted in Kofi Annan, *We the Peoples: A UN for the 21st Century*, edited by Edward Mortimer (London: Paradigm Publishers, 2014).

4 Gareth Evans, *The Responsibility to Protect: Ending Mass Atrocity Crimes Once and For All* (Washington, DC: Brookings Institution Press, 2008); Ramesh Thakur, *The United Nations, Peace and Security: From Collective Security to The Responsibility to Protect* (Cambridge: Cambridge University Press, 2006); and Thakur, *The Responsibility to Protect: Norms, Laws and the Use of Force in International Politics* (London: Routledge, 2011).

5 Thomas G. Weiss, *Humanitarian Intervention: Ideas in Action* (Cambridge: Polity, 2011). See also Ramesh Thakur and Thomas G. Weiss, 'R2P: From Idea to Norm – and Action?', *GR2P* 1:1 (2009), 22–53.

6 Edward C. Luck, 'Sovereignty, Choice, and the Responsibility to Protect', *GR2P* 1:1 (2009): 10–21; Luck, 'The Responsibility to Protect: Growing Pains or Early Promise?', *Ethics & International Affairs* 24:4 (2010), 349–65.

7 W. Andy Knight and Frazer Egerton, eds., *The Routledge Handbook of the Responsibility to Protect* (London: Routledge, 2012); and Alex J. Bellamy and Tim Dunne, eds., *The Oxford Handbook of the Responsibility to Protect* (Oxford: Oxford University Press, 2016).

8 Sabrina Hoeling, *Can R2P Practice What it Promises? A Case Study on the Syrian Civil War* (Hamburg: Anchor Academic Publishing, 2015); Spencer Zifcak, 'The Responsibility to Protect after Libya and Syria', *Melbourne Journal of International Law* 13:1 (2012), 59–93; Justin Morris, 'Libya and Syria: R2P and the Spectre of the Swinging Pendulum', *International Affairs* 89:5 (2013), 1265–83.

9 Spencer Zifcak, 'What Happened to the International Community? R2P and the Conflicts in South Sudan and the Central African Republic', *Melbourne Journal of International Law* 16:1 (2015), 52–85.

10 This section has been shortened from the original as Chapter 6 in this book is a more detailed exposition of the differences between humanitarian intervention and R2P.

11 This is a sparse summary of a public lecture delivered at Kings College London on 12 November 2015: Ramesh Thakur, 'R2P: The Old Wine of Humanitarian Intervention in a New Bottle?'. Audiotext available at: https://soundcloud.com/warstudies/a-case-of-old-wine-in-new-bottle-from-humanitarian-intervention-to-r2p.

12 Weiss, *Humanitarian Intervention*; Ramesh Thakur, 'Humanitarian Intervention', in Thomas G. Weiss and Sam Daws, eds., *The Oxford Handbook on the United Nations* (Oxford: Oxford University Press, 2007), 387–403; Ramesh Thakur, 'Non-Intervention: A Case Study', *Political Science* 42:1 (1990), 26–61.

13 See Alex J. Bellamy, 'The Responsibility to Protect and the Just War Tradition', in Ramesh Thakur and William Maley, eds., *Theorising the Responsibility to Protect* (Cambridge: Cambridge University Press, 2015), 181–99.
14 Ellery Stowell, *Intervention in International Law* (Washington, DC: J. Byrne, 1921); Natalino Ronzitti, *Rescuing Nationals Abroad through Military Coercion and Intervention on Grounds of Humanity* (Leiden: Brill, 1985).
15 Michael Doyle, *The Question of Intervention: John Stuart Mill and the Responsibility to Protect* (New Haven: Yale University Press, 2015).
16 Bjorn Gomes, 'The Duty to Oppose Violence: Humanitarian Intervention as a Question for Political Philosophy', *Review of International Studies* 37:3 (2011), 1045–67.
17 Luke Glanville, *Sovereignty and the Responsibility to Protect: A New History* (Chicago: University of Chicago Press, 2014). See also: Francis K. Abiew, *The Evolution of the Doctrine and Practice of Humanitarian Intervention* (The Hague: Kluwer Law International, 1999); Gary J. Bass, *Freedom's Battle: The Origins of Humanitarian Intervention* (New York: Vintage Books, 2009); Alexis Heraclides, 'Humanitarian Intervention Yesterday and Today: A History', *European Journal of International Studies* 2:1 (2015), 15–37; Davide Rodogno, *Against Massacre: Humanitarian Intervention in the Ottoman Empire, 1815–1914* (Princeton: Princeton University Press, 2012); and Brendan Simms and D.B.J. Trim, *Humanitarian Intervention: A History* (Cambridge: Cambridge University Press, 2011).
18 Luke Glanville, 'The Myth of "Traditional Sovereignty"', *International Studies Quarterly* 57:1 (2013), 79–90.
19 Jennifer Welsh, 'A Normative Case for Pluralism: Reassessing Vincent's Views on Humanitarian Intervention', *International Affairs* 87:5 (2011), 1193–1204.
20 Michael J. Glennon, *Limits of Law, Prerogatives of Power: Interventionism after Kosovo* (New York: Palgrave Macmillan, 2001).
21 J.L. Holzgrefe and Robert O. Keohane, eds., *Humanitarian Intervention: Ethical, Legal and Political Dilemmas* (Cambridge: Cambridge University Press, 2003).
22 Jennifer Welsh, ed., *Humanitarian Intervention and International Relations* (Oxford: Oxford University Press, 2004).
23 Don E. Scheid, ed., *The Ethics of Armed Humanitarian Intervention* (Cambridge: Cambridge University Press, 2014).
24 Norrie MacQueen, *Humanitarian Intervention and the United Nations* (Edinburgh: Edinburgh University Press, 2011).
25 Monica Serrano and Thomas G. Weiss, eds., *The International Politics of Human Rights: Rallying to the R2P Cause?* (London: Routledge, 2013); John Janzekovic and Daniel Silander, eds., *Responsibility to Protect and Prevent: Principles, Promises and Practicalities* (London: Anthem Press, 2013); Dan Kuwali and Frans Viljoen, eds., *Africa and the Responsibility to Protect: Article 4(h) of the African Union Constitutive Act* (London: Routledge, 2014), Chapters 13–16.
26 Alex Bellamy, *Massacres and Morality: Mass Atrocities in an Age of Civilian Immunity* (Oxford: Oxford University Press, 2012).
27 Sheri P. Rosenberg, Tibi Galis and Alex Zucker, eds., *Reconstructing Atrocity Prevention* (Cambridge: Cambridge University Press, 2015).
28 A useful contrast is Niv Horesch and Emilian Kavalski, eds., *Asian Thought on China's Changing International Relations* (Basingstoke: Palgrave Macmillan, 2014), which gives primacy to voices from China and its Asian neighbours in the intellectual and philosophical reflections on the rise of China. It builds on the earlier Amitav Acharya and Barry Buzan, eds., *Non-Western International Relations Theory: Perspectives On and Beyond Asia* (New York: Routledge, 2010).
29 Kishore Mahbubani, *Can Asians Think?* (Singapore: Marshall Cavendish, 2009).
30 Alex Bellamy, *Global Politics and the Responsibility to Protect: from Words to Deeds* (London: Routledge, 2011), Chapter 6.

31 Robert I. Rotberg, ed., *Mass Atrocity Crimes: Preventing Future Outrages* (Washington, DC: Brookings Institution Press, 2010).
32 For a critique and defence of Crisis Group methodology, see Peter Tikuisis and David R. Mandel, 'Is the World Deteriorating?', and International Crisis Group, 'Response to "Is the World Deteriorating?"', *Global Governance* 21:1 (2015), 9–18.
33 E.g. 'R2P Monitor', Issue 23, 15 September 2015, www.globalr2p.org/media/files/r2p_monitor_sept2015_final.pdf.
34 Frank Chalk, Kyle Matthews and Carla Barqueiro, *Mobilizing the Will to Intervene: Leadership to Prevent Mass Atrocities* (Montreal: McGill Queens University Press, 2010).
35 Adam Lupel and Ernesto Verdeja, eds., *Responding to Genocide: The Politics of International Action* (Boulder: Lynne Rienner, 2013).
36 Serena Sharma and Jennifer Welsh, eds., *The Responsibility to Prevent: Overcoming the Challenges of Atrocity Prevention* (Oxford: Oxford University Press, 2015).
37 'Declaration of the Latin American Network for Genocide and Mass Atrocity Prevention', Santiago, 29 May 2015, www.auschwitzinstitute.org/wp-content/uploads/2015/08/Network-Declaration-EN.pdf.
38 Asia-Pacific Centre for the Responsibility to Protect, www.r2pasiapacific.org/index.html?page=224295&pid=191756.
39 This is the main narrative storyline of Thakur, *United Nations, Peace and Security*.
40 Charles Sampford and Ramesh Thakur, 'From the Right to Persecute to the Responsibility to Protect: Feuerbachian Inversions of Rights and Responsibilities in State–Citizen Relations', in Thakur and Maley, eds., *Theorising the Responsibility to Protect*, 38–58. Reprinted in the present volume as Chapter 5.
41 Ban Ki-moon, *Implementing the Responsibility to Protect* (New York: United Nations, document A/63/677, 12 January 2009), paragraph 67.
42 Ramesh Thakur, 'The Development and Evolution of R2P as International Policy', *Global Policy* 6:3 (2015), 190–200.
43 Richard H. Cooper and Juliette Voinov Kohler, eds., *Responsibility to Protect: The Global Moral Compact for the 21st Century* (Basingstoke: Palgrave Macmillan, 2010).
44 Mary Ellen O'Connell, 'Responsibility to Peace: A Critique of R2P', *Journal of Intervention and Statebuilding* 4:1 (2010), 39–52.
45 Alex Bellamy, Sara Davies and Luke Glanville, eds., *The Responsibility to Protect and International Law* (Leiden: Brill, 2010); Carsten Stahn, 'Responsibility to Protect: Political Rhetoric or Emerging Legal Norm?', *American Journal of International Law* 101 (2007), 99–120; Michael Byers, 'International Law and the Responsibility to Protect' in Thakur and Maley, eds., *Theorising the Responsibility to Protect*, 101–24.
46 Amitav Acharya, 'The Responsibility to Protect and a Theory of Norm Circulation', in Thakur and Maley, eds., *Theorising the Responsibility to Protect*, 59–77.
47 Gentian Zyberi, 'Sharing the Responsibility to Protect: Taking Stock and Moving Forward', in Gentian Zyberi, ed., *An Institutional Approach to the Responsibility to Protect* (Cambridge: Cambridge University Press, 2013), 512.
48 Dieter Fleck, 'The Law Applicable to Peace Operations', in Andrew Clapham and Paola Gaeta, eds., *The Oxford Handbook of International Law in Armed Conflict* (Oxford: Oxford University Press, 2014), 216 (emphasis added).
49 William Bain, 'Responsibility and Obligation in the "Responsibility to Protect"', *Review of International Studies* 36 (2010), 25–46.
50 Peter Hilpold, ed., *The Responsibility to Protect (R2P): A New Paradigm of International Law?* (Leiden: Brill, 2014).
51 Jutta Brunée and Stephen Toope, 'R2P and the Use of Force: Building Legitimacy', *GR2P* 2:3 (2010), 191–212.

52 Heather Roff, *Global Justice, Kant and the Responsibility to Protect: A Provisional Duty* (London: Routledge, 2013).
53 Ines-Jacqueline Werkner and Dirk Rademacher, eds., *Protecting People – and Losing Just Peace? Debates on the Responsibility to Protect in the Context of Christian Peace Ethics* (Berlin: LIT Verlag, 2013).
54 Semegnish Asfaw, Guillermo Kerber and Peter Weiderud, eds., *Responsibility to Protect: Ethical and Theological Reflections* (Geneva: World Council of Churches, 2006).
55 Dan Bulley, 'The Politics of Ethical Foreign Policy: A Responsibility to Protect Whom?', *European Journal of International Relations* 16:3 (2010), 441–61; David Chandler, 'Rhetoric Without Responsibility: The Attraction of "Ethical" Foreign Policy', *British Journal of Politics and International Relations* 5:3 (2003), 295–316.
56 Theresa Reinold, *Sovereignty and the Responsibility to Protect: The Power of Norms and the Norms of the Powerful* (London: Routledge, 2013).
57 Cristina Badescu, *Humanitarian Intervention and the Responsibility to Protect: Security and Human Rights* (London: Routledge, 2012).
58 Hannes Peltonen, *International Responsibility and Grave Humanitarian Crises: Collective Provision for Human Security* (London: Routledge, 2012). See also: Thakur, *United Nations, Peace and Security*, Chapter 3; Cecilia Jacob, 'Practising Civilian Protection: Human Security in Myanmar and Cambodia', *Security Dialogue* 45:4 (2014), 391–408; David Chandler, 'Resilience and Human Security: The Post-Interventionist Paradigm', *Security Dialogue* 43:3 (2012), 213–29; and Nicholas Thomas and William T. Tow, 'The Utility of Human Security: Sovereignty and Humanitarian Intervention', *Security Dialogue* 33:2 (2002), 177–92.
59 Peter Hilpold, 'Intervening in the Name of Humanity: R2P and the Power of Ideas', *Journal of Conflict and Security Law* 17:1 (2012), 49–79.
60 Ramesh Thakur and Vesselin Popovski, 'The Responsibility to Protect and Prosecute: The Parallel Erosion of Sovereignty and Impunity', in Giuliana Ziccardi Capaldo, ed., *The Global Community: Yearbook of International Law and Jurisprudence 2007*, Vol. 1 (New York: Oxford University Press, 2008), 39–61; Kirsten Ainley, 'The Responsibility to Protect and the International Criminal Court: Counteracting the Crisis', *International Affairs* 91:1 (2015), 37–54; Jeremy Sarkin, 'The Role of the United Nations, the African Union and Africa's Sub-regional Organisations in Dealing with Africa's Human Rights Problems: Connecting Humanitarian Intervention and the Responsibility to Protect', *Journal of African Law* 53:1 (2009), 1–33.
61 Elizabeth G. Feris, *The Politics of Prevention: The Limits of Humanitarian Action* (Washington, DC: Brookings Institution Press, 2011); Ramesh Thakur, 'Protection Gaps for Civilian Victims of Political Violence', *South African Journal of International Affairs* 20:3 (2013), 321–38. Reprinted in the present volume as Chapter 10.
62 Ramesh Thakur, 'Israel's Serial Gaza Offensives are Offensive', *e-International Relations*, 24 July 2014, www.e-ir.info/2014/07/24/israels-serial-gaza-offensives-are-offensive.
63 Sara Davies and Luke Glanville, eds., *Protecting the Displaced: Deepening the Responsibility to Protect* (Leiden: Brill, 2010).
64 Agnes Hurwitz, *The Collective Responsibility to Protect Refugees* (Oxford: Oxford University Press, 2009); William Maley, 'Humanitarian Law, Refugee Protection, and the Responsibility to Protect', in Thakur and Maley, eds., *Theorising the Responsibility to Protect*, 249–65.
65 Walter Kemp, Vesselin Popovski and Ramesh Thakur, eds., *Blood and Borders: The Responsibility to Protect and the Problem of the Kin-State* (Tokyo: United Nations University Press, 2011).

66 Terry Nardin, 'Humanitarian Imperialism', *Ethics & International Affairs* 19:2 (2005), 21–26.
67 Thakur, *Responsibility to Protect*, Chapter 12.
68 Jennifer Welsh, 'Norm Contestation and R2P', *GR2P* 5:4 (2013), 365–96.
69 Bellamy, *Global Politics and the Responsibility to Protect*, 6.
70 Jared Genser and Irwin Cotler, eds., *The Responsibility to Protect: The Promise of Stopping Mass Atrocities in Our Time* (New York: Oxford University Press, 2011).
71 Charles Sampford and Ramesh Thakur, eds., *Responsibility to Protect and Sovereignty* (Aldershot: Ashgate, 2014).
72 Julia Hoffman and Andre Nollkaemper, eds., *Responsibility to Protect: From Principle to Practice* (Amsterdam: Pallas, 2012).
73 Bellamy, *Global Politics and the Responsibility to Protect.*
74 Roberto Belloni, 'The Tragedy in Darfur and the Limits of the "Responsibility to Protect"', *Ethnopolitics* 5:4 (2006), 327–46; Hugo Slim, 'Dithering over Darfur? A Preliminary Review of the International Response', *International Affairs* 80:5 (2004), 811–28; Nicholas Wheeler, 'A Victory for Common Humanity? The Responsibility to Protect after the 2005 World Summit', *Journal of International Law and International Relations* 2:1 (2005), 95–107.
75 Alex de Waal, 'Darfur and the Failure of the Responsibility to Protect', *International Affairs* 83:6 (2007), 1039–54.
76 Cristina Badescu and Linnea Bergholm, 'The Responsibility to Protect and the Conflict in Darfur: The Big Let-down', *Security Dialogue* 40:3 (2009), 287–309.
77 Nicolaas Smit, *The Evolution of the Responsibility to Protect: From the ICISS to the 2005 World Summit* (Hamburg: Anchor Academic Publishing, 2013).
78 Paul Williams and Alex Bellamy, 'The Responsibility to Protect and the Crisis in Darfur', *Security Dialogue* 36:1 (2005), 27–47.
79 Abdel Salam Sidahmed, Walter C. Soderlund and Donald E. Briggs, *The Responsibility to Protect in Darfur: The Role of the Mass Media* (Lanham: Lexington Books, 2010).
80 Evans, *Responsibility to Protect*, 61.
81 For an interesting argument on how even misuses and abuses of the R2P norm help to strengthen it, see Cristina Badescu and Thomas G. Weiss, 'Misrepresenting R2P and Advancing Norms: an Alternative Spiral' *International Studies Perspectives* 11:4 (2010), 354–74.
82 Damien Kingsbury, *Sri Lanka and the Responsibility to Protect: Politics, Ethnicity and Genocide* (London: Routledge, 2012). He also takes an unfortunate personal swipe at Amitav Acharya in describing the latter's localisation notion of norms as 'an intellectual juggling act' that is 'a prerequisite for public scholarship under Singapore's highly interventionist political order' (11).
83 Thakur, *Responsibility to Protect*, 155–56.
84 Adrian Gallagher, 'The Promise of Pillar II: Analysing International Assistance Under the Responsibility to Protect', *International Affairs* 91:6 (2015), 1259–75 at 1260.
85 *Report of the Commission of Inquiry on Human Rights in the Democratic People's Republic of Korea* (Geneva: Human Rights Council, UN document A/HRC/25/63, 7 February 2014).
86 Alex Bellamy, 'A Chronic Protection Problem: the DPRK and the Responsibility to Protect', *International Affairs* 91:2 (2015), 225–44.
87 Alex J. Bellamy, *The First Response: Peaceful Means in the Third Pillar of the Responsibility to Protect*. Policy Analysis (Muscatine IA: Stanley Foundation, December 2015), www.stanleyfoundation.org/resources.cfm?id=1586.
88 Aidan Hehir and Robert Murray, eds., *Libya, the Responsibility to Protect and the Future of Humanitarian Intervention* (Basingstoke: Palgrave Macmillan, 2013).

89 Paul Williams and Alex Bellamy, 'Principles, Politics, and Prudence: Libya, the Responsibility to Protect, and the Use of Military Force', *Global Governance* 18:3 (2012), 273–97; Zifcak, 'Responsibility to Protect after Libya and Syria'; Ivo H. Daalder and James Stavridis, 'NATO's Victory in Libya: The Right Way to Run an Intervention', *Foreign Affairs* 91:2 (2012), 2–7.

90 Alan Kuperman, 'A Model Humanitarian Intervention? Reassessing NATO's Libya Campaign', *International Security* 38:1 (2013), 105–36.

91 Roland Paris, 'The "Responsibility to Protect" and the Structural Problems of Preventive Humanitarian Intervention', *International Peacekeeping* 21:5 (2014), 569–603.

92 Ramesh Thakur, 'R2P's "Structural" Problems: A Response to Roland Paris', *International Peacekeeping* 22:1 (2015), 12–15. Reprinted in the present volume as Chapter 8.

93 Aidan Hehir, 'The Permanence of Inconsistency: Libya, the Security Council, and the Responsibility to Protect', *International Security* 38:1 (2013), 137–59.

94 Alex Bellamy, 'The Responsibility to Protect: Added Value or Hot Air?' *Cooperation and Conflict* 48:3 (2013), 333–57.

95 Alex de Waal, 'African Roles in the Libyan Conflict of 2011', *International Affairs* 89:2 (2013), 265–79.

96 Alex Bellamy and Paul Williams, 'The New Politics of Protection? Côte d'Ivoire, Libya and the Responsibility to Protect', *International Affairs* 87:4 (2011), 825–50; Luke Glanville, 'Intervention in Libya: From Sovereign Consent to Regional Consent', *International Studies Perspectives* 14:3 (2013), 325–42; Matthias Vanhullebusch, 'The Arab League and Military Operations: Prospects and Challenges in Syria', *International Peacekeeping* 22:2 (2015), 151–68; El Hassan bin Talal and R. Schwarz, 'The Responsibility to Protect and the Arab World: An Emerging International Norm?', *Contemporary Security Policy* 34:1 (2013), 1–15.

97 Hannes Peltonen, 'Modelling International Collective Responsibility: The Case of Grave Humanitarian Crises', *Review of International Studies* 36:2 (2010), 239–55.

98 Sara Davies, Zim Nwokora, Eli Stamnes and Sarah Teitt, eds., *Responsibility to Protect and Women, Peace, and Security: Aligning the Protection Agendas* (Leiden: Brill, 2013).

99 Laurel Bond and Jennifer Sherett, 'Mapping Gender and R2P', *GR2P* 4:2 (2012), 133–51; Susan Harris Rimmer, 'Is the Responsibility to Protect Doctrine Gender-neutral?', in Thakur and Maley, eds., *Theorising the Responsibility to Protect*, 266–84; Dursun Peksen, 'Foreign Military Intervention and Women's Rights', *Journal of Peace Research* 48:4 (2011), 455–68; Sara Davies, Sarah Teitt and Zim Nwokora, 'Bridging the Gap: Early Warning, Gender and the Responsibility To Protect', *Cooperation and Conflict* 50:2 (2015), 228–49.

100 Hitoshi Nasu, 'Operationalizing the Responsibility to Protect in the Context of Civilian Protection by UN Peacekeepers', *International Peacekeeping* 18:4 (2011), 364–78; Lisa Hultman, 'UN Peace Operations and Protection of Civilians: Cheap Talk or Norm Implementation?', *Journal of Peace Research* 50:1 (2013), 59–73; Thomas G. Weiss, 'Peace Operations and Humanitarian Interventions' in Joachim Koops, Norrie MacQueen, Thierry Tardy and Paul Williams, eds., *The Oxford Handbook of United Nations Peacekeeping Operations* (Oxford: Oxford University Press, 2015), 78–92.

101 Hugo Slim, 'Why Protect Civilians? Innocence, Immunity and Enmity in War', *International Affairs* 79:3 (2003), 481–501.

102 Vesselin Popovski, Charles Sampford and Angus Francis, eds., *Norms of Protection: Responsibility to Protect, Protection of Civilians, and Their Interaction* (Tokyo: UN University Press, 2012). See also Hugh Breakey, Angus Francis, Vesselin Popovski, Charles Sampford, Michael G. Smith, and Ramesh Thakur, *Enhancing Protection Capacity: A Policy Guide to the Responsibility to Protect and the Protection of Civilians in*

Armed Conflicts (Brisbane: Institute for Ethics, Governance and Law, 2012), www.griffith.edu.au/criminology-law/institute-ethics-governance-law/research/responsibility-to-protect-protection-of-civilians-policy-guide.

103 *GR2P* 6:2 (2014). The article by the former UN Under-Secretary-General for Humanitarian Affairs is especially noteworthy: John Holmes 'Responsibility to Protect', 126–45.

104 Susan Breau, 'The Impact of the Responsibility to Protect on Peacekeeping', *Journal of Conflict & Security Law* 11:3 (2006), 429–64.

105 Frédéric Mégret, 'From Peacekeeping to R2P: The Protection of Civilians as the UN's New Raison d'Être?' unpublished paper (September 2012); http://dx.doi.org/10.2139/ssrn.2154968.

106 Bellamy, *Responsibility to Protect: A Defense*, 150–69.

107 Thomas Weiss, *Military–Civilian Interactions: Humanitarian Crises and the Responsibility to Protect* (Lanham: Rowman & Littlefield Publishers, 2004).

108 Annie Herro, *UN Emergency Peace and the Responsibility to Protect* (London: Routledge, 2014).

109 Daniel Fiott and Joachim Koops, eds., *The Responsibility to Protect and the Third Pillar: Legitimacy and Operationalization* (Basingstoke: Palgrave Macmillan, 2014).

110 OAU, *Rwanda: The Preventable Genocide. Report of the OAU's International Panel of Eminent Personalities* (Addis Ababa: OAU, 31 May 2000), paragraph 15.87, www.refworld.org/pdfid/4d1da8752.pdf.

111 Toni Erskine, ed., *Can Institutions Have Responsibilities? Collective Moral Agency and International Relations* (Basingstoke: Palgrave Macmillan, 2004). See especially Daniela Kroslak, 'The Responsibility of Collective External Bystanders in Cases of Genocide: the French in Rwanda', 159–82; and Anthony Lang, 'The United Nations and the Fall of Srebrenica: Meaningful Responsibility and International Society', 183–206.

112 Richard Falk, Mark Juergensmeyer and Vesselin Popovski, eds., *Legality and Legitimacy in Global Affairs* (Oxford: Oxford University Press, 2012); Simon Chesterman, 'Legality Versus Legitimacy: Humanitarian Intervention, the Security Council, and the Rule of Law', *Security Dialogue* 33:3 (2002), 293–307; and Sylvia Lechner, 'Humanitarian Intervention: Moralism Versus Realism?' *International Studies Review* 12:3 (2010), 437–43.

113 David Fisher and Nigel Biggar, 'Was Iraq an Unjust War? A Debate on the Iraq War and Reflections on Libya', *International Affairs* 87:3 (2011), 687–707, especially Biggar's argument on 693–98 to justify the 2003 Iraq War; Fisher criticised the Iraq War but justified the 2011 NATO-led intervention in Libya.

114 Marc Weller, ed., *The Oxford Handbook of the Use of Force in International Law* (Oxford: Oxford University Press, 2015).

115 Simon Chesterman, *Just War or Just Peace? Humanitarian Intervention and International Law* (Oxford: Oxford University Press, 2001); Nicholas Wheeler, *Saving Strangers: Humanitarian Intervention in International Society* (Oxford: Oxford University Press, 2000); J. Peter Burgess, 'Ethics of Humanitarian Intervention: The Circle Closes', *Security Dialogue* 33:3 (2002), 261–64; John Williams, 'Space, Scale and Just War: Meeting the Challenge of Humanitarian Intervention and Transnational Terrorism', *Review of International Studies* 34:4 (2008), 581–600; Terry Nardin, 'The Moral Basis of Humanitarian Intervention', *Ethics & International Affairs* 16:1 (2002), 57–70.

116 Patrick Macklem, 'Humanitarian Intervention and the Distribution of Sovereignty in International Law', *Ethics & International Affairs* 22:4 (2006), 369–93.

117 Morten Abramowitz and Thomas Pickering, 'Making Intervention Work: Improving the UN's Ability to Act', *Foreign Affairs* 87:5 (2008), 100–08.

118 Daniel Silander and Don Wallace, eds., *International Organizations and the Implementation of the Responsibility to Protect: The Humanitarian Crisis in Syria* (London: Routledge, 2015).
119 Aidan Hehir, *The Responsibility to Protect: Rhetoric, Reality and the Future of Humanitarian Intervention* (Basingstoke: Palgrave Macmillan, 2012).
120 Ramesh Thakur, 'United Nations', in David Coates, ed., *The Oxford Companion to American Politics* (New York: Oxford University Press, 2012), Vol II, 388–96.
121 Madeleine Albright and Richard Williamson, *The United States and R2P: From Words to Action* (Washington, DC: US Institute of Peace, US Holocaust Memorial Museum, and Brookings Institution Press, 2013).
122 Cathinka Vik, *Moral Responsibility, Statecraft and Humanitarian Intervention: The US Response to Rwanda, Darfur, and Libya* (London: Routledge, 2015).
123 Hedley Bull, *Anarchical Society: A Study of Order in World Politics* (London: Macmillan, 1977), 200–29.
124 Alex Bellamy, 'Whither the Responsibility to Protect? Humanitarian Intervention and the 2005 World Summit', *Ethics & International Affairs* 20:2 (2006), 164.
125 Jennifer Welsh, 'Conclusion: Humanitarian Intervention after 11 September', in Welsh, ed., *Humanitarian Intervention and International Relations*, 180. See also: Colum Lynch, 'U.S. Wants Changes in U.N. Agreement', *Washington Post*, 25 August 2005; Alicia L. Bannon, 'The Responsibility to Protect: The U.N. World Summit and the Question of Unilateralism', *The Yale Law Journal* 115:5 (March 2006), 1157–66; Steven Groves, 'The U.S. Should Reject the U.N. "Responsibility to Protect" Doctrine', *Backgrounder* No. 2130 (Washington, DC: Heritage Foundation, 2008), www.heritage.org/research/reports/2008/05/the-us-should-reject-the-un-responsibility-to-protect-doctrine.
126 Bellamy, 'Whither the Responsibility to Protect?', 164; emphasis in original.
127 An alternative grouping would be 'global middle powers': Malte Brosig, ed., *The Responsibility to Protect – From Evasive to Reluctant Action? The Role of Global Middle Powers* (Johannesburg and Pretoria: Hans Seidel Foundation, Institute for Security Studies, Konrad-Adenauer-Stiftung, and South African Institute of International Affairs, 2012).
128 Ramesh Thakur, 'R2P after Libya and Syria: Engaging Emerging Powers', *Washington Quarterly* 36:2 (2013), 61–76. Reprinted in the present volume as Chapter 7.
129 Ramesh Thakur, 'How Representative are BRICS?' *Third World Quarterly* 35:10 (2014), 1791–1808.
130 Oliver Stuenkel, 'The BRICS and the Future of the Responsibility to Protect', *GR2P* 6:1 (2014), 3–28.
131 Thakur, *United Nations, Peace and Security*, 268–70.
132 Alex Bellamy and Sara Davies, 'The Responsibility to Protect in the Asia-Pacific Region', *Security Dialogue* 40 (2009), 547–74; David Capie, 'The Responsibility to Protect Norm in Southeast Asia: Framing, Resistance and the Localization Myth', *Pacific Review* 25:1 (2012), 75–93.
133 Ian Hall, 'Tilting at Windmills? The Indian Debate over Responsibility to Protect after UNSC Resolution 1973', *GR2P* 9:1 (2013), 84–108; Roopmati Khandekar, 'India and the Responsibility to Protect's Third Pillar', in Fiott and Koops, eds., *The Responsibility to Protect and the Third Pillar*, 115–29.
134 Ramesh Thakur, 'The Responsibility to Protect Revisited', *Daily Yomiuri*, 12 April 2007; reprinted in Ramesh Thakur, *The People vs. the State: Reflections on UN Authority, US Power and the Responsibility to Protect* (Tokyo: United Nations University Press, 2011), 151–53.
135 Kai Michael Kenkel and Philip Cunliffe, eds., *Brazil as a Rising Power: Intervention Norms and the Contestation of Global Order* (London: Routledge, 2016).
136 See, for example, *The Netherlands and the Responsibility to Protect: The Responsibility to Protect People from Mass Atrocities* (The Hague: Advisory Council on International Affairs, June 2010).

137 Natasha Kuhrt, 'Russia, the Responsibility to Protect, and Intervention', in Fiott and Koops, eds., *The Responsibility to Protect and the Third Pillar*, 97–114; Derek Averre and Lance Davies, 'Russia, Humanitarian Intervention and the Responsibility to Protect: The Case of Syria', *International Affairs* 91:2 (2015), 813–34.

138 Pu Xiaoyu, 'Socialisation as a Two-way Process: Emerging Powers and the Diffusion of International', *Chinese Journal of International Politics* 5:4 (2012), 341–67; Gregory Chin and Ramesh Thakur, 'Will China Change the Rules of Global Order?', *Washington Quarterly* 33:4 (2010), 119–38.

139 Yang Zewei, 'The Non-intervention Principle: Challenge and China's Response', *Global Review* (Shanghai) (Summer 2013), 65–83; Mordechai Chaziza and Ogen Goldman, 'Revisiting China's Non-interference Policy Towards Intrastate Wars', *Chinese Journal of International Politics* 7:1 (2014), 89–115; Tim Dunne and Sarah Teitt, 'Contested Intervention: India, China and the Responsibility to Protect', *Global Governance* 21:3 (2015), 371–91; Liu Tiewa and Haibin Zhang, 'Debates in China about the Responsibility to Protect as a Developing International Norm: A General Assessment', *Conflict, Security and Development* 14:4 (2014), 403–27; Peiran Wang, 'China and the Third Pillar', in Fiott and Koops, eds., *The Responsibility to Protect and the Third Pillar*, 78–96; Nicola P. Contessi, 'Multilateralism, Intervention and Norm Contestation: China's Stance on Darfur in the UN Security Council', *Security Dialogue* 41:3 (2010), 323–44; Jelena Cupac, 'Emerging International Norms and State Behavior: Chinese Foreign Policy Between "Pluralist Pull" and "Solidarist Push"', *CEU Political Science Journal* 9:1–2 (2014), 39–61; Sarah Teitt, 'The Responsibility to Protect and China's Peacekeeping Policy', *International Peacekeeping* 18:3 (2011), 298–312.

140 Pichamon Yeophantong, 'Governing the World: China's Evolving Conceptions of Responsibility', *Chinese Journal of International Politics* 6:4 (2013), 329–64.

141 Ruan Zongze, 'Responsible Protection: Building a Safer World', *China International Studies* (May/June 2012), 19–41.

142 Rama Mani and Thomas Weiss, eds., *Responsibility to Protect: Cultural Perspectives in the Global South* (London: Routledge, 2011).

143 Andrew Mack (director and editor-in-chief), *Human Security Report* (New York: Oxford University Press, 2005).

144 Dan Kuwali, *The Responsibility to Protect: Implementation of Article 4(h) Intervention* (Leiden: Brill, 2011).

145 Jason Ralph and James Souter, 'A Special Responsibility to Protect: The UK, Australia and the Rise of Islamic State', *International Affairs* 91:4 (2015), 709–23.

146 Ramesh Thakur, 'The Shock of the Iraq War and Awe at the Lingering Effects of the Folly', in Ramesh Thakur and Jack Cunningham, eds., *Australia, Canada, and Iraq: Perspectives on an Invasion* (Toronto: Dundurn Press, 2015), 77–99.

147 Edward Luck and Dana Luck, 'The Individual Responsibility to Protect', in Rosenberg, Galis and Zucker, eds., *Reconstructing Atrocity Prevention*, 207–48.

148 Alex Bellamy, *Responsibility to Protect* (Oxford: Polity Press, 2009); Bellamy, Davies and Glanville, eds., *Responsibility to Protect and International Law*; Bellamy, *Global Politics and the Responsibility to Protect*; Bellamy, *Massacres and Morality*.

149 Bellamy, 'Whither the Responsibility to Protect?', 143–69.

150 Alex Bellamy, *Responsibility to Protect: A Defense* (Oxford: Oxford University Press, 2014).

151 Thakur, 'R2P's "Structural" Problems: A Response to Roland Paris'.

152 Philip Cunliffe, ed., *Critical Perspectives on the Responsibility to Protect: Interrogating Theory and Practice* (London: Routledge, 2011).

153 Yang Razali Kassim, *The Geopolitics of Intervention: Asia and the Responsibility to Protect* (New York: Springer, 2014). See also Siddharth Mallavarapu, 'Colonialism and the Responsibility to Protect', in Thakur and Maley, eds., *Theorising the Responsibility to Protect*, 305–22.

154 Philip Cunliffe, 'Dangerous Duties: Power, Paternalism and the "Responsibility to Protect"', *Review of International Studies* 36:Supplement 1 (2010), 76–96.
155 Theresa Reinold, 'The Responsibility to Protect – Much Ado About Nothing?', *Review of International Studies* 36 (2010), 55–78.
156 Daniel Baer, 'The Ultimate Sacrifice and the Ethics of Humanitarian Intervention', *Review of International Studies* 37:1 (2011), 301–26.
157 Alan Kuperman, 'The Moral Hazard of Humanitarian Intervention: Lessons from the Balkans', *International Studies Quarterly* 52:1 (2008), 49–80.
158 Kofi A. Annan, '*We the Peoples': The Role of the United Nations in the Twenty-first Century.* Report of the Secretary-General (New York: UN document A/54/2000, 27 March 2000), paragraph 216.

Part I

Origins, meaning and evolution

Power, principles, ideas and the normative international architecture

Cognisant of the stern admonition from Athens to Melos that questions of right and justice apply only to relations among equals in power, while for others 'the strong do what they can and the weak suffer what they must',[1] 'Realism maintains that universal moral principles cannot be applied to the actions of states'.[2] Yet even Morgenthau, the intellectual godfather of Realism, hedged his bets when he wrote of 'the moral dignity of the national interest'.[3] Subsequent history has modified the Thucydides thesis with a steady reduction in societal, national and international violence from the hunter-gatherer civilisations to modern times, based on empathy, self-control, reason and moral sense as 'the better angels' of human nature.[4] Accordingly, to paraphrase and update the familiar mantra of Realism, international politics consists of the struggle for the ascendancy of competing normative architectures conducted on two axes. One axis consists of military muscle, economic weight and geopolitical clout. The second axis consists of values, principles and norms.

That is, over the centuries the pendulum of human behaviour has swung surely, albeit slowly and in a jagged rather than linear trajectory, from the 'pure' power towards the normative end of the arc of history. Of course, in every era, great powers have a disproportionate ability to influence the prevailing norms and laws. This is no different from domestic systems where also, even if every citizen has the same one vote, the political, social and financial elite has much greater access to the political process for writing the rules to govern society. Over the last few centuries, Western ideas and values have found expression as 'universal' norms and been embedded in the dominant institutions of global governance not necessarily because they are intrinsically superior, but more importantly behind battleships, missiles and tanks.

Acting as the hegemon, the United States took the lead in establishing the regimes and institutions of the post-1945 liberal international order for ensuring stability, promoting security and advancing prosperity in the international system as global public goods, albeit also taking care to embed its own set of preferences and values. The United States will remain the first among equals and retain an unmatched edge not just in military power, but also in the ability to form coalitions of allies and friends and mobilise networks of civil society actors and individuals. However, although the US is still the single most powerful and influential actor, US *primacy* – military, economic, ideological – is waning and global institutions will serve its power and purpose less and less, producing *a decline in the American order*.

The growth of the parallel global financial architecture by BRICS – the New Development Bank and the Asian Infrastructure Investment Bank[5] – is evidence of intent and ability to rewire the global governance system so that it no longer runs only through the West. The pendulum swing back to the historical norm is expected to accelerate, as by 2030 Asia could be bigger in economic size and strategic weight than Europe and the United States combined. Amitav Acharya deploys the metaphor of a multiplex theatre to make conceptual sense of the emerging system, with several different movies playing in different theatres with their own separate choice of plots, actors and action.[6] Order is maintained through decentralised arrangements with established and emerging state actors, global and regional organisations, and transnational non-state actors.

Over 1989–91 the end of the Cold War, the collapse of the former Soviet Union and the emergence of Russia as a shrink-wrapped successor state – many previous provinces spinning out of Moscow's orbit as independent states, the size of territory, population and economy all reduced, the people impoverished and the former 'superpower' increasingly weakened and humiliated – set in train a cascading set of multiple consequences. With the frozen geopolitical frame unlocked, many local conflicts emerged from the shadow of the Cold War and erupted into complex humanitarian emergencies. As the US-led West was the only grouping capable of alleviating the resulting mass suffering, demands grew correspondingly for the Western powers to 'do something'. Efforts to intervene based solely on humanitarian considerations where no national interests were engaged lacked sufficient motivation for sustained engagement when difficulties were encountered, as in Somalia in the early 1990s. Therefore, other crises crying out for 'humanitarian intervention' were ignored, as in the 1994 Rwanda genocide. But interventions were mounted with mixed-motive calculations where geostrategic interests coincided with humanitarian tragedies, as in the Balkans in the second half of the 1990s.

In the process, the North Atlantic community discovered that a defeated Russia could be safely ignored as a military rival even in its Balkans backyard and that its influence in the United Nations system had also greatly waned. The US kept expanding the borders of NATO ever eastward towards Russia's borders, contrary to the terms on which Moscow thought Germany's reunification and the admission of a united Germany into NATO had been agreed.[7] Several Western leaders at the highest levels had assured Mikhail Gorbachev, the last leader of the Soviet Union, that NATO would not expand even 'one inch eastward'. In 1999, Russia watched helplessly from the sidelines as its ally, Serbia, was dismembered by NATO that served as midwife to the birth of an independent Kosovo. But Moscow did not forget the lesson.[8] Meanwhile although China had begun its astonishingly rapid ascent up the ladder of economic growth and military modernisation, it was still two–three decades away from re-emerging as a comprehensive national power.

The inability of any other state actor or collective grouping to act as a check on the untrammelled exercise of US and NATO military power, combined with communism being totally discredited both as a political ideology and as an organising principle for the economy, in turn fostered growing faith in using US military power to refashion the world in its own image, bred triumphalism-cum-exceptionalism in the unipolar moment and blinded Washington to the concerns, fears and preferences of others. Exceptionalism still took two forms, as noted by Peter Beinart.[9] Some US administrations were prepared to accept that exceptionalism entailed the burden of special world order responsibilities alongside rights and act accordingly. But Presidents George W. Bush and, especially, Donald Trump, with John Bolton a common link across the two administrations, disclaimed any responsibility while asserting and exercising uniquely privileged rights to the maximum. 'The Trump administration's decision [of May 2018] to openly violate the Iran [nuclear] deal – and demand that Iran negotiate a new one more favorable to the U.S. – is a brazen example of this "rights exceptionalism"', Beinart concludes. Only the United States is permitted to act in material breach of binding international agreements and violate international law; all other actors, including China and Russia as great powers, must still abide by accords, conform to global norms and respect international law.

The darker sides of Western virtue signalling

The shift in power and influence, and in consequence in the geopolitical centre of gravity, from the previously ascendant North Atlantic countries to Asia and the Pacific has become a staple of analysis and commentary. The centrepiece of that is the relative waning of US power and the steady accretion of power, wealth and clout by China. As China fills out as a major power, uncontested US primacy will become increasingly unsustainable. There is a second dynamic at play in Asia with potentially far-reaching implications for global order also, namely the parallel rise of India in the shadow of China by 12–13 years. As other states become economically and militarily powerful, their trains of global interests expand, and they seek commensurate influence over international political and economic institutions.

Moreover, even in the moment of the US unipolar triumph at the end of the Cold War, developing countries still comprised a majority in the UN General Assembly and they could deny the West the imprimatur of collective legitimacy by using their numbers. They were motivated to do so because their historical narrative of colonialism was starkly different from that of the major European colonial powers who thought they had exported civilisation to the natives. It is not clear that even now many Westerners – leaders, scholars, media commentators, lay people – appreciate the cynicism among many of the non-Western rest about the hypocrisy and double standards that lie behind Western judgements of other countries' actions and policies on human rights. The Canadian government was instrumental in setting up, assembling and backstopping ICISS that gave birth to the principle of the Responsibility to Protect. Canadians generally self-identify themselves as being at the vanguard of the liberal internationalist states – the 'like-minded' progressives – with a deep attachment and commitment to the promotion of universal human rights norms and standards. Yet even the Liberal Party government led by the liberal-leaning and internationalist Prime Minister Justin Trudeau went through with a profitable arms sale to Saudi Arabia despite widespread domestic criticism of the potential for abuses by one of the most stiflingly repressive regimes in existence. The concern was especially pertinent in relation to the brutal Saudi campaign against Iran-backed opponents in Yemen. The government salvaged its social conscience by giving CAD 65 million in humanitarian aid to Yemen. An investigation by the Toronto *Star* found that in the meantime, since 2015 Canada had approved CAD '284 million in exports of Canadian weapons and military goods to countries bombing Yemen'.[10]

Earlier, in June 2011, the conservative Stephen Harper Government single-handedly blocked asbestos from being added to the hazardous-chemicals list of the UN's Rotterdam Convention.[11] Canada had also opposed the listing of asbestos at the convention's meetings in 2004, 2006 and 2008. Not that Canada did not believe in the science: asbestos could not legally be sold domestically at that time because of tough health regulations. But Canada was happy to mine, ship and make money from asbestos at the cost of large numbers of third world lives. On 14 September 2012, Ottawa finally announced an end to the asbestos mining industry in Quebec and said it would no longer block the listing of chrysotile asbestos as a hazardous substance under the Rotterdam Convention.[12] Canada then abstained at the subsequent meetings in 2013 and 2015. The same Harper government had the chutzpah to boast of conducting a 'principled' foreign policy, in the pursuit of which Harper unsuccessfully lobbied other Commonwealth prime ministers, in Perth for the 2011 summit (the same year that Ottawa blocked the effort to end international trade in asbestos), to boycott the 2013 Commonwealth summit to be held in Sri Lanka because of human rights abuses by Colombo. Harper refused to attend, with cynics suggesting he was courting the ethnic Tamil vote in Toronto more than suddenly elevating ethics as a priority goal in Canada's foreign policy.

It is difficult for many former colonies not to weigh present rhetoric against the historical record on human rights by the leading Western powers during the colonial period. During the Second World War, for example, in order to keep British troops supplied with food, the United Kingdom created an artificial famine in Bengal that killed around four million Indians – the greatest disaster of the twentieth century in the subcontinent. Prime Minister Winston Churchill rejected pleas from two successive viceroys, and the UK Secretary of State for India and Burma, to ship food urgently to Bengal.[13] Britain suppressed the Mau Mau rebellion in Kenya in the 1950s with savage brutality and has fiercely resisted any independent criminal investigation of the atrocities.[14] Instead the

British government systematically and deliberately destroyed the documents detailing the mistreatment of its colonial subjects and the Foreign Office deliberately lied about a secret cache of documents detailing lesser crimes.[15]

Anyone who wishes to understand the deep-seated cynicism of many people in the global South about the self-sustaining belief in an exceptional America and a virtuous West should read *The Blood Telegram.*[16] Reacting with shock and revulsion to the genocide in East Pakistan unfolding before their eyes in 1971, US Consul General Archer Blood (hence the title of the book) and 19 colleagues from the consulate, the US Aid Agency and Information Service in Dhaka sent a telegram to Washington expressing their conviction that turning a blind eye to the tragedy served neither the US broad moral interests nor its narrow national interests. President Richard Nixon and National Security Adviser Henry Kissinger, the latter in thrall to his own geopolitical genius, did not want to hear because they were busy prising China away from the Soviet Union on the global geopolitical chessboard. And so, the cry from the heart proved career-unfriendly to the signatories rather than result in a course correction in American foreign policy. Little wonder that in one of the most important as well as interesting studies published by Chatham House, of elite perceptions, in contrast to Europeans who emphasised America's historical 'moral leadership', the US is viewed by many Asian elites as hypocritical, overbearing, arrogant and disinterested in others' interests, aggressively pushing its own policy priorities instead.[17]

Origins and evolution of R2P

Sovereignty is the bedrock organising principle of modern international society and faith in it was strongly reaffirmed by the large number of countries that regained their independence from colonial bondage in the second half of the twentieth century. In the growing anti-colonial narrative, 'humanitarian intervention' as a doctrine was progressively discredited in large parts of the world in a new climate of international legitimacy unfavourable to intervention in general, and to Western intervention in particular.[18] At one level, the developing countries' attachment to sovereignty is deeply emotional, reflecting the lingering trauma of their colonial experience. At another level, the commitment to sovereignty is functional. The state is the cornerstone of the international system and state sovereignty provides order, stability and predictability in international relations. In the meantime, however, as the world steadily became a global village under the impact of rapid developments in information, telecommunications and transportation technology, the human rights norm also deepened and spread outwards from the Euro–Atlantic core to the farthest reaches of the increasingly interconnected international system.

In the use of force within and across borders, states have had to conform increasingly to international standards and normative benchmarks. The history of the twentieth century is in part the story of a twin-track approach to tame – through a series of normative, legislative and institutional fetters – impulses to armed criminality by states in the use of force domestically (to commit atrocities) and internationally (to commit aggression). Cumulatively, these attempted to translate an increasingly internationalised human conscience into a new normative architecture of world order, but one that still left a gap when victims of state-sanctioned atrocities needed international military force to protect them.

This produced normative dissonance between the norms of non-intervention in the internal affairs of sovereign states and the abusive practices and humanitarian atrocities perpetrated by some brutish thug-rulers on their own peoples shielding behind that norm. But when some states defied the norm of non-intervention in efforts to protect the victims of mass atrocity crimes, their claimed emerging norm of 'humanitarian intervention' collided with the existing norm of non-intervention. The majority of states rejected the effort to relegitimise the unilateral use of force internationally by some in order to circumscribe the arbitrary use of force internally by others. Thus, the existing normative consensus was no longer fit for purpose against the brutal facts of the real world. Under the impact of contrasting experiences in Rwanda and Kosovo, UN Secretary-General Kofi Annan urged member states to come up with a new consensus on the competing visions of national and popular sovereignty and the resulting 'challenge of humanitarian intervention'.[19] The policy community split between the major powers and the majority of states from the global South on the question of the continuing validity and relevance of the norm of non-intervention.

Responding to Annan's 'intervention dilemmas',[20] the Canadian government organised and convened ICISS to explore the possible pathways to a new normative consensus on the use of force, within the boundaries of both law and legitimacy, to save strangers. Chapter 3 describes how international commissions are a useful means of collating state of the art knowledge on particular problems and converting them into policy recommendations for improving the collective management of world affairs; that is, to make the world a better and safer place for all its peoples. Despite their popularity, nonetheless, most international commissions fail to leave an enduring legacy. ICISS was an exception. The chapter outlines measures of success with respect to ideational and institutional impact and normative and operational success. The overall success is explained with reference to its independence, international composition and inclusiveness, as well as its modus operandi, the focussed quality of its report and the follow-up work after the publication of the report. The chapter also identifies different categories of normative actors like entrepreneurs, brokers, champions, carriers and, of course, spoilers who have to be either co-opted or otherwise neutralised.

Roberta Cohen and Francis Deng had already begun to reconceptualise sovereignty as responsibility in the context of internally displaced persons amidst the proliferating humanitarian crises at the end of the Cold War.[21] The catalyst to the call for a new normative consensus on the use of force by outsiders to save strangers inside foreign jurisdictions was the shattering of the old consensus under the impact of several high-profile humanitarian emergencies in the aftermath of the end of the Cold War. Two of the most consequential for present purposes were the 1994 genocide in Rwanda and the 1999 NATO intervention in Kosovo. The first occurred despite the presence of a UN peacekeeping operation on the ground in Rwanda at the time. The second took pace without any explicit UN authorisation. Rwanda caused lasting damage to UN ideals and credibility when the organisation failed to stop a three-month long genocide; Kosovo showed the damage to the UN's credibility and the sharp polarisation of international opinion when NATO intervened militarily outside the UN framework. Doing nothing in Rwanda was no longer acceptable to a globally sensitised human conscience, but doing something militarily in Kosovo without UN sanction which would have been impossible to obtain in the prevailing circumstances was illegal. Rwanda and Kosovo generated intense international controversy and produced contrasting determination among ashamed 'like-minded' Western states not to look the other way again at the next outbreak of atrocities; and among developing countries to protect any further erosion of national sovereignty. Inevitably, the contrasting perspectives informed much of the internal discussions among ICISS members and this story is told in Chapter 4.

R2P was the ICISS answer to reconciling the visceral hostility of the global South to any revival of the notion of 'humanitarian intervention' with the North's determination to take forceful action to prevent and stop atrocities. As explained in Chapter 5, in effect ICISS performed a 'Feuerbachian inversion' of state–citizen relations on rights and responsibilities. The authoritarian states that emerged during the Westphalian era were concerned less with protection *of* civilians and more with protection *from* civilians. They used the state's monopoly of legitimate force against them and thus the heart of Westphalian sovereignty undermined citizens' rights. Where previously human rights violations occurred in efforts by autocratic rulers to prove and reassert sovereign legitimacy, henceforth citizens were to be treated as the bearers of rights while states had to accept responsibilities towards the people.

The key innovation in 2001 was the reconceptualisation of 'humanitarian intervention' as R2P; everything else in this discourse flows from that distinction. Yet far too many analysts continue to conflate the two.[22] Contrary to the criticism that R2P was merely old wine in a new bottle, the differences between them are real and consequential: politically, conceptually, normatively, procedurally and even operationally. Moreover, the answer to a critical question – responsibility to whom? – differs when we change lens from humanitarian intervention (to your own soldiers and citizens first) to R2P (to the victims and the international community). Chapter 5 provides a complete account of the key differences between humanitarian intervention and the Responsibility to Protect.

The unanimous endorsement of R2P by world leaders in 2005 limited the triggering events to war crimes, genocide, ethnic cleansing and crimes against humanity. By realigning the emerging global political norm to existing categories of international legal crimes, the added specificity brought greater rigour to the principle. Secretary-General Ban Ki-moon's special reports on R2P, issued annually since 2009 and continued by his successor Antonio Guterres, sustained and consolidated the international consensus.

The ICISS formulation of the three symbiotically interlinked responsibilities embedded in the overall R2P principle are inflection points along the arc of a conflict curve: the responsibility to prevent atrocities; the responsibility to react to calls on our internationalised human conscience to situations requiring compelling human protection; and the responsibility to rebuild robust and resilient peace through enduring structures of governance that harmoniously blend the co-equal imperatives of justice and order. In his first report on R2P in 2009,[23] which remains the most important and influential so far, Ban reframed R2P in the metaphor of three pillars: first, the responsibility of each sovereign state itself to protect (including prevention) its own populations from the atrocity crimes in question; second, the responsibility of other states to assist it to do so; and third, the responsibility of the wider international community to respond to atrocities in a 'timely and decisive' fashion and by all appropriate means (not excluding coercive military action). Although only Pillar Three permits a coercive R2P response, its ambit is not restricted solely to military and non-military coercive tools. Rather, even in Pillar Three the use of force is the option of last resort; the default first response is peaceful means of persuasion and dissuasion.

It has become obvious in successive annual General Assembly debates in and since 2009 that the three pillar frame of reference is now overwhelmingly accepted by the UN community. The annual debates have helped to forge a shared understanding of R2P and show that the R2P consensus is broadening, its legitimacy strengthening, and most states are concerned to move on to questions of implementation. Those questions, including the controversies surrounding both failures and efforts to implement R2P in various conflict theatres, will be taken up in Part II.

Notes

1 Thucydides, *History of the Peloponnesian War*, 'Melian Dialogue' (London: J. M. Dent, 1910), 5.89. English translation available online at the Perseus Project: www.perseus.tufts.edu/hopper/text?doc=Perseus%3Atext%3A1999.01.0200%3Abook%3D5%3Achapter%3D89%3Asection%3D1.
2 Hans J. Morgenthau, *Politics Among Nations: The Struggle for Power and Peace*, 4th ed. (New York: Alfred A. Knopf, 1967), 10.
3 Hans J. Morgenthau, *In Defense of the National Interest: A Critical Examination of American Foreign Policy* (New York: Alfred A. Knopf, 1951), 33.
4 Steven Pinker, *The Better Angels of Our Nature* (New York: Viking, 2011).
5 Gregory T. Chin, 'Asian Infrastructure Investment Bank: Governance Innovation and Prospects', *Global Governance* 22:1 (2016), 11–26; Miles Kahler, 'The Global Economic Multilaterals: Will Eighty Years Be Enough?' *Global Governance* 22:1 (2016), 1–10.
6 Amitav Acharya, *The End of American World Order* (Cambridge: Polity, 2014).
7 Joshua R. Itzkowitz Shifrinson, 'Put It in Writing: How the West Broke Its Promise to Moscow', *Foreign Affairs*, 29 October 2014, www.foreignaffairs.com/articles/united-states/2014-10-29/put-it-writing?
8 'NATO Expansion: What Gorbachev Heard', transcripts of declassified documents published by the National Security Archive, 12 December 2017, https://nsarchive.gwu.edu/briefing-book/russia-programs/2017-12-12/nato-expansion-what-gorbachev-heard-western-leaders-early.
9 Peter Beinart, 'The Iran Deal and the Dark Side of American Exceptionalism' *The Atlantic*, 9 May 2018, www.theatlantic.com/international/archive/2018/05/iran-deal-trump-American-exceptionalism/560063/.

10 Brendan Kennedy and Michelle Shephard, 'Canada's Dual Role in Yemen: Arms Exports to Saudi Coalition Dwarf Aid Sent to War-torn Country', *The Star* (Toronto), 30 April 2018, www.thestar.com/news/investigations/2018/04/30/canadas-dual-role-in-yemen-arms-exports-to-saudi-coalition-dwarfs-aid-sent-to-war-torn-country.html.

11 Steve Rennie, 'Harper Parties in Mining Town as Canada Keeps Asbestos off Hazardous List', *Globe and Mail*, 24 June 2011, www.theglobeandmail.com/news/politics/harper-parties-in-mining-town-as-canada-keeps-asbestos-off-hazardous-list/article590968/.

12 Kathleen Ruff, 'The Belated Demise of Canada's Asbestos Industry', *The Star*, 22 September 2012, www.thestar.com/opinion/editorialopinion/2012/09/22/the_belated_demise_of_canadas_asbestos_industry.html.

13 The grim story documenting Churchill's racist contempt for Indians is well told in Madhusree Mukerjee, *Churchill's Secret War: The British Empire and the Ravaging of India during World War II* (New York: Basic Books, 2010).

14 David Anderson, *Histories of the Hanged: The Dirty War in Kenya and the End of Empire* (London: Weidenfeld and Nicolson, 2005); Huw Bennett, *Fighting the Mau Mau: The British Army and Counter-Insurgency in the Kenya Emergency* (Cambridge: Cambridge University Press, 2012); Caroline Elkins, *Britain's Gulag: The Brutal End of Empire in Kenya* (London: Jonathan Cape, 2005); and John Newsinger, *The Blood Never Dried: A People's History of the British Empire* (London: Bookmarks, 2006).

15 George Monbiot, 'Deny the British Empire's Crimes? No, We Ignore Them', *Guardian*, 24 April 2012; Ian Cobain, 'Secret Archive Shames Britain' *Age* (Melbourne), 20 April 2012.

16 Gary J. Bass, *The Blood Telegram: Nixon, Kissinger and a Forgotten Genocide* (New York: Alfred A. Knopf, 2013).

17 Xenia Dormandy with Joshua Webb, *Elite Perceptions of the United States in Europe and Asia* (London: Royal Institute of International Affairs, May 2014).

18 Hedley Bull, 'Intervention in the Third World', in Hedley Bull, ed., *Intervention in World Politics* (Oxford: Clarendon, 1984), 135–56.

19 Kofi A. Annan, *Facing the Humanitarian Challenge: Towards a Culture of Prevention* (New York: United Nations Department of Public Information, 1999).

20 Charles Cater and David M. Malone, 'The Genesis of R2P: Kofi Annan's Intervention Dilemmas', in Alex J. Bellamy and Tim Dunne, eds., *The Oxford Handbook of the Responsibility to Protect* (Oxford: Oxford University Press, 2016), 114–32.

21 Roberta Cohen and Francis M. Deng, 'Sovereignty as Responsibility: Buildings Blocks for R2P', in Bellamy and Dunne, eds., *The Oxford Handbook of the Responsibility to Protect*, 74–93

22 For example, Rajan Menon, *The Conceit of Humanitarian Intervention* (New York: Oxford University Press, 2016).

23 Ban Ki-moon, *Implementing the Responsibility to Protect* (New York: United Nations, document A/63/677, 12 January 2009).

3 High-level panels*

Several contemporary international features are distinctive to the world of international organisations which have added greatly to the institutional congestion and complexity of international relations. In previous centuries, war and peace were the mainstay of interstate relations as symbolised by the ambassador and the general. Today, alongside the horde of diplomats and soldiers, the multinational merchant, international financier, World Bank technocrat, World Health Organisation (WHO) medical expert, UN peacekeeper, the International Atomic Energy Agency (IAEA) inspector, 'Eurocrats' and officials of other regional organisations, NGO humanitarian worker and global sports administrator – not to mention the international terrorist, human and drug trafficker, gun runner and money launderer – jostle for space on the increasingly crowded international stage.

This chapter proceeds in four parts. First, it situates international organisations in the context of the changing nature of international diplomacy, including in particular summits and conferences as modes of contemporary diplomacy. It then describes the proliferating number and types of high-level panels as instances of commission diplomacy. Third, it describes the ideational, normative, institutional and operational impacts of panels. Finally, it provides a menu of the ingredients for successful commission diplomacy, including the different types of norm actors.

The changing diplomatic landscape

International organisations are not merely sites of global governance but, in some limited yet important respects and the principal-agent problem notwithstanding, actors in their own right as well.[1] There has also been a spurt in the number of regional organisations and direct relations among them.[2] There has been an exponential growth in the number of civil society actors and the volume of transnational networks in which they are embedded.[3] They bridge the 'disconnect between the political geography of the state on the one side and the new geography of economic and social relations on the other'.[4] UN Secretary-General Kofi Annan noted that NGOs are not merely 'disseminators of information or providers of services but also … shapers of policy' in security, development and humanitarian affairs.[5]

The role, activities and impact of international organisations reflect and in turn shape the conduct of modern diplomacy. The world of international relations has changed substantially since the First World War. New diplomatic procedures consolidated and initiated by the League of Nations included multilateral diplomacy, public debates, international parliamentary procedures and collective decision-making. Today's global environment is vastly more challenging, complex and demanding than the worlds of 1919 and 1945 when the League of Nations and the United Nations were created. The subject matter of diplomacy has expanded commensurately, from the high politics of war and peace to health, environment, development, science and technology, education, law, and the arts.

Mark Malloch-Brown, the former UN Deputy Secretary-General and then a Foreign Office Minister in the UK, has written that 'Diplomacy has been multilateralised': Britain's power to influence events depends 'on our ability to orchestrate action in Washington, the UN, the European Union or corporate boards'.[6] Multilateral diplomacy has also brought in its wake new forms of diplomatic activity like public debates, extensive committee work, parliamentary procedures that back in the home country are the provenance of politicians, diplomatic caucusing akin to political caucusing in national parliaments, and forging coalitions and alliances. Many UN agencies, especially in the human rights, humanitarian and development fields, prefer to work directly with NGOs than governments in service delivery.

International organisations give form, content and meaning to multilateral diplomacy, described by the distinguished Singaporean diplomat-scholar Kishore Mahbubani as 'a sunrise industry'.[7] The UN system constitutes the core of the multilateral order, enjoying a unique legitimacy derived from universal membership. UN multilateral diplomacy differs from traditional interstate diplomacy in some important respects.[8] Guided by Charter principles, it partially offsets the unfavourable position of the weaker party. It aims to establish a just peace as well as a stable balance of power. And it takes into account the interests of member states collectively as well as the disputants. Thus, international organisations have tempered the dictum handed down to posterity by Thucydides that 'the strong do what they can and the weak suffer what they must'.[9] Multilateral diplomacy also expanded the toolkit of both peaceful and coercive instruments, spelt out in Chapters VI and VII of the UN Charter, to resolve conflicts and punish rule-breaking or norm-deviating states. Annan remarked that 'diplomacy has expanded its remit, moving far beyond bilateral political relations between states into a multilateral, multi-faceted enterprise encompassing almost every realm of human endeavour'.[10]

The international calendar is surprisingly crowded for the leaders of most countries who are expected to attend the regularly scheduled gatherings of the United Nations, regional and subregional organisations, and informal groupings like the G8, G20 and BRICS,[11] giving rise to summit diplomacy as a distinctive feature of the current global order.[12] International finance and trade, pandemics and terrorism, climate change and biodiversity, and nuclear security spill across national boundaries and defy local treatment. They are 'problems without passports'[13] in search of solutions without passports. Some summits offer little beyond symbolism, some can make genuine progress on shared global challenges and problems like nuclear security, but in any case, summits with their alphabet soup of acronyms are an inescapable feature of the contemporary diplomatic topography. With broad, overarching responsibilities, leaders, and only leaders, can best weigh priorities and seek to balance interests across competing goals, sectors, national and international objectives, and between the immediate, medium and long terms.[14] Summits should make the most difference in those problem areas where leadership commitment is the critical variable ('the pay grade test'[15]), the primary obstacle to identifying policy overlap and convergence and reaching consensus is the unavailability or inadequacy of an appropriate forum, and speedy resolution is essential.

The United Nations too sometimes hosts and organises special summits, for example the 2000 Summit which produced the Millennium Development Goals (MDGs) and the world summit in 2005 which unanimously endorsed the responsibility to protect (R2P) as a new normative principle.[16] A more frequent UN activity is conference diplomacy on designated topics, for example environmental conferences in Stockholm and Rio de Janeiro in 1972 and 1992. Universal membership and international legitimacy give the UN unmatched convening and mobilising power that has been used to organise a large number of global conferences on a diverse range of topics from women to human rights, population, social development and environmental conservation. Where the intergovernmental conferences are the sites for the growth of treaty law, for example the UN Conference on the Law of the Sea (1973–82), the global conferences have been prime sites for the evolution of norms and 'soft law' which over time begin to exert a binding effect in the form of customary international law. UN conferences have been crucial agents of change, of norms if not behaviour, policy and action. Their global and long-term impact often lies in raising a new issue, reframing an existing issue or even simply focusing more international attention on an issue, so that the existing consensus is shifted, and the boundaries of possible national and international action are expanded.[17]

Commission diplomacy

International summits and global conference are useful to greater and lesser degrees as occasions for mediating divergent interests and national policy perspectives in order to forge common collective policy priorities on particular global challenges. In addition, as the UN Intellectual History Project has so brilliantly documented in several volumes, the UN system has been remarkably productive and effective in channelling ideas into global policy. The impact of ideas on global governance is a largely neglected area of study, with scholars focusing more on international institutions – the 'body of global governance' – than on the ideas – the 'mind of global governance' – that drive them.[18] High-level panels and international commissions are a useful means of leveraging emerging ideas into new global norms and converting them into policy.[19] Their composition, remits and reports are wonderful representations of the 'three UNs': the world of UN member states who are the principals of the organisation; of international civil servants who are its staff; and of personnel from government, academe and civil society who interact actively and regularly with the UN system.[20]

Gareth Evans – who in various capacities at different times has set up, been a member of and co-chaired half a dozen commissions – has tabulated almost three dozen international commissions looking at global challenges in the security, development, environmental, social policy and governance dimensions.[21] Their distinguishing features are that they address policy problems of global scope. They may be created or convened by international organisations, national governments or private foundations, but their recommendations are always directed to the international community overall. Their members are expected to think and make decisions in their personal capacity and not advance any official agenda. And they are of finite duration (with open-ended and ongoing panels better described as organisations).

Examples of high-level panels include the UN Panel on Peace Operations chaired by Lakhdar Brahimi (report published in 2000) and the High-level Panel on Threats, Challenges and Change (2004), both of which were set up by UN Secretary-General Kofi Annan. Some of the better known international commissions include the Pearson (1969), Brandt (1980), Palme (1982), Brundtland (1987), Global Governance (1995), Canberra (1996), and Kosovo (2000) commissions, and the International Commission on Intervention and State Sovereignty (ICISS, 2001). Between them, they have shaped and influenced the global discourse on a wide range of international policy issues:[22] development, the global economic order and North–South inequalities; international security and the disutility of nuclear weapons; resource conservation, environmental protection and economic development; and the legality and legitimacy of the use of military force to protect civilians trapped inside sovereign jurisdictions. One of the most recent such bodies, the High-level Panel on the Post-2015 Development Agenda, acknowledging that the years since the millennium had seen the fastest poverty reduction in history, identified a two-step goal: elimination, not mere reduction, of extreme poverty in all its forms; and putting in place the building blocks of sustained prosperity for all.[23]

Other panels look to address regional issues and problems, for example the Zedillo–Pickering Partnership for the Americas Commission (2008) and the Latin American Commission on Drugs and Democracy (2009). Some high-level panels are convened to investigate specific past failures to prevent atrocities, or allegations of complicity in the perpetration of atrocities, by state and international actors. A good example of this is the one convened by the OAU to investigate the multiple failures with respect to the 1994 Rwanda genocide, which was chaired by Sir Quett Ketumile Joni Masire, the former President of Botswana, and submitted its report to the OAU summit in Lomé, Togo in 2000.[24] The Carlsson Report,[25] commissioned by the UN itself, had restricted its analysis largely to the role of the United Nations. The OAU Panel looked much more closely and critically at the roles of several African and European states, the

United States, the OAU and the UN. A second good example is the Goldstone Panel, chaired by the eminent international jurist Richard Goldstone, which marshalled evidence of wrongdoing by Hamas and Israel during the three-week 2008–09 Gaza war and in its 2009 report called on both to conduct good faith investigations in conformity with international standards.[26] Because these panels are specific to individual events and look to clarify facts and apportion blame, they are not considered in this chapter which is interested more in panels that seek to improve global governance in the future.

Impacts

High-level panels are a means of collating state of the art knowledge on particular problems and converting them into policy recommendations for improving the collective management of world affairs. Owing to historical inertia, path dependence and the often stable equilibrium of accumulated interests around the status quo, their reports rarely produce dramatic policy shifts. Sometimes their legacies can be more subtle and nuanced, but are nonetheless real. For example, the Brandt Commission's report did not produce any major reform of the international economic order, but it exercised an enduring influence on the development discourse.[27]

What then counts as success? *Ideational impact* is shown in the generation of new ideas that *reshape the existing discourse* on the topic. *Normative* success would come by promoting a new *standard* of behaviour. *Operational* success would be indicated by setting new action agendas and changing the prevailing *patterns* of behaviour. *Institutional* success would be shown by the creation of *new institutions* or the reconfiguration of existing ones. Must a panel demonstrate impact on all these measures, or will one alone suffice to consider it to have been successful? And how much time-lag is permissible in attributing results to commission recommendations? It is worth emphasising that independent bodies, precisely because they are not official, are advisory only and lack executive decision-making authority. In addition, unless their contributions are openly acknowledged, it may be difficult to trace their lineage in the creation of new norms, practices and institutions.

It is as rare for any panel to be a total failure as for it to be wholly successful in adding to the world's body of knowledge, creating new norms, producing demonstrable and measurable shifts in policy, embedding the new norms and behaviour expectations in purpose-built institutions, and generating effective compliance mechanisms; that is, going farther on the journey of global governance by filling the five core knowledge, normative, policy, institutional and compliance gaps.[28] It is helpful to divide the impacts into ideational, normative, institutional and operational.

Ideational

One of the most notable contributions that high-level panels can make is to generate potentially game-changing ideas: new ways of addressing long-standing and intractable problems that have defeated policymakers. Ideas matter and institutions matter as conduits for ideas.[29] In the broad sweep of history, empires rise and fall, kings and queens come and go. They are remembered only if they leave behind ideas, embedded in institutions or practices, for improved governance or quality of life. Ideas are influential if they have strong theoretical foundations and clear policy application. The support of powerful rulers and countries helps. The Palme Commission turned the logic of Cold War nuclear deterrence on its head by highlighting the interdependence of everyone's security; the Brundtland Commission broke major conceptual ground by bridging the previously irreconcilable pro-growth and environmental protection camps. The three central insights of the Canberra Commission – as long as any country has nuclear weapons, others will want them too; as long as they exist, they will be used again some day by design, accident or miscalculation; and a nuclear war anywhere will be globally catastrophic – has informed strategic discourse ever since. The Palme, Brandt and Canberra commissions proved to be ahead of their time, but their ideational legacy was kept alive by activists and intellectuals until such time as the context was more hospitable to their message. Panels can also contribute directly to the store of existing knowledge by commissioning cutting edge papers and publishing substantial volumes of authoritative data and analysis. Thus, ICISS published a 400-page supplementary volume in addition to its main report and the Carnegie Commission generated no fewer than 10 books and over 30 other publications.

Normative

Ideas are value neutral. A norm is a socially validated and community sanctioned standard of appropriate or prescribed behaviour. The idea that climate change is real and caused by human activity has produced the norm that the resulting rise on global temperature must be kept to within 2° Centigrade relative to pre-industrial levels, but also produced controversy on the best suite of policies (mitigation, adaptation, climate engineering, financial and technology transfers) in order to comply with the norm. Three particularly useful commissions to illustrate normative impacts are the Pearson Panel, Brundtland Commission and ICISS. With respect to the first, the globally endorsed norm of the developed countries denominating 0.7 per cent of their GDP as official development assistance (ODA) is rarely met yet cannot be formally abandoned because of the stigma that would attach to walking away from it.

The Brundtland Commission introduced the concept of 'sustainable development' – meeting the development needs of the present without destroying the environment and thus compromising the ability of future generations to meet their own needs. Its report *Our Common Future* was memorable for its opening sentence: 'The Earth is one but the world is not'.[30] This singular UN achievement has framed the dominant approach to development ever since. For many in the development community, 'sustainable development' is the most consequential normative shift since 1945. The continuing frictions between the North and the South with respect to the responsibility for having caused and for ameliorating the effects of climate change suggest that efforts to combat climate change will have to be integrated into the broader context of sustainable social and economic development.

Like counterparts in development, vis-à-vis 'sustainable development', many in the security field consider R2P to be one of the most significant normative advances in decades, if not centuries.[31] It is closely related, conceptually as well as chronologically, to the norm of protection of civilians (POC).[32] The Brahimi Panel did not introduce the POC norm as such, since the first Security Council resolution on POC was adopted in 1999, a year before the Brahimi Report. But the latter did help to consolidate the POC norm by questioning the long-established assumptions of neutrality and impartiality as they applied to civilian victims of violence perpetrated by armed challengers to UN peace operations.

'Peacekeeping' is a word that famously cannot be found in the UN Charter; the concept did not exist in 1945. Yet it has been the most visible symbol of the UN's role in international peace and security. The Brahimi Report on UN peace operations was unusual in the candour of its analysis and recommendations.[33] It came to the overall sound conclusion that 'when the United Nations does send its forces to uphold the peace, they must be prepared to confront the lingering forces of war and violence with the ability and determination to defeat them'. For in the final analysis, 'no amount of good intentions can substitute for the fundamental ability to project credible force if complex peacekeeping, in particular, is to succeed'.[34] The need for impartial peacekeeping should not translate automatically into moral equivalence among the conflict parties on the ground: in some cases local parties consist not of moral equals but obvious aggressors and victims.[35] The analysis and recommendations have had an unmistakable impact in the consolidation and evolution of the twin R2P and POC norms.

An institutional channel for the transmission of the recommendations of the Brahimi Panel and ICISS was the High-level Panel on Threats, Challenges and Change set up by Annan which submitted its report in late 2004.[36] Its four major conceptual-cum-normative advancements were the inter-connectedness of today's threats; legitimacy criteria for the use of military force; an agreed definition of terrorism; and the need to extend normative constraints to non-state actors. It identified the major threats as war and violence among and within states; the use and proliferation of weapons of mass destruction; terrorism; transnational organised crime; and poverty, infectious disease and environmental degradation. The threats can come from state and non-state actors and endanger human as well as national security. Collective security is necessary because today's threats cannot be contained within national boundaries; they are interconnected and have to be addressed simultaneously at all levels.

Institutional

Following the Brahimi Report, the staff complement of the Department of Peacekeeping Operations (DPKO) in New York was increased to provide better support to field missions, and the latter now has its own additional Under-Secretary-General. The officers of the military and police advisers were bolstered. The old and not so well-regarded lessons learned unit was restructured into a best practices unit. DPKO's logistics base in Brindisi (Italy) received funding to acquire strategic deployment stocks. The reorganised UN Standby Arrangements System provides for forces to be made available within 30–90 days of a new operation. The Report also recommended the establishment of an Information and Strategic Analysis Secretariat.[37] For reasons of political sensitivity towards any intelligence gathering capacity by the UN, however, this proved stillborn. ICISS did not recommend it, but its report was most likely the trigger to the creation down the line of the UN Joint Office of Genocide Prevention and R2P. Similarly, the 2004 Cardoso Panel's recommendations on structuring the UN's relations with civil society have been quite influential.

The 2004 High-level Panel published a raft of recommendations on institutional restructuring. It called for the formal disbanding of the Trusteeship Council and the abolition of the Military Staff Committee.[38] But it shied away from recommending the abolition of the Economic and Social Council (ECOSOC), even though the body 'is perceived nearly universally as ineffective, poorly structured, and not up to the task of taking decisive action'.[39] The 2005 summit agreed to wind up the obsolete Trusteeship Council, but with regard to the equally anachronistic Military Staff Committee, it merely asked the Security Council to consider the Committee's composition, mandate and working methods.[40] The most critical section dealt with the Security Council. The call for reforming it is justified by the need for greater credibility, legitimacy, representation and effectiveness. The panel noted that a decision on Security Council enlargement 'is now a necessity'.[41] But, unable to agree between them, the panellists outlined two models, inviting the question: if 16 distinguished world citizens acting as individuals cannot choose between the two models, can 191 separate governments do so? The answer from the 2005 summit was a resounding 'No'. The world leaders merely committed to continue the efforts to achieve a decision.[42] That is, after a decade of talks, they agreed to talk some more.

The panel recommended the establishment of a new Peace-building Commission (PBC) under Security Council authority to identify countries sliding towards state collapse, institute measures to halt the slide and plan for and assist in the transition from war and conflict to peace and post-conflict peace-building.[43] The 2005 summit agreed to establish a PBC as an intergovernmental advisory body with a dedicated Peace-building Support Office in the UN Secretariat. But the PBC's authority was weakened by not placing it under the Security Council and instead tasking it to report annually to the General Assembly.[44]

The most optimistic had hoped for a San Francisco moment in New York in September 2005, one no less decisive and momentous than the signing of the UN Charter 60 years earlier in the city by the bay. The most critical concluded that instead the UN had an Albert Einstein moment, recalling the man of the century's famous description of madness as doing something over and over again and expecting a different result each time, also known as the triumph of hope over experience. One could interpret the 2005 outcome document generously and, gathering rosebuds of consolation, note that it could have been worse. Thus, some of the achievements were genuine enough. But Gareth Evans, one of the HLP members, expressed his disappointment at the outcome in characteristically colourful language. Speaking at a conference in Paris in October 2005, he said that the UN was, 'still the piranha pool of diplomats enjoying tearing flesh off each other, to the total exclusion of any enthusiasm for high principle or effectiveness of the organisation'.[45]

Operational

With the exception of Northern European countries, few others have come close to approaching the Pearson Panel's norm of 0.7 per cent of ODA. The Brundtland Commission can be traced as the 'intellectual godfather' of the Rio Earth Summit in 1992, the 1997 Kyoto Protocol on climate, the Biodiversity Convention and Agenda 21, as well as numerous other ongoing international, regional, national and local initiatives. With 'sustainable development', in most cases the environmental movement has achieved modest successes in changing official policy and citizen practices in the developed countries, but most developing countries still prioritise rapid and sustained economic growth over resource conservation and environmental protection. The concept of 'governance' became common currency only after publication of the Commission on Global Governance's report in 1995,[46] although that was also the year in which the first issue of the journal *Global Governance* appeared.[47] The Commission's recommendations stimulated much debate, but one of its very few to have had an operational impact concerned the responsibility of business to promote good global governance. This found expression ultimately in the UN's 'Global Compact'.[48] The recommendations of the Cardoso Panel on multi-constituency processes and partnerships were accepted by Annan and implemented remarkably quickly in response to the Indian Ocean tsunami the same year.[49]

The POC agenda has had a considerable operational impact on UN peacekeeping missions. R2P was applied in its preventive dimension by former Secretary-General Annan in Kenya and coercive military force was authorised in Security Council Resolution 1973 (17 March 2011) in Libya. But this turned out to be contested and controversial. On the one hand, Libya in 2011 best showcased the mobilising power of the R2P norm that led to China and Russia abstaining from instead of voting against and thereby vetoing Resolution 1973. The initial response to the crisis was a textbook example of R2P Pillar Three military intervention. But the NATO operation very quickly went off the rails as those implementing Resolution 1973 crossed the limits set by the resolution and Libya's post-Gaddafi turmoil and volatility further complicated international responses to the ongoing humanitarian crisis in Syria. Other examples, from the long-running crisis in Darfur to disaster relief in Myanmar, the fate of civilians under foreign occupation in Fallujah and Palestine, and civilians caught in the middle of a brutal civil war in Sri Lanka, also highlight the persistence of major civilian protection gaps when it comes to implementing the normative advances of the Brahimi Panel and ICISS alike.[50]

Explaining success

Many high-level panels and blue-ribbon commissions end up forgotten, little remembered and even less implemented. Some have made a difference. Factors that help to explain success include independence, inclusive composition, permissive or prohibitive context, widely consultative process, product quality, innovation, sharp product differentiation, luck-dependent timing, and follow-up.

The three 'I's': independent, international, inclusive

The successful commissions tend to be genuinely independent, regardless of who established and funded them. It is not always easy for sponsoring governments and foundations to provide the organisational and financial support yet not get involved in the commissioners' deliberation and decisions. But if they do or are seen to control and manipulate the analysis and recommendations, the final product will lack credibility in the policy community and civil society. Japan's political culture seems to militate against sponsoring a genuinely independent commission. This can also be a troublesome requirement for panels created by major powers who have too many interests entwined in international controversies and the military muscle and economic clout to get their own way. Conversely, it might be one likely explanation for why international commissions seem to be a fruitful area of niche diplomacy by so-called middle powers. Unlike the major powers, they are compelled to rely on the power of persuasion and the force of creative ideas.

The members of a high-level global panel must be genuinely international, inclusive and diverse with regard to professional backgrounds (former heads of state and cabinet ministers, UN officials, generals, scholars, journalists), continents-cum-civilisations, industrialised-developing-country perspectives, and initial starting positions on the topic to hand. To the extent that the major global schism has metamorphosed from the East–West rivalry of the Cold War to a North–South divide since,[51] a deliberate effort must be made to bring in Southern voices and give them a respectful hearing. There is not much point in assembling a group of like-minded people who agree amicably among themselves but never actually engage others with different worldviews and priorities. One of the major flaws of the Canberra Commission, for example, was that its composition included members from every Nuclear Non-proliferation Treaty (NPT) nuclear weapons state (NWS: the target audience for recommendations on nuclear disarmament), and nationals of many NPT non-NWS, but not a single citizen of any of the non-NPT threshold NWS (the target audience for recommendations on nuclear non-proliferation). India and Pakistan – two threshold NWS – tested nuclear weapons within two years of its report.

Chair(s)

The requirement for a balanced composition begins with the chair. To report on policy issues which do divide along a North–South polarity, it has become a popular formula to have co-chairs from the North and the South. ICISS was fortunate in its co-chairs Mohamed Sahnoun and Gareth Evans who represented diverse continents, backgrounds and experiences, yet were equally passionate, skilled and committed humanitarian multilateralists. Their example shows the importance of chairs who are simultaneously active, patient and diplomatic. A commission will falter if the chairs dominate and bully. Everyone who wants to articulate a point of view should be given voice and vote in the commission. At the same time, deliberations cannot go on interminably and the process must be kept moving forward to forestall loss of momentum with a judicious harmonisation of differences of opinion. In addition to facilitating this by skilful chairing of panel meetings, chairs also have the primary responsibility for ensuring that the final report is crisp, the analysis sharp, the writing elegant yet accessible. Part of this includes the ability and the willingness to find common ground and language without fudging the issue or retreating into lowest common denominator default positions. Chairs are also crucial to promoting the product after publication of the report to the relevant constituencies and audiences. A household name in the form of a celebrity former president or prime minister might help garner initial attention but is no guarantee of a successful post-product marketing. Capability and competence will trump celebrity status every time.

Panel members

The selection of the commissioners is just as crucial. The willingness of commissioners to listen to one another and adapt and evolve their thinking, without necessarily giving up bottom lines, enabled ICISS to come up with a unanimous report that was more than a collection of clichés and platitudes. But not all commissioners contribute equally. Some are worth having for giving the enterprise credibility in diverse global and sectoral constituencies. Others willingly do the heavy lifting in internal debates, research and even writing, as well as post-publication selling of the product and its message, which 'can make up for a certain elegant lassitude at the top'.[52] Homogeneity of backgrounds, experience and political outlook can facilitate cohesion, but only at the cost of legitimacy and impact. It is important also to include representatives from the worlds of practitioners and ideas. The last group is not always included. Yet as already noted, ideas are the key drivers of history and a panel that does not include them will have a short shelf life. This deficiency was notable in the 2004 panel on UN reforms. Its composition was initially ridiculed for its average age (around 70) when the task was to look to the future: 'Alzheimer's commission',[53] 'relics trying to reform a relic'[54] and 'a cross between déjà vu and amnesia'[55] were among the choice descriptions.[56]

The calls for inclusiveness, representivity and diversity can collide with the demands for efficiency and timeliness of final product. Panels become more and more unwieldy beyond a good working size of 12–15 members. If it is accepted that a compact size makes for more efficient functioning, it makes it all the more urgent to avoid multiple names from the 'old boys club': Brahimi, Brundtland, Cardoso, Evans, Ogata, Zedillo *et al.* To be sure, there is merit in continuity, institutional memory and cross-pollination, but the optics of lasting cynicism have to be assessed against those of instant credibility. Of course, many of them can still be brought into the process through membership of international advisory boards and other consultative mechanisms.

Process and timeline

Panels do not fail or succeed simply on the strength of their ideas or the quality of their chairs and commissioners. Matters of organisation, structure, resources (funding package and professional support personnel), process and outreach can be just as crucial. The workload for the panel, research staff and secretariat must be manageable, and the deadlines have to balance being realistic and yet timely. Consultations with stakeholder constituencies is important for the opportunity to listen to what the 'market' is saying and can bear, for 'road-testing' ideas and recommendations as they emerge, develop and firm, and for enhancing the legitimacy of the final product and encouraging broad buy-in.[57] The pattern of international composition, high-prolife leadership, contracted research, site visits to many countries for consultations with governments and civil society, and a dedicated professional secretariat, was well established by the Brandt, Palme and Brundtland Commissions in the 1980s.

ICISS meetings and roundtables were held in almost all continents and major capitals, involving continent-wide representatives, over 200 in total, from all sectors and cross-section of views.[58] The Report reflected a genuine effort to incorporate many of the views that were expressed in Cairo, New Delhi and Santiago as well as Beijing, London, Paris and Washington. The views presented during the outreach exercise were sometimes used as tie-breakers during deadlocked discussions in the Commission. In retrospect, as a final contextual comment, the one-year timeframe was probably a very useful discipline. This meant the momentum never flagged, ICISS worked to a tight deadline and participants remembered where they had got to at the previous meeting and the progress that had already been made. Even for panels with more ambitious mandates like the High-level Panel on UN reforms, a two-year mandate should be adequate for the required research, consultations, production and post-publication marketing of a report.

Product

To have traction and impact in the real world of policy, a panel's report and recommendations must strive for several right balances: between a document that is comprehensive, substantial and intellectually weighty, and one that is readable in terms of brevity, succinctness and accessible writing style; between pushing the envelope by testing the limits of politics with adventurous ideas but not tearing it up by moving too far ahead of what is realistically possible within political and institutional constraints; and between staying focussed on the specific mandate of the panel instead of solving all the world's problems, but not ignoring the wider context in which the particular proposals must be nested. In short, a balance between that which is ideally conceivable and desirable, and that which is practically achievable and implementable.

The Brandt Commission suffered because its social-democratic vision of development was closely aligned to the 'UN paradigm' of social justice and development and too far removed from the neoliberal leanings of the Bretton Woods institutions that soon became dominant.[59] The Commission on Global Governance had just too many recommendations, several of them too diffuse to attract the attention of the policy community or even the support of the intended beneficiaries in civil society. Similarly, Evans notes that the Blix Commission – of which he was a member – of like-minded members ended up with a wish-list, whereas the International Commission on Nuclear Non-proliferation and Disarmament – which he co-chaired – converted the same goals into more sharply prioritised action agendas for the immediate, medium and long terms to a generally more favourable reception.[60]

The final product should be innovative and exciting. A bumper sticker phrase that encapsulates the complex innovation and captures policy attention and popular imagination is enormously helpful. Among the two best examples are sustainable development and R2P. Phrases like 'our global neighbourhood' (Carlsson–Ramphal) and 'a culture of prevention' (Carnegie) have lacked similar resonance, while 'human security' (Ogata–Sen) had been popularised already by the UN Development Programme a decade earlier. Packaging is also important. The publication should be visually attractive, contain a succinct executive summary and a good index.

Focus

Panels that have something to say on everything are unlikely to be remembered for anything. ICISS stuck narrowly to its core mandate. It resisted the temptation to recast its report in light of the terrorist attacks of 11 September 2001, concluding that horrific and urgent as the latter was, self-defence is conceptually and operationally distinct from the protection of at-risk foreign populations. Nor did it urge amendments to the Security Council structure. If a panel's mandated mission is too broad and fuzzy, the other details cannot compensate, and the final result will be unhappy. Sponsoring governments and organisations should pay close attention therefore to the nature and importance of the problem to be addressed, whether a high-level panel is the best instrument for addressing the problem, the clarity of the terms of reference for the panel in tackling the problem, the primary and secondary target audiences, and the chairs and panel members likely to have credibility in the target audiences.

Timing and luck

Sometimes panels may prove to have been ahead of their times and their ideational and normative impact may still exercise considerable influence years or decades later. The Palme Commission's analysis and recommendations for advancing our common security were presented to a particularly inauspicious environment at the height of the Cold War in 1982 while, as already noted, the Brand Commission's attempt to redefine North–South relations fell victim to the ascendancy of the neoliberal consensus on the dominance of market principles. But their ideas regained circulation with the end of the Cold War, the heightened concern with international terrorism and nuclear security, and the growing consciousness of North–South inequity – exacerbated by the process of globalisation – and the links between poverty and security.

Luck can prove critical with respect to the timing and outcome of elections and the movement of commission chairs and members into and out of government. The Canberra Commission delivered an excellent product but by then the Labor Government had lost office and its successor had little interest in promoting its predecessor's product. Without active government backing and advocacy, the report languished in the policy world, although it continued to attract considerable attention in civil society. The Brundtland Commission was fortunate in that its chair returned to Norway's prime ministership and was able to harness the added profile and prestige of the office to the cause of selling the message. ICISS fell between these two extremes. The foreign and prime ministers changed, but the Liberal Party stayed in power through the 2005 UN world summit. Prime Minister Paul Martin's engaged advocacy was crucial to the inclusion of R2P in the summit's outcome document. The change of government to the Conservatives in 2006 marked a retreat of Canada from visible ownership and active sponsorship of the norm.

Timing was important to ICISS in two other respects as well. First, the series of humanitarian atrocities committed in Africa (Rwanda), Europe (the Balkans) and Asia (East Timor) in the 1990s, and the contrasting outcomes of a lack of intervention in Rwanda, unilateral intervention in Kosovo and UN-authorised but fitful intervention in East Timor, meant that ICISS was grappling with very much a major current controversy. But well into its process and just three months before its report was published, second, the international agenda took a dramatic right-turn to deal with the consequences of the terrorist attacks of 11 September 2001. It took the highly controversial and widely opposed US-led invasion of Iraq in 2003 to rekindle passionate interest in a new global consensus on the circumstances in which the use of force to deal with humanitarian atrocities and serial atrocity perpetrators is both lawful and legitimate.[61]

Follow through, follow up, and norm entrepreneurs, brokers, champions, carriers and spoilers

A panel commissions and gathers research, deliberates, decides, writes and then publishes its report. Sustained engagement and advocacy by key actors remain critical to success in the post-report phase. The messages have to be communicated to multiple audiences around the world in policy and civil society settings. In addition to good communication skills, this also requires resources, organisation and champions. The report is neither the start nor the end of the process but the mid-point. For it to have impact, it must be followed with a range of activities in key capitals, international forums and other target audiences so that the story can be told of why the report matters, how its recommendations will address and solve the problem to hand and what is the best way forward in implementing the recommendations.

If the core problem was a gap in the normative architecture, as with the protection of atrocity victims, then the actors involved from start to finish might be divided into norm entrepreneurs, brokers, champions, carriers and spoilers.

An entrepreneur is someone who spots or identifies a gap or need in the market and organises an enterprise to produce the missing goods and sell them to potential buyers. In the case of R2P, the norm entrepreneurs, in this author's judgement, were Kofi Annan who first most visibly and powerfully identified the normative gap that needed filling in his famous challenge of humanitarian intervention; Lloyd Axworthy who as foreign minister of Canada spotted the market opportunity to 'organise the production' of the missing norm; and co-chairs Evans and Sahnoun. In addition, Francis Deng had earlier done yeoman's work in reconceptualising sovereignty as responsibility with respect to internally displaced persons.[62]

A broker is someone who bridges the needs and brings together the selling and purchasing price of the two parties involved in a transactional exchange, sometimes as an agent of one of the two parties. In an important sense this is the role that the Brundtland Commission and ICISS played in bridging development and conservation, and sovereignty and intervention, through their formulations of 'sustainable development' and the 'responsibility to protect' respectively. ICISS brought together a number of disparate trends over several decades – the change from interstate warfare by uniformed armies using tanks and battleships to international and transnational armed conflict fought with small arms, the deliberate targeting of civilians, the rise of an internationalised human conscience, the expansion of international humanitarian and human rights laws, the advances in technology that brought the horrors of atrocities into living rooms in real time – in an innovative and coherent conceptual framework. ICISS put words to decades of deeds signifying international executive authority by the United Nations.[63]

A champion is someone who supports a cause and is prepared to defend it and fight for it. The role of a state champion is especially important. Had Labor not lost power in 1996, Evans would have ensured that Australia remained a state champion of the report of the Canberra Commission, and its implementation fate might well have been different. Having Canada as a champion meant that the R2P principle had the necessary resources, organisation, platform and powerful voices advocating on behalf of it and seeing it through to unanimous endorsement in 2005. With individuals, in the Canberra Commission, this role was assumed by a previous sceptic on the cause of nuclear abolition, General Lee Butler, the former commander of the US Strategic Air Command.[64] Once ICISS had published its report, the role of champion was taken on by Annan, Evans, Sahnoun, and Martin in the 2005 world summit process. Since 2007, Annan's successor Ban Ki-moon has been an equally committed champion of R2P, helping to crystallise, consolidate and build broader consensus behind the norm.

A carrier is someone who carries, conveys and transmits a product from one place, person or entity to another without claiming ownership of it at any time in the process. Civil society organisations – in particular, the Global Centre for R2P and the International Coalition for RtoP in New York, and the Asia Pacific Centre for R2P in Brisbane, working with their own global and regional networks – have helped to disseminate, transmit and clarify the norm to a broad global audience. The national focal points for R2P can also be described as norm carriers as can also, if in a more qualified sense, the various research centres and dedicated journals and book series devoted to R2P. Similarly, the Centre for Nuclear Non-Proliferation and Disarmament based at the Australian National University is a carrier of the report of ICNND which had recommended the establishment of such a centre in order to monitor the implementation of authoritative outcomes and recommendations by the relevant states.[65]

A spoiler is someone opposed to the activity, agenda or norm being introduced and organises either overtly or behind the scenes to frustrate its implementation, and who must be co-opted or neutralised. The overt state-level spoilers who have consistently opposed R2P are just a handful: Cuba, Nicaragua, Sudan and Venezuela. In more recent times, since the NATO operation in Libya in wake of Security Council Resolution 1973, and particularly with respect to Syria in the 2011–13 period, China and Russia also fall into the category of norm spoilers, at least in so far as R2P's implementation is concerned.

Conclusion

Attributes and factors that condition and determine the success and failure of high-level panels include their structural and operational features, the quality of leadership provided by their chairs, the breadth, depth and diversity of expertise of their members, the organisation of adequate financial and personnel resources to enable the necessary research and consultations to be undertaken, mission clarity and focus, and the full range of follow-up dissemination, advocacy and championing of the recommendations. While their operational impact can be diffuse, uncertain and spread thinly over considerable periods of time, they can be important agents of change in global governance for projecting the power of ideas and processing them into new and improved policy, normative, institutional and operational outcomes. For that reason, high-level international panels and commissions will continue to be set up as an instrument for brokering the change from a deficient to an improved set of governance norms, arrangements and practices to tackle important and urgent problems. At the same time, history suggests that fewer rather than more will succeed, and even the successful will depend on fortune smiling on them with respect to some matters that are beyond control. That said, they can improve their prospects of success by learning, no less than those in charge of national diplomacy, to operate as networks rather than clubs.[66]

Notes

* Originally published in Jacob Cogan, Ian Hurd and Ian Johnstone, eds., *The Oxford Handbook of International Organizations* (Oxford: Oxford University Press, 2016), 859–80. Reprinted by permission of Oxford University Press.

1 Ramesh Thakur, 'Multilateral Diplomacy and the United Nations: Global Governance Venue or Actor?', in James P. Muldoon, JoAnn Fagot Aviel, Richard Reitano, and Earl Sullivan, eds., *The New Dynamics of Multilateralism: Diplomacy, International Organizations, and Global Governance* (Boulder: Westview, 2011), 249–65; Ramesh Thakur and Thomas G. Weiss, 'United Nations "Policy": An Argument with Three Illustrations', *International Studies Perspectives* 10:1 (January–April 2009), 18–35.

2 Ramesh Thakur and Luk van Langenhove, 'Enhancing Global Governance Through Regional Integration', *Global Governance* 12:3 (2006), 233–40.

3 See Mary Kaldor, *Global Civil Society: An Answer to War* (Cambridge: Polity Press, 2003), and John Keane, *Global Civil Society?* (Cambridge: Cambridge University Press, 2003).

4 Thorsten Benner, Wolfgang H. Reinecke, and Jan Martin Witte, *Shaping Globalization: The Role of Global Public Policy Networks* (2002), 4, www.globalpublicpolicy.net/.

5 Kofi A. Annan, *Renewing the United Nations: A Programme for Reform*. Report of the Secretary-General. (New York: United Nations, document A/51/950, 14 July 1997), paragraph 212.

6 Mark Malloch-Brown, 'How to Reform the British Foreign Office', *Financial Times*, 14 January 2010.

7 Kishore Mahbubani, 'Multilateral Diplomacy', in Andrew F. Cooper, Jorge Heine, and Ramesh Thakur, eds., *The Oxford Handbook of Modern Diplomacy* (Oxford: Oxford University Press, 2013), 248.

8 Javier Pérez de Cuéllar, 'The Role of the UN Secretary-General', in Adam Roberts and Benedict Kingsbury, eds., *United Nations, Divided World: The UN's Role in International Relations* (Oxford: Clarendon, 1988), 67–69.

9 Thucydides, *The Peloponnesian War*, quoted in Ivor Roberts, ed., *Satow's Diplomatic Practice*, 6th ed. (Oxford: Oxford University Press, 2009), 7.

10 'Address by Secretary-General Kofi Annan to the American Academy of Diplomacy Upon Receiving the Academy's "Excellence in Diplomacy" Award in Washington, DC, on 28 November', United Nations Press Release, 30 November 2001.

11 See Andrew F. Cooper and Ramesh Thakur, 'The BRICS in the New Global Economic Geography', in Thomas G. Weiss and Rorden Wilkinson, eds., *International Organization and Global Governance* (London: Routledge, 2014), 265–78.

12 This paragraph draws in particular on Andrew F. Cooper and Ramesh Thakur, *The Group of Twenty (G20)* (London: Routledge, 2013) and Richard Feinberg, 'Institutionalized Summitry', in Cooper, Heine and Thakur, eds., *Oxford Handbook of Modern Diplomacy*, 303–18.

13 Kofi A. Annan, 'Problems without Passports', *Foreign Policy* (1 September 2002), www.foreignpolicy.com/articles/2002/09/01/problems_without_passports.

14 For elaboration of a balance of interests as an alternative analytical construct to the national interest, see Ramesh Thakur, 'A Balance of Interests', in Cooper, Heine and Thakur, eds., *Oxford Handbook of Modern Diplomacy*, 70–87.

15 David Shorr, 'Making the G-20 a Reservoir of Global Leadership – A Maximalist Argument', *Policy Analysis Brief* (Muscatine, IA: Stanley Foundation, April 2011), 5.

16 Gareth Evans, *The Responsibility to Protect: Ending Mass Atrocities Once and For All* (Washington, DC: Brookings Institution Press, 2008); Alex. J. Bellamy, *Responsibility to Protect* (Cambridge: Polity, 2009); Ramesh Thakur, *The Responsibility to Protect: Norms, Laws and the Use of Force in International Politics* (London: Routledge, 2011); and Thomas G. Weiss, *Humanitarian Intervention: Ideas in Action*, 2nd ed. (Cambridge: Polity, 2011).

17 Peter Willetts, 'The Pattern of Conferences', in Paul Taylor and A.J.R. Groom, eds., *Global Issues in the United Nations' Framework* (New York: St. Martin's Press, 1989), 46.

18 Andrew F. Cooper and John English, 'International Commissions and the Mind of Global Governance', in Ramesh Thakur, Andrew F. Cooper and John English, eds., *International Commissions and the Power of Ideas* (Tokyo: United Nations University Press, 2005), 1–26.

19 See Thakur, Cooper and English, eds., *International Commissions and the Power of Ideas*.

20 Thomas G. Weiss, Tatiana Carayannis and Richard Jolly, 'The "Third" United Nations', *Global Governance* 15:1 (2009), 123–42.

21 Gareth Evans, 'Commission Diplomacy', in Cooper, Heine and Thakur, eds., *Oxford Handbook of Modern Diplomacy*, 278–302.

22 Reflecting the author's background and bias, this chapter focuses mostly, but not exclusively, on examples from international security.

23 *A New Global Partnership: Eradicate Poverty and Transform Economies through Sustainable Development*. Report of the High-Level Panel of Eminent Persons on the Post-2015 Development Agenda (New York: United Nations, 2013).

24 OAU, *Rwanda: The Preventable Genocide. Report of the OAU's International Panel of Eminent Personalities* (Addis Ababa: OAU, 31 May 2000), paragraph 15.87, www.refworld.org/pdfid/4d1da8752.pdf.

25 *Report of the Independent Inquiry into the Actions of the United Nations during the 1994 Genocide in Rwanda* (New York: United Nations, document S/1999/1257, 15 December 1999), www.securitycouncilreport.org/atf/cf/%7B65BFCF9B-6D27-4E9C-8CD3-CF6E4FF96FF9%7D/POC%20S19991257.pdf.

26 Richard Goldstone, Hina Jilani, Christine Chinkin and Desmond Travers, *Human Rights in Palestine and Other Occupied Arab Territories: Report of the United Nations Fact Finding Mission on the Gaza Conflict* (Geneva: United Nations Human Rights Council, A/HRC/12/48, 15 September 2009), www2.ohchr.org/english/bodies/hrcouncil/specialsession/9/docs/UNFFMGC_Report.pdf. For a discussion on the report, see commentaries by Tom Farer, Dinah PoKempner, Ed Morgan, Richard Falk, and Nigel S. Rodley, in *Global Governance* 16:2 (2010), 139–207.

27 Jean-Philippe Therien, 'The Brandt Commission: The End of an Era in North–South Politics', in Thakur, Cooper and English, eds., *International Commissions and the Power of Ideas*, 27–45.

28 Thomas G. Weiss and Ramesh Thakur, *Global Governance and the UN: An Unfinished Journey* (Bloomington: Indiana University Press, 2010).

29 See Daniel Philpott, *Revolutions in Sovereignty: How Ideas Shaped Modern International Relations* (Princeton: Princeton University Press, 2001).

30 World Commission on Environment and Development (Gro Harlem Brundtland, Chair), *Our Common Future. Report of the World Commission on Environment and Development*, (Oxford: Oxford University Press, 1987), 27.

31 See, for example, Anne Orford, *International Authority and the Responsibility to Protect* (Cambridge: Cambridge University Press, 2011), 41; Martin Gilbert, 'The Terrible 20th Century', *Globe and Mail* (Toronto), 31 January 2007.

32 See Hugh Breakey, Angus Francis, Vesselin Popovski, Charles Sampford, Michael G. Smith, and Ramesh Thakur, *Enhancing Protection Capacity: A Policy Guide to the Responsibility to Protect and the Protection of Civilians in Armed Conflicts* (Brisbane: Institute for Ethics, Governance and Law, 2012), www.griffith.edu.au/criminology-law/institute-ethics-governance-law/research/responsibility-to-protect-protection-of-civilians-policy-guide.

33 *Report of the Panel on United Nations Peace Operations* (New York: United Nations, document A/55/305-S/2000/809, 21 August 2000).

34 *Report of the Panel on United Nations Peace Operations*, viii.

35 *Report of the Panel on United Nations Peace Operations*, 9, paragraph 50.

36 High-level Panel on Threats, Challenges and Change (HLP), *A More Secure World: Our Shared Responsibility* (New York: United Nations, document A/59/565, December 2004).

37 *Report of the Panel on United Nations Peace Operations*, paragraphs 65–75.

38 HLP, *A More Secure World*, paragraphs 298–300.

39 The Stanley Foundation, *Capturing the 21st Century Security Agenda: Prospects for Collective Responses* (Muscatine, Iowa: Stanley Foundation, 2004), 50. This is the report of the discussions of a high-level group of UN hands.

40 *2005 World Summit Outcome*, resolution adopted by the UN General Assembly, A/RES/60/1 (New York: United Nations, 24 October 2005), paragraphs 176–78.

41 HLP, *A More Secure World*, paragraph 250.

42 *Outcome Document*, paragraph 153.

43 HLP, *A More Secure World*, paragraphs 261–69.

44 *Outcome Document*, paragraphs 97–105.

45 Quoted in Emma Kate-Symons, 'UN Reform a Disaster: Evans', *The Australian*, 19 October 2005.

46 Unto Vesa, ed., *Global Commissions Assessed* (Helsinki: Ministry for Foreign Affairs, 2005), 90.

47 Disclosure: the author was editor-in-chief of *Global Governance* for the five years 2013–17.

48 W. Andy Knight, 'The Commission on Global Governance', in Thakur, Cooper and English, *International Commissions*, 113–14; John Ruggie, *Just Business: Multinational Corporations and Human Rights* (New York: W. W. Norton, 2013).

49 Weiss and Thakur, *Global Governance and the UN*, 43–45.

50 See Ramesh Thakur, 'Protection Gaps for Civilian Victims of Political Violence', *South African Journal of International Affairs* 20:3 (2013), 321–38.

51 Ramesh Thakur, *Towards a Less Imperfect State of the World: The Gulf between North and South* (Berlin: Friedrich Ebert Stiftung, Dialogue on Globalization Briefing Paper 4, April 2008).

52 Evans, 'Commission Diplomacy', 291.

53 Personal conversation, 2004.

54 Unnamed UN ambassador quoted in 'United Nations: Fighting for Survival', *Economist*, 20 November 2004, 23.

55 Barbara Crossette, quoting a former high-ranking UN official, 'Sixteen Wise People and the Future of the U.N.', *U.N. Wire*, 1 December 2003.

56 No one questioned the eminence and distinction of any one of the members individually; it was the balance among the group that raised many eyebrows.

57 The ICISS effort 'to engage a broad range of scholars and NGOs from a wide range of countries … was an attempt to establish legitimacy by means other than simply depending on the reputation of the core members of the commission'; Jon Pedersen, 'Ideas, Think-Tanks, Commissions, and Global Politics', in Thakur, Cooper and English, *International Commissions and the Power of Ideas*, 274.

58 Commission meetings were held in Ottawa (November 2000), Maputo (March 2001), New Delhi (June 2001), Wakefield, Canada (August 2000), and Brussels (September

2001). Roundtables and consultative meetings were held, in chronological order, in Ottawa, Geneva, London, Maputo, Washington DC, Santiago, Cairo, Paris, New Delhi, Beijing and St. Petersburg.

59 Therien, 'Brandt Commission', 28–29.

60 Evans, 'Commission Diplomacy', 295–96.

61 See Ramesh Thakur and Waheguru Pal Singh Sidhu, eds., *The Iraq Crisis and World Order: Structural, Institutional and Normative Challenges* (Tokyo: United Nations University Press, 2006).

62 Francis Deng, Sadikiel Kimaro, Terrence Lyons, Donald Rothchild, and I. William Zartman, *Sovereignty as Responsibility: Conflict Management in Africa* (Washington, DC: Brookings Institution Press, 1996).

63 Orford, *International Authority and the Responsibility to Protect.*

64 Marianne Hanson, 'Regulating the Possession and Use of Nuclear Weapons', in Thakur, Cooper and English, eds., *International Commissions and the Power of Ideas*, 138; Evans, 'Commission Diplomacy', 297.

65 See Ramesh Thakur and Gareth Evans, eds., *Nuclear Weapons: The State of Play* (Canberra: CNND, 2013).

66 Jorge Heine, 'From Club to Network Diplomacy', in Cooper, Heine and Thakur, eds., *Oxford Handbook of Modern Diplomacy*, 54–69.

4 Rwanda, Kosovo and the International Commission on Intervention and State Sovereignty*

The history of the twentieth century is in part the story of the effort to translate an increasingly internationalised human conscience into a new normative architecture of world order governing the internal and international use of force by sovereign states. There was growing recognition of the authority of international consensus over individual state consent as the foundation of legal obligation. To that end, the notion of 'excess state violence' challenged the use of violence by any state in its internal and international behaviour beyond the level that international political actors consider to be legitimate.[1]

As the century drew to a close, three powerful forces converged to entrench non-intervention as a peremptory norm of International Relations. The first was the doctrine of state sovereignty which emphasised the independence and formal equality of all territorially-defined states with exclusive authority over the people and resources within their legal jurisdiction. The second was the principle of self-determination that underpinned decolonisation and produced an explosion in the number of independent states making up the family of nations, with a jealous determination to guard their newly-regained sovereignty. The third was the progressive delegitimisation of the use of international force except in self-defence against armed attack or when authorised by the United Nations as the sole agent of the international community.[2]

In the meantime, however, the human rights norm also deepened, and its geographical footprint expanded to cover the world. In an increasingly interconnected international system, it was entrenched as a universal global norm, producing normative dissonance with the competing norm of non-intervention. The paradigmatic case of shameful inaction amidst mass atrocities was the Rwanda genocide in 1994; that of unilateral intervention to try and halt mass atrocities was military action by NATO in Kosovo in 1999. Between them, the two cases showed that the existing normative consensus was no longer fit for purpose against the brutal facts of the real world. Responding to a clarion call from UN Secretary-General Kofi Annan, an independent blue-ribbon international commission was convened to try and recreate a new consensus and its report came up with the innovative formula of R2P that married the civilian protection agenda of the mid and late 1990s to the earlier reformulation of sovereignty as responsibility in the context of internally displaced persons (IDPs).

This chapter proceeds in four parts. The first describes the default policy setting of non-intervention that seemed firmly set in the 1990s. The second section discusses the policy challenge posed both by no action and unilateral action when faced with mass atrocities in Rwanda and the Balkans in the 1990s. The third part reviews the policy controversies provoked by the claim of an emerging new norm of humanitarian intervention to justify the military action in Kosovo in 1999. The final section concludes with the successful effort of ICISS to reconcile the humanitarian imperative to protect civilians from atrocities with the normative prohibition on the use of force inside sovereign jurisdictions without, or even against, the consent of national governments.

Policy setting: non-intervention as the default norm

Sovereignty, which has its philosophical and political roots in European thought and practice, is the bedrock organising principle of modern international society and faith in it was strongly reaffirmed by the large number of countries that regained their independence from colonial bondage in the second half of the twentieth century. Internally, sovereignty refers to the exclusive competence of the state to make authoritative decisions of government with regard to all people and resources within its territory. Externally, it means the legal identity of the state in international law, an equality of status with all other states and the claim to be the sole official agent acting in international relations on behalf of a society. A condition of any one state's sovereignty is a corresponding obligation to respect every other state's sovereignty; that is, not to intervene in others' internal affairs. Military intervention was circumscribed also by the gathering effort to put increasingly strict limits on the right of states to wage war as unilateral policy. The fetters of the Covenant of the League of Nations were reinforced normatively by the 1928 Kellogg–Briand Pact outlawing war and followed by stringent proscriptions on the use of force in the UN Charter.

Yet, juridical sovereignty notwithstanding, 'humanitarian intervention' too has a long history. Its supposed illegality was neither uncontested in academic discourse nor abandoned in state practice. Three European powers – England, France and Russia – intervened in Greece in 1827 to stop massacres by Turkey, and France intervened again in Syria in 1860 to stop the killings of Maronite Christians. Various European powers intervened in defence of Christians also in Crete (1866–68), the Balkans (1875–78) and Macedonia (1903–08). Doctrine – for example 'just war'[3] – followed to justify practice, with one analyst justifying humanitarian intervention as the use of force to protect victims of 'arbitrary and persistently abusive' treatment by their own governments.[4] Even during the Cold War, state practice reflected the unwillingness of many countries, including former colonies like India and Tanzania, to give up intervention as an instrument of policy. The US has an almost unbroken history of intervening in Latin America, the Middle East and elsewhere to effect regime change.

At the same time, some of the iconic events in Latin America – Cuba in the 1960s, Chile in the 1970s, Nicaragua and Panama in the 1980s – show how difficult it is to pinpoint with precision just what constitutes military intervention, let alone 'humanitarian' intervention. The International Court of Justice (ICJ) ruled against humanitarian intervention, for example in the 1986 case *Nicaragua vs. United States*. The court interpreted Article 2(4) of the UN Charter broadly to impose strict limits on the use of force, and Article 51 narrowly to limit the use of force against another state to self-defence against armed attack from that state. Prior to the Reagan doctrine, US lapses from Charter proscriptions on the use of force were occasional and partial: the Bay of Pigs invasion of Cuba (1961), the intervention in the Dominican Republic (1965–66). The Reagan doctrine, in seeking to make it general and wholesale, was 'untenable in law'.[5]

Thus, the many examples of intervention in actual state practice throughout the twentieth century did not lead to an abandonment of the norm of non-intervention. Often the breaches provoked such fierce controversy and aroused so much nationalistic passion that their net effect was to reinforce the norm more than to negate it. The difficulty with justifying intervention is that the real world is characterised by moral ambiguity rather than clarity. Intervention may be self-serving from the start, or begin as humanitarian but be transformed into self-aggrandisement. Interventions by India into East Pakistan in 1971 and by Vietnam into Cambodia in 1978 removed two regimes that were clearly guilty of having committed gross humanitarian atrocities. But neither action was incompatible with the national security interests of the two intervening powers. Because of the dominance of the non-intervention norm, both intervening powers justified their military action as self-defence, not humanitarian intervention.

State sovereignty and the correlative norm of non-intervention received their most emphatic affirmation from the newly independent states in the growing anti-colonial narrative after the Second World War. They pointed to the underlying reality of commercial and geopolitical calculations cloaked in the language of humanitarian and religious motives, as well as paternalism of the European colonial powers. Many re-emerged as independent states traumatised by their colonial experience. The long shadows cast by this are yet to disappear even though the surviving scars in their collective memory are difficult for many Westerners to comprehend. That said, the commitment to sovereignty is also functional. The state is the cornerstone of the international system and sovereignty mediates relations between the strong and weak, rich and poor, and former colonisers and colonised. Upon independence, state sovereignty was the constitutional device used by newly decolonised countries to try to reconstitute disrupted societies and polities and restart arrested economic development. UN membership was the final symbol of independent sovereign statehood and the organisation was the principal forum for collaborative action in the shared pursuit of the three goals of state building, nation building and economic development. The UN was therefore the main arena for the jealous protection of state sovereignty, not its casual abrogation.

However, the increasing internationalisation of the world steadily widened the gap between the legal status and empirical reality of statehood. As a result of agreements signed voluntarily, states accepted many external obligations and international scrutiny. The norms of human rights and international humanitarian law in particular became widely acknowledged and honoured in and among states. As memories of colonialism dimmed and became increasingly distant, the salience of sovereignty correspondingly diminished. Citizens and domestic groups instead began to use the international human rights norm and cross-national global coalitions to subject the actions of their own governments to increasingly critical international scrutiny.

The arguments against intervention held up less easily in principle than in pragmatism. A perennial difficulty in trying to justify intervention is that 'The use of force as a sanction for a breach of an international obligation may do more harm than the breach of the international obligation; the cure is often worse than the disease'.[6] Yet a decision not to intervene can have grave consequences. Allied powers in effect, even if not in intention, helped the cause of Franco by refusing to intervene in the Spanish Civil War (1936–39). In practice, the legitimacy of intervention often turned on the answer to four questions on actor, act, target, and purpose. Who or what was the subject or intervening *agent;* what was the mode or *form* of intervention; who or what was the putative *object* of intervention, and what degree of legitimacy attached to the target; and what was the motive for or *goal* of intervention? The most commonly accepted form of intervention was that authorised by the United Nations.

Policy challenge: mass atrocity crimes

Against this backdrop, a fierce debate on intervention was ignited in the closing decade of the last century by outbreaks of humanitarian crises in Africa, Asia and Europe that were handled neither well nor with any semblance of consistency by the international community. Instead they highlighted a dangerous gap between the codified best practice of international behaviour as articulated in the UN Charter and actual state practice as it had evolved in the six decades since the Charter was signed. The international community failed to rise to the challenge of the conscience-shocking atrocities of the 1990s and the price of failure was paid by large numbers of innocent men, women and children.

Rwanda

If the Gulf War (1990–91) marked the birth of the new world order, Somalia (1992–94) was the slide into the new world disorder, and Rwanda (1994) and Srebrenica (1995) marked the loss of innocence after the end of the Cold War. As genocide unfolded in Rwanda in early 1994 with ample forewarning to the UN and the major powers, the world bore silent and distant witness to apathy. That institutionalised international indifference remains one of the most shameful episodes since the Holocaust. This was not a matter of lack of knowledge and awareness, or even lack of capacity. Rather, it was a failure of collective conscience, of civic courage at the highest and most solemn levels of responsibility.

The question that champions of humanitarian intervention posed was: what if a coalition of the willing had been prepared to move in with military force, but the Security Council was deadlocked?

The genocide was the result of many factors that had been festering for decades. During Rwanda's colonial history under Germany and later Belgium, the smaller Tutsi ethnic group (about 14 per cent of the population in 1994) was favoured for advancement over the larger Hutu ethnic group (about 85 per cent of the population at the time).[7] This social, political and economic inequality was large and widening. Rwanda's demographic explosion exerted severe pressure on the land available for cultivation,[8] which was increasingly unable to support so many people; repatriated refugees from Uganda and Burundi, falling prices for cash crops and progressive deforestation exacerbated matters. Added to the witch's brew was a failed political system: authoritarian, corrupt and prone to create and manipulate ethnic tensions. Rwanda was one of the most heavily aided countries in the world, with almost a quarter of its GNP from outside financing.[9] However, most of this aid went to development projects that benefited the elite and exacerbated ethnic tensions.[10]

Against this combustible background, the 1994 slaughter had been foreshadowed by major outbreaks of ethnic violence in 1963 and 1988 between Hutus and Tutsis.[11] President Juvenal Habyarimana died in an airplane crash thought to be an assassination carried out by extremist Tutsis in the Rwandan Patriotic Front (RPF). In response, Hutu extremists in the armed militias massacred 800,000 people in under three months. From its base in Uganda, the RPF invaded and made steady gains, and by July controlled the country. Over two million refugees, both Hutus and Tutsis, fled into neighbouring countries. The Security Council's late and incomplete response – the latter was essentially subcontracted to France under Operation Turquoise – in the face of advance warning, helped nudge the international community of states towards revisiting the notion of prevention and the principle of non-intervention.

While the major powers were determined not to use the word 'genocide' in order to avoid obligations to prevent or halt it, the UN was determined to stick narrowly and rigidly to its mandate not to use force to help the victims of the unfolding genocide either. According to the report of the inquiry conducted by the OAU panel of eminent persons,

> both the Security Council and the UN Secretariat had compiled an entirely inglorious record in the months preceding the genocide … [and] the response after Habyarimana's plane was shot down on 6 April does little to add to the credit of either.[12]

On 7 April, Prime Minister Agathe Uwilingiyimana fled over the wall of her own Kigali residence and sought refuge at a nearby UN compound. The UN Force Commander Lt.-Gen. Roméo Dallaire called Assistant Secretary-General Iqbal Riza in New York to tell him that force might be required to save the prime minister, but was ordered not to do so beyond the mandate of protecting his troops. Within an hour Rwandan soldiers entered the UN compound and shot her dead.

But on 9 April a cable to Dallaire from the then-Under-Secretary-General for Peacekeeping Annan, signed by Riza, instructed him to facilitate French and Belgian commanders in evacuating their nationals and use his discretion to exceed his mandate for that purpose if necessary – the only occasion on which he was permitted such individual discretion, never to protect the Rwandans.[13] The skill, speed and logistical efficiency displayed by Belgium, France and the US in evacuating their soldiers and nationals during the early days of the genocide reinforced Dallaire's conviction that the rapid deployment of just 5,000 well-trained and well-armed professional troops in the early days of the genocide would have stopped or substantially reduced the tragedy. He sadly concluded that serving the UN goals is not high on the foreign policy priority of most countries. Instead, 'What they want is a weak, beholden, indebted scapegoat of an organization, which they can blame for their failures or steal victories from'.[14]

The storyline explains why some commentators held Annan responsible for the genocide and do not believe he paid an appropriate price for it: 'Kofi Annan, who was head of the DPKO at the time, went on to become Secretary-General, taking with him his closest staff (including Riza as chief of cabinet), who had been central in the decision-making process in Rwanda'.[15] Annan himself confessed, in a speech at the UN on 26 March 2004 to mark the tenth anniversary of the genocide, that at the time, he thought he had done everything possible to rally the international community and mobilise support for the UN force in Rwanda. But now he believes he could and should have done more.[16]

Still, the overall conclusion of the OAU inquiry panel was that the 'small number of major actors whose intervention could directly have prevented, halted or reduced the slaughter' consisted of France, the US, UK and Belgium.[17] In addition, 'the silence of the OAU and a large majority of African Heads of State constituted a shocking moral failure'.[18] The report of the UN's own inquiry panel, chaired by Sweden's former Prime Minister Ingvar Carlsson, also concluded that the international community failed either to stop the genocide or to halt it once it had begun. It attributed the responsibility for these two failings to several actors, 'in particular to the Secretary-General [Boutros Boutros-Ghali], the Secretariat, the Security Council, UNAMIR [UN Assistance Mission for Rwanda] and the broader' UN membership.[19]

There were two more conscience-troubling cases in 1999. East Timor was devastated after a UN-mandated referendum on independence when the occupying power, Indonesia, watched from the sidelines as armed militias backed by Indonesian troops unleashed mass killings and destruction on unarmed civilians. Kosovo became the last of a series of humanitarian disasters in the Balkans. Both were clearly predictable. Indonesia had routinely repressed its captive population since 1975, with an estimated 100,000 Timorese dead in the process. And President Slobodan Milosevic had routinely demonstrated his intentions, especially in the province where in 1989 he had launched the pursuit of 'Greater Serbia' with a jingoistic speech invoking the Turks' humiliating defeat of the

Serbs six centuries earlier. Incendiary events were ignored, massacres followed and afterwards both Timor and Kosovo were the objects of major and costly humanitarian military operations succeeded by a substantial military presence to keep the peace.

Kosovo

After Rwanda, the UN suffered its next reputational blow with the fall of the UN 'Safe Area' of Srebrenica in July 1995 and the slaughter of more than 7,000 Bosnian men and boys sheltering under the protection of Dutch UN peacekeepers. A peacekeeping operation in a theatre where there was no peace to keep, the UN Protection Force in former Yugoslavia (UNPROFOR) offered neither safety to the local people, solace to the displaced and dispossessed, nor even the consolation to the international community of having done the job to the best of their ability. It remains a stain on world conscience for passivity in the face of the calculated return of 'evil' to Europe. In the words of the official UN report, the Srebrenica tragedy 'will haunt our history forever'.[20]

The horror in Yugoslavia unfolded in the context of a confused and incoherent Europe and an indecisive UN. Like Slovenia, Croatia, Macedonia and Bosnia, Kosovo too wanted independence in the wake of the dissolution of Josip Tito's Yugoslavia. Instead Kosovo lost the little autonomy it had, and along with Montenegro and Serbia, became an integral part of 'rump-Yugoslavia', its predominantly Albanian population suppressed by a small Serb elite. As the Balkans war seemed to be grinding to a bloody stalemate, the Srebrenica massacre shamed NATO into bombing Bosnian Serb positions, which led in turn to the Dayton Accord (1995). NATO's SFOR (Stabilisation Force) and IFOR (Implementation Force) troops, along with the Organisation for Security and Cooperation in Europe (OSCE) as the main civilian peace-builder, with only minor UN involvement, underwrote slow progress in providing for basic stability and the rebuilding of Bosnia-Herzegovina. Concluding that their concerns had been disregarded at Dayton, some radicalised Kosovars began to support the development of a paramilitary underground force known as the Kosovo Liberation Army (KLA). Serbia's war against the KLA escalated between the years 1996–98, with increasingly serious repercussions for Kosovo's civilian population.

Sickened by Milosevic's record of brutality in the Balkans and evasions and deceit in dealings with the Europeans and the UN, in 1999 the US decided on 'humanitarian intervention' in Kosovo. The allies concluded that for decisive and effective action against Milosevic, the political solidarity and military cohesion of NATO was a more congenial framework for collective action than the UN Security Council. Following the Serb rejection of an ultimatum not crafted for acceptance, NATO began bombing Serb military facilities throughout Kosovo and Yugoslavia on 24 March 1999. In retaliation, during almost three months of bombing, Serb military and paramilitary forces terrorised the Albanian population in Kosovo, drove hundreds of thousands out of the country and committed unspeakable atrocities against the local population.

Yugoslavia bitterly denounced NATO strikes as illegal aggression on a sovereign state. Its traditional ally Russia strongly opposed NATO's war against Yugoslavia and distanced itself from previous *rapprochement* with the West. China was deeply wounded by the 'accidental' NATO bombing of its embassy in Belgrade. The UN found itself sidelined by NATO. Annan, who had been head of UN peacekeeping at the time of the Srebrenica tragedy as well as genocide in Rwanda, was torn between criticism of the illegality of NATO actions and sympathy for the victims of Serb atrocities. With Russian assistance and G8 (the group of seven industrialised states plus Russia) involvement, the war was brought to an end and Yugoslav troops withdrew from Kosovo. A UN-led peacekeeping mission established a de facto protectorate in Kosovo, supported by a military presence (KFOR) with a large NATO component but also a Russian element. Most refugees returned home. Bouts of reverse ethnic cleansing broke out against local Serb and Roma populations but gradually over the coming years the security situation stabilised.

Policy controversy: an emerging norm of humanitarian intervention?

Genocide in Rwanda had left the international community with a deep sense of shame at having averted its gaze from the unfolding slaughter. NATO intervention in Kosovo ignited a fierce international controversy on the Atlantic allies' claim of an emerging new norm of 'humanitarian intervention'. NATO may well have acted illegally in terms of its own constitution, the UN Charter and state practice. This position was articulated most forcefully by China, Russia and India (as well as Serbia). For most Westerners, NATO is an alliance of democracies and as such a standing validation of the democratic peace thesis. For former colonies, one of the more notable features of NATO is that it is a military alliance of former colonial powers. Although not all NATO members are former colonial powers, every major former European colonial power is a member of NATO. For Russia, NATO includes France and Germany and there is always the input of historical trauma with painful memories of the bitter invasions of Russia by Napoleon and Hitler. China too has suffered invasions and humiliations at the hands of the major Western powers. In the collective view of Russia, China and the Non-Aligned Movement (NAM), neither the UN Charter nor the corpus of modern international law incorporates the right to 'humanitarian intervention'. According to the weight of legal opinion and authority, the prohibition on the use of force had become a peremptory norm of international law from which no derogation is allowed, and NATO was not permitted to contract out even at the regional level.

The case for NATO intervention: filling a critical protection gap …

Kosovo was a setback to the cause of slowly but steadily outlawing the use of force in solving disputes except under UN authorisation. NATO action was neither explicitly authorised nor prohibited by any UN resolution. NATO leaders argued that military action outside the UN framework was not their preferred option of choice. Rather, NATO's resort to force was a critical comment on the institutional hurdles to effective and timely action by the UN. Serbian atrocities in Kosovo challenged some of the cherished UN values. Had Milosevic been allowed to get away with his murderous campaign of ethnic cleansing, the net result would have been a fundamental erosion of the idealistic base on which the UN structure rests. The campaign against Serbia took place in the context of a history of defiance of increasingly tough UN resolutions by Milosevic. Moreover, the Security Council had relied progressively on NATO as its enforcement arm in the Balkans over the 1990s. NATO actions in Kosovo were thus a logical extension and evolution of a role already sanctioned by the Security Council. Czech President Vaclav Havel famously described the Kosovo war as one fought over 'principles and values' rather than national interests that showed, not disrespect for international law, but respect for the higher law of human rights than of state sovereignty.[21] Similarly, NATO Secretary-General Javier Solana proclaimed that for the first time, 'an alliance of sovereign states fought not to conquer or preserve territory but to protect the values on which the alliance was founded'.[22]

Support for this line of argument can be found in the UN's official report on Srebrenica. Acknowledging at least partial responsibility for the tragedy, the report in effect concluded that the UN peacekeeping philosophy of neutrality and non-violence was unsuited to the conflict in Bosnia. The approach of the international community was wholly inadequate to the Serb campaign of ethnic cleansing and mass murder which culminated in Srebrenica. Evil must be recognised as such and confronted by the international community; the UN's commitment to ending conflicts, far from precluding moral judgement, makes it all the more necessary.[23]

... Or opening new international fault lines?

Mobilising domestic support for a short and swift war against an enemy who has been successfully demonised does not automatically translate into building a new regime for interventions that has general acceptance in the international community. As Michael Glennon noted, 'Justice ... requires legitimacy; without widespread acceptance of intervention as part of a formal justice system, the new interventionism will appear to be built on neither law nor justice, but on power alone'.[24] The template of robust 'humanitarian intervention' and foreign-led 'regime change' was indeed to prove too rusty to the task in Iraq in 2003.

Raju Thomas attributes the 'self-righteous and one-sided perspectives and policies' animating NATO in Kosovo to the end of the Cold War, the collapse of countervailing power and the ascendancy of 'a new moral liberalism which emphasised global humanitarianism'.[25] In rejecting UN constraints, NATO chose not to play by the rules of the game when the result was not to its liking. More worryingly, no system was put in place instead of the UN. If unilateral intervention in defence of the rights of minority *peoples* was permitted, the weak *states* could lose protection against the dominant and assertive international moral-majority big powers. The case for NATO strikes on Serbia was not made with persuasive enough force to overcome the presumption of doubt – the humanitarian case was asserted, not argued. Just as anyone who attempted to question the humanitarian warriors over the case for Iraq risked being branded an apologist for Saddam Hussein in 2003, so those critical of the NATO intervention in 1999 risked being accused of standing shoulder-to-shoulder with the butcher of Belgrade. 'Humanitarianism' was married to 'war' in a clever and successful ploy to label opponents of the war as anti-humanitarian. The moral urgency underpinning NATO actions, and the military success of those actions, would in due course shape legal justification to match the course of action.[26]

Efforts to demonise Milosevic deflected attention from those who until recently were branded terrorists by Western governments[27] and by the Security Council,[28] but in 1999 became the principal beneficiaries of the bombing. By fighting and defeating Serbia, NATO became the tool for the KLA policy of inciting Serb reprisals through terrorist attacks in order to provoke NATO intervention.[29] The role of outside intervention in promoting territorial disintegration rather than preventing genocide was downplayed. Annan subsequently acknowledged that his call for a debate on the challenge of humanitarian intervention led to fears that the concept 'might encourage secessionist movements deliberately to provoke governments into committing gross violations of human rights in order to trigger external interventions that would aid their cause'.[30]

Kosovo as precedent

Most NATO countries insisted their action did not set a precedent. The Iraq war proved the claim false: the attempt 'to limit the reach of the Kosovo precedent did not prevent the advocates of the Iraq war from invoking it to justify toppling Saddam'.[31] The argument that NATO had no intention to set a precedent is less relevant than that its actions were interpreted by others as having done so. Can the Arab League claim the commensurate right to determine on its own that Israel is guilty of gross human rights atrocities against Palestinians and the League should intervene with military force in their defence? To say that they lack the power or military capacity to do so is to say that might is right. The worst-case scenario would be to encourage states to acquire nuclear weapons. At the Third Preparatory Committee (PrepCom) meeting of the NPT 2000 Review Conference in New York in May 1999, 'though the Chinese were the only ones publicly to wonder if NATO would have bombed Belgrade if Yugoslavia had also been nuclear armed, there were many in the corridors who made the obvious connection'.[32] In India, the same point was made by a former foreign secretary[33] and a leading newspaper.[34]

Western criticisms of the Russian use of massive force against Chechnya later in 1999 drew angry reminders of NATO action in Kosovo: an international war, as opposed to Russia's actions within its borders, noted Russian commentators.

Fifteen years later the Kosovo 'precedent' was hurled at US and European criticism of Russia's actions in Crimea and eastern Ukraine. Speaking after the reincorporation of Crimea into Russia in March, President Vladimir Putin was both explicit and expansive in justifying Russia's actions by recalling Kosovo. According to Putin,

> the Crimean authorities referred to the well-known Kosovo precedent – a precedent our western colleagues created with their own hands in a very similar situation, when they agreed that the unilateral separation of Kosovo from Serbia, exactly what Crimea is doing now, was legitimate and did not require any permission from the country's central authorities.[35]

Furthermore, he said, in its ruling on 22 July 2010, the ICJ had held that ' "General international law contains no prohibition on declarations of independence." Crystal clear, as they say'. He also recalled that in its submission on the case, the US had argued that while unilateral declarations may violate domestic law of the parent country, 'this does not make them violations of international law'. Rejecting the US and European argument 'that Kosovo is some special case', he pointed to the severe casualties in Kosovo compared to the absence of casualties and concluded: 'This is not even double standards; this is amazing, primitive, blunt cynicism'.[36]

Speaking at the Valdai Club of Russia experts in Sochi on 24 October 2014, Putin mentioned Kosovo three times to repeat his arguments from March in forceful language.[37] Foreign Minister Sergei Lavrov echoed the argument that those who used military force to dismember Serbia in 1999 have little moral authority to insist Crimea must be returned to Ukraine regardless of its people's wishes: 'Attempts by those who staged the secession of Kosovo from Serbia … to question the free will of Crimeans cannot be viewed as anything but a flagrant display of double standards'.[38] It is worth recalling that in 1999, Ambassador Lavrov was Russia's Permanent Representative to the United Nations (1994–2004). Most poignantly in this context, the person most responsible for the transformation of the former Soviet Union into Russia, Mikhail Gorbachev, also shares this view. In an interview with *Der Spiegel*, he said: 'NATO intervened militarily in the Yugoslavian civil war without the consent of the United Nations. That was a precedent-setting case' that 'No Kremlin leader can ignore'.[39] It seems fair to conclude, therefore, that the NATO intervention in Kosovo is deeply seared into the Russian consciousness as a precedent.

Relitigating humanitarian intervention

Thus, Kosovo was the terrain on which the rules of post-Cold War intervention were rewritten, and the controversy resonates to this day. The Independent International Commission on Kosovo, chaired by Richard Goldstone and Carl Tham, concluded that NATO's intervention was illegal but legitimate.[40] The legality–legitimacy distinction is problematical for it rests on an implicit hierarchy of norms.[41] If UN Charter proscriptions on the threat and use of force can be set aside, the justification for this must necessarily rest on the existence of a higher order of norms which override Charter clauses.[42] Conceding to any regional organisation the authority to decide when political legitimacy may override legal technicality would make a mockery of the entire basis of the strictly limited and increasingly constricted recourse to force for settling international disputes. Conversely, restricting the right solely to NATO is 'an open argument for law-making by an elite group of Western powers sitting in judgement over their own actions'.[43] A normative commitment to the rule of law implies a commitment to the principle of relations being governed by law, not power. It also implies a willingness to accept the limitations and constraints of working within the law, in specific instances if necessary against individual notions of just or illegitimate outcome. The best that can be said of the NATO actions was that it fell into and enlarged a 'grey area' between lawfulness and legitimacy, where the use of force is neither condemned nor condoned, but tolerated.

Many Russians concluded that perhaps all these years the Warsaw Pact had held NATO in check and not the other way round. China was traumatised by the US bombing of its embassy in Belgrade and did not accept repeated assurances that the attack was an accident. Both China and Russia were shaken by the ease with which NATO evaded the requirement of UN authorisation for the international use of force and both, along with NAM, challenged any emerging doctrine of humanitarian intervention.[44] The majority of developing countries were strongly opposed to NATO intervention in Kosovo. Because the UN Charter encapsulates the international moral code and best-practice international behaviour, the urge to 'humanitarian intervention' by powerful states, coalitions of the willing or regional organisations outside their own area of operations had to be bridled by the legitimating authority of the international organisation.

Thus, the question of lawful-cum-legitimate intervention cannot be separated from the question of the authoritative determination of just cause and justified response: who, under what rules of evidence and procedure, can rightfully decide on what is to be done? Is UN authorisation a *sufficient* condition for overseas military action? If UN authorisation is not a *necessary* condition, then either we accept the resulting international anarchy and the law of the jungle in world affairs, or we spell out the preferred alternative set of rules and the institutions and regimes in which they are embedded.

Policy innovation: ICISS and the Responsibility to Protect

NATO's self-proclaimed 'humanitarian intervention' in Kosovo in 1999 set off a debate whose intensity and breadth failed to be appreciated by many Western commentators because they do not habitually read the opinions expressed outside the dominant trans-Atlantic policy, academic and media communities. The UN is an organisation dedicated to the territorial integrity, political independence and national sovereignty of its member states and the maintenance of international peace and security on that basis. But the overwhelming majority of contemporary armed conflicts are internal, and civilians comprise the dominant portion of casualties. This presents the UN with a great difficulty: how to reconcile its foundational principle of member states' sovereignty with the primary mandate to maintain international peace and security and the equally compelling mission to promote the interests and welfare of 'We the peoples of the United Nations'. Kofi Annan discussed the dilemma in the conceptual language of two sovereignties of the state and the people.[45] The 'policy trilemma' posed an uncomfortable choice between being complicit in humanitarian tragedies sometimes out of respect for sovereignty all the time; accepting paralysis by insisting on the requirement for UN Security Council authorisation, owing to the passivity and apathy of the Council as a whole, or to the most obstructionist of the five permanent members (P5) determined to use the veto clause; or acquiescing passively in the illegal use of force without UN authorisation.

The discomfort highlighted a critical gap between the needs and distress felt in the real world and the codified instruments and modalities for managing world order.[46] Faced with another Holocaust or Rwanda-type genocide on the one hand and a Security Council veto on the other, what would the world do? Under the impact of contrasting experiences in Rwanda and Kosovo, Annan urged member states to come up with a new consensus on the competing visions of national and popular sovereignty and the resulting 'challenge of humanitarian intervention'.[47] Responding to Annan's call for an urgently needed new consensus, Foreign Minister Lloyd Axworthy initiated the Canadian-sponsored but independent ICISS under the enlightened leadership of two wise, experienced and widely respected co-chairs, Gareth Evans and Mohamed Sahnoun.[48] ICISS wrestled with the whole gamut of difficult and complex issues involved in the debate. Its report sought to change the conceptual language from 'humanitarian intervention' to 'the responsibility to protect', pin that responsibility on state authorities at the national and the Security Council at the international level, and ensure that interventions, when they do take place, are done properly.[49]

In the extensive outreach and consultations exercise undertaken by ICISS in every continent over the course of 2001, nowhere was there an absolute rejection of intervention.[50] In all consultations, people were prepared to concede that sometimes, outsiders may indeed have to step in with military force to protect innocent victims from perpetrators of mass killings and ethnic cleansing. After the genocide in Rwanda, very few policymakers, pundits or practitioners excluded protective intervention in principle as a last resort that is necessary under some tragic contingency. In every single case, when pressed, people preferred the option of 'No more Rwanda' where genocide took place with no intervention, to 'No more Kosovo' where there was intervention outside the framework of UN authorisation.

The 12 members of ICISS reflected a wide spectrum of opinion on the necessity, legality, legitimacy and acceptability of NATO intervention in Kosovo. While some opinions might have softened and shifted over the course of the year as we listened to evidence and arguments from governments, international civil servants, humanitarian agencies, civil society and one another, no consensus would have been achievable even at the end of the process. This was indicated in the co-chairs' 'Foreword' wherein they noted that the Commissioners disagreed on the threshold for permissible intervention and on the flexibility to launch protective action when the Security Council was deadlocked. But the Commissioners were unanimous in their abhorrence of the passivity and inaction shown in Rwanda. To that extent, faced with a choice between no action in Rwanda and non-UN-authorised collective intervention in Kosovo, reflecting the overwhelming weight of international opinion, almost certainly the 12 would have unanimously chosen the former as the greater evil.

What can be said irrefutably is that the two episodes framed the discussion, thinking and evolution of a consensus in the Commission's deliberations and conclusions. This found expression in the formal report of the Commission. The first chapter framed the policy challenge. The two opening paragraphs noted that 'Rwanda in 1994 laid bare the full horror of inaction'[51] while 'Kosovo – where intervention *did* take place in 1999 – concentrated attention on all the other sides of the argument. The operation raised major questions about the legitimacy of military intervention in a sovereign state'.[52] Along with Bosnia and Somalia, these cases 'had a profound effect on how the problem of intervention is viewed, analysed and characterised'.[53] The report also recalled that Kofi Annan had been motivated by 'the failures of the Security Council to act in Rwanda and Kosovo' to challenge member states in 1999 'to "find common ground in upholding the principles of the Charter, and acting in defence of our common humanity"'.[54] Both the intervention dilemma and the challenge to find new common ground were repeated by Annan in his Millennium Report one year later:

> … if humanitarian intervention is, indeed, an unacceptable assault on sovereignty, how should we respond to a Rwanda, to a Srebrenica – to gross and systematic violations of human rights that offend every precept of our common humanity?[55]

The rest, as they say, is history. The impressive cast of well-known practitioners and academics brought together in *The Oxford Handbook on the Responsibility to Protect* is itself powerful testimony to the enduring policy and scholarly impact of the Commission's product.

Notes

* Originally published in Alex J. Bellamy and Tim Dunne, eds., *The Oxford Handbook of the Responsibility to Protect* (Oxford: Oxford University Press, 2016), 94–113. Reprinted by permission of Oxford University Press.

1 Bruce Cronin, 'International Legal Consensus and the Control of Excess State Violence', *Global Governance* 11:3 (2005), 300–11.

2 This journey is traced in Ramesh Thakur, *The United Nations, Peace and Security: From Collective Security to the Responsibility to Protect* (Cambridge: Cambridge University Press 2006).

3 See Alex Bellamy, 'The Responsibility to Protect and the Just War Tradition', in Ramesh Thakur and William Maley, eds., *Theorising the Responsibility to Protect* (Cambridge: Cambridge University Press, 2015), 181–99.

4 Ellery Stowell, *Intervention in International Law* (Washington, DC: J. Byrne, 1921), 53, quoted in Thomas G. Weiss, Don Hubert, *et al.*, *The Responsibility to Protect: Research, Bibliography, Background* (Ottawa: International Development Research Centre, 2001), 17.

5 Louis Henkin, 'Use of Force: Law and U.S. Policy', in Louis Henkin, Stanley Hoffmann, Jeane J. Kirkpatrick, Allan Gerson, William D. Rogers and David J. Scheffer, *Right v. Might: International Law and the Use of Force* (New York: Council on Foreign Relations, 1989), 47, 56.

6 Michael Akehurst, 'Humanitarian Intervention', in Hedley Bull, ed., *Intervention in World Politics* (Oxford: Clarendon, 1984), 111.

7 Thomas G. Weiss, *Military–Civilian Interactions: Humanitarian Crisis and the Responsibility to Protect*, 2nd ed., (Lanham, MD: Rowman & Littlefield, 2005), 97.

8 Jared Diamond, *Collapse: How Societies Choose to Fail or Succeed* (New York: Viking, 2005).

9 Weiss, *Military–Civilian Interactions*, 98.

10 Peter Uvin, *Aid and Violence: The Role of Development Assistance in the Rwandan Genocide* (West Hartford, Conn.: Kumarian, 1998).

11 Gérard Prunier, *The Rwanda Crisis: A History of a Genocide* (New York: Columbia University Press, 1995).

12 OAU, *Rwanda: The Preventable Genocide. Report of the OAU's International Panel of Eminent Personalities* (Addis Ababa: OAU, 31 May 2000), paragraph 15.1, www.refworld.org/pdfid/4d1da8752.pdf.

13 OAU, *Rwanda: The Preventable Genocide,* paragraphs 15.4, 15.6 and 15.7.

14 Roméo Dallaire, *Shake Hands with the Devil: The Failure of Humanity in Rwanda* (Toronto: Random House Canada, 2003), 90.

15 Howard Adelman and Astri Suhrke, 'Rwanda' in David M. Malone, ed., *The UN Security Council: From the Cold War to the 21st Century* (Boulder: Lynne Rienner, 2004), 495–96.

16 My own notes from that event.

17 OAU, *Rwanda: The Preventable Genocide*, paragraph 15.40.

18 OAU, *Rwanda: The Preventable Genocide*, paragraph 15.87. See also Mahmood Mamdani, *When Victims Become Killers: Colonialism, Nativism, and the Genocide in Rwanda* (Princeton: Princeton University Press, 2001); Linda Melvern, *A People Betrayed: The Role of the West in Rwanda's Genocide* (London and New York: Zed Books, 2000); and Samantha Power, *A Problem from Hell: America and the Age of Genocide* (New York: Harper, 2003).

19 *Report of the Independent Inquiry into the Actions of the United Nations during the 1994 Genocide in Rwanda* (New York: United Nations, document S/1999/1257, 16 December 1999), 30, www.un.org/en/ga/search/view_doc.asp?symbol=S/1999/1257.

20 *Report of the Secretary-General Pursuant to General Assembly Resolution 53/35: The Fall of Srebrenica* (New York: United Nations, document A/54/549, 15 November 1999), paragraph 503, www.un.org/en/ga/search/view_doc.asp?symbol=A/54/549.

21 In a speech originally delivered to a joint sitting of Canada's houses of parliament in Ottawa on 29 April 1999, subsequently reprinted as Vaclav Havel, 'Kosovo and the End of the Nation-state', *New York Review of Books*, 46:10 (10 June 1999), 6.

22 Javier Solana, 'NATO's Success in Kosovo', *Foreign Affairs* 78:6 (1999), 114.

23 *Report of the Secretary-General Pursuant to General Assembly Resolution 53/35 (1998)*, paragraph 502.

24 Michael J. Glennon, 'The New Interventionism: The Search for a Just International Law', *Foreign Affairs* 78:3 (1999), 7.

25 Raju G.C. Thomas, 'Prologue: Making War, Peace and History', in Raju G.C. Thomas, ed., *Yugoslavia Unraveled: Sovereignty, Self-determination, Intervention* (Lanham: Lexington Books, 2003), xi.

26 For development of this line of argumentation, see in particular Louis Henkin, 'Kosovo and the Law of "Humanitarian Intervention"', *American Journal of International Law* 93:4 (1999), 824–28, and Ruth Wedgwood, 'NATO's Campaign in Yugoslavia', *American Journal of International Law* 93:4 (1999), 828–34. For the structural link of Wedgwood's argument to Iraq, see her 'The Multinational Action in Iraq and International Law', in Ramesh Thakur and W.P.S. Sidhu, eds., *The Iraq Crisis and World Order: Structural, Institutional and Normative Challenges* (Tokyo: United Nations University Press, 2006), 413–25.

27 Thus a former US Ambassador to Yugoslavia (1977–81) and subsequently Secretary of State (1992–93), in an article not exactly friendly to Milosevic: 'The Kosovo Liberation Army *earned* its reputation as a terrorist group'; Lawrence S. Eagleburger, 'Taking a Stand Against the Milosevics of the Future', *International Herald Tribune*, 5 April 1999 (emphasis added).

28 Security Council Resolution 1160 (31 March 1998). Its preamble condemned 'the use of excessive force by Serbian police forces against civilian and peaceful demonstrators in Kosovo, as well as acts of terrorism by the Kosovo Liberation Army'.

29 'The KLA's success between 1997 and 1999 was a vintage demonstration of how to exploit the human rights conscience of the West in order to incite an intervention that resulted eventually in guerrilla victory'; Michael Ignatieff, *Human Rights as Politics and Idolatry*, edited and introduced by Amy Gutmann (Princeton: Princeton University Press, 2001), 45. For a succinct account of the KLA strategy as well as a discourse on the many 'subtexts' underlying NATO campaign, see Michael McGwire, 'Why did we bomb Belgrade?' *International Affairs* 76:1 (2000), 1–24. McGwire is sceptical of the claim that humanitarianism had displaced geopolitical interests as the principal motive.

30 Kofi A. Annan, *We the Peoples: The Role of the United Nations in the 21st Century* (New York: United Nations Department of Public Information, 2000), 48.

31 Robert W. Tucker and David C. Hendrickson, 'The Sources of American Legitimacy', *Foreign Affairs*, 83:6 (2004), 31.

32 Rebecca Johnson, 'NPT Report', *Disarmament Diplomacy* 37 (May 1999), 16, www.acronym.org.uk/dd/dd37/37npt.htm.

33 Muchkund Dubey, 'The NATO Juggernaut: Logic of an Indian Defence Deterrent', *Times of India* (Delhi), 8 April 1999.

34 *Times of India,* 'Might on Show', editorial, 2 April 1999.

35 Vladimir Putin, 'Address by President of the Russian Federation', The Kremlin, Moscow, 18 March 2014, http://eng.kremlin.ru/news/6889.

36 Putin, 'Address by President of the Russian Federation'.

37 Valdai International Discussion Club, *Transcript of the Meeting of the Valdai International Discussion Club*, Sochi, 24 October 2014, http://eng.kremlin.ru/news/23137.

38 Sergei Lavrov, 'It's not Russia that is destabilising Ukraine', *Guardian* (London), 8 April 2014.

39 Matthias Schepp and Britta Sandberg, interviewers, 'Gorbachev Interview: "I Am Truly and Deeply Concerned"', *Spiegel Online International*, 16 January 2015, www.spiegel.de/international/world/gorbachev-warns-of-decline-in-russian-western-ties-over-ukraine-a-1012992.html.

40 Independent International Commission on Kosovo, *Kosovo Report: Conflict, International Response, Lessons Learned* (Oxford: Oxford University Press, 2000). Other works that can be traced to the debate launched in the aftermath of the Kosovo crisis include *Humanitarian Intervention* (The Hague: Advisory Council on International Affairs, 2000); *Humanitarian Intervention: Legal and Political Aspects* (Copenhagen: Danish Institute of International Affairs, 1999); Alton Frye, *Humanitarian Intervention:*

Crafting a Workable Doctrine (New York: Council on Foreign Relations, 2000); and Kofi A. Annan, *The Question of Intervention: Statements by the Secretary-General* (New York: United Nations, 1999).

41 Hideaki Shinoda, 'The Politics of Legitimacy in International Relations: A Critical Examination of NATO's Intervention in Kosovo', *Alternatives* 25:4 (2000), 528–31.

42 The same applies when citizens' moral frameworks lead them to defy laws in the unshakeable conviction that their conscience answers to God, not to men. However, in apartheid South Africa, in colonial India and in any situation where conscience dictates that individuals resist laws they regard as unjust and illegitimate, citizens accept the resulting punishment meted out by the legal process as the necessary price for acting on the basis of their core beliefs. By contrast, in international affairs, the legitimacy–legality distinction is invoked to seek *escape* from any penalty for acting outside the law: Kosovo may have been illegal, but our intervention was legitimate, and we deserve praise and reward, not blame and punishment. This is why the distinction grated among critics of the NATO intervention, as did the dismissive response from those who waged war on Iraq in 2003 that they will answer to their Maker. Critics would prefer international criminal accountability in this world to eternal damnation in the next.

43 David Chandler, *From Kosovo to Kabul: Human Rights and International Intervention* (London: Pluto, 2002), 135.

44 See Vladimir Baranovsky, 'Russia: Reassessing National Interests'; Zhang Yunling, 'China: Whither the World Order after Kosovo?'; Satish Nambiar, 'India: An Uneasy Precedent'; and Philip Nel, 'South Africa: The Demand for Legitimate Multilateralism', in Albrecht Schnabel and Ramesh Thakur, eds., *Kosovo and the Challenge of Humanitarian Intervention: Selective Indignation, Collective Action, and International Citizenship* (Tokyo: United Nations University Press, 2000).

45 Kofi A. Annan, 'Two Concepts of Sovereignty', *The Economist*, 18 September 1999, 49–50.

46 For my analysis of protection gaps that remain post-R2P, see Ramesh Thakur, 'Protection Gaps for Civilian Victims of Political Violence', *South African Journal of International Affairs* 20:3 (2013), 321–82.

47 Kofi A. Annan, *Facing the Humanitarian Challenge: Towards a Culture of Prevention* (New York: United Nations Department of Public Information, 1999).

48 For an analysis of international commissions as norm and policy brokers in the Oxford handbooks series, see Ramesh Thakur, 'High-level Panels', in Jacob Cogan, Ian Hurd and Ian Johnstone, eds., *The Oxford Handbook of International Organizations* (Oxford: Oxford University Press, 2016), 859–80.

49 International Commission on Intervention and State Sovereignty, *The Responsibility to Protect* (Ottawa: International Development Research Centre, 2001).

50 See Thakur, *United Nations, Peace and Security*, 268–74.

51 ICISS, *The Responsibility to Protect*, paragraph 1.1.

52 ICISS, *The Responsibility to Protect*, paragraph 1.2.

53 ICISS, *The Responsibility to Protect*, paragraph 1.4.

54 ICISS, *The Responsibility to Protect*, paragraph 1.6.

55 Kofi A. Annan, *Report of the Secretary-General on the Work of the Organization*, UN document A/54/1 (1999), 48.

5 From the right to persecute to the Responsibility to Protect

Feuerbachian inversions of rights and responsibilities in state–citizen relations*

The Responsibility to Protect, commonly shortened to 'R2P', is widely seen as a quintessentially post-Westphalian, liberal internationalist norm. As such it is alternately the poster-boy and whipping-boy of the supporters and detractors of liberal internationalism. However, its relationship with Westphalian statehood is a little more complex. R2P owes it origins to a major push by UN Secretary-General Kofi Annan, scarred by the atrocities in Rwanda in 1994 and Srebrenica in 1995 that happened on his watch as the Under-Secretary-General for Peacekeeping, to forge a new normative consensus on when and how the international community should prevent and stop such tragedies. In his first report on R2P in 2009, his successor Ban Ki-moon reframed R2P in the metaphor of three pillars. Pillar One was defined as 'the enduring responsibility of the State to protect its populations, whether nationals or not, from genocide, war crimes, ethnic cleansing and crimes against humanity, and from their incitement'. Pillar Two was described as 'the commitment of the international community to assist States in meeting those obligations'. Pillar Three was defined as 'the responsibility of Member States to respond collectively in a timely and decisive manner when a State is manifestly failing to provide … protection'.[1] While primacy was to be given to peaceful means, should they prove inadequate to ensure protection, the international community should use more robust action: 'no strategy for fulfilling the responsibility to protect would be complete without the possibility of collective enforcement measures, including through sanctions or coercive military action in extreme cases'.[2]

The first pillar of R2P thus provides the core justification for the sovereign's claim to rule and the basis of the social contract that Hobbes posited for their subjects. However, the security of their subjects was doubly undermined: first by the fraudulent nature of the claims of many sovereigns to protect their subjects and second because the successful repression of civilians was one of the most common ways of establishing sovereignty and the basis of sovereign legitimacy. Seventeenth century 'R2P' was more likely to be the 'Right to Persecute' than a Responsibility to Protect.

The Enlightenment turned the relationship between sovereign and subject on its head in an inversion that Sampford has likened to Feuerbach's suggested reversal of the relationship between man and God.[3] While justifying democracy and human rights within democratic sovereign states, it raised questions about what democracies should do to states that trampled on rather than recognised the rights of their citizens – and about the putative right of humanitarian intervention. Unfortunately, however, this new right was as liable to abuse as the claims of sovereigns to protect them. The report of ICISS performed another Feuerbachian inversion to turn the right of other states to intervene into the Responsibility to Protect.[4]

In, *The Structure of Scientific Revolutions*, Thomas S. Kuhn outlined the process by which a dominant paradigm in science is replaced by a new paradigm. Normal science is concerned with solving puzzles within a particular framework. However, in the course of ongoing research, anomalies are uncovered, reflecting an empirical variance with the dominant theory that suggests deficiencies in the existing paradigm. This generates auxiliary hypotheses within the dominant paradigm to explain the anomalies. But if there comes a point where the old paradigm proves unable to accommodate the anomalies, the pressure grows for a new paradigm to emerge. At this point 'the anomalous has become the expected'.[5] In this chapter, we argue that a similar 'structure of philosophical revolution' occurred to flip the understandings, expectations, limitations and exercise of state sovereignty as the dominant paradigm of the contemporary world order. Accumulating anomalies and 'pockets of apparent disorder', or 'gaps' in common parlance (and sometimes 'disconnects' in more contemporary usage) were reconciled by reformulating sovereignty as state responsibility and citizen rights.

The Feuerbachian analogy

Emphasising Kuhn highlights the gradual drip of evidence on an inadequate theory leading to a permanent inversion in which support for the old theory withers quite rapidly. This chapter examines an alternative analogy to Kuhn's portrayal of scientific revolutions typified by the Copernican inversion of the Ptolemaic image of earth as the centre of the heavens. Emphasising Feuerbach highlights the dramatic philosophical insight which leads some to completely reorient their view, but which leaves others still holding on to the previous view as a matter of faith. The Enlightenment inversion of sovereign/subject relationships and the subsequent inversion of the right to intervene to the Responsibility to Protect display elements of each. One could distinguish between the two analogies in that matters of religion cannot be undermined by facts in a way that 'scientific' theories can. The Feuerbachian analogy is the more apt of the two metaphors also because of the clear, if for understandable political reasons unacknowledged, philosophical antecedents of R2P in the Christian tradition's just war theory.

Ludwig Andreas von Feuerbach (1804–72) was a German philosopher who is acknowledged as an intellectual bridge in the development of dialectical materialism from Friedrich Hegel to Karl Marx. An atheist, he pondered the relationship between God and man. Christians imagine that God created man in his own image. Feuerbach suggested that it was at least as likely that man created God in his own image. R2P represents just such a Feuerbachian reversal of the way rulers and ruled relate to each other. Enlightenment *philosophes* suggested a similar inversion for sovereignty. Before the Enlightenment, 'subjects' had to demonstrate their allegiance and loyalty to their 'sovereign'. The *philosophes* proclaimed that 'governments' had to justify their existence to 'citizens' who chose them. Once the reversal of the relationship was suggested in this 'great leap forward', it was very hard to go back to the pre-Enlightenment way of looking at things. Indeed, it became as broadly popular with civilians as Westphalian sovereignty was with some authoritarian states. This approach led, in the increasingly large number of democracies, to the new basis of sovereign legitimacy in domestic law and political theory – the acquiescence, then consent, then the active choice of the governed. It also had a profound impact on the way in which the ruler's right to use force was conceived and justified, initially with respect to subjects within territorial jurisdictions but eventually also with respect to the international use of force in the jurisdictions of other sovereigns.

The Westphalian protection racket

Rulers have long claimed that the protection of their subjects is the first duty of the sovereign's primary responsibility of the relevant sovereign state – an idea that is grounded in the long-standing attempts by rulers to legitimise their regimes based on the claim that they protected their people. While there were other claims to legitimacy, including the claim to be anointed by God (or, more directly, to be a God), this is always, at least, a supplementary claim of those who justify the power they wield.

Of course, with every grant of power comes the possibility of abuse. What happens if the rulers do not live up to their claims and it is not such a good deal for their subjects? What if they cannot or will not protect their subjects? Worse still, what if they become a threat to the very people whose defence is the core of their *raison d'être*?[6] There is a special obloquy for those who are entrusted with power for the benefit of another and use it against them – doctors who murder patients, parents who abuse their children, teachers who brainwash rather than educate their pupils, and priests who prey on children for whose moral enlightenment they are responsible. It is common for the law to treat such abuse of power as aggravating the offence. Some sovereigns turn out to be a greater threat to their peoples than the real or imagined enemies against whom they claim to protect their people from, and are rarely punished at all. Even when they kill thousands, prison doors do not generally open for them. The doors that open for them are those of the palace at home, the embassy abroad and the private jet in between – as well as the doors to bankers who lend the tyrant money to buy the plane and the palace and to pay for the persecution of civilians.[7] And after it is all over, the citizens will have the responsibility to repay this 'sovereign debt'.

Why is this tolerated? Why do other states not intervene to protect citizens from the tyrants who oppress them? The answer lies in the wars of religion culminating in the Thirty Year' War (1618–48) which involved frequent interventions, purportedly to protect co-religionists from persecution. Because such interventions were generally undertaken for other reasons, the plight of those to be protected often worsened and the intervening forces added to that plight. Indeed, the 1648 Treaty of Westphalia can be seen as based on the view that the consequences of intervention were so bad that it was better to let the tyrant do what tyrants do, and the principle of non-intervention was born in the presumption of the lesser evil. It was seen as better to have refugees streaming over the border out of the tyranny than to have troops going the other way to stop it. Hence the characterisation of the Treaty of Westphalia as 'a tyrant's charter' – written of the tyrants, by the tyrants and for the tyrants.[8]

Despite the claims of sovereigns to protect their peoples, the Westphalian concept of sovereignty and sovereign legitimacy is effectively predicated on its opposite. Sovereignty is based on control of territory. This concept had a number of different formulations – most notably Hans Kelsen's formulation that the regime had to be 'by and large effective'.[9] The effectiveness is initially established by the 'prior successful use of force'[10] to gain effective control against a previous sovereign. It is maintained by a continued perceived willingness and capacity to use that force against anyone who would seek to similarly supplant them. The main threat was traditionally other tyrants or groups demanding religious or other freedoms. Members of such groups are not protected from attack but subject to it. If people did not like the sovereign or what was done in his or her name, then it was necessary for the sovereign to impose his will and demonstrate his authority by massacring groups of subjects and gruesomely executing their leaders. Rather than giving way to the wishes of the people, sovereigns saw it as their duty to enforce their will and demonstrate their sovereignty. Their *raison d'être* was not the rights of citizens but the preservation of the dynasty and its authority.[11] Where the criterion of sovereignty was the prior successful use of force, human rights violations did not so much undermine sovereign legitimacy as prove and reassert it.

One may conclude that, despite traditional claims of sovereigns to protect their people, the heart of Westphalian sovereignty undermined it. The authoritarian states that were emerging during the century of Westphalia and those that followed were not so much concerned with protection of civilians but protection *from* civilians, and used their claimed monopoly of legitimate force against them.[12] If one were to formulate an R2P principle for Westphalian states, they would be more likely to refer to a right, indeed a responsibility, to use force against any of their people who disagreed with them (or were just insufficiently supportive). This was an assertion and exercise of power not in the name of, but over citizens. For some of the more religiously minded, it might be seen as the 'Responsibility to Persecute'. For those who just 'did it because they could', it became a 'Right to Persecute' that was recognised, if sometimes reluctantly, by other sovereign states.

This idea has been embraced by tyrants the world over. This is not an 'eastern' or 'Asian' value. It is a Western idea that has been picked up with obscene alacrity, sometimes displacing contrary traditions rooted in local conceptions of the proper relationship of duties and rights binding sovereigns and subjects. It has demonstrated its appeal to tyrants of countries large and small from all regions, religions, cultures, languages and climates. The tyrant's rule based in terror does not discriminate on grounds of race, religion or gender but is an equal opportunity offender and that is why it needs a universal norm to prohibit and end it.

Sovereign legitimacy – domestic and international

As we have seen, in 1648 legitimacy in both domestic and international law and political theory was based on the effectiveness of the sovereign's rule. Within some European states, it was challenged almost immediately and within 30 years concepts of sovereignty in domestic and international law started to diverge. John Locke argued that sovereigns were *entrusted* with power. If they abused that trust and became a threat to their people, the latter had a right to revolt. That was a pretty inefficient form of regime change and the right to revolt against governments that did not protect their citizens became a right to choose the government that best reflected their interests and values. The political system was held to embody, articulate and facilitate the achievement of the social purposes of a community. This shift was part of the Enlightenment's great leap forward in which a variety of governance values (liberty, equality, fraternity, democracy, human rights and the rule of law) were demanded and partly secured in the United States, United Kingdom and a growing number of European countries.

International law, however, has continued to recognise states and governments on the basis of who exercises effective political control over discrete territories. Even when a democratically elected government is overturned by a *coup d'état*, the ambassadors of the new regime are accredited by foreign powers and are allowed to take that country's seat at the United Nations and other international forums. In the last century, India and Vietnam were censured by the UN community for their interventions in Bangladesh and Cambodia respectively which rid the world of regimes that had carried out large-scale brutal massacres. This glaring inconsistency caused considerable tension and great soul searching within democratic states and led to the tentative and controversial claim that there was an emerging norm of humanitarian intervention.

Some of the most thoughtful soul searching was done in response to challenges acknowledged and articulated by Annan. In his annual address to the UN General Assembly in 1999 he challenged the international community to devise principles governing the exercise of sovereignty and the conditions under which 'humanitarian intervention', as it was then called, could be justified. In the inaugural Ministerial Conference of the Community of Democracies, Annan was 'delighted to associate' himself 'with a new coalition of democracies, dedicated to expanding the frontiers of freedom and to ensuring that, wherever democracy has taken root, it will not be reversed'.[13] ICISS responded to the first challenge in 2001 and a Council on Foreign Relations Task Force responded to the second challenge in 2002.[14]

These responses have stimulated rather than resolved debate between traditional state sovereignty based on power and popular sovereignty based on the active choice of the governed. The revival of pre-twentieth century ideas of intervention faced a lot of hostility that not only cited Westphalian norms but also the sorry history of interventions that helped stimulate it. One of the problems was that this was formulated as a right of states rather than civilians. One of the great achievements of ICISS was to effect a 'Feuerbachian inversion' on the 'Right to Intervene'. The relevant rights belonged to human beings. States had responsibilities to protect them – with the primary responsibility being of the state in which they reside and contingent responsibility on other states. It is radical because it denies tyrants the right to do what tyrants have always done and for which international law rewarded them. Accordingly, we see R2P not as a Western attempt to interfere in other people's problems, but as a global attempt to deal with a Western problem at the heart of the Westphalian system with deeply unfortunate attraction to some would-be tyrants. But it was also a legitimate concern of others who fear not only selfishly motivated interventions disguised in the language of humanitarian concerns, but also a breakdown of the very principle on which the present world order resting on a system of independent and autonomous states is organised.

Developing countries and sovereignty

One of the legitimate concerns was that the new enthusiasm for intervention might be directed at developing countries soon after they had wrested sovereignty back from their colonial overlords. The continued silencing of non-Western voices in the Western discourse on the historical memories and changing notions of sovereignty is at once rather surprising and deeply disrespectful of their experience. Thus a recent article points out that non-intervention in one another's internal affairs was only a twentieth century attribute of sovereignty and that indeed the right to intervene – for example to protect co-religionists under threat by a ruler from a different denomination – predates non-intervention as an *attribute* of sovereignty.[15] Of the 106 references cited in the article, just four are recognisably non-Westerners by name, of whom one is a Japanese: so only three might have some colonised-country background. Even Francis Deng, the intellectual godfather of sovereignty as responsibility, doesn't rate a mention. Scholars from former colonies remember only too well that their nations were invaded and subjugated by the European powers within the Westphalian paradigm of sovereign states. R2P never would have gained such rapid uptake and traction had ICISS not conducted its extensive outreach exercise, listened to and then reflected the voices heard in its final report.[16]

The input of historical trauma of the colonised societies makes them deeply suspicious of various concepts of suspended sovereignty,[17] interrupted sovereignty[18] and, most significantly, conditional sovereignty.[19] Western countries had justified invading them because of their supposed backwardness and newly unacceptable practices (such as the slave trade which Western countries had dominated a few decades before). Were they now to be invaded because they were practising milder forms of the human rights abuses perfected by Western nations?

Developing countries fear that in some sections of the West today, the view has gained ground that anyone *but* the legitimate authorities can use force. As already noted, the doctrines of sovereign equality and non-interference are distinctively European in origin and construct. In the era of decolonisation, the sovereign equality of states and the correlative norm of non-intervention received their most emphatic affirmation from the newly independent states. Ironically, while aspects of sovereignty were being progressively pooled, if not superseded, in the construction of the increasingly borderless European Union (EU), some of its most passionate defenders were to be found among developing countries. That said, the United States is second to none in the jealous defence of national sovereignty against international encroachments. Its 'sovereigntists' have launched three lines of attack: that the emerging international legal order is vague and illegitimately intrusive on domestic affairs; that the international law-making process is unaccountable and the resulting law unenforceable; and that Washington can opt out of international regimes as a matter of power, legal right and constitutional duty.[20]

The most important clue to understanding the developing countries' concerns is the history of Europe's encounter with Arabs, Africans and Asians. The relentless march of colonialism and imperialism is never based on anything so vulgar as commercial and geopolitical calculations: land and wealth grabs. No, it is always driven by a lofty purpose. The deployment of moral arguments to justify imperialist actions in Iraq in 2003, for example, had a direct structural counterpart in the British annexation of the Indian kingdom of Awadh (Oudh in its anglicised version) in the first half of the nineteenth century. The structure of justification makes use of a specific set of techniques for the mobilisation of democratic consent and international support – through political representatives, the press and the interested and attentive public – of decisions taken in pursuit of national interests by an elite group of policy-makers.

Tracing its origins to John Locke and John Stuart Mill, Chatterjee locates it in the paternalistic belief that people and nations who are morally handicapped or in a state of moral infancy deserve a benevolent despot who will protect and look after them.[21]

> What is remarkable is how many of the same arguments, including the evangelical fervour, the axiomatic assumption of the mantle of civilisation, the fig-leaf of legalism, the intelligence reports, the forgeries and subterfuges and the hard-headed calculations of national interest, remain exactly the same at the beginning of the 21st century … the liberal evangelical creed of taking democracy and human rights to backward cultures is still a potent ideological drive, and … the instrumental use of that ideological rhetoric for realist imperialist ends is entirely available, as we have seen in Iraq.[22]

Afro-Asian countries achieved independence on the back of extensive and protracted nationalist struggles. The parties and leaders at the forefront of the fight for independence helped to establish the new states and shape and guide the founding principles of their foreign policies. The anti-colonial impulse in their worldview was instilled in the countries' foreign policies and survives as a powerful sentiment in the corporate memory of the elites. All too often, developing-country views either fail to get a respectful hearing at all in Western policy and scholarly discourse, or are patronisingly dismissed.[23]

At the same time, state sovereignty is also the bedrock principle of contemporary international system that provides order and stability. The most important task on the agenda of the international community therefore should be not to weaken states nor to undermine the doctrine of state sovereignty, but to strengthen the institutions of state and make them legitimate and empowering of people and respectful and protective of their rights.[24] In the words of Kofi Annan, 'one of the great challenges of the new millennium is to ensure that all States are strong enough to meet the many challenges they face'.[25]

The debate over R2P is not and ought not to be a North–South issue. But it can be turned into one either because of wilful – and sometimes self-serving – obstinacy on the part of key emerging countries,[26] or because of calculated neglect of their legitimate concerns by a declining West. Many non-Western societies have a historical tradition of reciprocal rights and obligations that define the terms of engagement of sovereigns and their subjects. Contrary to what many developing country governments might claim, R2P is rooted as firmly in their own indigenous values and traditions as in abstract notions of sovereignty derived from European thought and practice. As argued by ICISS co-chair Mohamed Sahnoun, in many ways R2P is a distinctly African contribution to global human rights.[27] Asia too has its own rich traditions that vest sovereigns with responsibility for the lives and welfare of their subjects, while circumscribing the sovereign's exercise of power with the majesty of law that stands above the agents of the state. For example, modern India's constitution imposes R2P-type responsibility on governments in its chapters on fundamental rights and directive principles of state policy.[28]

This is not to deny that the concern that R2P may be abused to justify self-interested invasions should be fully acknowledged and addressed. The thoroughly Western Westphalian principle of non-intervention was generated by direct experience of the consequences of abuse. The ICISS report acknowledged the risk – a risk that materialised almost immediately when Commissioner Michael Ignatieff used it to justify the invasion of Iraq.[29] There are several ways of limiting the risk of abuse:[30] reaffirming the Westphalian formula because of the sorry track record of intervention, narrowing the scope, underlining the centrality of pillar one, and emphasising that the rights belong to those being persecuted rather than those going to their aid.

Concrete challenges

However, it would be a major mistake to treat sovereignty as mainly a function of the law and practice of state intervention. The Westphalian image of a state as the ultimate authority and power is also challenged by the realities of the twenty-first century. One set of challenges relates to recognising the power dynamics in the international system where the only superpower, the United States, has considerable power which it has been able to exercise virtually unchecked until very recently. However, probably more fundamental are the set of challenges from the rise and recognition of new actors playing significant roles and wielding significant power, including transnational corporations (several of which are wealthier than all but the top ten states), the United Nations itself,[31] international agencies like the World Bank and the International Monetary Fund (IMF) imposing aid conditionality, indigenous peoples, international NGOs, and powerful individuals.[32] Indeed, individuals have become objects of international law as bearers of duties since the Nuremberg trials, and subjects of international law as holders of rights under human rights instruments and some treaties.[33]

A third set of challenges comes from the apparent inability of some states to maintain the internal order and control that is central to sovereignty. Accordingly, state breakups and state failure may mean the end of viable central public authority and control so that the rights of citizens cannot be met, and inter-state relationships cannot be meaningfully pursued. A fourth set of challenges lies in the formal end of professed indifference to the internal governance of other states and the attempts to formulate norms for such internal governance that are intended to be enforced. Some argue for an emerging right of democratic governance[34] – at least where democracy has been established.[35] This highlights the disjunction already noted between International Relations and International Law conceptions of sovereignty as the prior successful use of force, and the internal conceptions of popular sovereignty that now dominate a majority of nations.

Of course, the consequences of transferring domestic and internal approaches to sovereign legitimacy to international relations would be so profound that there is a natural hesitation in linking international legitimacy to domestic democratic legitimacy. Nevertheless, there is clear movement in this direction with some states joining bodies – for example, the European Union and the African Union – that impose obligations concerning internal governance. While armed intervention is still relatively rare to enforce internal standards of governance and respect for human rights, there are increasing attempts to generate formal mechanisms for protecting human rights, from the UN Human Rights Council to the European Court of Human Rights which can give binding orders to sovereign states. As well, aid and trade can be tied to what is considered to be acceptable internal behaviour of states.

A fifth set of challenges is based on the fact that many issues cannot be dealt with within traditional boundaries, for example environmental and health problems such as AIDS, SARS and avian flu. The most pervasive set of challenges arises from the movement of people, ideas and goods. International communications weaken a state's control over its own people and more people are on the move, reducing loyalty to the state. For some, the participation in economic success, not coercive power or legal authority, becomes the primary source of identity. Commerce is boundary-less while the state's authority and ability to use its laws and coercive power stops at its borders as the most lucrative business of all, the 400 billion dollar trade in illicit drugs and human smuggling, grows exponentially. Transnational criminals use weak or failed states as bases and safe havens as well as sources to fund their operations.[36] Just when police officials in pursuit of a suspect must halt at a border, money launderers cross with ease and transfer millions of dollars all over the globe instantaneously. As the state weakens economically, so does any real threat to use its coercive power and its system of the rule of law to compel other states to follow its pattern. Instead, chimerical wars on drugs are launched at the same time as anti-terrorist wars unleash new sources for those same illicit drugs.

Many of these challenges are mutually reinforcing and produce contradictory behaviour. Countries that provide legal protection to refugees in flight from persecution also interdict refugees and prevent them from arriving on their shores. Radical Islamist rebels who would be captured or killed on a state's own territory are supplied arms in their fight against Arab dictators. The threats to sovereign states themselves heighten the debate over the conception of sovereignty. Accordingly, the sovereignty of states unwilling or unable to fulfil certain basic standards of human rights may be jeopardised,[37] while their actions may threaten the security of other states, for example by generating refugees or exporting environmental hazards.[38]

As states are weakened economically and become weaker sources of identity, individuals and groups may look to other ethnic and religious identities – either within states (for example in the Balkans) or across states (for example ideas of a new Islamic 'caliphate'). This is particularly likely for those excluded from, or alienated by, the international market economy. And as some states are weakened, the ability of more powerful states to intervene is increased – and the costs of doing so are considerably reduced. Where the power differential is limited, intervention is extremely costly and would rarely be exercised merely for the benefit of oppressed peoples – in which case interventions would only be undertaken where it significantly advanced the interests of the interveners. If there is a huge disparity in power, the costs might be sufficiently low for leaders to act for the benefit of those to be protected. However, there is a natural scepticism that powerful nations engaging in intervention might still only do so if it advanced their own interests and that the protection of other peoples might be at best a secondary goal that is not actively secured and at worse an excuse for action that worsens their condition.

The United Nations: an organisation of, by and for sovereign states?

As previously outlined, the Treaty of Westphalia was a tyrant's charter in which the prior successful use of internal force justified the continuing use of internal force for any purpose that the sovereign sought fit. In many ways, the United Nations continues this tradition as the chief agent of the system of states for exercising international authority in their name. For countries emerging from colonial bondage into independence, who soon after the UN's establishment constituted the majority in the organisation, UN membership was the final symbol of independent sovereign statehood and thus the seal of acceptance into the community of nations. It was also the international forum in which their combined numbers could compensate for individual weakness in seeking to protect their newly regained sovereignty.

The United Nations is an organisation dedicated to the territorial integrity, political independence and national sovereignty of its member states and the maintenance of international peace and security on that basis. But the overwhelming majority of today's armed conflicts are internal, not inter-state. Moreover, the proportion of civilians killed by the direct violence of war, and from conflict-related starvation and disease, increased over the course of the last century. This presented the organisation with a major problem: how to reconcile its foundational principle of member states' sovereignty with the primary mandate to maintain international peace and security and the equally compelling mission to promote the interests and welfare of 'We the peoples of the United Nations'. Annan discussed the dilemma in the conceptual language of two notions of sovereignty, one vesting in the state, the second in the people.[39]

The UN Charter is itself an example of an international obligation voluntarily accepted by member states. On the one hand, in granting membership to the United Nations, the international community welcomes the signatory state as a responsible member of the community of nations. On the other hand, by signing the Charter the state accepts the responsibilities of membership flowing from that signature. There is a de facto redefinition from sovereignty as right of exclusivity to sovereignty as responsibility in both internal functions and external duties.

While the UN Charter and subsequent treaties embrace human rights, Article 2(7) of the Charter prohibits the United Nations from intervening in 'matters that are essentially within the domestic jurisdiction' of any member state. Yet by the very fact of signing the Charter a country accepts collective obligations and international scrutiny. The restrictions of Article 2(7) can be set aside when the Security Council decides to act under the collective enforcement Chapter VII to meet threats to or breaches of international peace and security. The scope of what constitute such threats and breaches has steadily widened to include such matters as HIV/AIDS, terrorism and atrocity crimes. In any case, Article 2(7) is about matters 'essentially' within domestic jurisdiction. This immediately implies that the issue is subject to judgement, which may differ from one competent authority to another and may undergo evolutionary change over time. Moreover, as shown in Somalia in the early 1990s, the collapse of state authority means that there is no functioning government to fulfil an essential condition of sovereignty, on the one hand, and the violence, instability and disorder can spill over from that failed state to others, on the other. This is why the Security

Council dealt with Somalia under the coercive clauses of Chapter VII rather than the consensual Chapter VI. Applying this argument more broadly, some analysts have questioned just how many of today's states would meet the strict requirements of sovereign statehood, describing many countries as 'quasi-states' instead.[40]

Accordingly, the sovereignty recognised by the United Nations is far from being absolute and instead has generally been considered to be contingent. The more significant change of recent times is that it has been reconceived as being instrumental. Its validation rests not in a mystical reification of the state, but in its utility as a tool for the state serving the interests of the citizens – moving tentatively towards the Enlightenment Feuerbachian inversion. Internal forms and precepts of governance must conform to international norms and standards of state conduct. That is, sovereignty must be exercised with due responsibility. This crucial normative shift was articulated by Francis M. Deng, the Special Representative of the Secretary-General for Internally Displaced Persons.[41] States are responsible for providing life-protecting and life-sustaining services to the people. When unable to do so, as responsible members of the international community, they must seek and accept international help. If they fail to seek – or obstruct – international assistance and put large numbers of people at risk of grave harm, the world has an international responsibility to respond. In extreme circumstances, the response may include the use of military force.

It is easy to forget that the United Nations was never meant to be a pacifist organisation. Its origins lie in the anti-Nazi wartime military alliance among Britain, the United States and the Soviet Union. Its primary purpose is the maintenance of international peace and security. The UN Security Council is the world's one duly sworn in sheriff for enforcing international law and order. But the UN Charter contains an inherent tension between the intervention-proscribing principle of state sovereignty and the intervention-prescribing principle of human rights. The calls for and controversy over humanitarian intervention arose from this tension. On the one hand, as noted, individuals became bearers of duties and holders of rights under a growing corpus of human rights and international humanitarian law treaties and conventions: the UN Charter, Universal Declaration of Human Rights and the two covenants on civil-political and social, economic and cultural rights, the four Geneva Conventions plus the two prohibiting torture and genocide, and so on. On the other hand, the cluster of norms inhibiting, if not prohibiting, humanitarian intervention includes, alongside the norm of non-intervention, state sovereignty, domestic jurisdiction, pacific settlement of disputes, non-use of force and, in the case of UN-authorised force, impartiality.

In the first four decades, state sovereignty was privileged over human rights, with the one significant exception of apartheid. The balance tilted in the 1990s and was more delicately poised between the two competing principles at the start of the new millennium. After the end of the Cold War, the UN Security Council experienced a surge of enforcement activity within civil war contexts to provide international relief and assistance to victims of large-scale atrocities from perpetrator or failing states.[42] In a number of cases in the 1990s, the Council endorsed the use of force with the primary goal of humanitarian protection and assistance: in the (ineffectual) proclamation of UN safe areas in Bosnia, the delivery of humanitarian relief in Somalia, the restoration of the democratically elected government of Haiti, and the deployment of the multinational Kosovo Force.[43] A more activist UN Security Council engaged in de facto intervention in Iraq to protect the Kurds from the defeated Saddam Hussein's regime, and Britain and the United States enforced a no-fly zone to protect the Kurdish minority in Northern Iraq throughout the 1990s, albeit with questionable legal basis for it.[44]

From Liberia and the Balkans to Somalia, Kosovo and East Timor, the conscience-shocking humanitarian catastrophes were explicitly recognised as threats to international peace and security, requiring and justifying a forcible response by the international community. When the UN Security Council was unable to act owing to lack of enforcement capacity, it subcontracted the military operation to UN-authorised coalitions. And if it proved unwilling to act, sometimes groups of countries forged 'coalitions of the willing' to act anyway even without UN authorisation. The debate on intervention was ignited in particular by humanitarian crises in Somalia, Rwanda, Srebrenica, Kosovo, and East Timor which revealed a dangerous gap in civilian protection mandates and capacities and a sharp polarisation of international opinion.

There was a second change. From 1945 to the end of the Cold War in 1989–90, the preservation of peace was privileged over the protection of human rights. The Charter talks of both but provides concrete instruments for the maintenance of the former. The end of the Cold War lessened the fear that international action in defence of human rights would threaten world peace by cutting across the vital interests of Moscow or Washington vis-à-vis their allies. At the same time, the proliferation of complex humanitarian emergencies, and the inappropriateness of the classical tenets of UN peacekeeping for dealing with them, highlighted the inherent tension between the neutrality of traditional peacekeeping and the partial consequences of peace enforcement. The dilemma was confronted squarely in the Brahimi Report which concluded that political neutrality has often degenerated into military timidity and the abdication of the duty to protect civilians. Impartiality should not translate into complicity with evil. While striving to remain impartial, the United Nations should soften its principle of neutrality between belligerents in favour of 'adherence to the principles of the Charter and to the objectives of [the] mandate'.[45] In retrospect the Brahimi Report was an important milestone in the normative journey from humanitarian intervention to the responsibility to protect.

The logic of Feuerbachian inversion: sovereign rights are human rights

The final approach is to take the logic of the Enlightenment's Feuerbachian inversion to the next step. Much of the debate leading up to and stemming from the enunciation and endorsement of R2P is based on the potential conflict between human rights and sovereign rights. However, this is a false dichotomy.[46]

The Feuerbachian inversion places citizens above states rather than sovereigns over subjects and locates sovereignty in the citizens, with governments only exercising power as delegated to them via the procedures adopted by the citizens. Sovereignty can become a collective human right of the citizens (and arguably a broader right to citizenship in an effective state).[47] This reconception of the basis of international constitutional legitimacy, largely eliminates most of the conflict between sovereignty and the protection of human rights.[48] Conflict of this kind is always possible when the international community recognises, as the sovereign power, any group which has gained effective political control through the prior successful use of force. This formula does not deny the possibility that such force will be exercised to deny the human rights of the excluded groups. If anything, it actively encourages human rights abuses by rewarding the successful exercise of force to secure dominion over a particular territory. It rewards those who mount anti-democratic coups. It rewards those who rig elections. It rewards those who intimidate the population or who rule through and for one ethnic or social group against others.[49]

If sovereignty is seen as extending only over those to whom the sovereign power is democratically accountable, then this principle provides members of any group over which that sovereign power is claimed a right to democratic participation. It also accords a right to those who have been excluded to democratic participation in that or another state. Sovereignty is no longer the recognition of a power over a people, but the collective right of a people to participate in and benefit from an independent political community, participating as an equal in the community of nations. To put it another way, sovereignty becomes a human right.[50]

This would be a 'great leap forward' in the Maoist sense, if attempted in a single bound. However, we can take it in smaller steps. Once a people have secured their sovereign rights through the establishment of even a half-decent democracy, no one else can trump those sovereign rights. Democracies can, and should, protect each other – and the African Union has provided a lead by incorporating this principle into its constitutive document. Africans have had more than their fair share of tyrants, both home-grown and among European colonisers. They have had enough of tyrants exercising their right to persecute and are sometimes prepared to act in line with the more recent 'R2P'.

Notes

* Originally published in Ramesh Thakur and William Maley, eds., *Theorising the Responsibility to Protect* (Cambridge: Cambridge University Press, 2015), 38–58. Reprinted by permission of Cambridge University Press.

1 Ban Ki-moon, *Implementing the Responsibility to Protect.* Report of the Secretary-General (New York: United Nations, document A/63/677, 12 January 2009), 8–9, paragraph 11(a, b and c).

2 Ban, *Implementing the Responsibility to Protect.* Report of the Secretary-General, 25, paragraph 56.

3 Charles Sampford, 'Professions Without Borders: Global Ethics and the International Rule of Law', Public Lecture, Queensland University of Technology, 19 August 2009.

4 International Commission on Intervention and State Sovereignty, *The Responsibility to Protect* (Ottawa: International Development Research Centre, 2001).
5 Thomas S. Kuhn, *The Structure of Scientific Revolutions* (Chicago: University of Chicago Press, 1962), 53.
6 Locke's repudiation of Hobbes puts it quite nicely: 'This is to think, that men are so foolish, that they take care to avoid what mischiefs may be done them by *pole-cats*, or *foxes*; but are content, nay, think it safety, to be devoured by *lions*'. Locke (1947), II: 93.
7 An example of black humour in a similar vein: you kill one person, you get sent to trial for murder; kill ten, you get sent to a mental asylum; kill 10,000, you are invited to Geneva for UN peace talks.
8 With apologies to the United Dutch Provinces, the only signatory clearly not a tyranny and to Abraham Lincoln and his Gettysburg address.
9 Hans Kelsen, *Pure Theory of Law*, trans. M. Knight (Berkeley: UCLA Press, (1960) [1967]).
10 See Charles Sampford, 'Sovereignty and Intervention', Plenary Paper, World Congress of Legal and Social Philosophy, New York, June 1999; and later published in T. Campbells and B. Leiser, eds., *Human Rights in Theory and Practice* (London: Ashgate 2001).
11 If they claimed higher purposes and external responsibilities, these were likely to be to do with religion rather than human rights. Sovereigns might purport to be more concerned about the afterlife of their subjects than their present life – to the extent that some thoughtfully burned heretics.
12 Although Max Weber did not refer to the 'monopoly of legitimate force' until 250 years later, the seventeenth century rulers were very much concerned to establish such a monopoly against their 'over-mighty subjects'.
13 Kofi Annan, address delivered at the international conference 'Community of Democracies', United Nations Press Release SG/SM/7467, Warsaw, 28 June 2000, www.un.org/press/en/2000/sgsm7467.htm.
14 ICISS, *Responsibility to Protect*; Independent Task Force Sponsored by the Council on Foreign Relations, *Threats to Democracy: Prevention and Response* (Council on Foreign Relations, Washington, 2003). Thakur was a member of the first and Sampford of the second.
15 Luke Glanville, 'The Myth of "Traditional" Sovereignty', *International Studies Quarterly* 57:1 (2013), 79–90.
16 See Ramesh Thakur, 'Intervention, Sovereignty and the Responsibility to Protect: Experiences from ICISS', *Security Dialogue* 33:3 (2002), 323–40.
17 Alexandros Yannis, 'The Concept of Suspended Sovereignty in International Law', *European Journal of International Law* 13:5 (2002), 1037–52.
18 For example of trusteeships, see Simon Chesterman, *You, the People: The United Nations, Transitional Administration, and State-Building* (Oxford: Oxford University Press, 2004); and Richard Caplan, *International Governance of War-Torn Territories: Rule and Reconstruction* (Oxford: Oxford University Press, 2005).
19 ICISS, *Responsibility to Protect.*
20 Peter J. Spiro, 'The New Sovereigntists', *Foreign Affairs* 79:6 (2000), 9–15.
21 Partha Chatterjee, 'Empire after Globalisation', *Economic and Political Weekly* 39:37 (11 September 2004), 4158.
22 Chatterjee, 'Empire after Globalisation', 4163.
23 Ramesh Thakur, *Towards a Less Imperfect State of the World: The Gulf between North and South* (Berlin: Friedrich Ebert Stiftung, Dialogue on Globalization Briefing Paper 4, April 2008).
24 See Simon Chesterman, Michael Ignatieff and Ramesh Thakur, eds., *Making States Work: State Failure and the Crisis of Governance* (Tokyo: United Nations University Press, 2005).

25 Kofi A. Annan, *In Larger Freedom: Towards Development, Security and Human Rights for All*. Report of the Secretary-General (New York: United Nations, document A/59/2005, 21 March 2005), paragraph 19.
26 Ramesh Thakur, 'R2P after Libya and Syria: Engaging Emerging Powers', *The Washington Quarterly* 36:2 (2013), 61–76.
27 Mohamed Sahnoun, 'Africa: Uphold Continent's Contribution to Human Rights, Urges Top Diplomat', *allAfrica.com*, 21 July 2009, http://allafrica.com/stories/printable/200907210549.html. For another African perspective that also strongly supports R2P, see Samuel Atuobi, 'The Responsibility to Protect: The Time to Act is Now', *KAIPTC Policy Brief* No. 1 (Accra: Kofi Annan International Peacekeeping Training Centre, July 2009).
28 Ramesh Thakur, 'The Responsibility to Protect Revisited', *Daily Yomiuri*, 12 April 2007.
29 Michael Ignatieff, 'Why are we in Iraq?' *New York Times*, 7 September 2003, www.nytimes.com/2003/09/07/magazine/why-are-we-in-iraq-and-liberia-and-afghanistan.html?pagewanted=all&src=pm.
30 See Charles Sampford, 'A Tale of Two Norms', in A. Francis, V. Popovski and C. Sampford, eds., *The Norms of Protection* (Tokyo: UN University Press, 2012).
31 See Ramesh Thakur, 'Multilateral Diplomacy and the United Nations: Global Governance Venue or Actor?', in J.P. Muldoon, J. Fagot Aviel, R. Reitano, and E. Sullivan, eds., *The New Dynamics of Multilateralism: Diplomacy, International Organizations, and Global Governance* (Boulder: Westview, 2011), 249–65.
32 D. Josselin and W. Wallace, eds., *Non-State Actors in World Politics* (London: Palgrave, 2001).
33 Ronald A. Brand, 'Sovereignty: The State, the Individual, and the International Legal System in the Twenty-First Century', *Hastings International and Comparative Law Review* 25 (2002), 279–95.
34 Thomas M. Franck, 'The Emerging Right to Democratic Governance', *American Journal of International Law* 86:1 (1992), 46–91.
35 Kofi A. Annan, *We, the Peoples: The United Nations in the 21st Century*. Millennium Report of the Secretary-General (New York: United Nations, 2000).
36 J. Stern, *The Ultimate Terrorists* (Cambridge MA: Harvard University Press, 1999); M. Galeotti, *Cross-Border Crime in the Former Soviet Union* (Durham: Durham University Press, 1995); and Jorge Heine and Ramesh Thakur, eds., *The Dark Side of Globalization* (Tokyo: UN University Press, 2011).
37 Simon Chesterman, *Just War or Just Peace: Humanitarian Intervention and International Law* (Oxford: Oxford University Press, 2001).
38 Howard Adelman and Gil Loescher, *Refugee Movements and International Security*, Adelphi Paper 268 (London: Brassey's, 1992); Ramesh Thakur, 'Threats without Enemies, Security without Borders: Environmental Security in East Asia', *Journal of East Asian Studies* 1:2 (August 2001), 161–89.
39 Kofi A. Annan, 'Two Concepts of Sovereignty', *The Economist*, 18 September 1999, 49–50.
40 Robert H. Jackson, *Quasi-States: Sovereignty, International Relations, and the Third World* (Cambridge: Cambridge University Press, 1990). See also Stephen D. Krasner, *Sovereignty: Organized Hypocrisy* (Princeton: Princeton University Press, 1999).
41 Francis M. Deng, Sadikiel Kimaro, Terrence Lyons, Donald Rothchild and I. William Zartman, *Sovereignty as Responsibility: Conflict Management in Africa* (Washington, DC: Brookings Institution Press, 1996); and Francis M. Deng, 'Frontiers of Sovereignty', *Leiden Journal of International Law* 8:2 (June 1995), 249–86.
42 Thomas G. Weiss, Don Hubert, *et al.*, *The Responsibility to Protect: Research, Bibliography, Background* (Ottawa: International Development Research Centre, 2001), 79–126.
43 See Brian D. Lepard, *Rethinking Humanitarian Intervention* (University Park: Pennsylvania State University Press, 2002), 7–23.

44 Washington and London grounded their declaration and enforcement of the no-fly zone in UNSC Resolution 688 (5 April 1991). But the resolution contains no obvious basis for such a claim and the claim never was accepted by any relevant UN authority.

45 *Report of the Panel on United Nations Peace Operations* (New York: United Nations, document A/55/305-S/2000/809, 21 August 2000) paragraph 50.

46 Sampford, 'Sovereignty and Intervention'.

47 Charles Sampford, 'The Four Dimensions of Rights and the Means for their Protection', in C. Sampford and B. Galligan, *Rethinking Human Rights* (Sydney: Federation Press, 1997).

48 This does not deal with problems of human rights abuses by democratic states.

49 This overcomes the problem that Steven David highlights. Although some elites in developing countries may represent little more than themselves, use state power for their own ends and interests, and have come to power by illegitimate means (including support from abroad), they have all the benefits of sovereignty, including non-intervention without consent. Steven David, *Third World Coups d'État and International Security* (Baltimore: John Hopkins University Press, 1987), 4–6.

50 See Krasner, *Sovereignty: Organized Hypocrisy*, 231. Some would leave this as a collective right of the people. Others might like to conceive it in terms of individual rights – as a right of all persons to take part in a sovereign government, to be a part of the group to whom a government is accountable. See Sampford, 'The Four Dimensions of Rights and the Means for their Protection'. Either way the point is that every human being on the planet has the right to participate in such a community and denying that right constitutes an abuse of human rights.

6 From humanitarian intervention to R2P

Cosmetic or consequential?*

In 1999, when NATO asserted an emerging new norm of 'humanitarian intervention' to justify the bombing of Serbia, the ensuing controversy highlighted a lacuna in the existing legal regime governing the international use of force. R2P was formulated by ICISS in 2001 as the answer to reconciling the neuralgic rejection of 'humanitarian intervention' by the global South with the determination by the North to end atrocities. The final ICISS meeting was held in Wakefield, Ontario in August (an extraordinary meeting was subsequently scheduled in Brussels in late September to discuss the implications of 9/11 for the report on which the 12 Commissioners had signed off in August.) Towards the end of the meeting, Cornelio Sommaruga, an ICISS Commissioner who had served as president of the International Committee of the Red Cross for 13 years, commented: 'If nothing else, we have killed off "humanitarian intervention"'.

R2P was unanimously endorsed by the 2005 UN world summit[1] which accepted the ICISS argument about its substantial difference from humanitarian intervention. ICISS co-chairs argued for the distinction in an article in *Foreign Affairs*.[2] The substantive differences between 'humanitarian intervention' and R2P were also emphasised by ICISS co-chair Gareth Evans and I as a Commissioner in our respective books.[3] And research director Tom Weiss commented that 'ICISS sought to drive a stake through the heart of the term humanitarian intervention'.[4] Yet the pronouncement of the death of 'humanitarian intervention' proved premature. When queried on his use of 'humanitarian intervention', Roland Paris noted that the term 'continues to be widely employed in the academic literature' and 'should be regarded as analytically neutral'; a search for it on Google Scholar in January 2014 yielded 'about 10,600' results published since 2011 alone.[5]

As someone who has reflected, written (including the initial draft of the relevant sections of the original ICISS report) and spoken on the topic extensively around the world, I believe the differences between 'humanitarian intervention' and R2P to be both real and consequential.[6] Following Paris, a search of Google Scholar on 22 February 2016 yielded 23,200 results for 'humanitarian intervention' but 111,000 for 'responsibility to protect'. This suggests two conclusions. Most analysts have accepted the conceptual-cum-normative significance of the shift in terminology, but a substantial number still persist in using the old one.[7] It is difficult to know if the continued employment of 'humanitarian intervention' by some scholars as synonymous with R2P is due to carelessness, intellectual hubris, laziness or incompetence.

The older term has been discarded in UN circles by UN officials, national diplomats and civil society since 2005. R2P was not a principle adopted by the policy community after its conceptualisation by scholars. Rather, the scholarly literature on R2P has flourished following its adoption by the UN policy community in 2005.[8] If the ICISS distinction between humanitarian intervention and R2P is artificial, the constitutive predicate of R2P is false and the entire edifice of policy structures in the UN system and national capitals, as well as scholarly discourse since 2001/2005, collapses. The continued usage of the old framework by a few seeks to relitigate the debate that was lost and abandoned, and its major effect is to lengthen the distance between academic scholarship and the real world of international policy, with the accompanying risk of increasing irrelevance of scholarship to policy.

This chapter attempts to elaborate the many dimensions on which in fact R2P differs from 'humanitarian intervention'. I will begin by looking back at the controversy unleashed in 1999 by the term humanitarian intervention and then substantiate the differences on five dimensions: political, conceptual, normative, procedural and operational. The chapter would have been unnecessary if so many analysts did not still continue to confuse the two terms. That they do so may well reflect the fact that the different strands are scattered. Bringing them together in one coherent whole may show just how compelling the case is for acknowledging the two as substantially different, without pre-judging which is better.

Annan's 'challenge of humanitarian intervention'

The intellectual and political antecedents of R2P can be traced to the challenge of humanitarian intervention articulated by Secretary-General Kofi Annan in four landmark statements in 1998–99. In a speech at Ditchely Park, UK on 26 June 1998, he said: 'Sovereignty implies responsibility, not just power'. In a blunt sentence, he insisted: 'State frontiers ... should no longer be seen as a watertight protection for war criminals or mass murderers'.[9] The other three statements were made in 1999 against the backdrop of the NATO intervention in Kosovo. Addressing the Human Rights Commission in Geneva on 7 April, he said slowly but surely an international norm was emerging 'against the violent repression of minorities that will and must take precedence over concepts of sovereignty'. He added: 'No government has the right to hide behind national sovereignty in order to violate the human rights or fundamental freedoms of its peoples'.[10]

Building on the theme, in the introduction to his annual report on the work of the UN, Annan outlined his vision on 'Facing the Humanitarian Challenge'.[11] Presenting the report to the UN General Assembly in New York on 20 September 1999, Annan said that state sovereignty was being redefined and the state 'is now widely understood to be the servant of its people, and not vice versa'. The Rwanda genocide had defined the consequences of inaction in the face of mass murder, but Kosovo had raised uncomfortable questions about the consequences of action taken without international unity. The two together had

> cast in stark relief the dilemma of what has been called humanitarian intervention: on one side, the question of the legitimacy of an action taken by a regional organisation without a United Nations mandate; on the other, the universally recognised imperative of effectively halting gross and systematic violations of human rights with grave humanitarian consequences.

He asked: what if a group of states had been able and willing to take action in Rwanda but failed to receive UN Security Council authorisation, 'should such a coalition have stood aside and allowed the horror to unfold'? Conversely, to those who accepted that states could take military action 'outside established mechanisms for enforcing international law', he asked: what of the risk of 'setting dangerous precedents for future interventions without a clear criterion to decide who might invoke these precedents, and in what circumstances'?[12]

Annan's statements unleashed a chorus of harsh criticisms from many developing countries. On 23 September 1999, the final communiqué of the 113-member NAM Ministerial Meeting in New York emphatically rejected any 'so-called "right of humanitarian intervention" which has no legal basis in the UN Charter or in the general principles of international law'. The sentiment was repeated in an identical sentence in the Declaration of the South adopted by the Group of 77 (G77) summit in Havana in April 2000 by 133 countries.[13] Yet Annan's call also resonated powerfully among many Western governments and people. Recognising that the international community was split on the subject, the Canadian government set up an international commission[14] with the mandate to reconcile the two competing imperatives of state sovereignty and international interventions. The ICISS report argued that it had successfully reconciled the tension with the innovative formula of the Responsibility to Protect which was different from humanitarian intervention not just linguistically but substantively.[15]

Political

R2P can be discussed in any one of three aspects. As an analytical exercise, its three core concepts are sovereignty, responsibility and protection. Scholars can study these in the history of ideas and political thought, examine the relations among and tensions between them and scrutinise possibilities for conceptual refinement. A second approach would be to discuss R2P as a normative enterprise: how best to build, consolidate and institutionalise the atrocity prevention and human protection norm. There exists a fairly sophisticated literature on norms with respect to entrepreneurs, champions, carriers and spoilers; and also, regarding the rise, dissemination, circulation, tipping point, cascade, and retreat and replacement of norms. Or R2P can be studied as a political project: when, how and with what oversight and accountability measures to ensure a convergence between lawfulness and legitimacy in the use of force across borders in order to prevent, limit and halt the commission of atrocities inside sovereign borders. Who are the relevant actors; what are their collective and institutional memories, interests and values, and capacity to advance and implement or block and frustrate the implementation of R2P; where are the institutional points of resistance; which regional actors can function as key gatekeepers and framers of R2P situations; etc.?

The epicentre of R2P as an international political project is the United Nations, and ICISS never lost sight of this reality as its 'eye on the prize'. Since 2005, R2P has progressed along three parallel tracks in the UN system: in numerous UN Security Council resolutions and presidential statements, starting with Resolution 1674 (28 April 2006); in successive reports of the Secretary-General since 2009; and in annual debates in the General Assembly on these reports. In addition, it has been progressively institutionalised in the UN system and in some national governments and widely disseminated and promoted by civil society organisations.

The principle of non-intervention is the most important embodiment of the notion that states are autonomous entities, and its ancestry can be traced to the Treaty of Westphalia of 1648. As a consequence of the formal status of sovereignty, a state has certain legal rights, including against intervention in its internal affairs by other states. After NATO's actions in Kosovo, venerable commentators asserted that 'Intervention has become the new norm' in 'a climate in which non-intervention appears as a dereliction of duty, requiring explanation, excuse or apology'.[16] Contrary to what many European governments claimed, however, the application of a right to humanitarian intervention in Kosovo was not self-evidently (self-righteously?) based in law or morality. Agreement among Western scholars can neither hide nor overcome the deep divisions between Western and developing country diplomats. The powerful sense of grievance and resentment can be easily missed by Western academics who read and cite one another to the near total exclusion of colleagues from developing countries. This is how the journal-publishing requirement 'to engage with the literature' becomes a self-perpetuating mechanism for entrenching a fundamentally flawed conception.[17]

Humanitarian intervention

Because so many analysts seem unaware that the majority of the world's countries rejected the 'humanitarian intervention' justification of NATO intervention in Kosovo in 1999, it is worth briefly reviewing why its history renders it so toxic for developing countries. 'Humanitarian intervention' has a long lineage and people associated with ICISS, including Weiss and I,[18] have used it when discussing the phenomenon in its historical entirety. In fact I had used it much earlier in 1990, describing 'humanitarian intervention' as one of 11 separate 'legitimising principles of intervention'.[19] ICISS, too, recognised 'the long history, and continuing wide and popular usage, of the phrase "humanitarian intervention"', but 'made a deliberate decision not to adopt this terminology, preferring to refer either to "intervention," or as appropriate "military intervention," for human protection purposes'.[20] Its supplementary volume briefly described the many past humanitarian interventions, before 1990 and since the Cold War.[21]

Several European powers engaged in humanitarian intervention throughout the nineteenth century and doctrine followed to justify practice.[22] States engaged in intervention even during the Cold War, including former colonies like India and Tanzania. The US has a long – and seemingly continuing – history of intervening in the Middle East to effect regime change and in Latin America as its sphere of influence. Glanville notes that non-intervention in one another's internal affairs was only a twentieth century attribute of sovereignty and that indeed the right to wage a just war to punish tyranny and rescue the oppressed – for example to protect co-religionists under threat by a ruler from a different denomination – predates non-intervention as an *attribute* of sovereignty.[23]

The abuse of humanitarian arguments to justify interventions motivated mainly by strategic or commercial gains was a recurrent feature of state practice prior to 1945. Scholars from countries that were once European colonies are not likely to forget or overlook the brutal historical fact that their nations were invaded, conquered, annexed and ruled by the European powers through the height of the Westphalian order of traditional sovereignty. To understand the strength of visceral reactions to the so-called right to humanitarian intervention one has to grasp how the colonial experience is deeply internalised in their collective consciousness and continues to scar their memories. Their post-1945 elevation of non-intervention as a peremptory norm from which no derogation is permitted and their abiding attachment to the new norm rest on this memory.

In 2006 I asked:

> Should we be mute accomplices when they substitute their mythology of humanitarian intervention for our narratives of colonial oppression? Do they think we do not remember or do not care, or is it simply that they themselves do not care?[24]

An Indian scholar has highlighted the similarities in the structure of justifications deploying moral arguments to support the British annexation of the Indian kingdom of Awadh in the first half of the nineteenth century and the invasion of Iraq in 2003.[25] As for its great colonial competitor France: 'General Bonaparte ... would have entered India not as a devastating conqueror ... but as a liberator'. Having expelled the English from India, he 'would have restored independence, peace, and happiness.... All the Princes in India were longing for French intervention'.[26]

Today's norms restrict the rights of states both to violate citizens' rights arbitrarily and to use force abroad unilaterally. The UN Charter shows a tension between the principle of human rights that subjects domestic state conduct to external scrutiny, on the one hand and, on the other, the principle of sovereignty that shields a state from external interference. In case of conflict, therefore, should human rights violations justifying external intervention prevail over the doctrine of non-intervention? The prohibition in the plain words of Article 2(4) of the UN Charter[27] notwithstanding, can a doctrine of humanitarian intervention 'be insinuated into its interstices'? Zifcak holds that to locate a right of humanitarian intervention in the development of customary international law as a result of accumulating UN Security Council decisions and evolving state practice is problematical because it mixes 'legal justifications with political and security concerns'.[28]

Inevitably, the burden of leadership responsibility falls on the most powerful members of any given system of world order. It is because of frustrations induced by this dilemma that the Reagan doctrine rejected the idea that the US could be bound to UN Charter proscriptions on the use of force in international relations while others flouted such norms. Concerned with the moral legitimacy of US support for insurgencies under certain circumstances, the doctrine rejected 'the inviolability of sovereignty'.[29] In criticising the doctrine, Henkin argued that the most authoritative statement of the law on the use of force is the UN Charter which – while not neutral between democracy and totalitarianism, justice and injustice, human rights and their violation – does not sanction the use of unilateral force across international frontiers to redress such grievances. In practice states have followed a restrictive view of the Charter's law on the use of force, with virtually every use of force since World War II being condemned. Previous US lapses from Charter proscriptions on the use of force were occasional and partial. The Reagan doctrine, in seeking to make it general and wholesale, was 'untenable in law'.[30]

In the real world, intervention is typically characterised by mixed motives and moral ambiguity. Accordingly, the many examples of intervention in actual state practice over the centuries did not lead to an abandonment of the norm of non-intervention. As the UK Foreign Office affirmed in 1986:

> The overwhelming majority of contemporary legal opinion comes down against the existence of a right of humanitarian intervention for three main reasons. First, the UN Charter and the corpus of modern international law do not seem specifically to incorporate such a right; secondly, state practice in the last two centuries, and especially since 1945, at best provides only a handful of genuine cases of humanitarian intervention; and finally, on prudential grounds, that the scope for abusing such a right argues strongly against its creation.[31]

Yet the UK joined NATO allies in 1999 in justifying military intervention in Kosovo on humanitarian grounds. The ICISS report summarised the Kosovo controversy succinctly with regard to just cause, exhaustion of peaceful means, manipulation of humanitarian arguments, lawful authorisation and aggravation of the humanitarian crisis.[32] The case against Serbia was not framed in humanitarian language. NATO went to war because President Slobodan Milošević rejected the Rambouillet ultimatum. Air strikes did not prevent widespread atrocities against civilians on the ground in Kosovo nor the mass exodus of refugees into neighbouring countries. High altitude, zero-casualty air war shifted 'the entire burden of risk and harm' to life and limb completely to the target society, 'including the supposed beneficiaries and innocent civilians'. Expanding the list of bombing targets, such as water and electricity infrastructure and broadcasting stations, reversed progressive trends in the laws of war over the course of the twentieth century. And bombing mistakes, the increased risk of which was deliberately accepted by political leaders in order to minimise risks to their own soldiers, 'caused the finger of criminality to be pointed in NATO's direction'.[33]

The moral position was less clear-cut than NATO implied. The Kosovo Liberation Army's director of elite services was allegedly al-Qaeda's top operative in the Balkans, Mohammed al-Zawahiri, brother of Osama bin Laden's military chief of staff Ayman al-Zawahiri, according to Interpol and bin Laden's biographer Yossef Bodansky.[34] In addition, the costs of the war in Kosovo drained development funds away from needy populations in Africa and Asia; Nigeria's ambassador to the UN called it 'morally repugnant' that the international community spent $1.50 per day per refugee in Kosovo, but only $0.11 in Rwanda and Sierra Leone.[35]

Against this backdrop, Alex Bellamy notes:

> The principal objections to *The Responsibility to Protect* immediately after it was published came from states and commentators worried about the widened potential for abuse that may accompany any relaxing of the general prohibition on force contained in Article 2(4) of the Charter.[36]

The risk materialised shortly when ICISS Commissioner Michael Ignatieff justified the invasion of Iraq.[37] But co-chair Evans and I, as fellow-Commissioner, argued that Iraq did not satisfy R2P requirements.[38]

Disrespecting the rest

Leading into and during the 2005 world summit negotiations, Western countries were largely supportive of R2P being included in the outcome document, but so, crucially, was Africa, provided that interventions were rules-based and collectively authorised by the UN or regional organisations.[39] In April 2005, India's Ambassador Nirupam Sen warned against conferring legitimacy on a doctrine of humanitarian intervention dressed in the language of R2P and 'turning it into a new ideology of "military humanism"'. Pakistan's Munir Akram warned the General Assembly against adopting the doctrine of humanitarian intervention under the semantic cloak of R2P. Egypt thought R2P would be a licence for the strong to judge and attack the weak.[40]

In other words, the 2005 'unanimous' endorsement of R2P rested on shallow foundations. Many people from the 2005 negotiations confessed privately that

'For the sake of … overall consensus, they had been willing to endorse the new norm even though they did not support and would not adhere to it'.[41] This underlines the fact that the global consensus on R2P is tenuous and fragile rather than robust and resilient, and distinguishing it from humanitarian intervention was crucial for building, sustaining and consolidating the consensus. If political sensitivity is neglected or affronted, therefore, R2P would be at serious risk of falling apart. The developing countries remain deeply suspicious of the self-serving hidden agenda of geopolitical and commercial interests behind such claims. To dismiss their claims is to deny their historical encounter with the West and dismiss their worldviews rooted in that collective memory.

In fact, the charge of disrespect – by implication more than intention – could be considerably broader. To argue that R2P and humanitarian intervention are essentially interchangeable suggests that ICISS Commissioners were either intellectually challenged or else chose to 'spin' their report in order to deflect the deep hostility of the international political constituency by marketing the same old wine of humanitarian intervention in the shiny new bottle of R2P; that the NAM and G77 countries were intellectually challenged and politically naïve in accepting and endorsing the distinction; and that the international community as represented in the UN corridors continues to be similarly confused in rejecting humanitarian intervention but endorsing, promoting and reaffirming R2P. Every annual report on R2P by the Secretary-General since 2009 has been fraudulent and the annual General Assembly debate on the reports has been organised and conducted on a lie. To this widening circle should be added the vast array of civil society organisations actively disseminating and promoting R2P as a new principle or norm as well.

One final point is worth emphasising on the politics of the global North–South divide. China's Ambassador Liu Zhenmin warned in a UN Security Council debate on 4 December 2006 that the 2005 Outcome Document was 'a very cautious representation of the responsibility to protect … it is not appropriate to expand, wilfully to interpret or even abuse this concept'.[42] The principled underpinnings for adopting an R2P rather than a humanitarian intervention perspective are reinforced by the reality of the gradual but steady shift of power and influence from the West to the rest. The folly of disregarding the global South's sensitivities and preferences has only grown since R2P and was first articulated. Thus, regardless of whether or not 'humanitarian intervention' is analytically neutral, it comes with considerable political baggage and is anything but neutral in its effects in the world of international politics.

Conceptual

The prevailing norm of non-intervention proved no longer fit for purpose by the end of the last century and was discredited. But when some countries joined together to proclaim and launch humanitarian interventions as a new principle, they encountered stiff resistance from most of the world's countries. ICISS resolved the impasse through the innovative R2P that positioned itself between the institutionalised collective indifference of the old norm and the unilateralism of humanitarian intervention, and found near-universal acceptance on this distinction. The term is not used any longer by national diplomats or UN officials in UN debates and documents. Even so, deference to the political arguments by themselves would risk the dismissive comment of 'political correctness'. In fact, they are buttressed by weighty conceptual arguments. Thus, ICISS claimed it was making 'a principled, as well as a practical and political, case for conceptualising the intervention issue in terms of a responsibility to protect'.[43] R2P reconciled the moral responsibility of nations to end atrocities within borders with the constitutional principle of a world of territorially-defined and sovereignty-bound states.

Before considering the advantages of 'the responsibility to protect' as a concept, it is first worth highlighting the inherent euphemism of 'humanitarian intervention'. NATO's intervention in Kosovo in 1999 consisted of three months of bombing. If that was humanitarian intervention, it must necessarily also have been 'humanitarian bombing'. Such usage immediately points up the damaging contradiction in juxtaposing the two words. But that is exactly what NATO action amounted to, which explains the controversy that embroiled Czech President Vaclev Havel.[44] The phrase 'humanitarian intervention' is used to trump sovereignty with intervention at the outset of the debate by labelling and delegitimising dissent as anti-humanitarian. The effort to foreclose debate on the merits of a particular case by deploying the language of humanitarian intervention is 'wrong – intellectually as well as politically'.[45]

ICISS made two further arguments that effectively link the political to conceptual arguments. It noted that the language of a right or duty to intervene 'is intrinsically more confrontational' while the R2P concept 'bridges the divide between intervention and sovereignty'. Moreover, 'the humanitarian intervention terminology … had become irretrievably linked to the use of military force, and *only* military force'.[46] In choosing the phrase 'responsibility to protect' over 'humanitarian intervention', ICISS had responded also 'to the very strong opposition' from humanitarian agencies and workers to 'any militarisation of the word "humanitarian": whatever the motives of those engaging in the intervention, it is anathema for the humanitarian relief and assistance sector to have this word appropriated to describe any kind of military action'.[47]

In addition, by rooting military intervention in human solidarity, R2P provides conceptual, normative and operational linkages between assistance, intervention and reconstruction. If interventions are embedded conceptually in the rights and privileges of the intervening actors, then of course the fewer the constraints and obligations on them, the better. In that case, however, they can hardly be called 'humanitarian'. Conversely, if interventions are genuinely motivated by humanitarian concerns as the primary goal (accepting that the real world is usually characterised by mixed motive situations), then their implementation implies solidarity across borders. Such solidarity, however, cannot begin and end with military intervention. It must also find expression at the pre-crisis point and be continued after the immediate crisis is over.

While paraphrasing the Commission's three claims to what its report had done – pinning the principal responsibility on the state, holding the state responsible to the international community as well as its own people, and holding the state answerable and accountable for its responsibility failures[48] – Zifcak states: 'This *conceptual* shift was significant'. He then adds that ICISS 'developed its conceptual framework further by distinguishing between different classes of responsibility': prioritising prevention, highlighting the importance of prior non-forcible measures and emphasising the responsibility to rebuild after intervention.[49]

ICISS argued that reconceptualising sovereignty as responsibility had a three-fold significance: it implied the state authorities are responsible *for* the functions of protecting the safety and lives of citizens and promotion of their welfare; it suggested that national political authorities are responsible *to* citizens internally and the international community through the UN; and it meant that the agents of a state are responsible for their actions, that is to say, they are *accountable* for their acts of commission and omission: 'Would-be perpetrators of mass atrocities should fear the growth of universal justice as a result of which they will ultimately have nowhere else to run, no place left to hide'.[50]

Developing countries and emerging powers were suspicious and remain wary about a stealthy morphing of R2P into humanitarian intervention. Chinese commentators have remained consistent since in their criticism of unilateral military interventions:

> The main sources of today's refugees – Syria, Libya, Iraq and Afghanistan – are targets of U.S. intervention, which led to devastation, chaos, deteriorating domestic security and extensive displacements …
>
> The militants of the so-called Islamic State (IS), emerging from the Syrian oppositions which were supported by the U.S. to topple the Syrian government, have launched numerous attacks against Syrian civilians, who have become targets of kidnappings, suicide and car bombings, among others …
>
> On other fronts, although the United States has pulled out its troops from some countries like Iraq and Afghanistan, it should be still held accountable for having destabilized these countries in the first place and then leaving them in a hopeless mess.[51]

International executive authority: updating principle to align with evolving practice

Humanitarian intervention is fundamentally about the distribution of authority and jurisdiction between different individual and groups of states, and their respective rights vis-à-vis one another. By contrast, R2P is fundamentally about the distribution of rights and responsibilities between states and citizens domestically; and the distribution of authority between states on the one side, and the international community collectively on the other internationally. Internally, ICISS performed a 'Feuerbachian inversion' of state–citizen relations on rights and responsibilities in which citizens became rights holders and states are duty carriers.[52] Externally, R2P preserves to states the responsibility to protect their own populations but strengthens the UN's responsibility acting for the international community as a whole. The ancestry of this insight is traced by Orford, like so much of UN best practices, to former Secretary-General Dag Hammarskjöld.[53] As the European colonial powers withdrew, the weakness of state structures posed a threat to the law and order of many newly independent countries (who were at best quasi-sovereign[54]) and to the physical safety and security of their people. The instability also posed a potential threat to international peace and security and risked the intervention of major powers on opposing sides, thereby importing the global Cold War rivalry into local intrastate conflicts.

Hammarskjöld inserted the UN to fill the resulting power vacuum as the European colonial powers retreated from empire, using the authority of the international organisation to initiate several innovative practices both to underwrite public order and to protect the safety and security of the people. R2P's singular achievement was to integrate existing and evolving but dispersed practices of protection into a conceptually coherent account of international authority. That is, ICISS provided 'a detailed normative articulation' of the 'international authority to undertake executive action for protective ends'.[55] Hammarskjöld justified a special and rapidly growing role for the organisation by its neutrality, impartiality and technical competence. On the one hand, this meant that the UN was not encumbered by the baggage of special interests which guided the actions of individual member states. On the other hand, this neutrality permitted – perhaps even obligated – the UN to step in as a mediator and facilitator between the warring factions. Just as Hammarskjöld's notions of preventive diplomacy and peacekeeping were meant to avert great power intervention by inserting the UN as a neutral presence, so R2P came about in opposition to efforts to justify interventions by non-UN coalitions of the willing, led by powerful states, by inserting the UN as the only legitimate validator of interventions.

Normative

The key normative difference between 'humanitarian intervention' and R2P is one already mentioned, namely grounding international action in the privileges of the interveners versus in solidarity with the victims. ICISS argued that

> 'the right of humanitarian intervention' or the 'right to intervene' … necessarily focuses attention on the claims, rights and prerogatives of the potentially intervening states much more so than on the urgent needs of the potential beneficiaries of the action.[56]

By contrast, and equally necessarily, R2P impels an evaluation of the issues from the point of view of those seeking or needing support, rather than those who may be considering intervention.[57] Because 'humanitarian intervention' prioritises the perspectives and interests of the intervening states, it can accommodate regime change as a legitimate goal of intervention. Because R2P is based on solidarity with victims, it stays studiously neutral with respect to the political struggle for power among the different local contenders. Interventions cannot become the pretext for imposing external political preferences with regard to regimes and political and economic systems. NATO fell into this trap in Libya in 2011 and there was a de facto transformation of an R2P authorisation by the UN Security Council into a humanitarian intervention operation by NATO.

R2P represents a major normative advance second in redefining sovereignty as responsibility, and third in locating that responsibility in every sovereign state and the society of states collectively, as represented by and in the United Nations. Weiss observes that 'Reframing sovereignty as responsibility provided a way to navigate around the shoals of state sovereignty'.[58] Fourth, in addition to the new norm of sovereignty as responsibility, R2P also helps to link international interventions to the twin norm of civilian protection that emerged at about the same time. R2P and 'protection of civilians' have many overlaps and similarities, but also important differences and tensions.

ICISS successfully – although how durably remains to be tested – shifted the normative consensus on the use of deadly force to save strangers in harm's way. It pinned that responsibility first and foremost on state authorities themselves as part of their *sovereign* duties. And it located the fallback international responsibility, where states fail owing to incapacity, unwillingness or complicity in the perpetration of atrocities, in the UN Security Council. By contrast 'humanitarian intervention' explicitly and fundamentally asserted the right to be able to act outside the UN framework, either individually or in coalitions of the willing. As such it necessarily confronts and rejects the norm of non-intervention. R2P sidesteps and finesses, without frontally challenging, the norm of non-intervention, by being able to claim that because sovereignty has not been exercised with due responsibility, its exercise is being temporarily suspended without the status of sovereign statehood being revoked.

Military intervention for human protection purposes takes away the rights flowing from the status of sovereignty, but does not in itself challenge the status as such. It does supplant the rights of the state to *exercise* protective functions if the state has proven incapable or unwilling to do so with respect to war crimes, genocidal killings, crimes against humanity and ethnic cleansing; or to suspend the right of the state to conduct itself free of external interference if such conduct is the cause of the above atrocities. The prevention of the exercise of sovereign rights under R2P intervention is always limited in time to a temporary period, until the capacity of the state itself to resume its protective functions can be restored and institutionalised. It may also be limited geographically to the particular portion of the target state's territory where the atrocities are occurring; or it may be limited with respect to a particular group that is the target of abuse. Taking everything together, therefore, ICISS did not pronounce the 'demise' of sovereignty nor abandon 'the discourse of state sovereignty'. On the contrary:

'R2P actually reinforces the importance of state sovereignty' and 'reaffirms the non-intervention principle as default'.[59] Indeed two ICISS Commissioners collaborated in a subsequent project on how states could be made stronger, more effective, but also legitimate with respect to international normative benchmarks.[60]

Procedural

War is itself a major humanitarian tragedy that can be justified only under the most compelling circumstances regarding the provocation, the likelihood of success – bearing in mind that goals are metamorphosed in the crucible of war once started – and the risk of unintended and perverse consequences. The burden of proof rests on the proponents of force, not on dissenters. Given the enormous normative presumption against the use of deadly force to settle international quarrels, who has the right to authorise such force? On what basis, for what purpose and subject to what safeguards and limitations?

There was considerable support during the ICISS consultations, from Asia and the Middle East to Africa and Latin America, for the principles, safeguards and issues of the threshold and lawful agency for authorisation of intervention that came to be very largely reflected in R2P. ICISS concluded there is no better nor more appropriate body than the UN Security Council to authorise military intervention for human protection purposes. The task therefore is not to find alternatives to the UN Security Council as a source of authority, but to make it work better, on a more reliable and predictable basis, than it has.[61] When NATO powers subverted UN Security Council R2P authorisation into a humanitarian intervention operation in Libya, China and Russia, with considerable international sympathy, reacted by vetoing subsequent draft resolutions on Syria. Far from being a failing, this is a strength of R2P compared to humanitarian intervention: an abuse can be checked by withholding consent in follow-up cases. And Brazil's effort to ensure responsibility to the UN Security Council on the part of those implementing R2P attracted broad international interest.

Under the 2005 Outcome Document, while R2P implementation falls within the UN Security Council jurisdiction and authority, the refinement and development of R2P as principle is the General Assembly's responsibility. Ed Luck, SG Ban Ki-moon's first Special Adviser on R2P, remarks that a potential 'Achilles Heel of the Summit agreement – the General Assembly's "continuing consideration"' was turned 'into a series of annual reports and Assembly dialogues on different aspects of R2P that have both sharpened doctrine and advanced acceptance of the norm'.[62]

Attempts to enforce authority can only be made by the legitimate agents of that authority. The chief contemporary institution for building, consolidating and using the authority of the international community is the United Nations. The only alternative doctrine – that any one state or coalition can decide when to intervene with force in the internal affairs of other countries – is unacceptable, for down that path lies total chaos. A committee of academic experts does not make government decisions, the administration does. Consider a hypothetical case. What if a future Republican administration, captured by fundamentalist Christians who believe abortion is murder of the most innocent and defenceless unborn human beings, decides to launch 'humanitarian interventions' to stop abortions in other countries?

International intervention in the US?

Turning the issue on its head, might there be a case for interventions within domestic US jurisdiction? Within the US criminal justice system, one of the most horrific yet mostly neglected *systematic* atrocities is prisoner rape. The number of prisoners sexually abused in US jails annually is estimated to be 90,000 – without counting those abused in immigration detention, half-way houses, rehabilitation centres and other community corrections facilities.[63] In addition to the physical injuries and lifelong psychological damage, prison rape spreads diseases, including HIV/AIDS, out into families and communities as 95 per cent of inmates are eventually released.

Henry Porter facetiously drew on statistics compiled by the US Congressional Research Service and www.icasualties.org to the effect that a total of 1,171,177 Americans had been killed in all wars since the 1775 War of Independence. According to the Center for Disease Control and Prevention and the Federal Bureau of Investigation (FBI), the number killed by firearms (including suicides) since the assassination of Robert F. Kennedy stood at 1,384,171. That is, a staggering 212,994 more Americans lost their lives from firearms in the last 45 years (1968–2013) than in all wars involving the US. To take another benchmark, since 9/11 fewer than 20 people had been killed in the US in terrorist incidents and 364,000 had been killed in that period by privately owned guns. With annual death toll from firearms at 32,000, Porter said: 'If this perennial slaughter doesn't qualify for intercession by the UN and all relevant NGOs, it is hard to know what does'.[64]

From the time he became president in 2009 until December 2015, President Barack Obama had to respond to mass shootings – 'the new normal'[65] – in Fort Hood, Texas (twice); Tucson, Arizona; Aurora, Colorado; Oak Creek, Wisconsin; Sandy Hook, Connecticut; Washington, DC; and San Bernardino, California. Obama's repeated calls to effect meaningful gun reform, made with evident mounting frustration and exasperation, were ignored by Congress. Time and again, the US gun lobby has proven itself too powerful to challenge. A former Deputy Prime Minister of Australia, Tim Fischer, noting that a person was 15 times more likely to be shot dead in the US than in Australia, said the Australian government travel advisory to people visiting the US should be updated to reflect this graphic reality.[66]

American and world consciousness has also been sensitised to the reality of the US being the police killings capital of the democratic world. But because, incredibly, the police do not maintain records of civilians killed by police forces across the country, no reliable statistics exist on the exact numbers. But newspapers have begun to compile databases. According to the *Guardian*, US police killed more people (59) in the first 24 days of 2015 than police in England and Wales killed in the past 24 years (55); and more every week until mid-year in 2015 than by German police in all of 2011 (6) and 2012 (7).[67] According to their web page, The Counted, the number killed by law enforcement officers in 2015 was 1,138.[68] The *Washington Post's* database counts those killed by police officers and its total by the same date (31 December 2015) was 984.[69] In October 2015, FBI director James Comey conceded it was 'ridiculous and embarrassing' that the *Guardian* and *Washington Post* kept better data than the US government.[70] In December the FBI announced plans to implement a new system that would match the two newspapers' and be more authoritative for being official,[71] but is not expected to be operational until 2017. The US qualifies as an R2P-type situation under lack of capacity or willingness to end the preventable mass slaughter of civilians. The one qualification it would not meet, of course, is the balance of consequences test.

R2P constrains all major power unilateralism in use of force

The response from those with little patience for claims of UN monopoly on the legitimate use of international force is that the UN system of collective security was fatally flawed from the start. Peace was preserved, and justice advanced by the operation of institutions and the pursuit of values by coalitions of the right minded, able and willing to defend the international order against all challenges. The right or duty of 'humanitarian intervention' falls within a long tradition of the special responsibilities that major powers have for underwriting the stability of the existing international order, as very well summarised in Bull's still-influential *Anarchical Society*.[72] The most consequential actor, both as an enabling and a blocking power, remains the US. It has a global train of interests and the technological and military capacity to be able to pursue perceived enemies to the farthest reaches of the planet; R2P merely complicates its decision-making calculus. Many have placed a particular opprobrium on Washington for its recalcitrance in mounting an effective global response to halt the 1994 Rwanda genocide. Unsurprisingly, its role in addressing the various humanitarian crises afflicting the world continues to attract scholarly scrutiny in relation to the R2P agenda. This is especially so with the continued usage of 'humanitarian intervention' with its inbuilt bias towards unilateral interventions.

Those willing to accept the possibility of interventions outside the UN framework fall into the humanitarian intervention camp. Among those who wish to retain the flexibility to launch military intervention without UN authorisation if necessary, there is a further division of opinion between those who would like a 'doctrine' approach and others who want merely an 'exception' approach[73] – a signposted emergency exit from the existing norms as embedded in the UN Charter. Yet another variation would be to distinguish a 'red light', where interventions can take place unless and until specifically prohibited by the UN Security Council, from the entrenched 'green light' approach where intervention may not proceed until and unless it has been duly authorised by the Council.

Developing countries fear that with the former, the norm of non-intervention could become a roadkill on the highway of international power politics.

ICISS recommended the five permanent members of the UN Security Council (P5) should agree not to apply their veto power in atrocity cases where their vital state interests are not involved. The idea has been revived recently by France but has not really led anywhere, the sound logic notwithstanding.[74] Action in selected cases outside a veto-paralysed UN Security Council framework is less defensible by those who refuse to accept any dilution of the veto power. ICISS further argued that if the UN Security Council rejects a proposal or fails to deal with it in a reasonable time, alternative options are consideration of the matter by the UN General Assembly in Emergency Special Session under the 'Uniting for Peace' procedure; and action within area of jurisdiction by regional or sub-regional organisations. On the last possibility, in a strong affirmation of the key argument of this chapter, Kuwali and Viljoen note that under the Constitutive Act of the African Union, 'Article 4(h) intervention is not "humanitarian intervention," but is treaty-based, multilateral action by the AU in reaction to mass atrocities in a Member State'.[75]

For supporters of humanitarian intervention, UN inaction is not the end of the matter. If the crisis remains real, and urgent outside military action is still required to bring atrocities to an end, then unilateral action is legally permissible and may indeed be morally the responsible course of action.[76] This ignores the fundamental objection that R2P was formulated in response to the forceful opposition by the world's majority to humanitarian intervention asserted as a right by NATO. Moreover, precisely because R2P would circumscribe discretionary behaviour, the John Bolton-led US delegation at the negotiations successfully pressured the summit to drop language that would have called on the P5 to refrain from using the veto in cases of the four atrocity crimes.[77] In other words, Washington had used its considerable leverage in the UN system to abort efforts to reduce the likelihood of UN inaction because of the veto, but some US scholars were arguing that the resulting agreement strengthened the legal justification for unilateral action because of UN paralysis. Bellamy got this right instead: 'the majority of states shared the view that if the responsibility to protect was to *constrain* Western interventionism – a core component of the argument in favor of the concept – then the absolute primacy of the Security Council had to be reaffirmed'[78] – as it was.

R2P, like any law, norm, rule or code of behaviour, has both an enabling (licence) and a constraining (leash) function. Major powers were bound to resist it on both counts. Humanitarian intervention acts as an enabling without the restraining element norm. During the 2005 World Summit, Bolton argued, correctly, that the responsibility of host states to protect their populations was a legal obligation, whereas the UN Security Council was not legally obligated to protect endangered civilians.[79] Washington rejected the idea of criteria for the use of force, on the grounds that it could not offer pre-commitments to engage its military forces where it had no national interests; nor would it bind itself to criteria that would constrain its right to decide when and where to use force.[80]

All regional and global major powers would resist both the prescriptive elements of R2P, increasing the pressure on them to take protective measures in locations and contexts where they did not believe vital interests to be engaged; and the constraining elements of R2P, enfettering their discretionary latitude to engage with actors and issues in their regions or the world with policy tools of their choice, including coercive military force. Instead they would be more comfortable with the facilitative, enabling and discretionary attributes of unilateral humanitarian intervention. Russia has tried to corrupt R2P by invoking it to try and justify military interventions to protect ethnic Russians in its near abroad in South Ossetia and eastern Ukraine.[81] If the US can be the arbiter of the lawfulness and legitimacy of its own interventions in the Middle East, why not Russia in South Ossetia and eastern Ukraine? Or do Western analysts seriously expect the 'international community' to concede enlightened benevolence to US and NATO actions while denying it to Russian and Chinese? They are more likely to support calls for the US to collaborate with Russia and China within the framework of the UN Security Council to end the chaos along the periphery. India is surrounded by a string of fragile states with the potential for state failure and has a history of both cooperative and coercive diplomacy in its immediate neighbourhood. R2P was unlikely to be viewed as a facilitative and enabling normative tool expanding its freedom of action across South Asia, such as the commando raid into Myanmar in June 2015 to neutralise an alleged insurgent camp across the border.[82]

Operational

Two roundtables were organised for the humanitarian community in Geneva – the global capital of the humanitarian community – on 30–31 January 2001, one with the inter-governmental organisations and the second with NGOs. The context of the dialogue between them and the Commission was the recognition that when mass atrocities begin during messy armed conflicts, humanitarian agencies and actors are often the only neutral or international presence on the ground. Both groups were unanimous and forceful in their representation that 'humanitarian intervention' was a cruel misnomer, that *their* actions constituted humanitarian interventions and the politicised term was a euphemism for military intervention deliberately designed to conceal its ugliness behind the vocabulary of humanitarianism.

Traditional warfare is the use of force by rival armies of enemy states fighting over a clash of interests: us against them. Collective security rests on the use of force by the international community of states to defeat or punish an aggressor: all against one. Traditional peacekeeping involves the insertion of neutral and lightly armed third-party soldiers as a physical buffer between enemy combatants who have agreed to a ceasefire: us between them. R2P differs from all these in that it refers to the use of military force by outsiders for the protection of victims of mass atrocities. Mats Berdal has recorded how the requirement for civilian protection in a peacekeeping operational context was foreshadowed by

Hammarskjöld during the Congo crisis in the 1960s. He informed Katanga's secessionist leader, Moïse Tshombe, in 1960 that it was 'the duty of the United Nations Force to protect the civilian populations and [that] this duty is … in no way restricted by the rule of non-intervention applied by the Force in relation to domestic conflicts'.[83]

The protection of victims from mass atrocities requires different guidelines and rules of engagement as well as different relationships to civil authorities and humanitarian actors that need to be identified, articulated and incorporated into officer training manuals and courses.[84] Operationalising R2P with respect to the protection agenda in the field will mean adopting a bottom-up approach that brings together the humanitarian actors on the ground in conflict zones in a distinct protection cluster to assess needs and priorities for each vulnerable group and identifying, in advance, the custom-tailored responses for prevention and rebuilding.[85]

The Commission's deliberations and views on military doctrine[86] were strongly influenced by General Klaus Naumann, former Chief of Staff of Germany's armed forces and Chair of NATO's North Atlantic Military Committee that oversaw the Kosovo intervention in 1999. In war, the neutralisation of an opponent's military or industrial capabilities is often the instrument to force surrender. By contrast, the basic objective of protective military interventions is always to achieve quick success with as little cost as possible in civilian lives, and inflicting as little damage as possible so as to enhance recovery prospects in the post-conflict phase. The rules of engagement of an R2P preventive operation will primarily be of a defensive nature and only reluctantly allow forcing an opponent to comply. If prevention fails and the force is transformed into an intervention tool, the rules of engagement will be more flexible than for traditional peacekeeping missions, but more restrictive than for combat operations in war.

Nor can force protection override protection of civilians as the primary criterion for determining the type of force employed. NATO's exclusive reliance on bombing strikes in Kosovo was not the result of belief in the superior efficacy of air power, but rather of the extreme reluctance to risk casualties to the NATO troops from any 'boots on the ground'. After the intervention operation, the main mission of R2P military forces is transformed to provide the safe environment necessary for the restoration of good governance and the rule of law. This requires a transition of responsibility from the military authorities to the civilian authorities as soon as possible after the cessation of hostilities. And because the responsibility to rebuild is an integral component of R2P, the intervening countries must be prepared to remain engaged during the post-intervention phase as long as necessary to achieve stability.

While R2P might differ from traditional UN peacekeeping missions, it owes an intellectual and political debt to the Brahimi Panel on UN Peace Operations that submitted its report in 2000, just months before ICISS was brought together. Indeed, two ICISS members – Naumann and Sommaruga – had also been members of the Brahimi Panel. In highlighting the uneven impact of the neutrality of traditional peacekeeping on perpetrators and victims, the Brahimi Report was an important milestone on the road to R2P.[87] Given this shared intellectual ancestry, it is not surprising that the subsequent evolution of peacekeeping doctrine and practice has closely tracked the development of R2P policy.[88] Both were outgrowths of the inadequacies of traditional peacekeeping based on the three cardinal principles of consent, impartiality and non-use of force in addressing the deliberate resort to violence and atrocities by some conflict parties in the post-Cold War environment of fluid and ambiguous conflict theatres, constant violence and armed challenges to international authority, diffuse and shifting power equations, and fickle and tenuous consent. ICISS itself explicitly acknowledged the failures of UN peacekeeping in Rwanda and the Balkans as the spur to its creation and to its thinking.[89] In the decade and a half since the Brahimi Report, just as reference to R2P has become a staple of many UN Security Council resolutions and presidential statements, civilian protection too has become an integral component of many UN peacekeeping mandates, now issued as often as not under the coercive Chapter VII of the UN Charter.[90]

All peacekeeping missions operationalise R2P Pillar One in underwriting the security and assisting with local capacity development. If the UN assumes trusteeship type administration as in Kosovo and East Timor, it takes over Pillar One responsibility. And when it authorises peace enforcement, it has transitioned into Pillar Three operations. This reached its zenith with Resolution 2098 (28 March 2013) authorising the creation of a ‘Force Intervention Brigade’ in the Democratic Republic of Congo (DRC). The trigger was the embarrassment caused to the UN when despite 17,000 peacekeepers in the DRC, rebels occupied Goma, the country’s second largest city, in December 2012. The Intervention Brigade was tasked ‘with the responsibility of neutralising armed groups’ and ‘contributing to reducing the threat posed by armed groups to state authority and civilian security’ in eastern DRC. The 3,000-strong brigade, an integral component of the United Nations Organization Stabilization Mission in the Democratic Republic of the Congo (MONUSCO) and made up of units from South Africa, Malawi and Tanzania, was mandated to undertake ‘targeted offensive operations’ in support of the DRC authorities. It was involved in several military operations in 2013 and 2014. Resolution 2277 (30 March 2016) extended its mandate until 31 March 2017.[91]

Conclusion

This chapter has explained why the language of humanitarian intervention is an affront to the political sensitivity of many countries whose voice is unfortunately silenced in the global discourse dominated by Western scholarship. R2P is an improvement on humanitarian intervention on almost all dimensions that the international community finds objectionable. Consequently, military intervention under R2P has much better prospects of a convergence of legality and legitimacy in the use of force than humanitarian intervention. This does not mean, however, that R2P resolves all the dilemmas of how outsiders can provide timely, decisive and effective assistance to all groups in need of protection. R2P may be deep, but it remains so narrow that many areas beyond the four atrocity crimes fall outside its scope.[92] It remains subject to UN Security Council veto and paralysis. Certainly, no group at risk of atrocities can be confident of outside assistance in timely fashion.[93] To many people and countries, 'humanitarian intervention' will remain attractive as an alternative moral framework for trying to respond effectively and in time. But this can only be at the cost of immediate global controversy and long-term damage to the principle of an international order governed by the rule of law. Domestically, a firmly established rule of law offers more reliable protection for the poor, weak and marginalised members of society than either the discretionary beneficence of an enlightened despot or justice meted out by groups of self-appointed vigilantes. Similarly, in international affairs too, a rules-based R2P is a better normative protection instrument than the unilateralism of humanitarian intervention. But, because of the inescapable problems of humanitarian intervention and in the absence of reliable, predictable and consistent provision of international protection to victims of atrocities within borders, the need remains for an 'R2P Plus' protection normative architecture.

The chapter began with a comment from Commissioner Sommaruga at the final ICISS meeting in August 2001. In a fitting symmetry, I conclude with an apposite African folktale from co-chair Mohamed Sahnoun at the inaugural meeting in Ottawa in November 2000. A man had grown up in a desert-like inland environment and never seen a fish. One day as he was walking along, he spied a fish swimming in a pond. 'This little animal has fallen into the water and will surely drown. I had better rescue it'. So, he caught it, plucked it out of the water, put it in his pocket and kept walking. A little later he thought to check on the rescued fish, only to discover it had died in the meantime. 'Alas, I did not rescue it in time', he concluded. Humanitarian intervention can be a lot like that, Sahnoun cautioned us: well-intentioned but completely oblivious to differences in context and capable of inflicting fatal harm.

Notes

* Originally published in Ramesh Thakur, *The United Nations, Peace and Security: From Collective Security to the Responsibility to Protect*, 2nd ed. (Cambridge: Cambridge University Press, 2017), 272–300. Reprinted by permission of Cambridge University Press.

1 UN General Assembly, sixtieth session, *World Summit Outcome, 2005*, resolution adopted by the General Assembly, 24 October 2005, paragraphs 138–39.

2 Gareth Evans and Mohamed Sahnoun, 'The Responsibility to Protect', *Foreign Affairs* 81:6 (2002), 99–110.

3 Gareth Evans, *The Responsibility to Protect: Ending Mass Atrocity Crimes Once and For All* (Washington, DC: Brookings Institution Press, 2008), 38–42; Ramesh Thakur, *The United Nations, Peace and Security: From Collective Security to The Responsibility to Protect* (Cambridge: Cambridge University Press, 2006), 250–51.

4 Thomas G. Weiss, *Humanitarian Intervention: Ideas in Action* (Cambridge: Polity, 2011), 111.

5 Roland Paris, 'Responsibility to Protect: The Debate Continues', *International Peacekeeping* 22:2 (2015), 144, 149 n4.

6 This is based on a public lecture delivered at Kings College London on 12 November 2015: Ramesh Thakur, 'R2P: The Old Wine of Humanitarian Intervention in a New Bottle?' and to the Canadian Centre for R2P, Munk School, University of Toronto, 21 March 2016.

7 Aidan Hehir, *Humanitarian Intervention: An Introduction*, 2nd ed. (Basingstoke: Palgrave Macmillan, 2013); James Pattison, *Humanitarian Intervention and the Responsibility to Protect: Who Should Intervene?* (Oxford: Oxford University Press, 2012); Norrie MacQueen, *Humanitarian Intervention and the United Nations* (Edinburgh: Edinburgh University Press, 2011); Don E. Scheid, ed., *The Ethics of Armed Humanitarian Intervention* (Cambridge: Cambridge University Press, 2014); Derek Averre and Lance Davies, 'Russia, Humanitarian Intervention and the Responsibility to Protect: The Case of Syria', *International Affairs* 91:2 (2015), 813–34; Ian Hurd, 'Is Humanitarian Intervention Legal? The Rule of Law in an Incoherent World', *Ethics & International Affairs* 25:3 (2011), 293–313; and Jon Western and Joshua S. Goldstein, 'Humanitarian Intervention Comes of Age: Lessons from Somalia to Libya', *Foreign Affairs* 90:6 (2011), 48–59.

8 For a guide to the burgeoning literature, see Ramesh Thakur, 'The Responsibility to Protect at 15', *International Affairs* 92:2 (2016), 415–34.

9 The text of the speech is reprinted in Kofi Annan, *We the Peoples: A UN for the 21st Century*, edited by Edward Mortimer (London: Paradigm Publishers, 2014), 196–97.

10 Annan, *We the Peoples: A UN for the 21st Century*, 204–06.

11 Kofi Annan, *Report of the Secretary-General on the Work of the Organisation* (New York: United Nations, document A/54/1, 31 August 1999), 1–7.

12 United Nations Press Release, 'Secretary-General presents his report to General Assembly', (New York: United Nations, document SG/SM/7136, GA/9596, 20 September 1999).

13 Quoted in the ICISS supplementary volume, Thomas G. Weiss, Don Hubert, *et al.*, *The Responsibility to Protect: Research, Bibliography, Background* (Ottawa: International Development Research Centre, 2001), 162.

14 Of the 12 Commissioners, I was the sole serving UN official.

15 International Commission on Intervention and State Sovereignty, *The Responsibility to Protect* (Ottawa: International Development Research Centre, 2001).

16 Inis L. Claude, 'The Evolution of Concepts of Global Governance and the State in the Twentieth Century', paper delivered at the annual conference of the Academic Council on the United Nations System (ACUNS), Oslo, 16–18 June 2000. See also Michael Byers and Simon Chesterman, 'Changing the Rules about Rules? Unilateral Humanitarian Intervention and the Future of International Law', in J.L. Holzgrefe and Robert O. Keohane, eds., *Humanitarian Intervention: Ethical, Legal and Political Dilemmas* (Cambridge: Cambridge University Press, 2003), 177–203; and Thomas M. Franck, 'Interpretation and Change in the Law of Humanitarian Intervention', in Holzgrefe and Keohane, eds., 204–31.

17 Having been back in academia for a decade, I sometimes shudder to think: What if the 2001 ICISS report had been peer reviewed – what would its final shape have been?

18 Weiss, *Humanitarian Intervention*; Ramesh Thakur, 'Humanitarian Intervention', in Thomas G. Weiss and Sam Daws, eds., *The Oxford Handbook on the United Nations* (Oxford: Oxford University Press, 2007), 387–403.

19 Ramesh Thakur, 'Non-Intervention: A Case Study', *Political Science* 42:1 (1990), 26–61, reprinted in Ramesh Thakur, *The Responsibility to Protect: Norms, Laws and the Use of Force in International Politics* (London: Routledge, 2011), Chapter 2.

20 ICISS, *Responsibility to Protect*, paragraph 1.39.

21 Weiss, Hubert, *et al.*, *Responsibility to Protect: Research, Bibliography, Background*, 47–126.

22 Brendan Simms and D.B.J. Trim, *Humanitarian Intervention: A History* (Cambridge: Cambridge University Press, 2011); Ellery Stowell, *Intervention in International Law* (Washington, DC: J. Byrne, 1921); Natalino Ronzitti, *Rescuing Nationals Abroad Through Military Coercion and Intervention on Grounds of Humanity* (Leiden: Brill, 1985); Davide Rodogno, *Against Massacre: Humanitarian Intervention in the Ottoman Empire, 1815–1914* (Princeton: Princeton University Press, 2012).

23 Luke Glanville, 'The Myth of "Traditional Sovereignty"', *International Studies Quarterly* 57:1 (2013), 79–90. See also: Francis K. Abiew, *The Evolution of the Doctrine and Practice of Humanitarian Intervention* (The Hague: Kluwer Law International, 1999); Gary J. Bass, *Freedom's Battle: The Origins of Humanitarian Intervention* (New York: Vintage Books, 2009); Simon Chesterman, *Just War or Just Peace? Humanitarian Intervention and International Law* (Oxford: Oxford University Press, 2001); Alexis Heraclides, 'Humanitarian Intervention Yesterday and Today: A History', *European Journal of International Studies* 2:1 (2015), 15–37; Luke Glanville, *Sovereignty and the Responsibility to Protect: A New History* (Chicago: University of Chicago Press, 2014); and Nicholas Wheeler, *Saving Strangers: Humanitarian Intervention in International Society* (Oxford: Oxford University Press, 2000).

24 Thakur, *The United Nations, Peace and Security*, 267; emphasis in original.

25 Partha Chatterjee, 'Empire after Globalisation', *Economic and Political Weekly* 39:37 (11 September 2004), 4158–63.

26 Louis Bourquien, in an article published in 1923 on the failed effort by Napoleon Bonaparte to take India from the British towards the end of the eighteenth century; quoted in William Dalrymple, *The White Mughals: Love and Betrayal in Eighteenth Century India* (New Delhi: Viking, 2002), 147–48.

27 'All Members shall refrain in their international relations from the threat or use of force against the territorial integrity or political independence of any state, or in any other manner inconsistent with the Purposes of the United Nations'.

28 Spencer Zifcak, *United Nations Reform: Heading North or South?* (London: Routledge, 2009), 107–08.

29 Jeane J. Kirkpatrick and Allan Gerson, 'The Reagan Doctrine, Human Rights, and International Law', in Louis Henkin, Stanley Hoffmann, Jeane J. Kirkpatrick, Allan Gerson, William D. Rogers and David J. Scheffer, *Right v. Might: International Law and the Use of Force* (New York: Council on Foreign Relations, 1989), 21.

30 Louis Henkin, 'Use of Force: Law and U.S. Policy', in Henkin, *Right v. Might*, 47, 56.

31 British Foreign Office, 'Policy Document No. 148', *British Year Book of International Law* 57 (1986), 614.

32 ICISS, *Responsibility to Protect*, paragraph 1.2.

33 Richard Falk, 'Reflections on the Kosovo War', *Global Dialogue* 1:2 (1999), 93–94.

34 George Bogdanich, 'An eye for an eye?' *Chicago Tribune*, 11 July 2004.

35 Statement by the Permanent Representative of Nigeria, H.E. Ibrahim Gambari, to the United Nations Security Council, 30 September 1999.

36 Alex J. Bellamy, 'Whither the Responsibility to Protect? Humanitarian Intervention and the 2005 World Summit', *Ethics & International Affairs* 20:2 (2006), 147.

37 Michael Ignatieff, 'Why are we in Iraq? (And Liberia? And Afghanistan?)', *New York Times Magazine*, 7 September 2003.

38 Gareth Evans, 'Humanity Did Not Justify This War', *Financial Times*, 15 May 2003; Ramesh Thakur, 'Chrétien Was Right: It's Time to Redefine a "Just War"', *Globe and Mail* (Toronto), 22 July 2003.

39 See the extract from a speech by the Tanzanian president in Zifcak, *United Nations Reform*, 114.

40 Zifcak, *United Nations Reform*, 115–16.

41 Zifcak, *United Nations Reform*, 119–20.

42 Quoted in Zifcak, *United Nations Reform*, 122.
43 ICISS, *Responsibility to Protect*, paragraphs 2.4–2.6 and 2.28–2.29.
44 See the entry under 'Humanitarian bombing' in Wikipedia, http://en.wikipedia.org/wiki/Humanitarian_bombing.
45 Weiss, *Humanitarian Intervention*, 112.
46 Evans, *Responsibility to Protect*, 40; emphasis in original.
47 ICISS, *Responsibility to Protect*, paragraph 1.40.
48 ICISS, *Responsibility to Protect*, paragraph 2.15.
49 Zifcak, *United Nations Reform*, 111; emphasis added.
50 Ramesh Thakur, 'Intervention, Sovereignty and the Responsibility to Protect: Experiences from the ICISS', *Security Dialogue* 33:3 (2002), 227.
51 Hu Yao, 'U.S. Should Bear Blame for European Refugee, Humanitarian Crisis', *Xinhua*, 5 September 2015; http://news.xinhuanet.com/english/2015-09/05/c_134591925.htm.
52 Charles Sampford and Ramesh Thakur, 'From the Right to Persecute to the Responsibility to Protect: Feuerbachian Inversions of Rights and Responsibilities in State–Citizen Relations', in Ramesh Thakur and William Maley, eds., *Theorising the Responsibility to Protect* (Cambridge: Cambridge University Press, 2015), 38–58.
53 Anne Orford, *International Authority and the Responsibility to Protect* (Cambridge: Cambridge University Press, 2011).
54 Robert H. Jackson, *Quasi-States: Sovereignty, International Relations, and the Third World* (Cambridge: Cambridge University Press, 1990).
55 Orford, *International Authority and the Responsibility to Protect*, 1.
56 ICISS, *Responsibility to Protect*, paragraph 2.28.
57 ICISS, *Responsibility to Protect*, paragraph 2.29.
58 Weiss, *Humanitarian Intervention*, 103.
59 Cristina Gabriela Badescu, *Humanitarian Intervention and the Responsibility to Protect: Security and Human Rights* (New York: Routledge, 2011), 41.
60 Simon Chesterman, Michael Ignatieff and Ramesh Thakur, eds., *Making States Work: State Failure and the Crisis of Governance* (Tokyo: United Nations University Press, 2005).
61 ICISS, *Responsibility to Protect*, 47–55.
62 Edward C. Luck, 'R2P at Ten: A New Mindset for a New Era?' *Global Governance* 23:4 (2015), 500.
63 David Kaiser and Lovisa Stannow, 'The Rape of American Prisoners', *New York Review of Books*, 11 March 2010, 16–19. See also Allen J. Beck and Paige M. Harrison, *Sexual Victimization in Local Jails Reported by Inmates* (Washington, DC: Bureau of Justice Statistics, 2008); and *National Prison Rape Elimination Commission Report* (Washington, DC: June 2009), www.ncjrs.gov/pdffiles1/226680.pdf.
64 Henry Porter, 'American Gun Use is Out of Control. Shouldn't the World Intervene?', *The Observer* (London), 22 September 2013.
65 Alex Abramovich, 'The New Normal', *London Review of Books*, 29 November 2015, www.lrb.co.uk/blog/2015/11/29/alex-abramovich/the-new-normal-us-edition/?utm_source=LRB+online+email&utm_medium=email&utm_campaign=20151103+online&utm_content=ukrw_nonsubs&hq_e=el&hq_m=4050997&hq_l=12&hq_v=0c8007cc35.
66 Fergus Hunter, '"Sick and Tired": Tim Fischer Calls for Better Australian Travel Warnings after US Shooting', *Canberra Times*, 3 December 2015.
67 Jamiles Lartey, 'By the Numbers: US Police Kill More in Days Than Other Countries do in Years', *Guardian*, 9 June 2015.
68 *Guardian*, 'The Counted: People Killed by Police in the US', www.theguardian.com/us-news/ng-interactive/2015/jun/01/the-counted-police-killings-us-database#.
69 *Washington Post*, 'Police Shootings Database', www.washingtonpost.com/graphics/national/police-shootings/.

70 Quoted in Tom McCarthy, Jon Swaine and Oliver Laughland, 'FBI to Launch New System to Count People Killed by Police Officers', *Guardian*, 10 December 2015.
71 McCarthy, Swaine and Laughland, 'FBI to Launch New System to Count People Killed by Police Officers'.
72 Hedley Bull, *Anarchical Society: A Study of Order in World Politics* (London: Macmillan, 1977), 200–29.
73 See especially Chesterman, *Just War or Just Peace?*, 226–32, and Wheeler, *Saving Strangers*, 33–51.
74 Gareth Evans, 'Limiting the Security Council's Veto Power', *Japan Times*, 6 February 2015.
75 Dan Kuwali and Frans Viljoen, 'Conclusion', in Kuwali and Viljoen, eds., *Africa and the Responsibility to Protect: Article 4(h) of the African Union Constitutive Act* (Abingdon: Routledge, 2014), 341.
76 See especially Alicia L. Bannon, 'The Responsibility to Protect: The U.N. World Summit and the Question of Unilateralism', *The Yale Law Journal* 115:5 (2006), 1157–65.
77 Colum Lynch, 'U.S. Wants Changes in U.N. Agreement', *Washington Post*, 25 August 2005.
78 Bellamy, 'Whither the Responsibility to Protect?', 164; emphasis in original.
79 Bellamy, 'Whither the Responsibility to Protect?'.
80 Jennifer M. Welsh, 'Conclusion: Humanitarian Intervention after 11 September', in Jennifer M. Welsh, ed., *Humanitarian Intervention and International Relations* (Oxford: Oxford University Press, 2004), 180. See also Steven Groves, 'The U.S. Should Reject the U.N. "Responsibility to Protect" Doctrine', *Backgrounder* No. 2130 (Washington, DC: Heritage Foundation, 2008), www.heritage.org/research/reports/2008/05/the-us-should-reject-the-un-responsibility-to-protect-doctrine.
81 For a discussion of R2P in the context of the tension between cartographic lines denoting statehood and bloodlines of ethnically-defined nationhood, see Walter Kemp, Vesselin Popovski and Ramesh Thakur, eds., *Blood and Borders: The Responsibility to Protect and the Problem of the Kin-State* (Tokyo: United Nations University Press, 2011).
82 Sachin Parashar, 'India's Sensational Cross-border Raid', *Times of India*, 9 June 2015.
83 Mats Berdal, 'United Nations Peacekeeping and the Responsibility to Protect', in Thakur and Maley, eds., *Theorising the Responsibility to Protect*, 227.
84 Victoria K. Holt and Tobias C. Berkman, *The Impossible Mandate? Military Preparedness, the Responsibility to Protect and Modern Peace Operations* (Washington, DC: Stimson Center, 2006).
85 Jaya Murthy, 'Mandating the Protection Cluster with the Responsibility to Protect: A Policy Recommendation Based on the Protection Cluster's Implementation in South Kivu, DRC', *Journal of Humanitarian Assistance* (5 October 2008); https://sites.tufts.edu/jha/archives/55.
86 ICISS, *Responsibility to Protect*, Chapter 7.
87 *Report of the Panel on United Nations Peace Operations* (New York: United Nations, document A/55/305-S/2000/809, 21 August 2000).
88 Susan C. Breau, 'The Impact of the Responsibility to Protect on Peacekeeping', *Journal of Conflict & Security Law* 11:3 (2006), 429–64; Hitoshi Nasu, 'Operationalizing the Responsibility to Protect in the Context of Civilian Protection by UN Peacekeepers', *International Peacekeeping* 18:4 (2011), 364–78; Lisa Hultman, 'UN Peace Operations and Protection of Civilians: Cheap Talk or Norm Implementation?', *Journal of Peace Research* 50:1 (2013), 59–73; and Thomas G. Weiss, 'Peace Operations and Humanitarian Interventions' in Joachim Koops, Norrie MacQueen, Thierry Tardy and Paul D. Williams, eds., *The Oxford Handbook of United Nations Peacekeeping Operations* (Oxford: Oxford University Press, 2015), 78–92.

89 ICISS, *Responsibility to Protect*: vii, 1.
90 See Frédéric Mégret, 'From Peacekeeping to R2P: The Protection of Civilians as the UN's New Raison d'Être?' unpublished paper (September 2012); https://papers.ssrn.com/sol3/papers.cfm?abstract_id=2154968.
91 This description of the Force Intervention Brigade is taken from the UN's website: www.un.org/en/peacekeeping/missions/monusco/background.shtml.
92 But for a robust defence of R2P against many misconceived criticisms, see Alex. J. Bellamy, *Responsibility to Protect: A Defense* (Oxford: Oxford University Press, 2014).
93 Ramesh Thakur, 'Protection Gaps for Civilian Victims of Political Violence', *South African Journal of International Affairs* 20:3 (December 2013), 321–38.

Part II

Implementation controversies

The Sanskrit word and Hindu concept of 'karma' has been gradually mainstreamed in cosmopolitan Western consciousness in its English translation as destiny. Yet in the mass understanding in India as much as in the West, the popular definition inverts the correct meaning. It does not mean that an otherworldly and unknowable 'fate' is going to determine one's destiny irrespective of one's actions. Rather, one cannot escape the consequences of one's actions, cause and effect are immutably linked, and this is why we should practice good and abjure bad behaviour. The code of conduct for good behaviour in every relevant social context – duty – is summed up in the matching concept of 'dharma'.

This has a twofold relevance to the still simmering undercurrents of controversy over R2P. First, tyrants, dictators and other would-be perpetrators of mass atrocities are learning that the consequences of their brutal behaviour might after all perhaps have to be paid in this life; they need not wait for the afterlife. And those who would implement R2P as an international norm when its domestic analogue has been violated, are learning that the manner of implementation in one crisis has consequences for the prospects for securing international authorisation to implement it in a different crisis: they too cannot escape the consequences of their choices and actions.

The human rights norm has grown so powerful that those who would violate it in the privacy of their torture chambers are compelled to swear fealty to it in global public discourse. The resilience of the norm has contributed to changes in the nature of state sovereignty. But there is a dramatic discrepancy between commitments on paper and actual improvements in human rights conditions. The human rights norm and international humanitarian law are ever more firmly established, yet actual protections have come under growing stress in state practice.[1]

The debate over when and how force may be used to defend human rights and protect against humanitarian atrocities lies at the intersection of law, norms and politics. The United Nations lies at the centre of the international law enforcement system and its unique legitimacy, based on universal membership, also places it at the core of the global normative order. It is also the forum of choice for debating and deciding on collective action requiring the use of military force across borders and inside sovereign jurisdictions. At the 2005 summit of world leaders, R2P repaired a broken UN paradigm and created a new policy template that repositions the global consensus between institutionalised indifference to mass killings of the 'Other' and unilateral interventions based on the 'Self's' arrogance of power.

As noted in previous chapters, in the pre-R2P era until the end of the last century, the two cases that most vividly highlighted the flaws of the then-existing normative architecture were Rwanda in 1994, where there was no international action to avert or stop the genocide, and Kosovo, where intervention by NATO to end alleged Serbian atrocities lacked UN authorisation. In the post-R2P era in this century, the two cases that best highlight its mobilising power but also underline its problems are the UN-authorised and NATO-led R2P intervention in Libya in 2011, and Syria since 2011 where large numbers of civilian deaths, massive population displacements and the use of chemical weapons have failed to elicit robust and effective action by the United Nations. The Syrian example will be taken up in Part III under civilian protection gaps that remain despite the adoption of R2P as a new normative instrument. For now, a preliminary comment worth noting is that R2P implementation is an ineluctably contested normative terrain because it lies at the intersection of tensions between national and human security, state and human rights, and peace and justice: all of which are themselves essentially contested concepts.

Libya

We begin with a discussion of Libya in the next chapter. What the example shows above all is that success in an R2P intervention is no more self-guaranteeing than in any other type of external intervention. Since the Treaty of Westphalia, sovereignty has been backed by the norm of non-intervention. By contrast, R2P strikes a balance between unauthorised unilateral interventions and institutionalised indifference. With a rapidly deteriorating humanitarian situation in Libya in early 2011, the UN Security Council authorised the use of force to protect an imminent slaughter of civilians but, importantly, it also called for a ceasefire with the mediation of the African Union and prohibited taking sides in the internal civil war, intervening with ground troops, or effecting forcible regime change (Resolution 1973, 17 March 2011). Crucially, five Council members abstained: China, Russia, Brazil, Germany and India, reportedly at the persuasion of China.[2] According to Hardeep Singh Puri, India's senior delegate on the Security Council at the time, South Africa wavered until the last moment between abstaining and voting in support of the resolution while Nigeria's delegate had been issued standing instructions by her government to side with South Africa regardless of how the latter voted. That is, if South Africa had abstained and Nigeria followed suit, Resolution 1973 would not have had the requisite nine affirmative votes needed for it to be adopted.[3]

The R2P consensus on Libya was damaged by the way in which NATO was seen by those who mandated the operation to have exploited the enabling licence function of Resolution 1973 while ignoring the equally important restrictive leash function. The record of NATO actions in Libya mark a triumph for R2P but also raise questions about how to prevent the abuse of UN authority to use international force for purposes beyond human protection. As Secretary-General Ban Ki-moon put it, Libya in 2011 'demonstrated that human protection is a defining purpose of the United Nations'. But 'the execution of our collective responsibilities was not always perfect' and some innocent lives were lost in the name of R2P.[4]

Puri is clear in his mind that the 'passage of Resolution 1973 would have been jeopardised if regime change had been specifically mentioned in the text' – yet no sooner had the resolution been adopted than regime change became the all-consuming goal.[5] As well, while killing Libyan leader Muammar Gaddafi helped NATO to win the war, it may have cost them the peace.[6] One important result of the gaps in understanding, communication and accountability was a split in the international response to the worsening crisis in Syria. China and Russia, still smarting from the over-interpretation of Resolution 1973 in Libya, remained defiantly opposed to any resolution that could set in train a sequence of events leading to a 1973-type authorisation for outside military operations in Syria and have vetoed numerous draft Security Council resolutions since 2011. As with any great power, their positions reflect a mix of principled, commercial and geopolitical calculations.

Thus, Libya marks an important milestone on the journey to tame atrocities on their own people by tyrants, initially demonstrating the mobilising power of R2P as a new norm but then showing both how easy it was for NATO powers to abuse UN authorisation and the resulting backlash from key players. Disrespecting the restrictions of Resolution 1973 came at considerable political cost. In other words, almost inevitably, the first UN-authorised military intervention under R2P Pillar Three showed flaws and imperfections in the machinery of implementation that will need to be addressed. In something of a historical irony, the illegal-but-legitimate conclusion by the Western bloc regarding the 1999 NATO intervention in Kosovo discredited the pre-R2P normative architecture. The NATO actions in Libya in 2011 were deemed by most developing countries to have been legal (because UN-authorised) but illegitimate in implementation for exceeding the mandate. This discredited R2P implementation.

Although this is not the place to explore the subject, it is worth recording that the much broader gap between the Charter-based legal authority of the Security Council and its perceived illegitimacy for performance and representational flaws can damage future R2P operations also. With respect to nuclear weapons, for example, issues of legality and legitimacy have come to the fore much more prominently with the adoption of the UN Nuclear-Weapon Prohibition Treaty in July 2017.[7] And yet, urgent as the requirement for major Security Council reform is, it seems as elusive as ever, with one analyst comparing it to Samuel Beckett's *Waiting for Godot*.[8] Meanwhile inordinate attention is paid to the Secretary-General's efforts to rearrange the deckchairs on the Titanic through essentially trivial reforms of the UN Secretariat by comparison.

Structural flaws as the explanation for R2P failures in Libya

The post-Libya intervention refusal by Russia and China to cooperate in robust resolutions against President Bashar al-Assad's brutal crackdown in Syria led to a widespread perception that inaction on Syria proved the hollowness of R2P as an inherent flaw. In a major critique, Roland Paris argued that the core explanation for the failures in Libya were structural weaknesses in the R2P normative architecture.[9] Chapter 8 explains how this conflates the structural dilemmas inherent in *any* contemporary use of international force into a central dilemma of R2P. Other critics insist that the intervention did not satisfy the just cause and last resort criteria,[10] which is far more difficult to sustain on the evidence available in real time.

The real question is: does R2P make the structural dilemmas more or less acute? In no case does R2P worsen the dilemma; in almost every case it makes the dilemma less acute. In a brutal civil war like the one that has raged in Syria since 2011, the state cannot be prohibited from employing force to fend off armed challenges to its authority. Outsiders confront the moral hazard of encouraging opposition and secessionist groups to take up arms against governments elsewhere in the world. Yet the moral hazard argument can itself be exaggerated. It is intuitive to believe that some groups may be encouraged by examples elsewhere to provoke government forces to commit atrocities that would otherwise not occur, as a means of drawing in outside powers on their behalf. It is equally intuitive to believe that governments would be more reluctant to initiate atrocities knowing there was greater chance of international intervention to stop them. The net impact on the incidence of atrocities therefore could just as easily be negative or neutral as positive.[11]

Resuscitating the responsibility to rebuild

The prevention and reaction components of the original ICISS formulation were endorsed and reaffirmed by the UN in 2005, but the third component, namely the responsibility to rebuild, got lost in translation. Building on the 2005 Outcome Document, Ban's reports too neglected peace-building as an integral component of R2P despite the substantial similarities in the core tasks of both normative agendas, such as promoting inter-communal dialogue and reconciliation; legitimate and inclusive political institutions; and effective and impartial justice mechanisms. The 2001 ICISS version had dissected the principle into three interlinked responsibilities to prevent, respond and rebuild. Ban's 2009 report reformulated it in the metaphor of three pillars which in general is superior to the original ICISS formulation. But it does lose sight of the third responsibility to reconstruct and rebuild. Arguably, this was a critical failure in Libya, one which US President Barack Obama later was to blame on the Europeans who, 'given Libya's proximity', should have been more 'invested in the follow-up'.[12]

Chapter 9 argues that the responsibility to rebuild needs to be re-elevated to prominence as an integral component of R2P: conceptually, normatively and operationally; and its institutional homes in the UN system and the Secretary-General's role clarified. The 2009 three pillar formulation of R2P works well in most contexts, but is problematic in that it buries and loses sight of the critical importance of the original ICISS third 'responsibility to rebuild' and reconstruct war-raved societies to the point of being viable and self-sustaining once again. Recalling the context in which R2P was originally formulated in order to highlight the distinctive features of its contribution to international policy, the chapter describes the three dimensions of the responsibility to rebuild – recovery, reconstruction and reconciliation – and the strategies and steps needed for the rebuilding agenda. Recalling that Security Council authorisation of R2P coercive operations is a non-negotiable prerequisite, it suggests that the responsibility to rebuild can be reintroduced and implemented through the administrative and political leadership roles of the Secretary-General.

R2P is a global normative answer to a universal moral failing

The political impasse over coercive R2P intervention is often explained with reference to North–South schisms. Yet R2P is not, and ought not to be, a North–South issue. The persistent criticism, that R2P is a neo-colonial updated version of the old White Man's burden, can itself be racist in assumptions and consequences. It denies agency to developing countries, insisting they can only be victims. It would deny to peoples of developing countries the benefits of good governance that Westerners take for granted, preferring either to leave them to the tender mercies of thugs masquerading as government leaders, or to leave any efforts to alleviate their suffering to the ad hoc geopolitical calculations of powerful Western countries rather than to globally validated norms and due process. It ignores the origins of R2P in the demands for protection by atrocity victims in Africa and Europe, and in the norm entrepreneurship of people form the global South in developing the principle. It also ignores the rich history of indigenous traditions in many parts of Asia and Africa that hold rulers owe duties for the safety, welfare and protection of subjects in return for the latter's allegiance.

Consider the two heavyweight countries among the emerging powers. Notions of responsibility and the corollary concept of responsible governance have deep roots in Chinese traditions of statecraft and corresponding visions of world order.[13] In turn this suggests that 'responsible protection'[14] resonates in Chinese political thought and could conceivably anchor its engagement with global governance. Similarly, the Hindu-Buddhist concept of *dharma* – the code of right conduct based on duty – applies to kings as much as to subjects. The companion notion of *rajdharma* means duty of rulers. In 2002, the pro-Hindu Bharatiya Janata Party (BJP) was in power in the state of Gujarat as well as federally in New Delhi. Gujarat's Chief Minister Narendra Modi was widely blamed for not instituting effective measures to protect up to 2,000 Muslims who were killed in anti-Muslim riots that erupted when a group of Hindu pilgrims were deliberately burnt alive in a railway carriage. It was a classic R2P case of a mass atrocity due to the responsible government being unable or unwilling to institute effective preventive and reactive measures. Appearing on a dais with Modi and speaking in Hindi, Atal Bihari Vajpayee, the recently deceased Prime Minister of India at the time, pointedly reminded Modi of every ruler's *rajdharma*.[15]

The Genocide Convention converted the moral revulsion of the Holocaust – a failure of *Western* civilisation – into a binding universal norm. The two humanitarian crises that most drove the push for R2P were the Rwanda genocide in 1994, and the Balkans atrocities bookended by the Srebrenica massacre in 1995 and the Kosovo intervention in 1999; one African, the other European. R2P is a global norm that, in the allocation of solemn responsibilities of protection, does not discriminate on grounds of nationality, race or religion, but applies equally to all. As such it speaks eloquently to the highest UN ideals of international solidarity.

By contrast, the theory and practice of sovereignty is decidedly European in origin and flavour. The major European colonial powers acquired far-flung overseas territories while also intervening against nearby small states on a variety of pretexts. Clearly, Westphalian principles of sovereignty were no bar to such interventions even at the height of this order. The colonised countries were effectively treated as lacking the identity of states in the Eurocentric world order of the time, just as slavery was justified despite all men being created equal by some people being denied their essential human identity. But at least the powers that be paid lip service to the principle of sovereignty and the norm of non-intervention while rejecting its applicability to the case at hand. This dual-track approach continued after 1945 and the practice was by no means limited to Western powers. For example, India used its full military power to help Bangladesh secede from united Pakistan in 1971. Its legal justification did not invoke any right to humanitarian intervention, instead pointing to self-defence against 'demographic aggression' with the influx of ten million refugees from Bangladesh.

This is where the NATO intervention in Kosovo in 1999 was a radical departure, as discussed in Chapter 4. For the first time, the major Western powers challenged the validity and relevance of the norm of non-intervention itself and proclaimed an emerging new norm of 'humanitarian intervention' instead. But the others still had the numbers to reject the self-interested claim and did so in no uncertain terms in congenial forums like the Non-aligned Movement and the UN General Assembly.

The as-yet unsettled debate on how best to operationalise R2P requires a respectful conversation among proponents and sceptics over when, how, by whom and under what accountability mechanisms to execute the international responsibility to protect. The 2001/2005 consensus on R2P resulted from a genuine dialogue within the ICISS, an extensive outreach and consultation exercise in every continent and successive rounds of intensive consultations across the UN membership in and since 2005. The global South's comfort level with R2P grew steadily as they studied the principle closely and recognised that all legitimate concerns had been incorporated. An important part of the explanation for the principle resonating across the global North–South divide is that instead of merely repackaging the Western humanitarian warriors' worldviews, as noted in the last chapter, it accommodated the sensitivities of the formerly colonised countries. This helped R2P to gain rapid uptake and unanimous endorsement by world leaders in 2005.

Learning from that the leading NATO powers, instead of being disdainful and disrespectful of the critics of how R2P was implemented in Libya, should listen, acknowledge and accommodate legitimate concerns. This is desirable in principle. It is also required as a matter of pragmatism as the world order is rebalanced militarily, economically, geopolitically and even morally, with power and influence shifting from the North to the South.

The China–Russia resort to the veto for addressing the slaughter in Syria does not prove the irrelevance of the UN Security Council. Rather, what it proves is that the politics of the Security Council must be got right before an R2P military intervention; and the political equilibrium should be maintained during the operation. The veto is a constitutional device to compel the powerful countries to accommodate one another's policy priorities and forge a common interest different from the national interest of any dominant power. Besides, as many vetoes are cast by Washington as by Moscow and Beijing.

The emerging powers like BRICS are the countries where R2P implementation remains most controversial and political resistance can be most expected. Because of their mediating role between developing countries and the global North,[16] they have a particular responsibility to ensure that, through global governance mechanisms and international accountability instruments, the normative gains of new tools to protect civilians and punish the perpetrators of atrocities are not lost in the fog of mutual recriminations.

While R2P preserves to states the responsibility to protect their own populations, it strengthens the UN's responsibility for the international community as a whole. In a speech on 18 January 2012 to a conference to honour ICISS on the tenth anniversary of the R2P report, Secretary-General Ban Ki-moon noted that historically, the international community's 'chief failing... has been the reluctance to act in the face of serious threats', not too much intervention.[17] The price has been the loss of far too many lives and an erosion of UN credibility. As Tom Weiss reminds us in a sharply argued but far from uncritical book, the world would not be better off without the United Nations.[18]

Notes

1 See Ramesh Thakur, 'A Civil Libertarian's Lament for a Lost Decade of Human Rights', in Rowena Maguire, Bridget Lewis and Charles Sampford, eds., *Shifting Global Powers and International Law: Challenges and Opportunities* (London: Routledge, 2013), 173–92.

2 Hardeep Singh Puri (India's Permanent Representative to the United Nations while India was on the Security Council in 2011–2012), *Perilous Interventions: The Security Council and the Politics of Chaos* (Noida: HarperCollins India, 2016), 79.

3 Puri, *Perilous Interventions*, 90–91.

4 Ban Ki-moon, 'Address to Stanley Foundation Conference on the Responsibility to Protect', New York, 18 January 2012 (New York: UN News Centre, 18 January 2012).
5 Puri, *Perilous Interventions*, 91–92.
6 Arash Heydarian Pashakhanlou, 'Decapitation in Libya: Winning the Conflict and Losing the Peace', *The Washington Quarterly* 40:4 (2018), 135–49.
7 See Ramesh Thakur, 'The Nuclear Ban Treaty: Recasting a Normative Framework for Disarmament', *The Washington Quarterly* 40:4 (2018), 71–95.
8 Rajeesh Kumar, 'Waiting for Godot: India and United Nations Security Council reform', *Strategic Analysis* 41:6 (2017), 546–58.
9 Roland Paris, 'The "Responsibility to Protect" and the Structural Problems of Preventive Humanitarian Intervention', *International Peacekeeping* 21:5 (2014), 569–603.
10 Arif Saba and Shahram Akbarzadeh, 'The Responsibility to Protect and the Use of Force: An Assessment of the Just Cause and Last Resort Criteria in the Case of Libya', *International Peacekeeping* 25:2 (2018), 242–65.
11 See: Alex J. Bellamy and Paul D. Williams, 'On the Limits of Moral Hazard: The "Responsibility to Protect", Armed Conflict and Mass Atrocities', *European Journal of International Relations* 18:3 (2012), 539–71; and Jon Western, 'Illusions of Moral Hazard: A Conceptual and Empirical Critique', *Ethnopolitics* 4:2 (2005), 225–36.
12 Quoted in Jeffrey Goldberg, 'The Obama Doctrine', *The Atlantic*, April 2016, www.theatlantic.com/magazine/archive/2016/04/the-obama-doctrine/471525/.
13 Pichamon Yeophantong, 'Governing the World: China's Evolving Conceptions of Responsibility', *Chinese Journal of International Politics* 6:4 (2013), 329–64.
14 Ruan Zongze, 'Responsible Protection: Building a Safer World', *China International Studies* (May/June 2012), 19–41.
15 The video is available at: www.youtube.com/watch?v=HJBItuHzUR0.
16 Ramesh Thakur, 'How Representative Are BRICS?' *Third World Quarterly* 35:10 (2014), 1791–1808.
17 Ban, 'Address to Stanley Foundation Conference on the Responsibility to Protect'.
18 Thomas G. Weiss, *Would the World Be Better without the UN?* (Cambridge: Polity, 2018).

7 R2P after Libya and Syria

Engaging emerging powers*

The use of force – no matter how benevolent, enlightened, or impartial in intent – has dramatic consequences. In particular, it shapes the struggle for power and helps to determine the outcome of political contests. This is why it is inherently controversial and contested. It also explains why international debates about Libya – the first road test of R2P's coercive element under Pillar Three – were understandably contentious.[1] Libya proved to be almost a textbook illustration justifying R2P principles, but its implementation also demonstrated the need for legitimacy criteria to guide decisions on authorising and overseeing international military intervention. Although successful, the Libyan operation proved particularly controversial among the emerging powers, and the price of exceeding the mandate there has been paid by Syrians. Nevertheless, it would be premature to conclude that R2P can be branded 'RIP'.

The global diffusion of power underway means that Westerners have lost their previous capacity to set global standards and rules of behaviour. Brazil, China and India, among others, are emerging as important growth centres in the world economy, but so far, the signs show that these new players are more interested in the status and trappings of power than in assuming burdens of leadership. Nor do they clearly have the institutional capacity to connect national aspirations of rapid economic development and political stability to breaking global gridlocks on issues such as democratisation, political and market freedoms, civil liberties and human rights. Even the democratic rising powers – Brazil, South Africa and, especially, India with its more than six decades of constitutional democratic governance – do not demonstrate that hard or soft human rights promotion is an integral element of their foreign policy. As power and influence seep out of the US-led trans-Atlantic order and migrate towards Asia and elsewhere, how – and who – will manage the transition from the Westphalian system of world affairs to an alternative system?[2] One aspect of that transition is the shift from the norm of non-intervention to the principle-cum-norm of R2P.

Through global governance mechanisms and international accountability instruments, the emerging powers – more than any other group of states because of their increasing influence – will determine:

1 whether vulnerable groups receive protection from predations by brutish rulers domestically;

2 whether weak countries receive protection from predations by regional or global major powers; and
3 whether violators of both the above are made to answer for their transgressions.

Before looking more closely at how these states' views on R2P are evolving, given recent experiences such as Libya and Syria, it is important to understand three preliminary things. First, external interventions were frequent in the past, before R2P's 2001 formulation, and are not guaranteed in the future, despite R2P's unanimous adoption in 2005. The choice therefore is not *if* intervention, but *whether* an intervention will be ad hoc or rules-based, unilateral or multilateral, and divisive or consensual. R2P, especially when backed by agreed-upon legitimacy criteria, will help shift the balance towards interventions which are rules-based, multilateral and consensual. Thus, the international community should prepare itself normatively, organisationally and operationally to deal with humanitarian crises rather than bury its head and belatedly make up responses when crises inevitably happen.

Second, the debate over R2P is not, and should not be, a North–South issue. But it can turn into one, either because of wilful – and sometimes self-serving – obstinacy on the part of key emerging countries or because of calculated neglect of their legitimate concerns by a declining West. Despite impressions that non-Western societies resist R2P, many have a historical tradition of reciprocal rights and obligations which bind sovereigns and subjects. As argued by Mohamed Sahnoun, co-chair of ICISS, in many ways R2P is actually a distinctly African contribution to global human rights.[3] Many traditional Asian cultures also stress the symbiotic link between duties owed by kings to subjects and loyalty of citizens to sovereigns, a point made by civil society representatives who accordingly conclude that, far from abridging sovereignty, R2P *enhances* it.[4] In India, for example, Emperor Ashoka (third-century BC) inscribed the following message on a rock edict: 'this is my rule: government by the law, administration according to the law, gratification of my subjects under the law, and protection through the law'.[5]

Third, the realities are that the only likely sites and targets of intervention in the foreseeable future will be developing countries. It is the *people in developing countries* therefore who will suffer if mass atrocities are committed and outsiders refuse (or fail) to help, or if primarily geopolitical or commercial interventions are disguised as humanitarian ones. Conversely, people in developing countries will be the principal beneficiaries if interventions are motivated chiefly by humanitarian concerns and executed responsibly. Since the interveners will likely come from a spectrum of advanced and/or developing countries, conversations on R2P should occur first among the civil societies and governments of developing countries, and second between developing and advanced countries. This will forge common norms and standards of international citizenship consistent with contemporary principles of national and global good governance. The relevance of this diversity seems to be surprisingly ignored in UN circles in

New York and many opinion capitals/journals, with a near exclusive dominance of Western names, faces and voices on the subject. A recent roundtable on R2P after Libya, for example, had exclusively Western writers. Each one of the five is individually very qualified – with most being personal friends, co-authors or co-editors – but the collective optics are damaging,[6] to the point where the first instinctive response of even an author-supporter of R2P is: how could they, what were they thinking?

For all these reasons, engaging the emerging powers on developing the criteria for, and conduct of, R2P interventions as we learn from recent experiences such as Libya and Syria are in the mutual interest of both the emerging powers themselves and all those who support the principle of R2P to protect the world's vulnerable populations from genocide, war crimes, ethnic cleansing and crimes against humanity.

R2P: between unilateral intervention and institutional indifference

In the decades after 1945, the nature of armed conflict transformed as inter-state warfare between uniformed armies gave way to irregular conflict between rival armed groups.[7] The nature of the state also departed from its idealised European version. Many communist and some newly-decolonised countries were states whose regimes ruled through terror, sometimes even propped up by the US national security state.[8] Thus, the principal victims of both regular and irregular warfare have increasingly been civilians. And advances in telecommunications have brought the unadulterated horror in the world into our living rooms.

Simultaneously, the goals of promoting human rights and democratic governance, protecting civilian victims of humanitarian atrocities and punishing governmental perpetrators of mass crimes have become more important. R2P spoke eloquently to the need to change the UN's normative framework to account for the changed reality of threats and victims.[9] R2P now provides an entry point for the international community to step in and take up the moral as well as military slack. Pared down to its essence, R2P is the acceptance of a duty by all those who live in zones of safety to care for those trapped in zones of danger.

Engaging the developing world: the 2001 ICISS debates

The practice of intervention, and the belief that it is in the best interests of natives who will warmly welcome and benefit from it, has a long but not necessarily distinguished lineage. The European colonial powers in particular, convinced of the moral as well as material superiority of their own civilisations, often justified their conquests and rule over 'savages' and 'natives' with reference to the 'white man's burden' to spread the 'standards of civilisation' to non-Western societies.[10] When NATO took military action against Serbia's atrocities in Kosovo in 1999, the West justified the action as 'humanitarian intervention' while the NAM – the largest grouping in the word outside the United Nations –

rejected any so-called right to humanitarian intervention.[11] Secretary-General Kofi Annan, mindful of the controversy also when there was no intervention to halt the genocide in Rwanda in 1994, acknowledged that the UN Charter-based regime for regulating the use of military force in such circumstances was broken and called for a new normative consensus on the subject. Canada responded to his call by setting up the independent ICISS which was successful in repositioning the international consensus on intervention to prevent and halt atrocities because it rejected the language and discourse of 'humanitarian intervention'. In 2001, ICISS conducted extensive consultations around the globe to better understand the problems in reconciling intervention with state sovereignty. During this process, ICISS quickly discovered a visceral hostility across the developing world to any so-called 'right of humanitarian intervention', often rooted in colonialism.[12]

This hostility is a reflection of a real world reality: the concept of 'intervention' is a euphemism. Going back to 1999, NATO's 'humanitarian intervention' in Kosovo was actually three months of bombing. Just using the term 'humanitarian bombing' starkly highlights the damaging contradiction of the two words. But that is exactly what NATO action amounted to, which explains the controversy that embroiled no less a person than Vaclev Havel of the Czech Republic.[13] ICISS argued however that, unlike humanitarian intervention, R2P would put the needs and interests of the victims of atrocities ahead of those of the intervening powers. It is victim- and people-centred, while 'humanitarian intervention' privileges the perspectives, preferences, and priorities of the intervening states. Beyond this general guidance, I drew eight inferences from the ICISS consultations with opinion leaders from governments, media and civil society in the developing world:[14]

1 The term 'humanitarian' should never be associated with war. Humanitarianism is good, but interventionism is bad; 'humanitarian intervention' therefore marries evil to good. Far from humanitarianism burnishing interventions, it will itself be tarnished by interventionism.
2 The UN Charter recognises only self-defence and the maintenance and restoration of international peace and security as legitimate grounds for the use of force. The use of force for moral reasons is dangerous and counterproductive in its practical effects: it can encourage warring parties inside a country to be rigid and irresponsible in the hope of internationalising the conflict,[15] or facilitate interventions by those exploiting the cloak of legality for their own purposes. Both can cause or prolong large-scale killings.
3 The Western concept of human rights animating 'humanitarian interventions' has an internal incoherence: human rights for the individual somehow mystically transforms into collective rights (protecting groups of people), at the same time as the collective rights of the entire nation as a sovereign entity are still denied legitimacy.
4 The inconsistent practice, double standards and the sporadic nature of Western powers' interest in protecting human rights shows that noble principles are often convenient cloaks for hegemonic interests.

5 The results of Western intervention have not always been beneficial and sometimes have aggravated the crises, for example in Indochina, Iran and Latin America.
6 The UN is the central and indispensable agency to lawfully authorise the use of military force.
7 Interventions cannot become the pretext for imposing external political preferences (a.k.a. regime change). Cases justifying intervention must be tightly restricted to such heinous crimes as genocide and mass murders, must always be the option of last resort, must be temporary and must be guided by considerations of political impartiality and neutrality between the domestic political contenders.
8 Interveners must respect and ensure the territorial integrity of the target state.[16]

There were of course significant differences across the developing world. In Latin America in the twentieth century, for example, interventions were most frequently conducted by the great and powerful neighbour to the north. The continent also had its share of rogue regimes (sometimes backed by Washington) that brutalised their own people in the 1970s and 1980s. The dual experience has shaped its response to the tension between sovereignty and intervention more sharply than in Africa and Asia.[17] Geography and history ensure that in Latin America, 'the contrast between [US] hard power and [UN] legitimacy is viewed in even more vivid colours than in other regions of the globe'.[18]

Meanwhile, if Asia had the hardest line in defence of state sovereignty, Africa took the softest: Article 4(h) of the Constitutive Act of the Africa Union, adopted in Lomé on 11 July 2000, spells out the principle of intervention: the 'right of the Union to intervene in a Member State' with respect to the commission of 'war crimes, genocide, and crimes against humanity'.[19] Author Dan Kuwali calls this a shift from 'humanitarian' to 'statutory' intervention, wherein African states 'have themselves accepted sovereignty not as a shield but as a responsibility'.[20]

There are many possible explanations for the greater willingness of Africans to accept intervention than Asians. State failure is a more widespread problem – the polarisation between society and the state makes sovereignty elusive. In effect, in parts of Africa, sovereignty has become restricted to an international relational dimension (the negative conception of non-interference rather than the positive one of enabling attributes and assets). Many weak African states consequently lack real experience with sovereignty, being subject instead to warlords, robber barons and gun and drug runners, among other criminal elements.[21] Recent African history may also explain Africa's greater openness to intervention: far too many regimes had abused the shield of sovereignty to treat African people as objects not actors.

R2P since 2001

Shaped in part by the ICISS consultations, The Responsibility to Protect report was published in December 2001 and endorsed by the UN High-level Panel on

Threats, Challenges, and Change in 2004, and by UN Secretary-General Kofi Annan in 2005.[22] In a significant breakthrough for the growing acceptance of the new norm, China's official paper on UN reforms, published on 7 June 2005, noted that '[e]ach state shoulders the primary responsibility to protect its own population … When a massive humanitarian crisis occurs, it is the legitimate concern of the international community to ease and defuse the crisis'.[23] It went on to list the conditions and safeguards, including Security Council authorisation, which form the core of R2P. Unanimous endorsement by world leaders in 2005 added clarity, rigour and specificity, limiting the triggering events to war crimes, genocide, ethnic cleansing and crimes against humanity, and thus realigning the emerging global political norm to existing categories of international legal crimes.[24]

UN Secretary-General Ban Ki-moon has subsequently released four special reports that have sustained and consolidated the new international consensus on the subject.[25] The annual debates by the UN General Assembly on Ban's special reports have helped to forge a shared understanding of R2P to distinguish it from humanitarian intervention and align it with efforts to build capacity to help states exercise their sovereignty more effectively. Meanwhile, civil society organisations have promoted a vigorous process of R2P norm socialisation and crystallisation.

Four actual test cases in 2008–09 demonstrated the growing understandings and clarifications of the meaning and limits of R2P, even though at times it was abused and misapplied.[26] With Burma's deadly Cyclone Nargis in 2008, principles, politics and practicality converged to counsel caution in invoking R2P. When the military regime rejected outside assistance to help alleviate the suffering caused by the humanitarian disaster, France proposed that R2P should be invoked to forcibly overcome the government's recalcitrance. But the 2005 formulation on R2P did not cover humanitarian disasters (principle); the developing countries were not prepared to broaden R2P's scope beyond the four atrocity crimes specified in 2005 (politics); and no country was prepared to send troops into another land war in the jungles of Southeast Asia (practicality).

When Russia claimed an R2P mandate in intervening against Georgia in South Ossetia in 2008, it drew attention to the relationship of R2P to the problem of the kin state.[27] A group that constitutes the majority or a substantial population in one state might find itself in an ethnic minority in another, especially neighbouring, state: Chinese in Indonesia, Tamils in Sri Lanka, Indians in Fiji, whites in Zimbabwe or South Africa, Russians in the former Soviet bloc in eastern Europe and Central Asia. If these minority groups are attacked and risk being killed in large numbers based on their ethnic identity, then do their kin overseas have any special rights or duties to protect them? The kin-state has a strong interest to defend its fellow-ethnics under attack. Yet, history shows that the intervention of a so-called 'kin state' or 'motherland' to defend a threatened minority in a neighbouring state can increase rather than defuse conflict. Instead of helping find a solution, the interested party exacerbates the problem.

Israel's offensive in Hamas-ruled Gaza in 2008–09 demonstrated the risks of seeking remedy in R2P when better or more appropriate tools and instruments are available, for example international humanitarian law (IHL). Under international law, an occupying power has the responsibility to protect not just citizens and residents on its own territory, but all peoples living under its occupation. But R2P does not cover situations of inter-state armed conflict; its scope is limited to atrocities committed or anticipated inside sovereign jurisdictions. By contrast, IHL regulates the use of force in all armed conflicts.

Finally, the May 2009 climax of the Sri Lankan civil war, when the government mercilessly crushed the ruthless terrorist organisation the Tamil Tigers, raised troubling questions about the applicability of R2P to a brutal civil war and about the limits to the authority of the legitimate government to use force when confronted with armed challenge. Should the United Nations have invoked R2P to protect the tens of thousands of civilians caught in the cross-fire against large-scale killings by both the government forces and the Tamil Tigers? The debate in the Human Rights Council in Geneva showed that most developing countries, to the shock of Westerners, back a government's right to suppress armed insurgencies and terrorist groups with military force.[28] At the same time, it is worth noting that Foreign Minister (and now President) Pranab Mukherjee of India – a country that was among the most resistant to R2P in 2001 – found it useful to remind Colombo of its responsibility to protect all its citizens.[29]

The General Assembly debate in July 2009 on Ban Ki-moon's report on R2P, *Implementing the Responsibility to Protect*, was held against the backdrop of these four cases. Yet, 94 speakers, almost two-thirds of them from Africa, Asia and Latin America, mostly reaffirmed the 2005 consensus, expressed opposition to any effort to reopen it and insisted that its scope be restricted to the four crimes of genocide, crimes against humanity, war crimes and ethnic cleansing.

This had been foreshadowed by China's Ambassador Liu Zhenmin in a Security Council debate on 4 December 2006, when he warned that the 2005 Outcome Document in which the UN General Assembly affirmed R2P was 'a very cautious representation of the responsibility to protect … it is not appropriate to expand, wilfully to interpret or even abuse this concept'.[30] Ban also warned in his 2009 report that 'it would be counter-productive, and possibly even destructive, to try to revisit the negotiations that led to the provisions of paragraphs 138 and 139 of the Summit Outcome'.[31] In an interview with *Time* magazine, Liberia's President Ellen Johnson Sirleaf captured the broad consensus as of 2009: 'Look at how we have gone from [a stance] of non-interference in our internal affairs to respect for the principle of the responsibility to protect'.[32]

Libya 2011

Two years later, Libya would demonstrate both the potential mobilising power and the limitations of R2P as a call to international arms. R2P was the discourse of choice in debating how best to respond to the crisis and the Security Council for the first time invoked R2P under the coercive Chapter VII of the Charter.[33] The Libyan experience would also confirm that the debate on military interventions cannot avoid questions of regime legitimacy, state capacity and state-building.

Resolution 1973, adopted on 17 March 2011 by a 10–0-5 vote (China, Russia, Brazil, Germany and India abstained), authorised the use of 'all necessary measures … to protect civilians and civilian-populated areas'.[34] NATO took almost a full decade to intervene with air power in Kosovo in 1999. In Libya, it took just one month to mobilise a broad coalition, secure a UN mandate to protect civilians, establish and enforce no-kill zones, stop Gaddafi's advancing army and prevent a massacre of the innocents in Benghazi. By year's end, Gaddafi had been ousted and killed. The outcome was thus a triumph for R2P. It showed it *is* possible for the international community, working through the authenticated, UN-centred structures and procedures of organised multilateralism, to deploy international force to neutralise the military might of a thug and intervene between him and his victims.

The Libyan people's euphoria and NATO's relief over the successful military campaign tempered criticisms of the manner in which NATO over-interpreted UN authorisation to protect civilians. Carefully crafted both to authorise and delimit the scope of intervention, Resolution 1973 specified the purpose of military action as humanitarian protection and limited the means to that goal. Yet, NATO ignored the restrictions to target Gaddafi directly in a transparent effort at regime change, spurned hints of any willingness by the Gaddafi regime to negotiate a ceasefire, intervened in the internal civil war and broke the UN's arms embargo by supplying weaponry to the rebels. If 1973 restrictions had been respected, the civil war and the international intervention could well have been longer and messier. Ignoring them may thus well have been justified on the logic of military necessity and efficiency. But the insistence by some NATO powers that they fully adhered to UN-authorised 'all necessary measures' to protect civilians and civilian-populated areas is not credible. In his speech to the General Assembly in September 2011, Prime Minister Manmohan Singh of India made a thinly-veiled attack on the expansive interpretation of Resolution 1973: 'Actions taken under the authority of the United Nations must respect the unity, territorial integrity, sovereignty and independence of individual states'.[35] All the BRICS countries objected strongly to the shift from the politically neutral posture of civilian protection to the partial goal of assisting the rebels and pursuing regime change.[36]

Furthermore, volatility and violence continue to cast a long shadow over post-Gaddafi Libya's stability and commitment to a liberal democratic culture. Gadaffi's death brought a wave of questions: Who are the rebels? What do they stand for? For whom do they speak? How much popular support do they command? How committed are they to eschewing rule by terror? The same questions have been highly pertinent with respect to the ongoing crisis in Syria and have complicated international responses to it.

Syria 2012

Syrians have paid the price of NATO excesses in Libya.[37] By the end of 2011, the peaceful Arab Spring in Syria had mutated into a bloody armed uprising and then a full-fledged civil war, in which, according to a study commissioned by the UN Office of the High Commissioner for Human Rights, 60,000 people had been killed as of November 2012.[38] Possible courses of action in Syria cannot be contemplated without acknowledging that the crisis is also about relations with Iran, Russia, and China. Furthermore, there is heightened caution about yet another Western invasion of another Muslim country, especially since this is a more formidable enemy in a more volatile strategic environment.

Arab and Western countries introduced draft resolutions in October 2011 and February as well as July 2012 calling for an end to the flow of arms into Syria, for President Bashar al-Assad to yield key powers to a deputy, for a government of national unity, and preparations for free presidential and parliamentary elections. China and Russia vetoed all three, while Brazil, India and South Africa have shifted from initial abstention to subsequent support.[39]

China and Russia remain resolutely opposed to any resolution which could set off a chain of events leading to a 1973-type authorisation for outside military operations in Syria. They have several arguments, including: such a resolution would put Syria on the path to civil war; the Security Council should not dictate internal politics and succession; opposition groups must also receive condemnation for perpetrating violence (the moral hazard argument) and exhorted to engage constructively with the government;[40] the draft resolutions would have inflamed, not calmed the situation; and the only solution to the Syrian crisis is through an inclusive, Syrian-led process to address the legitimate aspirations of the people in an environment free of violence and human rights abuses. In other words, while there are unquestionably strategic and economic imperatives behind Russia's policy in particular, the strength of the Sino-Russian opposition also reflects a conflict of political approaches and rejects armed domestic confrontation backed by international enablers.

India and South Africa have emphasised the primary responsibility of the Security Council to resolve internal differences through peaceful means while Brazil has played a more constructive role by tabling a possible compromise paper (discussed below). They noted that the October 2011 draft resolution failed to condemn the rebel-perpetrated violence and failed to require rebels to engage with the government in seeking a peaceful solution through political processes.[41] Both voted in favour of the draft resolution on 4 February 2012, which China and Russia also vetoed on the grounds that it was unbalanced and a thinly-veiled attempt to impose regime change in Damascus through armed struggle. Ambassador Hardeep Singh Puri explained India's vote by noting that the resolution called on the Syrian government to protect its population.[42] A more realpolitik explanation is that India did not wish to antagonise six Gulf Arab neighbours (including Saudi Arabia), where almost six million Indians work and live. Saudi Arabia was also promising to make up India's energy imports from Iran which was proving problematical with the tightening US and European sanctions on Iran in the unrelated impasse over Tehran's suspected nuclear weapons programme.[43] Riyadh had also begun handing over suspected foreign-based terrorists for questioning by Indian agencies as part of the broader realignment of India's relations with key Middle Eastern countries.[44] Nevertheless, the underlying Indian assessment is unlikely to have changed significantly: while the Assad regime has given hints of being open to discussions, the rebels have been intransigent in insisting on his departure as a precondition for negotiations. Because the opposition's regional and international backers do not press them to drop this condition, 'the obsession with regime change has come in the way of a search for political dialogue'.[45]

Rebalancing the normative order?

The debate on how best to operationalise R2P requires a respectful conversation among proponents and sceptics over when, how and by whom to execute the international Responsibility to Protect. The consensus on R2P in ICISS in 2001 and at the UN since 2005 resulted from a genuine North–South dialogue. Had R2P merely repackaged the Western humanitarian warriors' wishes and brushed aside the sensitivities of the formerly colonised, it never would have gained rapid uptake and traction culminating in unanimous endorsement by world leaders in 2005.

The R2P consensus underpinning Resolution 1973 on Libya was damaged by gaps in expectation, communication and accountability between those who mandated the operation and those who executed it. Brazil subsequently offered a paper on 'Responsibility while Protecting' with the potential to bring in some agreed parameters on the conditions to govern the use of UN-authorised R2P operations.[46] Its two key elements are to formulate an agreed set of guidelines to help the UN Security Council achieve consensus in future debates before authorising an R2P military intervention; and a monitoring or review mechanism to help sustain that consensus by ensuring that the Council has an oversight role over the operation during implementation.

As exemplified by the Brazilian initiative, critics should engage with R2P and seek to improve the means and manner of implementation. This way, the Southern players will become joint and responsible stakeholders in the emerging new world order. On the other hand, if new, rising powers remain more concerned with consolidating their national power aspirations than developing norms and institutions of global governance,[47] they will remain incomplete powers, limited by these narrow ambitions, with their material grasp longer than their normative reach.

The collision of different UN Charter norms that produced the heated and tense debates over 'humanitarian intervention' in 1999 between the global North, as represented by NATO, and the global South, as articulated by NAM, reflected a growing erosion of the sense of community among the different members of the family of nations. States and peoples no longer share a common belief in the means and procedures by which their differences can be mediated and reconciled. This suggests that the response of states to atrocities will continue to be ad hoc and on a case-by-case basis, rather than principled and consistent.[48]

Reframing 'humanitarian intervention' as the Responsibility to Protect at least re-established an international consensus on the legitimate ends of the use of military power. However, the implementation of the sharp, military end of Pillar Three of R2P in Libya in 2011 shows that the global consensus on R2P is tenuous and fragile rather than robust and resilient. Above all, the Libyan example confirms that success in an R2P intervention, even if internationally approved, is not guaranteed any more than in any other type of external intervention. Good intentions do not automatically shape good outcomes.

Because there is no humanitarian crisis so grave that an outside military intervention cannot make it worse, the use of military force cannot be the option of first resort but only that of the last. However, its use cannot be excluded as part of the toolkit for dealing with threatened or occurring atrocities: that would offer comfort to the atrocity perpetrators without solace to the victims. The key is to engage emerging countries in continually shaping the means of implementing R2P interventions, when necessary, and for those emerging countries to seek to shape global normative guidelines rather than looking only to their own national ambitions.

Notes

* Originally published in *The Washington Quarterly* 36:2 (2013), 61–76. Reprinted by permission of Taylor & Francis Ltd, www.tandfonline.com on behalf of The Elliott School of International Affairs.

1 Pillar Three is defined as 'the responsibility of Member States to respond collectively in a timely and decisive manner when a State is manifestly failing to provide … protection'; Ban Ki-moon, *Implementing the Responsibility to Protect*, A/63/677, (New York: United Nations, 12 January 2009, www.unrol.org/files/SG_reportA_63_677_en.pdf), 9, paragraph 11(c). While primacy is given to peaceful means, should they prove inadequate to ensure protection, the international community should use more robust action: 'no strategy for fulfilling the responsibility to protect would be complete without the possibility of collective enforcement measures, including through sanctions or coercive military action in extreme cases'; Ban, *Implementing the Responsibility to Protect*, 25, paragraph 56.

2 See Sung Won Kim, David P. Fidler, and Sumit Ganguly, 'Eastphalia Rising? Asian Influence and the Fate of Human Security', *World Policy Journal* 26:2 (2009), 53–64.

3 Mohamed Sahnoun 'Africa: Uphold Continent's Contribution to Human Rights, Urges Top Diplomat', *allAfrica.com*, 21 July 2009, http://allafrica.com/stories/printable/200907210549.html. For another African perspective that also strongly supports R2P, see Samuel Atuobi, 'The Responsibility to Protect: The Time to Act is Now', *KAIPTC Policy Brief* no. 1, July 2009, www.responsibilitytoprotect.org/index.php/component/content/article/35-r2pcs-topics/2633-kaiptc-policy-brief-the-responsibility-to-protect-the-time-to-act-is-now.

4 See World Federalist Movement, *Global Consultative Roundtables on the Responsibility to Protect: Civil Society Perspectives and Recommendations for Action, Interim Report*, (New York: WFM, January 2009), 8.

5 Quoted in Stanley Wolpert, *A New History of India*, (New York: Oxford University Press, 1977), 66–67.

6 See *Ethics & International Affairs* 25:3 (2011).

7 See Andrew Mack (director and editor-in-chief), *Human Security Report 2005*, (Oxford: Oxford University Press, 2005).

8 See Michael J. Hogan, *A Cross of Iron: Harry S. Truman and the Origins of the National Security State, 1945–1954* (Cambridge: Cambridge University Press, 2000);

Seth G. Jones, Olga Oliker, Peter Chalk, C. Christine Fair, Rollie Lal, and James Dobbins, *Securing Tyrants or Fostering Reform? U.S. Internal Security Assistance to Repressive and Transitioning Regimes* (Santa Monica CA: Rand, 2006); Norrin M. Ripsman and T.V. Paul, *Globalization and the National Security State* (Oxford: Oxford University Press, 2010); Douglas C. Stuart, *Creating the National Security State: A History of the Law That Transformed America* (Princeton: Princeton University Press, 2008); and Gary Wills, *Bomb Power: The Modern Presidency and the National Security State* (London: Penguin, 2010).

9 For an account of the UN's transformation since 1945, see Ramesh Thakur, *The United Nations, Peace and Security: From Collective Security to the Responsibility to Protect* (Cambridge: Cambridge University Press, 2006).

10 See Gerrit W. Gong, *The 'Standard' of Civilization in International Society* (New York: Oxford University Press, 1984).

11 Albrecht Schnabel and Ramesh Thakur, eds., *Kosovo and the Challenge of Humanitarian Intervention: Selective Indignation, Collective Action, and International Citizenship* (Tokyo: United Nations University Press, 2000).

12 International Commission on Intervention and State Sovereignty, *The Responsibility to Protect* (Ottawa: International Development Research Centre, 2001) can be downloaded as an ebook from: www.idrc.ca/EN/Resources/Publications/Pages/IDRCBookDetails.aspx?PublicationID=240.

13 See, for example, the entry under 'Humanitarian bombing' in Wikipedia, http://en.wikipedia.org/wiki/Humanitarian_bombing.

14 These are drawn from the author's notes from the various meetings. The reports from all the ICISS regional discussions are available on the Commission's website. Adonia Ayebare, 'Regional Perspectives on Sovereignty and Intervention', discussion paper prepared for the ICISS Round Table Consultation, Maputo, 10 March 2001; Emmanuel Kwesi Aning, 'Rapporteur's Report, ICISS Round Table Consultation, Maputo, 10 March 2001'; Luis Bitencourt, 'Rapporteur's Report, ICISS Round Table Consultation, Santiago, 4 May 2001'; Ahmed T. Khalil, 'Rapporteur's Report, ICISS Round Table Consultation, Cairo, 21 May 2001'; Omran el-Shafie, 'Intervention and State Sovereignty', discussion paper for the ICISS Round Table consultation in Cairo, 21 May 2001; Sripapha Petcharamesree, 'Rapporteur's Report, ICISS Round Table Consultation, New Delhi, June 10, 2001'; and unattributed, 'Rapporteur's Report, ICISS Round Table Consultation, Beijing, 14 June 2001'. [The ICISS website for a decade was www.iciss.gc.ca. This now seems to have become inactive].

15 For a discussion of the moral hazard argument, see Alan J. Kuperman, 'The Moral Hazard of Humanitarian Intervention: Lessons from the Balkans', *International Studies Quarterly* 52:1 (2008), 49–80.

16 These were the argument advanced by various participants during the ICISS outreach consultations; they do not necessarily reflect the author's views.

17 See Jorge Heine, 'The Responsibility to Protect: Humanitarian Intervention and the Principle of Non-intervention in the Americas', in Ramesh Thakur, Andrew F. Cooper and John English, eds., *International Commissions and the Power of Ideas* (Tokyo: United Nations University Press, 2005), 221–45.

18 Bitencourt, 'Rapporteur's Report'.

19 African Union, 'Constitutive Act', (Lomé, Togo, 11 July 2000), www.au.int/en/about/constitutive_act.

20 Dan Kuwali, 'The End of Humanitarian Intervention: Evaluation of the African Union's Right of Intervention', *African Journal of Conflict Resolution* 9:1 (2009), 41.

21 Ayebare, 'Regional Perspectives on Sovereignty and Intervention'.

22 ICISS, *The Responsibility to Protect*; High-level Panel on Threats, Challenges and Change, *A More Secure World: Our Shared Responsibility* (New York: United Nations, A/59/565, December 2004); Kofi Annan, *In Larger Freedom: Towards*

Development, Security and Human Rights for All, Report of the Secretary-General, A/59/2005 (New York, United Nations, March 21, 2005).

23 'Full Text of China's Position Paper UN Reforms', Part III.1, *Xinhua*, 7 June 2005, http://news.xinhuanet.com/english/2005-06/08/content_3056817_3.htm.

24 *2005 World Summit Outcome*, resolution adopted by the General Assembly, A/RES/60/1 (New York: United Nations, 24 October 2005), paragraphs 138–40.

25 Ban, *Implementing the Responsibility to Protect*; Ban Ki-moon, *Early Warning, Assessment, and the Responsibility to Protect*, A/64/864 (New York: United Nations, 14 July 2010); Ban Ki-moon, *The Role of Regional and Subregional Arrangements in Implementing the Responsibility to Protect*, A/65/877-S/2011/393 (New York: United Nations, 28 June 2011); Ban Ki-moon, *Timely and Decisive Response*, A/66/874–S/2012/578 (New York: United Nations, 25 July 2012).

26 Cristina Badescu and Thomas G. Weiss, 'Misrepresenting R2P and Advancing Norms: An Alternative Spiral?' *International Studies Perspectives* 11:4 (2010), 354–74.

27 Walter Kemp, Vesselin Popovski, and Ramesh Thakur, eds., *Blood and Borders: The Responsibility to Protect and the Problem of the Kin-State* (Tokyo: United Nations University Press, 2011).

28 See Catherine Philp, 'Sri Lanka Forces West to Retreat Over "War Crimes" with Victory at UN', *The Times*, 28 May 2009, www.timesonline.co.uk/tol/news/world/us_and_americas/article6375044.ece?.

29 Pranab Mukherjee quoted in 'UN says 6,500 civilians have been killed in Sri Lankan violence', *Telegraph*, 24 April 2009, www.telegraph.co.uk/news/worldnews/asia/srilanka/5211742/UN-says-6500-civilians-have-been-killed-in-Sri-Lankan-violence.html; and 'India to Sri Lanka: killings of Tamil civilians must stop', *Sindh Today*, 22 April 2009, www.responsibilitytoprotect.org/index.php/crises/177-crisis-in-sri-lanka/2324-india-to-sri-lanka-killings-of-tamil-civilians-must-stop.

30 UN Security Council, 'Security Council Open Debate on Protection of Civilians in Armed Conflict', S/PV.5577, Verbatim Record (New York: United Nations, 4 December 2006), 8; quoted in Sarah Teitt, 'Assessing Polemics, Principles and Practices: China and the Responsibility to Protect', *Global Responsibility to Protect* 1, no. 2 (2009), 216.

31 Ban, *Implementing the Responsibility to Protect.* Paragraph 67.

32 Ellen Johnson Sirleaf quoted in 'Look across Africa and see the major changes that are happening', *Time*, 13 July 2009, www.time.com/magazine/article/0,9171,1908312,00.html.

33 For a range of diverse opinions and perspectives on R2P and Libya, see the collection of essays in e-International Relations: Alex Stark, ed., *The Responsibility to Protect: Challenges and Opportunities in Light of the Libyan Intervention*, (eInternational-Relations: 21 November 2011), www.e-ir.info/2011/11/21/the-responsibility-to-protect-challenges-opportunities-in-light-of-the-libyan-intervention/comment-page-1/#comment-37850.

34 S/RES/1973 (17 March 2011).

35 Manmohan Singh quoted in 'Manmohan Slams West for Using Force to Change Regimes', *Times of India*, 25 September 2011, http://articles.timesofindia.indiatimes.com/2011-09-25/india/30200524_1_libya-sovereignty-countries.

36 See the debates in UN Security Council, 66th session, 6528th meeting, S/PV.6528, Official Record (New York: United Nations, 4 May 2011), 7–10. On the BRICS grouping, see Andrew F. Cooper and Ramesh Thakur, 'The BRICS in the New Global Economic Geography', in Thomas G. Weiss and Rorden Wilkinson, eds., *International Organizations and Global Governance* (London: Routledge, 2014), 265–78.

37 Joshua Foust, 'Syria and the Pernicious Consequences of our Libya Intervention', *Atlantic*, 6 February 2012, www.theatlantic.com/international/archive/2012/02/syria-and-the-pernicious-consequences-of-our-libya-intervention/252631.

38 Megan Price, Jeff Klingner and Patrick Ball, *Preliminary Statistical Analysis of Documentation of Killings in the Syrian Arab Republic* (Geneva: Benetech Human Rights Program, 2 January 2013), www.ohchr.org/Documents/Countries/SY/PreliminaryStatAnalysisKillingsInSyria.pdf.

39 UN Department of Public Information, 'Security Council Fails to Adopt Draft Resolution Condemning Syria's Crackdown on Anti-Government Protestors, Owing to Veto by Russian Federation, China', Press Release, SC/10403, New York, 4 October 2011, www.un.org/News/Press/docs/2011/sc10403.doc.htm.

40 This ignored the November 2011 report of the UN Human Rights Council-appointed independent commission of the significant asymmetry of responsibility for the violence in Syria; UN Human Rights Council, 'Report of the Independent International Commission on the Syrian Arab Republic', A/HRC/S-17/2/Add.1, 23 November 2011, www.ohchr.org/Documents/Countries/SY/A.HRC.S-17.2.Add.1_en.pdf.

41 UN Security Council, 66th session, 6617th meeting, S/PV.6627 (New York: United Nations, 4 October 2011), 6–7, remarks by Hardeep Singh Puri; and p. 11, remarks by Baso Sangqu. See also UN Security Council, 66th session, 6524th meeting, S/PV.6524, remarks by Hardeep Singh Puri, (New York: United Nations, 27 April 2011), 8.

42 UN Security Council, 66th session, 6524th meeting, S/PV.6524, remarks by Hardeep Singh Puri, 8. See also Spencer Zifcak, 'The Responsibility to Protect after Libya and Syria', *Melbourne Journal of International Law* 13, no. 1 (2012), 59–93.

43 See Ramesh Thakur, 'To Stop Iran Getting the Bomb, Must We Learn to Live with Its Nuclear Capability?' *Strategic Analysis* 36, no. 2 (March 2012), 328–34

44 Personal conversation by author with retired senior Indian ambassador, Canberra, July 2012.

45 Chinmaya R. Gharekhan, 'A Civil War Set to Escalate', *The Hindu*, 26 November 2012. A retired senior ambassador and a former UN Under-Secretary-General, Gharekhan can be assumed to reflect the dominant viewpoint of the Indian foreign policy establishment.

46 Permanent Mission of Brazil to the United Nations, 'Responsibility while Protecting: Elements for the Development and Promotion of a Concept', A/66/551, S/2011/701, (New York: United Nations, 11 November 2011).

47 Amitav Acharya, 'Can Asia lead? Power Ambitions and Global Governance in the Twenty-first Century', *International Affairs* 87:4 (2011), 851–69.

48 See Lori Fisler Damrosch, 'The inevitability of selective response? Principles to guide urgent international action', in Schnabel and Thakur, eds., *Kosovo and the Challenge of Humanitarian Intervention*, 405–19.

8 R2P's 'structural' problems

A response to Roland Paris*

Roland Paris is a formidable intellectual, one of Canada's foremost mid-career scholars with an enviable international reputation already, who thinks deeply and writes cogently on some pressing contemporary challenges of global governance at the intersection of scholarship and policy – as well as a friend and professional colleague. That I am no longer able to interact with him as easily as when I was based in Canada is a keenly felt loss. This chapter highlights many of his impressive strengths as an analytical scholar on policy relevant topics.

Before responding to points with which I disagree, let me begin with some preliminary remarks. First, R2P is not a principle/norm in search of a self-validating crisis. Rather, it is an attempt to find new consensus on a rare but recurring problem, namely humanitarian atrocities which, in the age of an internationalised human conscience, are an increasing affront to modern sensibility for a growing number of people and countries.

Second, R2P remains conceptually contested and politically controversial. But it is contentious as a principle in academic circles. In the policy community, the principle per se is no longer contested but how best to implement it, and with what oversight and safeguards in order to prevent abuse, continues to attract controversy. So when Paris writes, quoting Phil Orchard, that 'both the study and practice of R2P have arrived "at a crossroads"',[1] he is correct with regard to the study but not the practice.

Third, part of the explanation for the discrepant status of the R2P principle between the scholarly and policy communities, in my view as someone who has straddled both, is that conceptual purity and analytical consistency is a requirement of academic rigour divorced from the untidy and messy real world of politics inhabited by policymakers. An easy way to grasp this is to ask: if consistency of principle was an absolute requirement, how many of the UN's 193 member states would still be left standing as we knock down inconsistent national foreign policies one by one? Every country has to trade off value goals and material interests (values against values, interests against interests, and values against interests), which is why 'a balance of interests' is a more satisfactory analytical construct than the stale and no longer fit for purpose 'the national interest'.[2] That is, far from a fatal flaw, policy inconsistency is the norm, which is why the five permanent members of the UN Security Council (P5) feel no embarrassment in demanding the right to enforce non-proliferation on Iran while hanging on indefinitely themselves to nuclear weapons in defiance of their own obligations under Article VI of the NPT.

Fourth, although R2P (along with its sibling norms POC and international criminal justice) is an important normative innovation, it does not fill all the gaps in the normative architecture of world order. Both R2P and POC resulted from growing shame at the accumulating list of atrocities in which the international community stood by as passive onlookers, frustrations at the 'constitutional' constraints and normative inadequacies rather than indifference and apathy to the plight of civilian victims that produced the passivity, and a determination to reposition the UN system to be empowered and capacitated to be able to respond better on both the timeliness and effectiveness dimensions when confronted by repeat occurrences of similar tragedies. Despite these two valuable additions to the repertoire of the international community in dealing with atrocities perpetrated on civilians, there remain many gaps in the protection agenda's normative architecture.[3]

Fifth, Paris writes that 'the literature on R2P, which has traced the emergence of the doctrine since 2001, and explored R2P's normative and legal aspects … has largely overlooked the question of how coercive force may be used to avert mass atrocities'.[4] Two comments: (a) The 1999–2001–05 period is in fact largely ignored in the literature. Yet this was the period of the heaviest lifting for shifting the existing global normative consensus so visibly and violently fractured by NATO's unilateral (that is, not UN-authorised) intervention in Kosovo, and the visceral hostility to Kofi Annan's challenge of humanitarian intervention, in 1999. The heavy lifting was done by ICISS, its co-chair Gareth Evans, ICISS Commissioner Ramesh Thakur and ICISS research co-director Tom Weiss. Many enthusiasts clambered aboard the bandwagon post-2005; (b) for prevention, the use of coercive force is least relevant, albeit still important.

Sixth but not least, interventions were frequent before R2P was formulated in 2001 and are not guaranteed after R2P's unanimous adoption in 2005. The choice therefore is not if intervention, but whether the intervention will be ad hoc or rules-based, unilateral or multilateral, and divisive or consensual. R2P, especially when backed by legitimacy criteria that have been agreed in advance, will help to shift the balance towards interventions that are rules-based, multilateral and consensual. To that extent it will help the world to be better prepared – normatively, organisationally and operationally – to deal with crises of humanitarian atrocities as, when and wherever they arise, without guaranteeing good outcomes.

Next, I address four issues: the choice of terminology; the core argument on the structural problems hardwired into R2P; Libya and Syria as case studies to illustrate the inescapable problems; and the different attempts to rescue R2P.

R2P vs. humanitarian intervention, protective or otherwise

It is both surprising and troubling to see the persistent hold of the terminology of 'humanitarian intervention' in the title and body of the article. The phrase 'humanitarian intervention' is used to trump sovereignty with intervention at the outset of the debate: it loads the dice in favour of intervention before the argument has even begun, by labelling and delegitimising dissent as anti-humanitarian. Of course, the term has a long historical pedigree and to that extent it is fair enough to use it when analysing the concept in its historical entirety, as even people closely associated with ICISS have done.[5] But when the discussion is restricted to or principally about R2P since formulation and adoption in 2001/2005, the reversion to the humanitarian intervention terminology is less defensible analytically and provokes a neuralgic rejection politically from the global South based on their traumatic colonial history.

'Humanitarian intervention' is what humanitarian agencies like the International Committee of the Red Cross (ICRC) and the UN High Commissioner for Refugees (UNHCR) do. In our pre-report consultations, they objected to the phrase being appropriated by states engaged in military intervention. 'Humanitarian intervention' conveys to most Western minds the idea that the principle underlying the intervention is not self-interested power politics but the disinterested one of protecting human life. It conjures up in many non-Western minds historical memories of the strong imposing their will on the weak in the name of the prevailing universal principles of the day, from the civilising mission of spreading Christianity to the cultivation and promotion of human rights.

Where humanitarian intervention raises fears of domination based on the international power hierarchy, R2P encapsulates the element of international solidarity and implies an evaluation of the issues from the point of view of those seeking or needing support, rather than those who may be considering intervention. It is victim- and people-centred, whereas humanitarian intervention privileges the perspectives, preferences and priorities of the intervening states. Unlike humanitarian intervention, which is only about military coercion, R2P embraces a whole spectrum of preventive and reactive responses, with coercive military action reserved only for the most extreme and exceptional cases. The focus on the 'right to intervene' does not adequately take into account the prevention and follow-up assistance components of external action. Moreover, the concept is a euphemism in the real world. In 1999, NATO's 'humanitarian intervention' in Kosovo in reality consisted of three months of bombing. The phrase 'humanitarian bombing' is such an obvious oxymoron that it does not pass the laugh test, as President Vaclev Havel of the Czech Republic discovered.[6]

The debate over R2P should not be framed as a North–South issue. Many non-Western societies have a historical tradition of reciprocal rights and obligations that bind sovereigns and subjects. It is very much in the interests of developing countries. The key questions are (1) shared understandings and expectations among states about the circumstances in which the use of international force across sovereign borders is both legal and legitimate, and (2) the authorising and implementing agency: who has the legal authority to approve and the material capacity to undertake protective interventions? The emerging powers, for example BRICS are the countries where R2P implementation remains most controversial, political resistance can be most expected, and whose power and influence is growing, especially the capacity to form blocking coalitions. Their 'emerging power' status ensures them of a distinctive mediating role between developing countries and the global North.

In the period of decolonisation after the Second World War, as European empires crumbled and retreated from around the world, the UN steadily expanded the range of executive actions it undertook to fill power vacuums in many newly-independent countries. These 'practices of governing' were not always accompanied by clearly articulated forms or bases of authority. Instead, it fell to ICISS to provide 'a detailed normative articulation' of the 'international authority to undertake executive action for protective ends'.[7] R2P does not address the distribution of jurisdiction and authority among states, but between states and international actors.[8] While R2P preserves to states the responsibility to protect their own populations, it strengthens the UN's responsibility for the international community as a whole, and in doing so 'represents one of the most significant normative shifts in international relations since the creation of the UN in 1945'.[9]

ICISS was successful in repositioning the international consensus because we made the core, sustaining idea not the 'right to intervene' but the 'responsibility to protect'. We quickly discovered the visceral hostility across the developing world to any so-called right of intervention, for any purpose, rooted in these countries' experience of Western *missions civilisatrice* in the era of colonialism. The developing countries remain deeply suspicious of the self-serving hidden agenda of geopolitical and commercial interests behind such claims. To dismiss their claims is to deny their history and disrespect their collective memory. In the foreseeable future the advanced developed countries will comprise the ranks of the powers doing most military interventions, not the targets of such interventions. The latter will mostly consist of developing countries.

This has a threefold importance to the people of developing countries that is of critical importance. They will be the victims of atrocities if outsiders refuse to save strangers; the victims of self-interested interventions where the language of humanitarianism is invoked to mask darker commercial and geopolitical motivations; but also the principal beneficiaries if interventions are motivated mainly by humanitarian concerns and executed responsibly. In turn this points to the need to hold mutually respectful conversations between the governments and civil society of both Western and developing countries. Only so can the community of nations forge shared understandings and common norms and standards of good international citizenship consistent with contemporary principles of national and global good governance.

Confusing the structural dilemmas of the use of force and R2P implementation

The second big error into which Paris falls is to conflate the structural dilemmas of *any use of force* in the contemporary world into the implementation difficulties of the coercive military edge of R2P. Paris refers to this as an 'unwinnable dilemma' or 'unavoidable paradox'.[10] A more familiar colloquialism describes the dilemmas as damned if you do and damned if you don't. It arises from the continuing need to use force sometimes, whether for national/collective self-defence or in order to enforce international/collective security, in an age of a deepening delegitimisation of the use of force. Because the dilemma is neither specific nor restricted to R2P, the 'structural' explanation is less than convincing.

A good example of normative inconsistency on the use of force comes from two recent statements by the US president. In his commencement speech at West Point on 28 May 2014, Barack Obama insisted: 'The United States will use military force, unilaterally if necessary, when our core interests demand it'.[11] But in his speech to the opening of the annual session of the UN General Assembly on 24 September, he demanded that 'all of us – big nations and small – must meet our responsibility to observe and enforce international norms'.[12] The two statements, less than five months apart, are not compatible and indeed the second was an admonition to Russia for acting in implementation of the first in using force to protect its core interests in the Crimea. The use of force is legally permissible only in self-defence against armed attack or when authorised by the United Nations. Therefore, no country that reserves the right to use military force unilaterally can claim to be committed to obeying global norms.

Paris is right that the use of military force is the defining element of R2P. Ban Ki-moon's first special report on its implementation[13] downplayed this element, as do many other reports and discussions. Far from helping, this does long-term damage in generating false understandings of a key element of R2P. Paris does a great job in tackling this in its preventive role. That said, the basic structural dilemma arises from the inescapable fact that any use of force produces material consequences. These do not always coincide with the benevolent intentions of the author of the use of force. Where force is used in the middle of a struggle for power by political actors, whether the contest is taking place in the domestic or global arena, it can tilt the balance decisively for and against the contestants. And this means that the recourse to force will attract charges of bias and partiality from the losing side. The use of force in the exercise of the international responsibility to protect cannot be quarantined from this structurally determined controversy but the dilemma is not derived from or limited to R2P.

A hundred years ago, war was an accepted institution with distinctive rules, etiquette, norms and stable patterns of practices. Now there are significant restrictions on the authority of states to use force either domestically or internationally and the UN has overseen the development of a robust corpus of laws and norms against the unilateral resort to force by states except in self-defence. The human rights movement grew as an effort to curb arbitrary excesses by states against the liberties and rights of their own citizens. International humanitarian law emerged as an effort to place limits on the behaviour of belligerent forces during armed conflict. The convergence of the interests of human rights and humanitarian communities with respect to protecting victims of atrocity crimes (crimes against humanity, large-scale killings, ethnic cleansing and genocide) is a logical extension of their original impulses. At the same time, it produces the paradox of humanitarianism – 'an endless struggle to contain war in the name of civilization'[14] – encouraging, even demanding, the use of force. 'Far from being a defense of the individual against the state', therefore, 'human rights has become a standard part of the justification for the external use of force by the state against other states and individuals'.[15]

Therein lies the 'structural' explanation for the split in the humanitarian community over the NATO military intervention in Kosovo. In a remarkable passage in 1960, UN Secretary-General Dag Hammarskjöld informed Katanga's secessionist leader, Moïse Tshombe, that it was 'the duty of the United Nations Force to protect the civilian populations and [that] this duty is … in no way restricted by the rule of non-intervention applied by the Force in relation to domestic conflicts'.[16] Even though ONUC used force to prevent the secession of Katanga and not to protect civilians, Hammarskjöld was foreshadowing the conscience as well as the controversies that were to be awakened and generated around the turn of the century. In a number of cases in the 1990s, the UN Security Council endorsed the use of force with the primary goal of humanitarian protection and assistance: in the (ineffectual) proclamation of UN safe areas in Bosnia, the delivery of humanitarian relief in Somalia, the restoration of the democratically elected government of Haiti, and the deployment of the multinational Kosovo Force.

Mixed motives problem

I'm not sure who would disagree with the claim about major powers being motivated by several considerations in any use of force, or about the interplay between material self-interest and humanitarian norms in driving their action. I am fairly certain that all 12 ICISS members would agree also that 'unless humanitarian operations are at least partly rooted in self-interest, intervening states may lack the political commitment and resolve to complete the humanitarian tasks they undertake, especially if these involve combat'.[17] This is exactly why we used the phrase 'primary purpose' in the Commission report. Paris is guilty of a mild dose of reinventing the wheel in these arguments. In my 2006 book, I wrote: 'The primary purpose of the intervention, whatever other motives intervening states may have, must be to halt or avert human suffering', adding: 'Right intention is better assured with multilateral operations'.[18] And a footnote to the qualification of 'whatever other motives' noted: 'For an intervention to be sustained, at least one state with the requisite military capacity must also have a stake in stabilising the situation, as with Australia in East Timor'.[19]

This is also why the follow-up argument does not hold: 'If self-interest is an unavoidable (and, to some extent, desirable and necessary) feature of such operations, and if the legitimacy of such missions rests on their perceived altruism, we should expect these operations to be *especially prone to delegitimization*'.[20] The 'backlash against R2P, particularly if the doctrine is viewed as a "cover" for imperialism, pre-emptive war, or other ulterior motives'[21] will come more from the use of the language of humanitarian intervention than from mixed motives.

The counterfactual problem

This is another example of a non-issue in the policy world. Precisely because it is impossible to know how many would have been killed without external intervention in any given conflict, the only alternative is to permit preventable atrocities simply to provide irrefutable proof of intent to kill. Even then it would still be impossible to prove how many further killings were prevented after the intervention. In Libya, Muammar Gaddafi had form on atrocities and his threats and choice of words were indeed chilling – a point made very well by Paris himself.[22] Perhaps dictators will avoid the use of such words/threats in future. Certainly, Bashar al-Assad has not made the same mistake in Syria.

The conspicuous harm problem

> No matter how carefully coercive operations may be planned and conducted, they almost always cause collateral damage and accidental deaths – they break things and kill innocent people – which is bound to have a more immediate impact on public debates than a conjectured counterfactual scenario.[23]

This is an absolutist position. All interventions must be subject to the balance of consequences test, erring on the side of caution:

> The risks of unintended and perverse consequences remain only too real. There is no humanitarian crisis so grave that it cannot be made worse by an outside military intervention. Hence the due diligence imperative: on an informed assessment, are we reasonably confident of doing more good than harm?[24]

Paris is correct in saying that

> outside actors may be held responsible for the behaviour of groups under their protection. Any form of external military intervention in a civil conflict is likely to favour one party or another, and thus will tend to be seen as biased by the local parties, even if the interveners, themselves, seek to remain impartial.[25]

But these are two separate problems, and both are more serious than conspicuous harm.

The end state problem

> In cases where outside forces set out to secure a population under threat, the mission may achieve its initial objective but then face a quandary: how to disengage or withdraw without recreating the same threatening conditions that prompted military action in the first place.[26]

This is a problem for humanitarian intervention but one of the major advantages of R2P (lost a bit in the three pillar formulation of 2009). My answer? The eminent and highly respected Professor Adam Roberts of Oxford University had written an early critique of R2P and I was tasked to write the reply on behalf of, but not in the name of, ICISS. I explained that:

> The substance of the responsibility to protect is the provision of life-supporting protection and assistance to populations at risk. The goal of intervention for human protection purposes is not to wage war on a state in order to destroy it and eliminate its statehood, but to protect victims of atrocities inside the state, to embed the protection in reconstituted institutions after the intervention, and then to withdraw all foreign troops. Thus military intervention for human protection purposes takes away the rights flowing from the status of sovereignty, but does not in itself challenge the status as such. It does supplant the rights of the state to *exercise* protective functions if the state has proven incapable or unwilling to do so with respect to genocidal killings, humanitarian atrocities and ethnic cleansing; or to suspend the right of the state to conduct itself free of external interference if such conduct is the cause of the above atrocities. The prevention of the exercise of sovereign rights under intervention for human protection purposes is always limited in time to a temporary period, until the capacity of the state itself to resume its protective functions can be restored and institutionalised. The scale, duration and intensity of the planned military intervention should therefore be the minimum necessary to secure the defined human protection objective…[27]

Twelve years later, Libya notwithstanding, I would not change a word in the above extract. '[I]f the threat is the government of the country (which is likely to be the case, since coercive intervention, by definition, is against the wishes of the target state), such a strategy would amount to regime change'.[28] Again, we foreshadowed and dealt with this problem:

> If defeat of a noncompliant state or regime is the only way to achieve the human protection goals, then so be it. But the primary motivation behind intervention – the cause rather than the necessary condition – must not be defeating an enemy state.[29]

The inconsistency problem

'A measure of selectivity, based on calculations of expected consequences, already seems to be built into the doctrine'.[30] In itself this is not a problem. It will 'produce the appearance of "double standards"' only if selection is based, not on the balance of consequences test, but on friends vs. foes. By way of analogy, consider citizen safety, law and order, and crime as part of the responsibilities of states. No country can guarantee perfect law and order or that every criminal and murderer will be apprehended, prosecuted and punished after conviction. But if whites/gentiles are given de facto impunity when victims are blacks/Jews, then the administration of justice falls into disrepute. It is wrong therefore to say that: 'R2P is thus caught in a confounding logical trap of its own making: whether prospective interveners act, or refrain from acting, they risk bringing the doctrine into disrepute'.[31]

Libya and Syria as R2P hard cases

The allegations of inconsistency and double standards have been particularly prevalent among the commentators with regard to Libya (intervention) and Syria (no intervention), but mostly they miss the nuances. There was only one example of a successful road testing of the non-military side of R2P before 2011. When post-election violence broke out in Kenya in 2007–08, called in to mediate, Kofi Annan saw and handled the crisis in R2P terms.[32] Both the potential mobilising power and the limitations of R2P as a call to international arms were demonstrated in Libya in 2011 which served as a stark reminder that the debate on military intervention is inextricably entangled with questions of regime legitimacy, state capacity and state-building.

Libya

UN Security Council Resolution 1973, adopted on 17 March by a 10–0-5 (China, Russia, Brazil, Germany, India) vote, authorised the use of 'all necessary measures … to protect civilians and civilian-populated areas'. This proved that it *is* possible for the international community, working through the authenticated, UN-centred structures and procedures of organised multilateralism, to deploy international force to neutralise the military might of a thug and intervene between him and his victims.

Subsequently, however, Libya highlighted the tensions inherent in any international use of force, including for implementing R2P. I agree that post-Gaddafi violence, killings and anarchy have retroactively delegitimised the NATO intervention under Resolution 1973.[33] But it is an exaggeration to say it exposed structural problems that are inevitable with all such operations.[34] As Margaret Macmillan reminds us with the concluding sentence of her magisterial account of the outbreak of the First World War, 'there are always choices'.[35] The same is true of NATO action in Libya in 2011. Gaddafi could have been defanged and contained but left in place to rule. The best example is Saddam Hussein from 1991 to 2003, a period in which Iraq was better off than in the 12 years before or after. A no-fly-zone enforced when required could have ensured the protection of civilians in Benghazi and elsewhere at less cost and controversy. While all options might have been problematic,[36] such an option would have been the least bad one.

Syria

The charge that inaction on Syria has proven the hollowness and emptiness of R2P[37] has been laid mainly by the old-fashioned humanitarian warriors. In any war, critical question marks must be substituted for excitable exclamation points regarding facts and responses. Too often slogans pass for policy: something must be done; this is something; therefore, this must be done. The failure to act in Syria stemmed from five factors.

The first is the difficulty of the boundary between permissible and illegitimate force by the state in dealing with an armed rebellion in a violent civil war. In Syria this posed a threefold challenge: is a state prohibited from employing force to fend off armed challenges to its authority; how can the moral hazard of encouraging other opposition and secessionist groups to take up arms against governments elsewhere be avoided; and what is the appropriate division of labour between R2P and international humanitarian and human rights laws in regulating the conduct of conflict parties in civil wars?[38]

Second, the Syrian crisis has been characterised with confused facts (for example on the numbers killed and by whom) and shared culpability, including for the use of chemical weapons. With regard to chemical weapons use – a qualitative escalation that does cross the 'atrocity threshold' – the West did not help its credibility problem by jumping from the fact that they were used to conclusions that they were used by the regime. Seymour Hersh argues that, like President George W. Bush in Iraq in 2003, Obama cherry-picked facts and intelligence, presented assumptions as facts, implied a sequence that reversed reality and omitted important intelligence pointing to the jihadist al-Nusra Front's capability to make and mount a chemical weapon attack with sarin gas.[39]

Third, it was far from obvious how the world could respond without further inflaming an extremely volatile situation. The fluid and confused internal situation; question marks over the identity, intent and methods of the rebels; the risk of atrocities against minority groups if the regime collapsed; relations with Iran, China and Russia; and the deepening Sunni–Shia divide all around the Islamic crescent made it impossible to assess the balance of consequences of outside intervention. A war-weary US public doubted the West has any dog in the fight where a rebel commander filmed himself eating the heart of a government soldier and almost half the rebel fighters are jihadists. There is the added risk of blowback as radicalised Western Muslims take up arms to go and fight in Syria and return with an extremist ideology and battle experience. By late 2014 a frightening thought was the possibility of the ultra-extremist Islamic State being in power in Syria if Assad had been toppled.

Fourth, the post-Gaddafi turmoil and volatility in Libya further complicated international responses to the ongoing crisis in Syria by raising doubts about the long-term results of military action based on visceral rather than cerebral calculations.

Fifth, at least some worried about the further damage to the fabric of international law if Syria – which had not attacked a foreign country – was attacked by a US-led coalition. China and Russia were adamantly opposed to UN authorisation and to any resolution that could set in motion a sequence of events leading to Libya-style military operations in Syria. Without UN authorisation, military strikes would be neither lawful nor legitimate, just another instance of vigilante justice by a trigger-happy and seemingly out-of-control West. To the non-West rest, enforcing humanitarian norms inside another country's sovereign jurisdictions means flouting higher-order global norms on restrictions on the unilateral threat and use of force internationally. Those norms are critical to most countries' national security and international stability.

Ways forward?

Paris undervalues the importance of efforts being made in several quarters to try and find ways to move forward on how best to prevent and halt atrocities. In particular he underestimates the importance of initiatives from within the global South, including Brazil's paper on 'Responsibility while Protecting'.[40] This would require an agreed set of guidelines to assist the Security Council in determining if the crisis warranted an R2P-type response including military intervention before the mandating resolution was approved. And it would also institute an oversight and monitoring mechanism to govern the use of UN-authorised R2P operations in order to prevent abuse of the international community's sanction for a limited use of force through mission creep. In speaking directly to the Brazilian initiative,[41] Secretary-General Ban emphasised the 'shared determination to ensure that implementation' of R2P 'will be carried out in a way that is consistent with the purposes, principles and provisions of the Charter and with the intent of the Heads of State and Government expressed at the 2005 World Summit'.[42]

My views on Pape's 'pragmatic standard'[43] are already on record.[44] In discussing Gareth Evans's efforts at rebuilding R2P consensus,[45] Paris comments that 'Evans' recommendations do not deal with the structural problems described above'.[46] That's because we do not see them as real. Evans lists three reasons for rejecting pessimism about the future of R2P.[47] First, there is near-universal consensus in the UN policy community on basic R2P principles. Second, the Security Council continues to endorse R2P as a principle and to draw on its language in several resolutions and presidential statements. And third, initiatives like Brazil's RWP and the Chinese notion of 'responsible protection'[48] point to a new dynamic of refining rather than rejecting the principle. In October 2013, even the Diplomatic Academy of the Russian Ministry of Foreign Affairs convened a one-day meeting on R2P in Moscow. The key point about all this activity is how the so-called critics are actually trying to engage with rather than reject outright R2P as a new global principle.

Conclusion

In some ways the most dispiriting aspect of the debate is how repetitive it can be. There is little if anything in the above analysis that we have not said before.[49]

Paris is right: what ultimately matters is how ideas are translated into practice,[50] including with respect to R2P. Hence the emphasis on policy rather than academic community. To call for R2P implementation to be reliable, predictable, certain and universal in application is to set an impossibly high bar. Rather, the key question is: on balance, does it help to get it right more often than not? And the answer to that is: yes, because it is rules-based, multilateral and consensual when compared to the opposite alternative of unilateral interventions by the powerful.

The collision of different UN Charter norms that produced the heated and tense debates over 'humanitarian intervention' in 1999 reflected a growing erosion of the sense of community among the different members of the family of nations with respect to the internal and international use of force by states. As well as strongly held beliefs in contrary directions, states and peoples no longer share a common belief in the means and procedures by which their differences can be mediated and reconciled. This suggests that the response of states to atrocities will continue to be ad hoc and on a case by case basis, rather than principled and consistent. Reframing 'humanitarian intervention' as the responsibility to protect at least re-established an international consensus. However, the implementation of the sharp, military end of Pillar Three in Libya shows that the global consensus on R2P is tenuous and fragile rather than robust and resilient.

Notes

* Originally published in *International Peacekeeping* 22:1 (2015), 11–25. Reprinted by permission of Taylor & Francis Ltd.

1 Roland Paris, 'The "Responsibility to Protect" and the Structural Problems of Preventive Humanitarian Intervention', *International Peacekeeping* 21:5 (2014), 570.

2 Ramesh Thakur, 'A Balance of Interests', in Andrew F. Cooper, Jorge Heine and Ramesh Thakur, eds., *The Oxford Handbook of Modern Diplomacy* (Oxford: Oxford University Press, 2013), 70–87.

3 Ramesh Thakur, 'Protection Gaps for Civilian Victims of Political Violence', *South African Journal of International Affairs* 20:3 (December 2013), 321–38.

4 Paris, 'The "Responsibility to Protect" and the Structural Problems of Preventive Humanitarian Intervention', 571.

5 Thomas G. Weiss, *Humanitarian Intervention: Ideas in Action*, 2nd ed. (Cambridge: Polity, 2011); Ramesh Thakur 'Humanitarian Intervention', in Thomas G. Weiss and Sam Daws, eds., *The Oxford Handbook on the United Nations* (Oxford: Oxford University Press, 2007), 387–403.

6 See the entry under 'Humanitarian bombing' in Wikipedia, http://en.wikipedia.org/wiki/Humanitarian_bombing.

7 Anne Orford, *International Authority and the Responsibility to Protect* (Cambridge: Cambridge University Press, 2011), 1.

8 Orford, *International Authority and the Responsibility to Protect*, 25–27.

9 Orford, *International Authority and the Responsibility to Protect*, 41.

10 Paris, 'The "Responsibility to Protect" and the Structural Problems of Preventive Humanitarian Intervention', 570.

11 Barack Obama, 'Remarks by the President at the United States Military Academy Commencement Ceremony', 28 May 2014, www.whitehouse.gov/the-press-office/2014/05/28/remarks-president-united-states-military-academy-commencement-ceremony.

12 Barack Obama, 'Remarks by President Obama in Address to the United Nations General Assembly', 24 September 2014, www.whitehouse.gov/the-press-office/2014/09/24/remarks-president-obama-address-united-nations-general-assembly.

13 Ban Ki-moon, *Implementing The Responsibility to Protect*, Report of the Secretary-General (New York: United Nations, document A/63/677, 12 January 2009).

14 David Kennedy, *The Dark Sides of Virtue: Reassessing International Humanitarianism* (Princeton: Princeton University Press, 2004), 323.

15 Kennedy, *The Dark Sides of Virtue: Reassessing International Humanitarianism*, 25.

16 Quoted in Mats Berdal, 'United Nations Peacekeeping and the Responsibility to Protect', in Ramesh Thakur and William Maley, eds., *Theorising the Responsibility to Protect* (Cambridge: Cambridge University Press, 2015), 227.

17 Paris, 'The "Responsibility to Protect" and the Structural Problems of Preventive Humanitarian Intervention', 573.

18 Ramesh Thakur, *The United Nations, Peace and Security: From Collective Security to the Responsibility to Protect* (Cambridge: Cambridge University Press, 2006), 258.

19 Thakur, The United Nations, Peace and Security, n18.

20 Paris, 'The "Responsibility to Protect" and the Structural Problems of Preventive Humanitarian Intervention', 574.

21 Paris, 'The "Responsibility to Protect" and the Structural Problems of Preventive Humanitarian Intervention', 574.

22 Paris, 'The "Responsibility to Protect" and the Structural Problems of Preventive Humanitarian Intervention', 582–83.

23 Paris, 'The "Responsibility to Protect" and the Structural Problems of Preventive Humanitarian Intervention', 575.

24 Thakur, 'Protection Gaps for Civilian Victims of Political Violence', 334.

25 Paris, 'The "Responsibility to Protect" and the Structural Problems of Preventive Humanitarian Intervention', 576.

26 Paris, 'The "Responsibility to Protect" and the Structural Problems of Preventive Humanitarian Intervention', 576.

27 Ramesh Thakur, 'Reply in Defence of the Responsibility to Protect', *International Journal of Human Rights* 7:3 (Autumn 2003), 163.

28 Paris, 'The "Responsibility to Protect" and the Structural Problems of Preventive Humanitarian Intervention', 577.

29 Thakur, 'Reply in Defence of the Responsibility to Protect'.

30 Paris, 'The "Responsibility to Protect" and the Structural Problems of Preventive Humanitarian Intervention', 578.

31 Paris, 'The "Responsibility to Protect" and the Structural Problems of Preventive Humanitarian Intervention', 579.

32 Roger Cohen, 'How Kofi Annan Rescued Kenya', *New York Review of Books*, 14 August 2008, 51–53.

33 Paris, 'The "Responsibility to Protect" and the Structural Problems of Preventive Humanitarian Intervention', 585.

34 Paris, 'The "Responsibility to Protect" and the Structural Problems of Preventive Humanitarian Intervention', 585–91.

35 Margaret Macmillan, *The War that Ended Peace: The Road to 1914* (New York: Random House, 2013), 645.

36 Paris, 'The "Responsibility to Protect" and the Structural Problems of Preventive Humanitarian Intervention', 583.

37 Paris, 'The "Responsibility to Protect" and the Structural Problems of Preventive Humanitarian Intervention', 588.

38 Similar 'structural' questions are raised every time Israel launches a military assault in Gaza: Ramesh Thakur, 'Israel's Serial Gaza Offensives Are Offensive', *e-International Relations*, 24 July 2014, www.e-ir.info/2014/07/24/israels-serial-gaza-offensives-are-offensive.

39 Seymour M. Hersh, 'Whose Sarin?', *London Review of Books*, 8 December 2013, www.lrb.co.uk/2013/12/08/seymour-m-hersh/whose-sarin.

40 Permanent Mission of Brazil to the United Nations, *Responsibility While Protecting: Elements for the Development and Promotion of a Concept* (New York: United Nations, General Assembly and Security Council, document A/66/551-S/2011/701, 11 November 2011).

41 Ban Ki-moon, *Responsibility to Protect: Timely and Decisive Response* (New York: United Nations, document A/66/874–S/2012/578, 25 July 2012), 13–15.

42 Ban, *Responsibility to Protect: Timely and Decisive Response*, paragraph 49.

43 Paris, 'The "Responsibility to Protect" and the Structural Problems of Preventive Humanitarian Intervention', 590–91.

44 Gareth Evans and Ramesh Thakur, 'Correspondence: Humanitarian Intervention and the Responsibility to Protect', *International Security* 37:4 (2013), 199–207.

45 Paris, 'The "Responsibility to Protect" and the Structural Problems of Preventive Humanitarian Intervention', 592.

46 Paris, 'The "Responsibility to Protect" and the Structural Problems of Preventive Humanitarian Intervention', 592.

47 Gareth Evans, 'The Evolution of the Responsibility to Protect: From Concept and Principle to Actionable Norm', in Thakur and Maley, eds., *Theorising the Responsibility to Protect.*

48 See Ramesh Thakur, 'A Chinese Vision of "Responsible Protection"', *Japan Times*, 1 November 2013.

49 For the works of Gareth Evans, see his book *The Responsibility to Protect: Ending Mass Atrocity Crimes Once and for All* (Washington, DC: Brookings Institution Press, 2008), and for his vast collection of journal articles, op-eds and speeches on the subject, see his website www.gevans.org. For my works, see: Thakur, *The United Nations, Peace and Security*; for the collection of my journal articles, see Ramesh Thakur, *The Responsibility to Protect: Norms, Laws and the Use of Force in International Politics* (London: Routledge, 2011), and two important articles since then, Ramesh Thakur, 'R2P after Libya and Syria: Engaging Emerging Powers', *The Washington Quarterly* 36:2 (Spring 2013), 61–76, and Thakur, 'Protection Gaps for Civilian Victims of Political Violence'; for the collection of newspaper op-eds, see Ramesh Thakur, *People vs. the State: Reflections on UN Authority, US Power and the Responsibility to Protect* (Tokyo: United Nations University Press, 2011). For the views of Thomas G. Weiss, see his *Humanitarian Intervention.*

50 Paris, 'The "Responsibility to Protect" and the Structural Problems of Preventive Humanitarian Intervention', 570.

9 The UN Secretary-General and the forgotten third R2P responsibility*

The failure of the UN's principal political organs – the UN Security Council and General Assembly – to function as envisaged in the UN Charter, places a disproportionate burden on the shoulders of the Secretary-General, turning the office into one with little power, but considerable influence. This has been particularly evident in the story of the origins, adoption and development of R2P as the central organising principle for the international community to respond to humanitarian atrocities being committed inside sovereign jurisdictions. First articulated in the report of ICISS in 2001,[1] as an 'umbrella' principle, R2P was broken down into three constituent responsibilities, each being given a chapter in the report: to prevent, react and rebuild. The principle was endorsed unanimously at the 2005 UN world summit – by historical standards, an astonishingly rapid advance from an innovative principle proposed by an independent international commission to a globally endorsed norm-in-waiting.[2]

Paragraphs 138 and 139 of the summit's outcome document serve as the functional equivalent of the 'constitution' of R2P. Eight crucial features pertinent to the core arguments in this chapter are worth highlighting:

1 They emphasise the primary responsibility of the state to protect populations from atrocity crimes and all UN member states 'accept that responsibility';
2 Member states collectively agreed to 'encourage and help States to exercise this responsibility', including help in building the capacity of states 'under stress';
3 The international community 'also has the responsibility to use appropriate diplomatic, humanitarian and other peaceful means';
4 However, 'should peaceful means be inadequate and national authorities are manifestly failing to protect their populations' from the atrocity crimes, all states 'are prepared to take collective action, in a timely and decisive manner, through the Security Council, in accordance with the Charter, including Chapter VII';
5 R2P 'entails the prevention of such crimes, including their incitement';
6 The UN Security Council would be responsible for implementing R2P;
7 The General Assembly would 'continue consideration of the responsibility to protect … and its implications';
8 The Secretary-General is not mentioned in either paragraph.

The prevention and reaction components of the original ICISS formulation were thus endorsed and reaffirmed. But the third and equally critical component, namely the responsibility to rebuild, fell through the cracks. Taking the 2005 document as the agreed inter-governmental text, Ban Ki-moon's subsequent reports have similarly disregarded peace-building as an integral component of R2P – even though, as noted by Paris, there are remarkable similarities in the core tasks of both normative agendas in the separate reports by the Secretary-General on them (promoting inter-communal dialogue and reconciliation, effective, legitimate and inclusive political institutions, effective and impartial justice mechanisms, etc.).[3] The 2001 ICISS version had sliced the principle into three cognate responsibilities to prevent, respond and rebuild. The Secretary-General's special report in 2009 reformulated it in the metaphor of three pillars: the state's responsibilities; international assistance to the state; and collective international action when the state is unable or unwilling to discharge its sovereign responsibility to international standards and satisfaction.[4]

We contend that the responsibility to rebuild needs to be re-elevated to prominence as an integral component of R2P conceptually, normatively and operationally; its institutional home(s) in the UN system clarified; and the Secretary-General's role clarified and understood by all relevant actors. We assert, without developing the argument in this chapter, that the 2005 version is the only authoritative statement of R2P; that the 2009 three pillar formulation is the most widely accepted description of the content of R2P in the policy and scholarly communities; and that in almost all respects this works better and more elegantly than the original sequential three slices. But in one respect, the three pillar formulation has proven to be problematic. Namely, it buries and loses sight of the critical importance of the third responsibility to rebuild and reconstruct the war-ravaged society to the point of being viable and self-sustaining once again. But because the three pillar conceptualisation works better in most respects, any effort to reverse the current global understandings would be damaging and counter-productive. Instead, recalling that UN Security Council authorisation of R2P coercive operations is a non-negotiable prerequisite, we suggest that the original ICISS third responsibility can be reintroduced through the administrative and political leadership roles of the Secretary-General.

We first derive some key lessons from the major international interventions of this century. Next, we recall the context in which R2P was originally formulated in order to highlight the distinctive features of its contribution to international policy. In the third section, we describe the three dimensions of the responsibility to rebuild and the strategies and steps needed for the rebuilding agenda. Fourth, we look at the Secretary-General as an actor and point out the bases of the Secretary-General's authority, power and influence that can be exploited to lay out and implement the rebuilding agenda.

Twenty-first century international interventions

As of August 2016, the twenty-first century had witnessed major international interventions in Afghanistan, Iraq, Libya and Syria.[5] (Yemen too was subjected to military intervention but by regional powers, and so is excluded from the discussion for present purposes.) The US war on Taliban-ruled Afghanistan after the terrorist attacks of 11 September 2001 was widely accepted as a legitimate act of self-defence against armed attack. Despite donors contributing vast resources, however, state-building and peace-building soon unravelled. The Taliban reorganised as an insurgency in 2003, the fragile peace fragmented revealing cracks and divisions in the clientelist political system,[6] and the state continued to be extractive and predatory.[7] President Hamid Karzai's rule (2001–14) was routinely described as corrupt and inept. By 2016 Afghanistan had become a lost cause. The International Crisis Group described the dominant Western approach as 'a market-bazaar approach to negotiations. Bargains are cut with any and all comers, regardless of their political relevance or ability to influence outcomes'.[8] The exodus of Western countries from Afghanistan quickly acquired the appearance of being 'all exit and no strategy'[9] – accurately if unkindly summed up as 'surge, bribe and run'.[10]

The invasion and occupation of Iraq by a US-led coalition in 2003 was a stark example of unauthorised unilateral intervention that proved to be a richly foretold mega-disaster.[11] The decade after did little to soften the criticism and much to validate and deepen it. As in Afghanistan, Washington left behind a country radically different from one envisaged when it was attacked and invaded. Occupation proved different from and more difficult than invasion, and nation-building proved more challenging and protracted still. Conventional wisdom seems to have settled into the conclusion that the war was one of the gravest foreign policy blunders of modern times. The long-awaited Chilcot Report on the reasons for and management of the British part of the Iraq war further seared conventional wisdom deep into the public consciousness.[12]

In responding to the Libya crisis in 2011, the UN Security Council invoked R2P under the coercive Chapter VII of the Charter. By year's end Gaddafi had been ousted, captured and killed. But ongoing volatility, violence and instability in Libya continued to cast a long shadow about the country's viability and commitment to a liberal democratic culture.[13] By 2016 few would dissent from the judgement that the first R2P military intervention had left 'Libya a failed state and a terrorist haven'.[14] US President Barack Obama later was to blame the Libya debacle on the Europeans who, 'given Libya's proximity', should have been more 'invested in the follow-up'.[15] In a subsequent interview, Obama said the biggest mistake of his presidency was failing to anticipate the fallout and prepare for the aftermath of Gaddafi's ouster. Because of that failure, the intervention – which he still believes to have been the right thing to have done – 'didn't work'.[16]

The post-intervention chaos, volatility and killings in Libya led to pronouncements that R2P had morphed into RIP. The failure to intervene effectively in Syria led to similar pronouncements. China and Russia did not veto UN Security Council Resolution 1973 (2011) authorising military action for the protection of civilians in Libya on the understanding that the NATO-led intervention would be limited to the humanitarian objective of civilian protection and would eschew regime change.[17] The perceived US 'bait-and-switch' over Libya entrenched their sense of betrayal. Although Western forces have not intervened in the Syrian conflict with their own troops on the ground, they have helped to arm the anti-government rebels and later launched air strikes against Islamic State targets inside Syria. Russia's air intervention in Syria in 2015 in support of the Assad regime – its first military intervention since 1989 outside the borders of the former Soviet Union – marked the breakout of Moscow from the post-Cold War international order constructed by the West and imposed on Russia: Moscow was no longer prepared 'to submit to the norms and practices laid down, policed and arbitrated by the West'.[18]

As of mid-2016, thus, Afghanistan, Iraq, Libya and Syria had stopped functioning as sovereign states. It has been well and truly said: 'When you destroy a state the gates to every corner of hell are opened – no frontiers, no police, no law, no education, no infrastructure, no government, a Hobbesian war of all against all'.[19] The entire region was consumed by sectarian, tribal and jihadist violence. It now seems safe to conclude that Saddam Hussein, Muammar Gaddafi and Hafez and Bashar Assad were and are the lids on their respective cauldrons of sectarian tensions that boil over into large-scale violence, killings and displacement if the lid is removed. All the cases involved foreign interventions in badly fragmented countries that deepened the sectarian fissures and tipped the hostile groups into open civil war. In all cases the justification included humanitarian goals that downplayed the presence of jihadist elements among groups opposing the local authoritarian regimes. But in no case did the regimes installed by force of foreign arms succeed in consolidating power and state authority to the point they could survive a total military withdrawal of their foreign backers. By 2016, the collapse of humanitarian ideals into sectarian bloodbaths had discredited externally directed liberal state-building as a normative enterprise, regardless of whether it is UN-authorised or unilateral.

Four common lessons can be drawn from these cases. The most important is the limited utility of the use of force in contemporary conditions. Non-R2P operations in Iraq and Afghanistan have been no more successful than the R2P-authorised mission in Libya. Syria (and other conflicts as in Sudan) prove that R2P does not guarantee collective UN action on all occasions when it is needed and justified. Nor, as Libya proved, does it guarantee successful outcomes when the UN does approve military action to protect populations at risk of slaughter. But nothing in recent history suggests going around the UN ensures success either. The use of force today is inherently controversial and problematic. No humanitarian crisis is so grave that the plight of the trapped civilians cannot be made even worse with outside military intervention: the swath of ungoverned territories from Afghanistan through the Middle East to North Africa is graphic evidence of that.

If the primary pathology in the region is the lack of local good governance institutions, the military is not just ineffectual; it is counter-productive, for it destroys and degrades the fragile physical and institutional infrastructure that does exist. The second critical lesson therefore is that for the major powers, going through the UN reduces the diplomatic transaction costs and contributes to the consolidation of the principle of a world governed by the rule of law in the use of force. The main focus should be on improving R2P implementation to safeguard against abuses and failures while channelling individual outrage to rid the world of atrocities through UN-centred collective action.

The third important lesson, conversely, is that unilaterally reinterpreting a UN Security Council mandate to expand the mission and the means builds resistance; other countries resent being exploited as useful idiots and will withhold cooperation on future issues until such time as credible checks are put in place to prevent self-interested expansive reinterpretations of collectively authorised operations. The fourth lesson is the invaluable utility of multilateral treaty-based arms control agreements and verification machinery for ensuring conformity with global norms on weapons of mass destruction. Without the Chemical Weapons Convention and the Organisation for the Prohibition of Chemical Weapons, it would have been much more difficult to resolve the crisis over allegations of chemical weapons use in Syria in 2013. In Iraq a major reason for the international legitimacy deficit, that doomed the war and the occupation, was the widespread sentiment that UN inspectors, instead of being given the time to do their job, had been deliberately sidelined by a coalition hell bent on regime change.

The shift from 'humanitarian intervention' to 'the Responsibility to Protect'

R2P emerged against the backdrop of a highly charged international controversy over NATO's self-proclaimed emerging new norm of 'humanitarian intervention' in Kosovo in 1999 that could trump national sovereignty. ICISS calmed the troubled waters by redefining sovereignty as responsibility and argued that states, as part of their sovereign duties, had the primary responsibility to protect all populations inside their borders; and the international community had a fall-back responsibility if the state authorities proved unable or unwilling, or if they were themselves complicit in the atrocities. One of the key arguments for R2P was that while humanitarian intervention highlighted the rights and privileges of the intervening powers, R2P prioritised the needs of the victims. By rooting military intervention in human solidarity, R2P provided 'conceptual, normative and operational linkages between assistance, intervention and reconstruction'.[20] If interventions are genuinely motivated by humanitarian concerns as the primary goal (accepting that the real world is usually characterised by mixed-motives situations), then their implementation implies solidarity across borders. Such solidarity, however, cannot begin and end with military intervention. It must also find expression at the pre-crisis point and be continued after the immediate crisis is over.

There are three other critical points of difference between humanitarian intervention and R2P relevant to this chapter.[21] First, conceptually humanitarian intervention is fundamentally about the distribution of authority and jurisdiction between different individual and groups of states, and their respective rights vis-à-vis one another. By contrast, internally R2P is fundamentally about the distribution of rights and responsibilities between states and citizens. ICISS performed a 'Feuerbachian inversion' whereby citizens became rights holders and states duty carriers.[22] Externally, R2P redefines the distribution of authority between states on the one side, and the international community collectively on the other. It preserves to states the responsibility to protect their own populations but strengthens the UN's responsibility acting for the international community as a whole.

Second, procedurally, attempts to enforce authority can only be made by the legitimate agents of that authority and the only legitimate agent of the contemporary international community is the United Nations. To concede to any one state or coalition the unilateral right to decide when to intervene with force in the internal affairs of other countries is tantamount to international anarchy. R2P, like any law or rule, has both an enabling (licence) and a constraining (leash) function. Humanitarian intervention is more great power friendly in that it acts as an enabling norm without the restraining element.

Third, operationally R2P can be aligned to supplement UN peace operations whereas humanitarian interventions are closer to war fighting.[23] The basic objective of protective military interventions is to achieve quick success with as little cost as possible in civilian lives, and inflicting as little damage as possible so as to enhance recovery prospects in the post-conflict phase. The rules of engagement of an R2P preventive operation will primarily be of a defensive nature and only reluctantly allow forcing an opponent to comply. After intervention, the main mission of R2P military forces is transformed to provide the safe environment necessary for the restoration of good governance and the rule of law, with a transition of responsibility from military to civilian authorities as soon as possible. Moreover, because the responsibility to rebuild is an integral component of R2P, the intervening countries must be prepared to remain engaged during the post-intervention phase as long as necessary to achieve stability.

The responsibility to rebuild

Post-conflict societies have special needs in order to avoid a return to conflict while laying a solid foundation for development. The UN has not generally been able to move from initial stabilisation, infrastructural reconstruction and the re-establishment of local governance institutions, to the more demanding goal of leaving behind self-sustaining structures of state that can implement rapid economic growth and social transformation. Bosnia, East Timor, Afghanistan and Iraq are examples of countries coming out of protracted conflicts that have left their people deeply traumatised, their economies wrecked, their infrastructure gutted, their political institutions highly stressed and in some cases their communities bitterly divided. The history of international missions in these places confirm that there are major gaps in the planning, financing and implementation capacities for the critical civilian components of such complex nation-building missions.

'Peace-building' gives us the conceptual bridge to connect the two great normative agendas of the UN, security and development. A good definition of peace-building is in the Brahimi Report: 'activities undertaken on the far side of conflict to reassemble the foundations of peace and provide the tools for building on those foundations something that is more than just the absence of war'.[24] In the 2001 ICISS formulation, R2P rebuilding is conceptually and operationally indistinguishable from peace-building which has an earlier pedigree going back to Secretary-General Boutros Boutros-Ghali's *Agenda for Peace*.[25] The distinct ICISS contribution lay in elevating this into a *political-cum-moral responsibility*, co-equal with the responsibilities to prevent and react. But there is one significant difference in consequence. Under the ICISS R2P, prevention and intervention are general responsibilities shared by all states, but the responsibility to rebuild is particular to states undertaking military intervention. Similarly, while the responsibility for peace-building is diffuse and shared among all states, that for R2P rebuilding is restricted to the intervening states.

Ban Ki-moon set out his vision for peace-building in a 2009 report that identified five priority areas of action: support for basic safety and security; political processes; provision of basic services; restoration of core government functions; and economic revitalisation.[26] The goals are often deeply interlinked. For example, the institutional reconstruction of a war-torn country often needs a prior reconciliation process to address the wounds of a traumatic and deeply unjust past. Intra-state conflicts often arise from inherited and accumulated hatred, transmitted across generations, and focussed around group-identity issues of dispossession, access to land, economic, cultural and religious resources, and the memory of prior aggression. External support for reconciliation efforts must be conscious of the need to encourage this cooperation and linked dynamically to joint development efforts between former adversaries.

The survey of twenty-first century interventions confirmed that without successful post-intervention peace-building, the countries subject to interventions can become stuck in a 'conflict trap' of a cycle of ongoing armed conflict and economic decline. Almost half of all countries coming out of conflict relapse into armed violence within a decade of a peace agreement, owing both to pre-conflict characteristics that led to conflict in the first place and to the post-violence legacy of the conflict itself.[27] Most armed conflicts of this century have been repeat civil wars.[28] This persisting reality makes peace-building a conflict prevention tool also in order to break the self-replicating cycles of violence. Conversely, targeted interventions by the international community can help to break the conflict trap. The presence of a UN peace operation in a post-conflict country significantly reduces the chances of it slipping back into violence.[29]

ICISS understood the responsibility to rebuild as the 'commitment to helping to build a durable peace, and promoting good governance and sustainable development'.[30] An R2P intervention either prevents or halts the commission of group-based atrocities. Thereafter, actions must be taken to consolidate the peace and create the institutions to prevent a recurrence of armed confrontation between former enemy groups. The underlying strategic vision informing all peace-building missions should be the restoration and development of effective, efficient and legitimate public institutions capable of delivering the necessary goods and services, assuring public safety and order, exercising monopoly control over the legitimate use of force, mediating inter-group competition, facilitating economic growth and development and so on. National institutions may have to be built and strengthened; participation and inclusiveness in the political process must be ensured; refugees and the displaced must be resettled; human rights laws enacted with the administrative and judicial structures to enforce them; demobilised combatants will need to be gainfully reintegrated into the economy and society; and conditions have to be created and policies instituted to resume economic growth and promote sustainable development.

In the long run, international actors in a post-conflict situation should aim 'to do themselves out of a job'.[31] While they have the requisite resources to build a secure environment and begin the reconstruction process, the responsibility for their future lies ultimately with the local actors and populations.[32] Locals are not only a vital source of peace-building resource, but also a vital actor in shaping peace-building methodology. Programs that do not take account of local priorities and exclude local personnel can create an unhealthy dependency on the intervening authority, stultify the regrowth of local institutions and the economy and infinitely delay the population's desire or ability to assume responsibility for its own government.

In Afghanistan, the failure to include locals (other than a small clique of elites[33]) meant interveners had little understanding of the complex conflict dynamics, especially the political economy of war. The external intervention overthrew a stable if brutal order under the Taliban and replaced it with an inherently unstable and violent order.[34] Eager to avoid further conflict, the Bonn accords facilitated a distribution of power among the victors rather than negotiate a genuine peace agreement, with the result that the invasion re-empowered the jihadi leaders whom the Taliban had pushed out in 1996.[35] The redesigned formal institutions failed to provide meaningful constraints on state power at the local level; instead, they institutionalised extractive and predatory politics. The extension of state power into the periphery can lead individuals and groups to either rebel, resist or even exit the state.

Recovery

Like R2P itself, ICISS also disaggregated the responsibility to rebuild into three constituent components: 'to provide, particularly after a military intervention, full assistance with recovery, reconstruction and reconciliation'.[36] A major and urgent peace-building responsibility of any intervening force is to encourage economic growth, the recreation of markets and sustainable development. Rapid economic growth is dramatically effective in reducing post-conflict risks.[37] Such growth can be promoted by international actors through aid and assistance in creating institutions and practices of good governance. Importantly, Collier points out that aid is highly effective, but only in the middle period of the first decade after a conflict has been terminated. It may be, he speculated, that in the beginning the country simply lacks the capacity to absorb and utilise aid optimally. Thus while the need is for external aid to taper in, politically the easiest time to justify aid is immediately after the intervention and so the usual practice is for aid to taper out as donors give up in frustration at the lack of demonstrable progress in generating economic growth.[38] The 2011 World Development Report recommended that international efforts need to be sustained for a minimum of 15 years to support most long-term institutional transformations, albeit in a support role to national authorities.[39]

An urgent post-intervention task relates to the disarmament, demobilisation and reintegration (DDR) of local security forces. The importance of this was starkly highlighted by the folly of the US occupying authority in disbanding Saddam Hussein's army with no effort to reintegrate the large number of soldiers. Security vacuums must be filled, and conditions of public safety and order have to be reconstituted for all members of a population, regardless of ethnic origin or relation to the previous source of power in the territory. Revenge killings and 'reverse ethnic cleansing', only too common as victimised groups attack those aligned to former oppressors, discredits and retrospectively delegitimises the intervention.

Reconstruction

Ensuring sustainable reconstruction and rehabilitation will involve the commitment of sufficient funds and resource and close cooperation with local people. Following DDR in the first phase, new national armed forces and police have to be rebuilt, integrating as far as possible elements of the formerly competing armed factions or military forces. It is just as important to build a non-corrupt and properly functioning judicial system, including both the courts and police. The importance of transitional justice arrangements during an operation is now generally acknowledged, and to restore judicial systems as soon as possible thereafter. Several NGOs have developed 'justice packages' and model penal codes that can be adapted to the specific conditions of a wide variety of operations.

Reconciliation

In post-conflict countries, groups engaged in killing one another must be socialised to live together peacefully once again, sharing power, engaging in bargaining, negotiation and accommodation instead of armed violence, and agreeing to resolve differences by constitutionally mandated peaceful means. The liberal peace paradigm has proven to be unduly optimistic in some core assumptions. Transitions from war to peace often reproduce rather than the transform wartime dynamics: violence may continue, mutate or intensify.[40] Hasty democracy promotion often generates perverse effects. For example, elections, far from signifying and embedding the peace dividend, can create losers and winners and increase the likelihood of violence if the victors govern with a winner-take-all mentality that actively discriminates against defeated groups and drives them to resume armed opposition.

The exclusion of former rebel groups from the post-conflict political order is often a significant causal factor in relapses into violent conflict and civil war.[41] Warring local groups and communities must be brought into the peace process, and this requires political solutions that aim to engender national unity and sustainable peace and ensuring former rebel actors are included in the processes of governance.[42]

In East Timor, the transition from peacekeeping to peace-building was relatively coherent. A crowning post-intervention achievement was the reconciliation effort. The Commission for Reception, Truth and Reconciliation was an all-Timorese body that emphasised forgiveness and reintegration of militia leaders and followers, 'welcoming them to return to rebuild their lives after engaging with traditional processes of apology and compensation'.[43] As the 2015 expert review of UN peace-building architecture noted:

> In building national reconciliation, Timorese leadership used their traditional and culturally supported systems effectively to address recurrent tensions. Through these efforts Timor-Leste was able to address problems at the human level, including the division of families, the lack of livelihoods and at least to some extent, individual trauma.[44]

Higashi argues that the construction of legitimacy is an integral component of peace-building. In addition to securing compliance through the use of force and resource distribution by the state, there are additional factors such as inclusive governments, post-conflict reconciliation of former enemies and the substantial role of international organisations as credible third party intermediaries, mediators and deal brokers.[45] That said, the post-intervention peace-building agenda has also to be sensitive to the often competing bases and imperatives of domestic as opposed to international sources of legitimacy, a factor that proved to be critically important in undermining international efforts to establish a viable state and institute sustainable peace in Afghanistan.[46]

The Secretary-General as an actor

Edward Luck describes the office of the Secretary-General as 'the repository of international authority on the meaning and application of R2P'.[47] With respect to global norms, universal values and international standards in particular, the Secretary-General has a unique bully pulpit both allowing and demanding a role and influence above and beyond the powers conferred on the office by the Charter and developed through inter-governmental practice. The two best exemplars of this have been Dag Hammarskjöld and Kofi Annan.[48]

In the first part of this chapter, we noted how any use of force across international borders is deeply problematical, intensely controversial and risks being *ex post facto* discredited if the intervention leads to entrenched instability. In the second part, we pointed out that two of the putative benefits of the shift from humanitarian intervention to R2P were making states and citizens duty and rights bearers respectively, and embedding external interventions in international solidarity. In the third section we identified the peace-building goals to include economic development, state-building and nation-building, and the patient efforts required to create a state that is both effective in providing public goods and services, including basic safety and security for all peoples, and legitimate with regards to representation of and responsiveness and accountability to citizens.

In this final part we ask: what role can and should the Secretary-General play in this? The first background point to note in answer is that the UN is both a site of and an actor in global governance.[49] Second, the principal-agent relationship notwithstanding, the UN often has its own suite of policies.[50] Previous works have analysed the role of the Secretary-General as norm champion in general and as R2P norm entrepreneur in particular.[51] Annan (1997–2006) played a key role in the development of R2P as a global norm, while Ban (2007–16) promised to engage in 'the effort to turn promise into practice, words into deeds'.[52]

The Secretary-General can draw on the different elements of UN identity and exploit his position at the centre of a complex network of diplomatic relationships to be an active player in the construction and mid-course corrections of peace-building mandates as core components of R2P operations, in providing broad overall management and oversight of their implementation and in coordinating the vast UN institutional machinery engaged in this multilevel and multi-stakeholder enterprise. The Secretary-General's first avenue of influence to this end is through three key institutional entities that are part of the UN system today: the special adviser on R2P, the PBC, and the Special Representatives of the Secretary-General (SRSGs).

Special Adviser

Luck, the inaugural Special Adviser on R2P, took 'the lead in framing both the normative and operational dimensions of R2P'.[53] It may be argued that the two dimensions – which are indeed 'interactive and interdependent'[54] – converge in peace-building and one of the early tasks for the new Special Adviser of the new Secretary-General should be to draft a special report on this missing third responsibility, promoting international understanding of its importance as an integral element of R2P and also encouraging UN implementing agencies and member states to make it part of international practice and national policy respectively. Because R2P was a novel principle, Luck enjoyed an exceptional opportunity to help shape its conceptual and normative development. Nevertheless, the authority of the special adviser is derived entirely from the Secretary-General. For any significant progress and advance, the special adviser must be close enough to the Secretary-General to engage him or her in articulating the key tenets of the principle and giving weight to peace-building, explaining why they matter to the institutional integrity and credibility of the UN as *the* international organisation. The Secretary-General must constantly strive to inject R2P perspectives into conversations with senior UN officials, CEOs of other international organisations, national leaders and business CEOs.

Peace-building Commission

The 2005 summit approved the creation of the PBC to fill a critical gap in the UN's institutional architecture. Its purpose is to identify countries sliding towards state collapse, institute measures to halt the slide and plan for and assist in the transition from war and conflict to peace and post-conflict peace-building. It is serviced by a modest Peace-building Support Office in the Secretariat that is responsible also for overseeing the Peace-building Fund, set up as a revolving and replenishable fund from voluntary contributions so that the necessary resources can be released immediately to launch peace-building activities without delay. Established in 2006 with a target goal of $250 million, the Fund's portfolio in early 2016 stood at $693 million,[55] supporting 222 projects spread across 31 countries. The major advantages of the new set-up were expected to be that a dedicated body will try to anticipate post-conflict requirements, pre-empt the collapse of peace settlements, promote reconstruction, reconciliation and institution-building through integrated strategies backed by necessary finances, and lay the foundations for sustainable development.

By being made a subsidiary body of both the Economic and Social Council and the UN Security Council, however, the PBC was lumbered with confused reporting lines. There are areas of overlap and duplication with the departments of political affairs and peacekeeping: the new peace-building architecture did not supplant the existing one so much as was grafted on top and alongside the old one.[56] Not surprisingly the UN Security Council questioned the value of the PBC's advice and input, while the SRSGs complained of duplicating roles and responsibilities.[57] The result is a confusing 'archipelago of unconnected units in the UN system, dealing with a variety of peace-building issues in a fragmented and inefficient way. The system still lacks the integration of strategy and purpose'.[58] In sum, the PBC suffers from a crisis of credibility-cum-legitimacy.

Special Representatives of the Secretary-General

The practice of the Secretary-General appointing trusted special envoys to represent him in the field in various trouble spots around the world began shortly after the establishment of the UN and expanded after the end of the Cold War in line with the spike in UN activism. Most, but not all, SRSGs are appointed to lead peace operations. The 'template' is that the UN Security Council will authorise the creation, mandate and size of the operation; the General Assembly determines the funding formula; and the Secretary-General appoints both the SRSG and the Force Commander to head the military component. In practice the

Secretary-General will consult with the UN Security Council, especially the five permanent members of the UN Security Council (P5), as well as the conflict parties, key regional stakeholders and the Under-Secretaries-General for Political Affairs and Peacekeeping Operations – the two departments through whom in most cases the SRSG will report back to New York.

In the field in many ways the SRSG replicates the nature of the office of the Secretary-General in New York. As head of mission, the SRSG exercises delegated administrative and executive authority over all its components, functions and personnel. The mandate has to be translated and 'operationalised' into mission tasks; the multinational, multilingual, multiethnic and multicultural (professional as well as civilisational) force has to be coaxed and cajoled into operating as one cohesive force; the conflict parties, civilian populations, potential spoilers and key regional players have to be persuaded to back the operation; and the UN personnel have to be motivated to assist the local communities on behalf of the international community.

Usually the SRSG is also the lead UN official in charge of the various UN agencies operating in the local theatre. This gives the SRSG, working under the Secretary-General and through him to the UN Security Council, the PBC and the General Assembly, both the opportunity and the responsibility to work with the UN humanitarian and development agencies, the World Bank, the bilateral and multilateral donor community and the regional stakeholders, to identify strategies for building peace in order to convert the ceasefire agreement and/or peace settlement into sustainable peace that is more than just the absence of war. If deemed necessary, the SRSG can also leverage the unique international authority and legitimacy of the Secretary-General to get buy-in from the private sector for regenerating economic activities and creating a functioning market once again. This is why Connie Peck, with extensive experience in briefing and debriefing SRSGs, believes they 'require excellent political, negotiation, leadership, and management skills' along with 'optimism, persistence, and patience'.[59] Just as with the Secretary-General vis-à-vis the UN Security Council, in 'triangulating' relations between the mission, the Secretariat/Secretary-General and the UN Security Council, the SRSG cannot function simply as a passive recipient and implementer of mandates and orders. Instead, through accurate and timely analysis of sensitive information and recommendations based thereon, SRSGs can actively shape both the peacekeeping and peace-building agendas.

The Secretary-General as embodiment of the international community

The United Nations is the epicentre of R2P as an international political project. The UN Security Council has the primary responsibility for maintaining peace and security, the General Assembly has a residual responsibility and the Secretary-General has a discretionary responsibility. The office of Secretary-General combines the role of politician, diplomat and public sector CEO. The status, authority and powers of the Secretary-General are derived chiefly from the clauses of the UN Charter, but depend also invariably on the skills and personality of the incumbent and the state of relations among the major powers of the world.[60] ICISS paid 'homage to the cardinal role a Secretary-General and her/his bully pulpit can play as a norm entrepreneur and catalyst for international action'.[61] For present purposes the Secretary-General's primary roles can usefully be disaggregated into administrative and political.

Administrative. Article 98 of the Charter requires the Secretary-General and the Secretariat – itself designated a principal organ – to discharge normative and operational mandates entrusted by the other principal organs. In practice this has evolved into the delegation of considerable authority to the Secretary-General in the implementation of those burgeoning mandates. The Secretary-General can expand his power and influence through allocating resources among the departments and activities, appointing senior staff and mediating the pulls and pressures of member states through creative interpretations that maximise his scope for privileging his own preferences and priorities. Thus, the Secretary-General as chief administrative officer at the head of the Secretariat has a vast reservoir of authority, powers, functions and reporting opportunities for pointing to needs and requirements, and interpreting mandates in their operationalisation and implementation.

The next Secretary-General should give urgent and careful consideration to Luck's argument that the relative rank and roles of the special advisers on genocide prevention and R2P have been back to front.[62] Genocide is after all but one and indeed the rarest of the four R2P atrocity crimes. The Joint Office should be headed by an Under-Secretary-General in charge of both R2P and Genocide Prevention, to lead the efforts at conceptual and normative development in New York and also to represent the Secretary-General in the field and be able to access national, civil society and conflict party leaders. The person chosen should be someone with high-level political judgement, diplomatic skills, intellectual heft, credibility in both the global North and South, belief in R2P and with the commitment and energy to drive the R2P agenda for the next five-ten years. There may not be a need for a second special adviser at the next rank of Assistant Secretary-General. Instead it may be better to increase the professional staff complement.

The second urgent R2P task for the new Secretary-General will be to end the 'estrangement of peace-building and R2P at the UN'.[63] More, the Secretary-General can designate the new special adviser as the lead official in bringing together *all* relevant UN departments and agencies to the common cause of integrating peace-building into R2P operations, including inserting appropriate clauses in the mandating resolution. This would be a good issue on which to follow the Brahimi Panel's advice to tell the UN Security Council what it needs to hear, not what it wants to hear. As part of this, those responsible for drafting the Secretary-General's periodic reports on R2P and peace-building must communicate with each other prior to finalising the reports to ensure they are mutually reinforcing in their core messages. In addition, the Secretary-General can direct UN officials to consult closely with relevant civil society organisations, led by the Global Centre for R2P, the International Coalition for RtoP and the Asia Pacific Centre for R2P.

Political. The most crucial source of authority for the Secretary-General's political role is that the office-holder is the only person in the world who can claim to be the embodiment of the international interest and the personification and spokesperson of the international community. Any Secretary-General has multiple avenues to shape the institutional context and normative milieu within which personal influence can be wielded. The Secretary-General has the right to be present and take part in the debates in the political organs and often does. S/he provides the logistical and intellectual basis for many UN Security Council and General Assembly resolutions and may urge particular courses of action. S/he is expected to implement the most controversial decisions with the most scrupulous impartiality, neither inflating nor deflating the role of the office.

R2P proved exciting from the start in 2001–02 because it was fresh, challenging and potentially invaluable in saving strangers' lives. But because its hard edge involved the use of force inside sovereign jurisdictions, it was inevitably also provocative, controversial and confronting. In consequence, politics is at the heart of efforts to analyse and respond to crises through the R2P lens. This shapes the Secretary-General's interaction with the UN Security Council. For the P5, R2P is but one among several interest and value goals competing for priority attention. The more an event touches the geopolitical and security interests of the major powers, the less the room for discretion by the Secretary-General. If the P5 are united, the Secretary-General cannot be an alternative locus of dissent. If they are deeply engaged but divided, the Secretary-General cannot construct an artificial consensus. But if they are relatively disengaged and detached, the Secretary-General may be able to navigate a tricky pathway through to an imaginative solution.

Along with other clauses, Article 99 of the Charter, which both permits and obligates the Secretary-General to bring to the attention of the UN Security Council any matter that in his opinion may threaten international peace and security, can be interpreted expansively by a Secretary-General under the doctrine of implied powers. During the Cold War, deadlock in the Council often produced an authority and policy vacuum that only the Secretary-General could fill through creative interpretations of his role and expansion of his remit to include the establishment and oversight of peacekeeping operations and mediation efforts. It was a Secretary-General – Dag Hammarskjöld – who conceived the novel institution of UN peacekeeping operations and became the lynchpin of their management and the critical channel of communication between the several actors. Peacekeeping requires leadership by the Secretary-General precisely because it falls conceptually between war-fighting and diplomatic negotiations, both of which are undertaken primarily by states.

With the end of the Cold War, great power agreement in the UN Security Council translated into a greatly expanded agenda of the UN and a multiplication of peacekeeping and conflict resolution missions and activities. As their nature changed to reflect the more demanding challenges of complex humanitarian emergencies, the Secretary-General found himself at the heart of a complex web of several peace operations, directing the military and humanitarian operations, engaging in conflict prevention and resolution activities, and supervising elections and post-conflict reconstruction efforts. The rise in activism and agenda of the UN Security Council coincided with the decline of the role and influence of the General Assembly and the fate of the UN's peace and security agenda often hinged on the relationship between the UN Security Council and the Secretary-General. Sometimes, in the most volatile and conflict-riven areas of the world, the Secretary-General is the only channel of communication between the parties concerned and the only interlocutor between them and outside actors. Together with the SRSGs, the Secretary-General is engaged in the process and substance of multilateral diplomacy on a 24/7 basis around the world.

Conclusion

All controversies notwithstanding, R2P has a secure future because in origins it was essentially demand, not supply driven and, unhappily, the demand for it is unlikely to disappear.[64] For peoples of developing countries, terrorism is a second-order security threat. Civil war, internal and trans-regional armed conflicts have taken a far heavier security toll on their quotidian lives. The high intensity end of this is when atrocities occur as part of the inter-group armed conflicts. Over a decade ago, Paul Collier calculated the cost of civil wars to developing countries at $100 billion.[65] The costs of interventions and post-intervention peace-building should be assessed against this benchmark.

R2P must be 'understood to include post-intervention peace-building, not as an optional add-on but as an integral part of the doctrine, just as the ICISS had suggested'.[66] Peace-building can continue to be ad hoc, with post-intervention strategies of economic aid and policy design being provided with *ex post* conditions. Or they can be accompanied by systematic *ex ante* requirements. The latter will almost always deliver better and more effective results, however defined and measured. And the UN has a huge comparative advantage in designing the template for post-intervention rebuilding strategies; the amount, type and timing of the required international economic, military and governance assistance; and oversight of delivery and implementation.

Because of the unique legitimacy of the United Nations and the unique attributes of the Secretary-General as an administrative manager and political actor, the development of R2P as principle and its implementation in practice are exceptionally dependent on the choices, decisions and actions of the Secretary-General and his entrusted aides. In turn, success or failure in the R2P agenda will be an important criterion for assessing the legacy of the new Secretary-General. For all our sakes, let us hope the Secretary-General passes the test with flying colours.

Notes

* Originally published in *Global Responsibility to Protect* 8:4 (2016), 343–65. Reprinted by permission of Brill Nijhoff Publishers.

1 International Commission on Intervention and State Sovereignty, *The Responsibility to Protect* (Ottawa: International Development Research Centre, 2001).

2 *2005 World Summit Outcome*, resolution adopted by the General Assembly, A/RES/60/1 (New York: United Nations, 24 October 2005).

3 Roland Paris, 'The Blurry Boundary between Peacebuilding and R2P', in Alex J. Bellamy and Tim Dunne, eds., *The Oxford Handbook of the Responsibility to Protect* (Oxford: Oxford University Press, 2016), 513–16.

4 Ban Ki-moon, *Implementing the Responsibility to Protect* (New York: United Nations, document A/63/677, 12 January 2009).

5 This section summarises Ramesh Thakur, *The United Nations, Peace and Security: From Collective Security to the Responsibility to Protect*, 2nd. ed. (Cambridge: Cambridge University Press, 2016), Chapters 8 and 9.

6 Timor Sharan, 'The Dynamics of Elite Networks and Patron-Client Relations in Afghanistan', *Europe-Asia Studies* 63:6 (2011), 1109–27.

7 Nazif Shahrani, 'Center-Periphery Relations in Afghanistan', in Conrad Schetter, ed., *Local Politics in Afghanistan* (London: Hurst & Co., 2012), 23–37.

8 International Crisis Group, *Talking About Talks: Toward a Political Settlement in Afghanistan*. Asia Report No. 221 (Kabul and Brussels: 26 March 2012), 'Executive Summary'.

9 Ahmed Rashid, 'Why are we abandoning the Afghans?', *NYRblog*, 22 May 2012, www.nybooks.com/blogs/nyrblog/2012/may/22/why-are-we-abandoning-afghans.

10 Brahma Chellaney, 'Surge, Bribe and Run', *Times of India*, 3 February 2010.

11 See Cole Moreton, 'Iraq Invasion 2003: The Bloody Warnings Six Wise Men Gave to Tony Blair as he Prepared to Launch Poorly Planned Campaign', *Independent*, 25 January 2015. For my own collection of newspaper op-eds, see Ramesh Thakur, *War in Our Time: Reflections on Iraq, Terrorism and Weapons of Mass Destruction* (Tokyo: United Nations University Press, 2007).

12 John Chilcot, *et al.*, *The Report of the Iraq Inquiry* (London: Her Majesty's Government, 2016), www.iraqinquiry.org.uk/the-report/.

13 Peter Cole and Brian McQuinn, eds., *The Libyan Revolution and Its Aftermath* (Oxford: Oxford University Press, 2015).

14 Jo Becker and Scott Shane, 'The Libya Gamble – Part 1: Hillary Clinton, "Smart Power" and a Dictator's Fall', *New York Times Magazine*, 27 February 2016.

15 Quoted in Jeffrey Goldberg, 'The Obama Doctrine', *The Atlantic*, April 2016, www.theatlantic.com/magazine/archive/2016/04/the-obama-doctrine/471525/.

16 Guardian staff and agencies, 'Barack Obama Says Libya Was "Worst Mistake" of His Presidency', *Guardian*, 12 April 2016. See also Outi Keranen, 'What Happened to the Responsibility to Rebuild?', *Global Governance* 22:3 (2016), 331–48.

17 Even the Special Adviser on R2P claims to have 'expressed doubts about the appropriateness of stretching the mandate to justify regime change by forceful means'; Edward C. Luck, 'Getting There, Being There: The Dual Roles of the Special Adviser', in Bellamy and Dunne, eds., *Oxford Handbook of the Responsibility to Protect*, 301.

18 Dmitri Trenin, *Russia's Break-out from the Post-Cold War System: The Drivers of Putin's Course* (Moscow: Carnegie Moscow Center, December 2014), 4.

19 Denis Macshane, 'Let Internal Politics Replace Intervention', letter to the editor, *Financial Times*, 15 February 2016.

20 ICISS, *Responsibility to Protect*, paragraph 2.29.

21 For a full discussion of the differences between the two, see Thakur, *United Nations, Peace and Security*, 2nd ed., 272–300.

22 Charles Sampford and Ramesh Thakur, 'From the Right to Persecute to the Responsibility to Protect: Feuerbachian Inversions of Rights and Responsibilities in State–Citizen Relations', in Ramesh Thakur and William Maley, eds., *Theorising the Responsibility to Protect* (Cambridge: Cambridge University Press, 2015), 38–58.
23 ICISS, *Responsibility to Protect*, Chapter 7.
24 *Report of the Panel on United Nations Peace Operations* (New York: United Nations, document A/55/305-S/2000/809, 21 August 2000), paragraph 13.
25 Boutros Boutros-Ghali, *An Agenda for Peace* (New York: United Nations, 1992).
26 Ban Ki-moon, *Report of the Secretary-General on Peacebuilding in the Immediate Aftermath of Conflict* (A/63/881–S/2009/304, 11 June 2009), paragraph 17.
27 Paul Collier, 'Development and Conflict' (Oxford: Centre for the Study of African Economies, Department of Economics, Oxford University, 1 October 2004), 8–9, www.un.org/esa/documents/Development.and.Conflict2.pdf; Paul Collier, Lani Elliot, Havard Hegre, Anke Hoeffler, Marta Reynal-Querol and Nicholas Sambanis, *Breaking the Conflict Trap: Civil War and Development Policy*. World Bank Policy Research Report (Oxford: Oxford University Press, 2003).
28 Lotta Themnér and Peter Wallensteen, 'Armed Conflicts 1946–2014', *Journal of Peace Research* 52:4 (2015), 536–50.
29 Michael C. Doyle and Nicolas Sambanis, *Making War and Building Peace: The United Nations Since the 1990s* (Princeton: Princeton University Press, 2006); Virginia Page Fortna, *Does Peacekeeping Work? Shaping Belligerents' Choices after Civil War* (Princeton: Princeton University Press, 2008).
30 ICISS, *Responsibility to Protect*, paragraph 5.1.
31 ICISS, *Responsibility to Protect*, paragraph 5.31.
32 Timothy Donais, *Peacebuilding and Local Ownership: Post-Conflict Consensus Building* (London: Routledge, 2012).
33 Jonathan Goodhand and Mark Sedra, 'Who Owns the Peace? Aid, Reconstruction, and Peacebuilding in Afghanistan', *Disasters* 10:Supplement 1 (April 2009), S78–S102.
34 Carter Malkasian, *War Comes to Gamser: Thirty Years of Conflict on the Afghan Frontier* (Oxford: Oxford University Press, 2013).
35 William Maley, 'Challenges of Political Development in Afghanistan', *International Studies* 48:1 (2011), 21–41.
36 ICISS, *Responsibility to Protect*, xi, paragraph 3.C.
37 Betty Bigombe, Paul Collier and Nicholas Sambanis, 'Policies for Building Post-Conflict Peace', *Journal of African Economies* 9:3 (2000), 323–48.
38 Collier, 'Development and Conflict', 8–9.
39 World Bank, *World Development Report 2011: Conflict, Security, and Development* (Washington, DC: World Bank, 2011), 193.
40 Astri Suhrke and Mats Berdal, *The Peace in Between: Post-War Violence and Peacebuilding* (London: Routledge, 2012). See also Jonathan Goodhand, Astri Suhrke and Srinjoy Bose, 'Flooding the Lake? International Democracy Promotion and the Political Economy of the 2014 Presidential Election in Afghanistan', *Conflict, Security and Development* 6:6 (2016), 481–500.
41 Charles T. Call, *Why Peace Fails: The Causes and Prevention of Civil War Recurrence* (Washington, DC: Georgetown University Press, 2012).
42 Michael Christopher Marshall and John Ishiyama, 'Does Political Inclusion of Rebel Parties Promote Peace after Conflict?', *Democratization* 23:6 (2016), 1010.
43 John Braithwaite, 'Evaluating the Timor-Leste Peace Operation', *Journal of International Peacekeeping* 16 (2012), 291.
44 *The Challenge of Sustaining Peace*. Report of the Advisory Group of Experts for the 2015 Review of the United Nations Peacebuilding Architecture. (New York: United Nations, 29 June 2015), 35, italics in original, www.un.org/en/peacebuilding/pdf/150630%20Report%20of%20the%20AGE%20on%20the%202015%20Peacebuilding%20Review%20FINAL.pdf.

45 Daisaku Higashi, *Challenges of Constructing Legitimacy in Peacebuilding: Afghanistan, Iraq, Sierra Leone, and East Timor* (London: Routledge, 2015).
46 Srinjoy Bose, 'Death by a Thousand Cuts or Dance of the Seven Veils? Legitimacy and Generation of Authority in Afghanistan's Statebuilding Enterprise, 2001–2014', PhD thesis (Canberra: Australian National University, 2016).
47 Luck, 'Getting There, Being There', 303.
48 See especially Carsten Stahn and Henning Melber, eds., *Peace Diplomacy, Global Justice and International Agency: Rethinking Human Security and Ethics in the Spirit of Dag Hammarskjöld* (Cambridge: Cambridge University Press, 2014), and Kofi Annan, *We the Peoples: A UN for the 21st Century*, edited by Edward Mortimer (London: Paradigm Publishers, 2014).
49 Ramesh Thakur, 'Multilateral Diplomacy and the United Nations: Global Governance Venue or Actor?', in James P. Muldoon, JoAnn Fagot Aviel, Richard Reitano and Earl Sullivan, eds., *The New Dynamics of Multilateralism: Diplomacy, International Organizations, and Global Governance* (Boulder: Westview, 2011), 249–65.
50 Ramesh Thakur and Thomas G. Weiss, 'United Nations "Policy": An Argument with Three Illustrations', *International Studies Perspectives* 10:1 (2009), 18–35.
51 Daisuke Madokoro, 'How the United Nations Secretary-General Promotes International Norms: Persuasion, Collective Legitimisation, and the Responsibility to Protect', *Global R2P* 7:1 (2015), 31–55; Luck, 'Getting There, Being There', 288–314.
52 Ban Ki-moon, 'Secretary-General Defends, Clarifies "Responsibility to Protect" at Berlin Event on "Responsible Sovereignty: International Cooperation for a Changed World"' (New York: United Nations, Press Release, 15 July 2008).
53 Luck, 'Getting There, Being There', 291.
54 Luck, 'Getting There, Being There', 294.
55 United Nations Peacebuilding Fund, 'Key Figures', www.unpbf.org/donors/key-figures/.
56 Rob Jenkins, *Peacebuilding: From Concept to Commission* (New York: Routledge, 2013), 12.
57 Judy Cheng-Hopkins, 'Epilogue: The UN Peacebuilding Architecture – Good Intentions, Confused Expectations, Faulty Assumption', in Cedric de Coning and Eli Stamnes, eds., *The UN Peacebuilding Architecture: The First 10 Years* (London: Routledge, 2016), 199–212.
58 Alvaro de Soto and Graciana del Castillo, 'Obstacles to Peacebuilding: Revisiting History and Moving Forward', *Global Governance* 22:2 (2016), 209–27.
59 Connie Peck, 'Special Representatives of the Secretary-General', in Sebastian von Einsiedel, David M. Malone and Bruno Ugarte, eds., *The UN Security Council in the 21st Century* (Boulder, CO: Lynne Rienner, 2016), 461.
60 This sub-section draws on Thakur, *United Nations, Peace and Security*, 2nd ed., 357–83.
61 Luck, 'Getting There, Being There', 290.
62 Luck, 'Getting There, Being There', 306–07.
63 Paris, 'The Blurry Boundary between Peacebuilding and R2P', 513.
64 Ramesh Thakur, 'Atrocity Crimes and Global Governance', in Amitav Acharya, ed., *Why Govern: Rethinking Demand and Progress in Global Governance* (Cambridge: Cambridge University Press, 2016), 138–56.
65 Collier, 'Development and Conflict', 1.
66 Paris, 'The Blurry Boundary between Peacebuilding and R2P', 519.

Part III

Gaps in and demands for atrocity prevention

The main point of a new norm is not merely to promote the adoption of a new organising principle of world order to address a particular issue, but to reshape international behaviour by altering state practice. When post-election violence broke out in Kenya in 2007–08, called in to mediate, former UN Secretary-General Kofi Annan saw and handled the crisis within the framework of R2P.[1] But it was Libya in 2011 that showcased both the potential mobilising power and the limitations of R2P in the service of liberal internationalism. Security Council Resolution 1973 (17 March 2011) authorised the use of 'all necessary measures … to protect civilians and civilian-populated areas'. Subsequently, as we saw in Chapter 7, the consensus underpinning Resolution 1973 fell apart as several Security Council members concluded that the military mission in Libya went well beyond the civilian protection agenda that had been mandated, in pursuit of unauthorised regime change instead. The post-Gaddafi turmoil and volatility in Libya, that also cross-infected neighbouring countries like Mali, further complicated international responses to the ongoing crisis in Syria by raising doubts about the long-term results of military action.

Wars have not become history and disputes between organised political groups are still widely prevalent. Simultaneously with outlawing war, except in self-defence against armed attack or when authorised by the UN Security Council, the society of states has tried to 'civilise' the manner in which wars are fought. From the different theatres of the killing fields in Africa, to the brutality of the war waged by and against the Tamil Tigers in Sri Lanka and the actions of Islamist insurgents and counter-insurgency operations from Afghanistan through the Middle East to North Africa, the norms of international law, international humanitarian law and international human rights law seem to have suffered serial reverses.

Unfortunately, the language of the three norms of protection of civilians, R2P and international criminal justice generates expectations of protection-cum-punishment that the UN and ICC often struggle to deliver. All three represent important normative advances in the civilian protection agenda. The world would be an even more cruel place for civilian victims without them. Equally, however, the world remains cruel for civilian victims even with the three norms which impose moral obligations to act but do not by themselves indicate what courses of action to follow in order to achieve the best outcomes, or how to overcome the political obstacles of divergent perspectives and clashing interests. Chapter 10 explores how limitations inherent in the civilian protection norms perpetuate protection gaps with respect, for example, to the situation of civilians caught in occupied territories, natural disasters, kin states, and armed civil wars and insurgencies.

To that list, one could also add gaps in the normative architecture to protect cultural heritage,[2] especially artefacts and monuments that are the 'common heritage of mankind';[3] and the dignity, rights and lives of refugees.[4] The inhumane cruelty to which refugees and asylum seekers undertaking hazardous ocean voyages to reach Australia are subjected has prompted former Foreign Minister and co-chair of ICISS, Gareth Evans, to call for Australia's conduct to be referred to the ICC.[5] This would have the additional, and far from insignificant, effect of neutralising the optics of only Africans being persons of interest to the ICC. But it was in the context of the mass outflow of refugees from Syria to Europe in 2014 that the gaps in their protection requirements really came to the fore of public consciousness, as noted by Edward Newman.[6] This was followed by conscience shocking atrocities against the Rohingya Muslims in Myanmar in what Zeid Ra'ad Al Hussein, the UN High Commissioner for Human Rights, called 'a textbook case of ethnic cleansing'.[7] On the one hand, in this instance the Association of South East Asian Nations (ASEAN) seemed to be largely missing in action as the relevant regional organisation for tackling the humanitarian crisis. On the other hand, the Western world largely ignored the government's complaint about the terrorist infiltration of the Rohingya community. Yet in May 2018 Amnesty International concluded that the Rohingya military group Arsa was indeed guilty of deadly massacres and abductions of Hindus in Myanmar's Rakhine state in 2017.[8]

Who will protect the Palestinians?

History, religious nationalism, zero sum territorial claims and local and global politics are all hopelessly entangled in the vexed Israeli–Palestinian conflict. Many criticise Israel's policy of creating new facts on the ground with its settlement policy. This is curious, for the original and most consequential new fact on the ground was the creation of the State of Israel back in 1948, made possible by Britain facilitating the resettlement of Jews in historic Palestine and 'consummated' with the unilateral declaration of independence backed by a military campaign when attacked by surrounding Arab regimes. Israel is a state imposed on the region by the Western powers in the dying days of their colonial dominance but now backed without qualification by the United States, surrounded by many enemies unreconciled to its existence and sworn to its destruction. In an act of brazen effrontery, Palestinians were made to pay the price of Christendom's guilt on the Jewish question and the West continues to act as the enforcer of this historically unjust redrawing of demographic equations in territorial jurisdictions. Burdened by Holocaust guilt, the West seems unable to draw any moral red lines that Israel may not cross. Instead, the setting of the West's moral compass on the region's conflicts is outsourced to Israel. The result is that conduct that many Western governments would consider unacceptable for themselves or others is rationalised or not opposed when done by Israel.

Equally, because of the powerful continuing resonance of the Holocaust, the Jewish nation is not prepared to tolerate existential threats to its only homeland, nor willing to depend ever again on others' goodwill for its survival. Instead, Israel is determined to ensure its continued existence – as a Jewish nation and as the only state for the Jews – by its own means, including whatever brute force it takes. Thus, Israel is as grimly determined to defend, protect and preserve its existence as its enemies are to destroy it. This explains the paradox of more Nobel peace prizes for efforts to resolve the Middle East conflict than for any other, but more outbreaks of war in the Middle East than anywhere else.

At the time of writing in mid-2018, following President Donald Trump's calculatingly inflammatory decision to shift the US embassy to Jerusalem, Israeli forces had once again killed scores of Palestinians who took to the street to protest against the move. The regular eruptions of violent conflict between Israel and Palestinians buck the historical trend of falling conflict numbers and casualties. R2P does not seem to be the most pressing or helpful international instrument for addressing the cycle. When we formulated R2P back in 2001, during the Commission deliberations we were clear in our mind that R2P did not apply to regular warfare between states. In conversations with regional interlocutors in the Middle East during the outreach conversations, most Commissioners also held that the Israeli–Palestinian conflict had more inter-state than internal conflict characteristics.

In an earlier round of uprisings and violence in 2014, analysts debated whether R2P applied in Gaza. At one level, that was a silly question – of course it does. R2P is a universal principle, not a light switch to be turned on and off on whim or convenience. It is always a requirement for every state with respect to the population living in its territory, 24/7. It is also always a call on the world's conscience, taking the form of assisting the state to build its protection capacity and providing timely and decisive protection to victims whenever any state anywhere has manifestly failed in its sovereign responsibility.

The more pertinent question is: in the Gaza conflict, was R2P the best normative instrument for dealing with the critical dimensions of the crisis? Here the answer is more ambivalent. In particular, there is a real danger of slipping into an analogue of judicial romanticism, where normative tools are called into play to resolve a conflict which at core is fundamentally political. Politics explain the creation of the state of Israel, the life threatening hostility directed at it by various groups in the region and its grim determination to defend its very existence by any means of its own choosing, stretching the boundaries of permissibility in the process by unilateral interpretation. Never again is Israel likely to outsource its moral compass on national (as in the Jewish nation, not the state of Israel) security to anyone else, friend or foe. And global politics explain the failure to hold the main conflict parties accountable for their acts of illegality and possible criminality in the self-repeating cycles of escalation and impunity.

The debate over Gaza did of course raise the question of occupying powers' responsibility to protect all peoples living under their occupation. True, Israel withdrew from Gaza in 2005. But because it retained authority over the borders, sea and airspace, making Gaza 'the world's largest open-air prison',[9] most international organisations, governments and human rights groups continued to regard Gaza as an occupied territory and Israel as the occupying authority. The responsibility to protect the population of Gaza would thus be split between the Palestinian Authority as the de jure government, Israel as the occupying power and Hamas as a de facto military governing authority, although the exact division of responsibility would be impossible to specify.

More importantly, Israel's cycle of offensive military operations in Gaza raised issues of international and UN Charter law: the well-established rights to self defence against armed attack and to resist foreign occupation, the validity of these justifications for the resort to violence by Israel and Palestinians, and the limits to the exercise of these rights. Second, the serial provocations and incursions also raise issues of international humanitarian law: regardless of whether the use of force itself is lawful or not, the conduct of hostilities is still governed by the Geneva laws with respect to proportionality, necessity, distinction between combatants and civilians, and the avoidance of unnecessary suffering, including with respect to the choice of munitions. Consequently, in every outbreak of hostilities, there are charges and counter-charges of possible war crimes committed by Hamas and Israel. And during the periods of cessation of hostilities, there are issues of international human rights law. Critics of Israeli laws, administrative practices and security forces behaviour hurl emotive charges of apartheid at one end of the spectrum while, at the other end, sympathisers and supporters accuse Palestinians of terrorism and Israel's critics of overt or closet anti-Semitism.

All these issues of international, humanitarian and human rights laws being raised with respect to Israel's 2014 offensive in Gaza were intensely debated the last time round in 2008–09 also. There was a furore in Israel as some soldiers claimed they shot unarmed civilians, sometimes under orders from their officers.[10] There can be no moral equivalence between a group that is sworn to the destruction of an existing country and commits acts of terror on civilians, and a state that uses military power to defend its existence and its citizens from the former. Under its national security responsibility, the Government of Israel has a duty to defend its population from external attack and daily harassment. Hamas employs the tactic of hiding its fighters and weapons amidst civilians, knowing that that will risk the death of innocents as Israelis return fire. Hamas blows up busloads of school children, hides behind human shields and fires rockets indiscriminately targeted at civilians.

The UN Human Rights Council (HRC)-mandated Goldstone Report marshalled evidence of wrongdoing by Hamas and Israel during that Gaza war and called on both to conduct good faith investigations in conformity with international standards.[11] Israel refused to cooperate with the Goldstone inquiry, thereby ensuring an imbalance of narrative in favour of those claiming to be the victims of Israeli attacks, occupation and policy. The Goldstone Report called on the Security Council to monitor these and only if credible inquiries were not carried out within six months, to refer them to the ICC. Both recommendations were in line with what European and US governments regularly advocate elsewhere. Failure to follow them in the Gaza context undermined the broader international legal principles and also 'the Obama administration's ability to press for justice in places such as Kenya, the Congo and Darfur'.[12]

On 16 October 2009, the 47-member HRC endorsed the Goldstone Report by a vote of 25–6, with the US being one of the six to vote against. Britain and France were among five countries that did not vote, while 11 countries abstained.[13] On 5 November, the General Assembly voted 114–18 (with 44 abstentions and 16 not voting) to endorse the Goldstone Report. While most Western countries abstained, Australia, Canada, Germany, Italy and the US joined Israel in voting against it.[14] In February 2010, the International Committee of the Red Cross (ICRC) condemned Israeli occupation of two million Palestinians in the West Bank, calling for 'action to be taken to allow Palestinians to live their lives in dignity'. The ICRC reiterated the call for

> Israel to do more to protect Palestinians in the West Bank against settler violence, to safeguard their land and crops, to allow families to repair their houses and to assure that all Palestinians can get to hospital or to school without delay.[15]

But in the end, to few analysts' surprise, Israel escaped any international accountability once again thanks to the efforts of the Western powers as its essential enablers.

Non-intervention in Syria

The poster child for the inadequacies of R2P in the last seven years has been the savage civil war in Syria. As the war grinds on the outside world continues to look the other way. Why the continued inaction in the face of such atrocities? In Chapter 8 above, I offered five explanations for the failure of effective intervention. It is worth repeating them briefly. But first, by way of preamble, it should be emphasised that the Syrian crisis was not just an internal civil war. The internal dynamics could not be disentangled from relations with and between Israel, Iran, Russia and China; nor from Arab/non-Arab and Sunni/Shiite divisions in the Middle East. Outsiders also had to assess the balance of consequences against the low odds of success and the high risks of unintended and perverse consequences in attacking a more formidable enemy than Libya's Muammar Gaddafi, and that too in a more volatile strategic environment. On top of all this, against the dominant narrative in much of the Islamic world, they had to ponder the long-term wisdom of another Western invasion of yet another Muslim country.

First, there have been multiple confirmations of just how problematical it is to seek to invoke R2P in the context of an armed civil war. When President Bashar al-Assad launched a fierce crackdown on the initially peaceful pro-democracy protests, the country swiftly descended into full-fledged civil war that sucked in various foreign jihadists and rival outside backers. Most countries of the world would strongly resist the claim that a state – which in practice means the recognised government of the day – is prohibited from employing force to fend off armed challenges to its authority. Many would also worry about the potential for opposition and secessionist groups elsewhere in the world being encouraged to take up arms against their governments. It would be success enough perhaps if the international community could insist on international humanitarian law being scrupulously observed; dragging in R2P is more likely to confuse the situation further instead of ensuring compliance with global normative standards.

Second, like most civil wars, Syria too has been characterised with an abundance of confused facts and shared culpability. All sides deliberately manipulate and misuse casualty figures through casual elision, for example implying that one side is responsible for the total casualty toll. With regard to chemical weapons use – a qualitative escalation that does cross the 'atrocity threshold' – there is a further problem. Even if incontrovertible evidence exists to prove the fact of chemical weapons having been used, the forensic examination to establish which agents were used, what their origins might have been, and how they were delivered, before assessing which conflict party might have used them based on the first set of conclusions, is time consuming and requires reasonably prompt access to the site(s) and victims of attacks. But by then it becomes correspondingly harder to mobilise domestic and international sentiment in support of robust military or other punitive action.

Third, amidst the confusion of the fog of civil wars where culpability for atrocities is spread among multiple actors, it is nonsensical for outsiders to intervene against several opposing conflict parties in proportion to their degree of culpability. But to intervene against only one conflict party is a partial use of force. If interventions are to be guided by an honest appraisal in advance of the balance of consequences, then it was impossible to be confident that forceful outside action would not inflame an already volatile situation. Not only was the rebellion quickly appropriated by competing jihadist groups to whom the overthrow of Assad was but a prelude to the establishment of an Islamist regime and the ethnic cleansing of Syria. In addition, in the early years it was the Assad regime that showed some flexibility towards a negotiated compromise while the rebels were completely intransigent – a point repeatedly emphasised by China and Russia in Security Council debates. India's Permanent Representative on the Council in 2011–2012, Hardeep Singh Puri, ascribes the rebels' uncompromising stance to the fact that they were 'emboldened by the three seemingly conventional steps of intervention witnessed in the case of Libya – a Security Council resolution, the arming of rebels and military action'.[16] Yet, in his view, 'intervention on behalf of an armed opposition with barely distinguishable links to terrorist groups … did not merit serious consideration'.[17]

Fourth, diplomatic ennui was the result of the very pronounced Libya fatigue. The 2011 NATO operation in Libya exposed a critical gap between the proclamation of a no-fly-zone, prohibition of regime change and the effective provision of civilian protection.

Fifth, there was a clash of norms. China and Russia were adamantly opposed to such authorisation without host-state consent, insisted that the continuation and deterioration of the civil war owed as much to rebel intransigence and tactics, and were determined to veto any resolution that could set in motion a sequence of events leading to a Libya-style military operation in Syria. The Assad regime had not attacked any other country and Russian and Chinese opposition ensured that no UN authorisation was forthcoming for external involvement either. In these circumstances, military strikes would be neither lawful nor legitimate, but a breach of the normative prohibition against the use of force against sovereign states that is critical to most countries' national security and international stability.

Of course there were commercial and geopolitical calculations behind China's and, especially, Russia's determination to protect the Assad regime, including arms sales to Syria, the reopening of a Russian naval supply base at Tartus, fears of a loss of international credibility if an ally is abandoned under pressure from abroad, and a sense of frustration and humiliation at how Resolution 1973 was abused to effect regime change in Libya.[18] After the death of Gaddafi, the new Libyan government cancelled Russia's existing commercial contracts and failed to give Russia the smallest slice of the Libyan reconstruction pie despite the tangible goodwill in not vetoing Resolution 1973. Instead the West took the inch given them by the UN and grabbed miles of prime political real estate in Libya. In a presidential election year, Vladimir Putin was not going to lose votes by pointing the finger of blame for Syria's mess at Western intelligence and special forces. A Security Council veto is a risk-free assertion of Russian boldness, independence and defiance that does not commit Moscow to a show of force which would expose its military weakness. It is a useful reminder that Russia still matters on the world stage, even if as a spoiler.

That said, the Chinese and Russian positions also reflected their principled opposition. They dislike intrusions into sovereign affairs and fear an intensification-cum-internationalisation of an internal civil war if external troops are injected. They prefer measures to calm the situation, not inflame it further. They also have concerns about the moral hazard of outside interventions and so like to issue calls for an end to violence by all sides.[19] They firmly reject any UN right to impose political settlements on sovereign societies.[20] And to their minds the greater damage to the UN has been done by Western violations of the UN Charter and their efforts to capture and subvert the international organisation.[21]

All controversies, shortcomings and flaws notwithstanding, not unlike the United Nations itself, R2P has a secure future because its origin was essentially demand and not supply driven; the demand for it is unlikely to disappear. World order will remain organised around the sovereign state as the basic entity. Some states will continue to exhibit the worst of human nature and engage in atrocities. Others will want to respond and help innocent victims. Success can never be guaranteed by any principle or formula for international interventions. But the chances of success can be enhanced and the controversy surrounding interventions can be muted if they are based on an agreed normative framework with regard to a triggering threshold, an authorising agent and implementation guidelines. One way or another, R2P addressed these concerns and requirements, and while inevitably it will be tweaked, it is unlikely to be discarded in the foreseeable future.

Notes

1 Roger Cohen, 'How Kofi Annan Rescued Kenya', *New York Review of Books*, 14 August 2008, 51–53; Abdullahi Boru Halakhe, '"R2P in Practice": Ethnic Violence, Elections and Atrocity Prevention in Kenya', Occasional Paper 4 (New York: Global Centre for R2P, December 2013).

2 See Thomas G. Weiss and Nina Connelly, *Cultural Cleansing and Mass Atrocities* (Los Angeles: J. Paul Getty Trust Occasional Papers in Cultural Heritage Policy No. 1, 2017), www.getty.edu/publications/pdfs/CulturalCleansing_Weiss_Connelly.pdf.

3 As a matter of record, I first used the R2P vocabulary in print in the context of the destruction of Afghanistan's famous Bamiyan Buddha statues by the Taliban, as an ICISS Commissioner at the time, in a co-authored op-ed in early 2001: Amin Saikal and Ramesh Thakur, 'Who has Responsibility for Protecting Humanity's Common Heritage?', *International Herald Tribune*, 6 March 2001, www.nytimes.com/2001/03/06/opinion/vandalism-in-afghanistan-and-no-one-to-stop-it.html. The commission at that time was developing this concept first formulated in this precise language by co-chair Gareth Evans.

4 See William Maley, 'Humanitarian Law, Refugee Protection and the Responsibility to Protect', in Ramesh Thakur and William Maley, eds., *Theorising the Responsibility to Protect* (Cambridge: Cambridge University Press, 2015), 249–65.

5 Gareth Evans, *Incorrigible Optimist: A Political Memoir* (Melbourne: Melbourne University Press, 2017), 249.

6 See Edward Newman, 'The Limits of Liberal Humanitarianism in Europe: The "Responsibility to Protect" and Forced Migration', *European Review of International Studies* 4: 2–3 (2017), 59–77.

7 Zeid Ra'ad Al Hussein, In opening remarks to the 36th session of the UN Human Rights Council, Geneva, 11 September 2017, www.ohchr.org/EN/NewsEvents/Pages/DisplayNews.aspx?NewsID=22041&LangID=E.

8 Amnesty International, 'Myanmar: New Evidence Reveals Rohingya Armed Group Massacred Scores in Rakhine State' (London: 22 May 2018), www.amnesty.org/en/latest/news/2018/05/myanmar-new-evidence-reveals-rohingya-armed-group-massacred-scores-in-rakhine-state/.

9 Seumas Milne, 'Gaza: This Shameful Injustice Will Only End if the Cost of it Rises', *Guardian*, 17 July 2014.

10 Ethan Bronner, 'Soldiers' Accounts of Gaza Killings Raise Furor in Israel', *New York Times*, 20 March 2009, and Rory McCarthy, 'Israeli Troops Describe Shooting Gaza Civilians', *Guardian*, 20 March 2009.

11 Richard Goldstone, Hina Jilani, Christine Chinkin and Desmond Travers, *Human Rights in Palestine and Other Occupied Arab Territories: Report of the United Nations Fact Finding Mission on the Gaza Conflict* (Geneva: United Nations Human Rights Council, A/HRC/12/48, 15 September 2009), www2.ohchr.org/english/bodies/hrcouncil/specialsession/9/docs/UNFFMGC_Report.pdf. In April 2011 Richard Goldstone, chair of the inquiry commission, wrote an opinion article retracting some of the harshest conclusions against Israel: 'Reconsidering the Goldstone Report on Israel and War Crimes', *Washington Post*, 2 April 2011. But the other members of the

commission strongly repudiated his retraction and stood by the original report: Hina Jilani, Christine Chinkin and Desmond Travers, 'Goldstone Report: Statement Issued by Members of UN Mission on Gaza War', *Guardian*, 14 April 2011.

12 Antonio Cassese (President of the Special Tribunal for Lebanon and past president of the International Criminal Tribunal for Former Yugoslavia), 'We Must Stand Behind the UN Report on Gaza', *Financial Times*, 14 October 2009.

13 Howard Schneider and Colum Lynch, 'U.N. Panel Backs Gaza Report', *Washington Post*, 17 October 2009.

14 United Nations, Press Release, 'By Recorded Vote, General Assembly Urges Israel, Palestinians to Conduct Credible, Independent Investigations into Alleged War Crimes in Gaza', Document GA/10883, 5 November 2009, www.un.org/News/Press/docs/2009/ga10883.doc.htm.

15 BBC, 'Israel Makes Life Very Hard for Palestinians, says ICRC', *BBC News*, 17 February 2010, http://news.bbc.co.uk/2/hi/middle_east/8519921.stm.

16 Hardeep Singh Puri, *Perilous Interventions: The Security Council and the Politics of Chaos* (Noida: HarperCollins India, 2016), 125.

17 Puri, *Perilous Interventions: The Security Council and the Politics of Chaos*, 126.

18 See Fyodor Lukyanov, 'Why Does Russia's Stance on Syria Baffle Everyone?', *Russia in Global Affairs*, 23 February 2012.

19 This ignored the report of the UN Human Rights Council-appointed independent commission of the significant asymmetry of responsibility for the violence in Syria; *Report of the Independent International Commission on the Syrian Arab Republic*, UN Doc A/HRC/S-17/2/Add.1, 23 November 2011.

20 Liu Xiaoming (China's ambassador to the UK), 'China Believes Syria Needs a Peaceful Solution', *Guardian*, 10 February 2012.

21 This is portrayed with surprising vividness in an imaginary essay on the death of the UN in a near-term dystopian future: Andrey Kortunov, 'The Day the United Nations Ceased to Exist', Valdai Discussion Club, 3 May 2018, http://valdaiclub.com/a/highlights/the-day-the-united-nations-ceased-to-exist/.

10 Protection gaps for civilian victims of political violence*

> [T]here are substantial gaps in capacity, imagination and will across the whole spectrum of prevention and protection measures relating to the responsibility to protect. Nowhere is that gap more pronounced or more damaging than in the realm of forceful and timely response to the most flagrant crimes and violations relating to the responsibility to protect. Here, weaknesses of capacity and the paucity of will, including in many capitals that speak in favour of advancing goals relating to the responsibility to protect, feed off each other in a particularly vicious cycle of hesitation and finger-pointing in the face of unfolding atrocities.[1]

The above quote from the United Nations Secretary-General Ban Ki-moon's first report on R2P shows three things. First, it demonstrates the importance of civilian protection to the UN's contemporary security agenda. Second, it acknowledges that there are still many significant gaps in the protection response capacity of the organisation. And third, it confirms that the demand–supply civilian protection gap continues to be a matter of concern at the highest level of the UN system.

Created from the ashes of the Second World War, with the allies determined to prevent a repeat of Adolf Hitler's horrors, the United Nations for most of its existence has focussed far more on external aggression than internal mass killings. Yet Nazi Germany was guilty of both. Unlike aggression against other countries, the systematic and large-scale extermination of Jews with industrial efficiency was a new horror. In the new century, the organisation is at long last elevating the doctrine of preventing mass atrocities against people to the same level of collective responsibility as preventing and repelling armed aggression against states. Given the changing nature and victims of armed conflict, the need for clarity, consistency and reliability in the use of armed force for civilian protection now lies at the heart of the UN's credibility in the maintenance of peace and security.

The proportion of civilians killed in armed conflict, either from direct violence or from 'excess deaths'[2] caused by conflict-related hunger and disease, has risen over the last two centuries. The international community has responded to the calls to protect innocent victims by developing two parallel principles, POC and R2P. Both grew out of critical shortcomings ('gaps') in the theory and practice of UN peacekeeping – in particular the collapse of the core assumptions of traditional consent-based peacekeeping amidst the violence of messy post-Cold War intra-state armed conflicts – and in turn contributed to the evolution of the understanding, doctrinal reshaping and practices of contemporary UN and UN-authorised peace operations.

The tragedy of the Rwanda genocide in 1994 and the cruel paradox of the Serbian massacre of Bosnian civilians sheltering in UN-protected safe areas in Srebrenica in 1995 were powerful stimuli to the normative shift from neutral, combat-averse and passive peacekeeping to the mandate to protect civilians under imminent threat. The fact that Kofi Annan was the UN Under-Secretary-General for Peacekeeping in 1994 and 1995 is fundamental to his championing of new normative understandings from 1999 onwards that led directly to the two new, mutually reinforcing norms of POC and R2P. This explains his comment after retirement as Secretary-General that R2P was one of his 'most precious of all' achievements.[3] The norm brokers in the two cases were the Report of the Brahimi Panel in 2000 on UN peace operations set up by Annan as an internal UN high-level panel,[4] and the report of ICISS set up as an independent commission by Canada in response to Annan's challenge of humanitarian intervention.[5] Several UN resolutions and statements now routinely insert both POC and R2P language, and sometimes POC and/or R2P tasks, in the mandate creating new UN peace operations or renewing existing ones.[6] Unfortunately, the language of R2P generates expectations of UN protection that the organisation often is unable to deliver. To date, Libya in 2011, and the less-noticed Cote d'Ivoire resolution at the same time,[7] are the sole examples of coercive action being authorised by the United Nations under the rubric of POC/R2P.

This chapter begins by explaining why the civilian protection agenda is particularly relevant and important for Africa and why R2P might be said to be an African norm export to the rest of the world. Next, it traces the reasons for peace operations' reluctance to use force. It then shows how the civilian protection agenda has tried to fill critical gaps in the existing normative architecture. The fourth section discusses the merits of the R2P and POC norms in responding to the challenge of civilian protection. The final part notes that despite these two valuable additions to the repertoire of the international community in dealing with atrocities perpetrated on civilians, there remain many gaps in the protection agenda as shown in several recent cases.

Africa and the civilian protection agenda

The future of R2P will depend on how the big emerging powers engage with it, and on conversations among them and between them and the relatively declining Western powers.[8] R2P is a distinctively *African* response to the problem of atrocities in part because it spoke to a distinctively African need. The structural coercion of colonial rule, often backed by sectarian feud-perpetuating policies of group-based divide-and-rule, the delineation of inter-state boundaries based more on military equations and political accommodations among colonial capitals than on ground realities in the colonies, and the uneven and messy timing, means, terms and processes of independence from the European colonial powers (and liberation from white minority rule) produced a cascade of violent transitions across Africa in the second half of the last century. After independence, inherited problems were often exacerbated by bad governance, the creation of rent-seeking internal security states ruled by family or clan dynasties through terror, and grievance and resource wars.[9] The points at which these intersected with external Cold War and post-Cold War dynamics intensified the insecurity dividends for African peoples while enriching the entrenched elites. All of which help to explain why, by the end of the last century, Africa was home to the overwhelming proportion of violent armed conflicts and associated civilian casualties.[10]

So far at least in the twenty-first century, Africa has been a continent of hope and optimism. Growth rates have been impressive, albeit from a low base. Investments in health, education and provision of safe water and sanitation; improved commitment to good governance norms, democratic institutions, the shift of political contestation from armed insurgency to the ballot box, power sharing, human rights; creation of markets and business-friendly laws and policies; increasing ownership of responsibility and mechanisms for preventing and muting conflict in the continent etc.: all these have underpinned rising and spreading income levels and distribution, encouraged investment, lifted people out of poverty, decreased the incidence and deadly tentacles of armed conflict and raised confidence in the continent and abroad that the benefits and gains can be sustained.

Yet challenges remain, including the increasingly blurred lines between interstate and intra-state armed conflict, on the one hand, and criminal violence, on the other; the risks of resource wars as populations grow and food and water scarcity rise with dwindling resources, likely to be exacerbated with the impacts of climate change; cross-infections from persisting pockets of 'bad neighbourhoods', particularly in the Great Lakes region and the Horn of Africa; growing numbers of and factionalised rivalry between non-state armed challengers to 'legitimate governments'; and, in the shadow of globalisation, the growth of globally networked uncivil society engaged in trafficking people, guns, drug and money laundering, and terrorism.[11] Moreover, the African success story has been dependent since the global financial crisis on robust and resilient growth in China and India in particular and is vulnerable to these two economies faltering. The civilian protection agenda thus could well remain Africa-centric. The caveats notwithstanding, a systematic examination of the literature on conflicts and trends opts in the end for optimistic rather than gloomy assessments of Africa's economic, human and traditional security prospects, with a gradually fading impact of the inertia of past conflict determining the trajectory of future relations.[12]

Limitations on the use of force in UN peace operations

The United Nations was set up but failed to develop as a collective security system. The primary UN purpose is to maintain international peace and security. The Charter specifies two chief means to this end, namely pacific settlement of disputes (Chapter VI) and collective enforcement against threats to or breaches of the peace (Chapter VII). Secretary-General Dag Hammarskjöld's priority in the 1950s–early 1960s was to localise conflicts. Peacekeeping, which famously finds no mention in the UN Charter, evolved in the grey zone between pacific settlement and military enforcement, hence the quip about it being grounded in Chapter 6.5. Lester Pearson, one of the originators of UN peacekeeping, described it as 'an intermediate technique between merely passing resolutions and actually fighting'.[13]

UN peacekeeping based on consent was thus an innovative attempt to circumvent the failure to realise a workable collective security system. The consensus on traditional, consent-based missions was that peacekeepers should not have the obligation, soldiers or equipment to engage violators in hostilities. Using them as a fighting force would erode international consensus on their function, encourage withdrawals by contributing contingents, convert them into a factional participant in the internal power struggle and turn them into targets of attack from rival factions. The consensus on classical peacekeeping held through the Cambodia operation but began to fray in Somalia under the strains of the post-Cold War messy internal conflicts in the early 1990s.[14]

The end of the Cold War did not mark the start of a successful collective security system. Even with UN authorisation, states are reluctant to transfer control over their national armed forces to the organisation because of doubts over its managerial capacity for military operations,[15] scepticism about its institutional capacity to police the world wisely and effectively and the fear of creating a military monster that one day might turn against them. Continuing inhibitions on the use of UN force include an inoperative Military Staff Committee, non-fulfilment of Articles 42 and 43 requiring national troop contingents to be placed at UN disposal, and recurring suspicions of transient majority coalitions in the UN Security Council.

Humanitarian, peacekeeping, electioneering and enforcement measures by the UN face distinctive difficulties when they have to be undertaken with regard to civil rather than international wars.[16] States provide troops to UN missions in the belief and expectation that the environment into which they are being deployed is benign, permissive and low risk. When the operational environment was transformed after the Cold War in messy civil and sectarian armed conflicts, rather than meet the new operational requirements, state contributors continued to find innovative ways of reducing risks to their peacekeepers by evacuating them at the first signs of danger and rejecting requests for fresh contributions. One consequence has been a creeping apartheid in UN peace operations where troops are provided overwhelmingly by developing countries.

Attempts to convert peacekeeping missions into collective enforcement operations remain fraught with grave risks resulting from the conceptual confusion.

Most civil conflicts have deep historical roots and are characterised by broad and mutual suspicions based on past traumatic experiences. The distinctions between combatants and civilians are often blurred and UN intervention necessitates measures to protect widely dispersed and highly vulnerable populations that are bitterly hostile towards one another. UN use of force cannot be politically neutral insofar as the outcomes of civil conflicts are concerned. The resort to overt force also entails certain 'opportunity costs', including a reduced ability to make the peace.

A gap analysis

Global governance advances and retreats by filling or widening five analytical gaps: knowledge, norms, policies, institutions and compliance.[17] Over the past decade and a half, concerned citizens, engaged academics and reflective practitioners have joined mandated and non-governmental organisations in becoming exercised about a much more acute empirical gap, namely the protection gap. With the benefit of hindsight, another striking observation to note is that neither the provision of humanitarian relief nor the protection of civilians was an explicit or primary concern of traditional UN peacekeeping. In a prescient note in 1960, Hammarskjöld anticipated both the internationalised human conscience being shocked and the controversies that were to arise by the end of the century. He wrote that it was 'the duty of the United Nations Force [in the Congo] to protect the civilian populations and [that] this duty is … in no way restricted by the rule of non-intervention applied by the Force in relation to domestic conflicts'.[18] In a number of cases in the 1990s, the UN Security Council endorsed the use of force with the primary goal of humanitarian protection and assistance: in the (ineffectual) proclamation of UN safe areas in Bosnia, the delivery of humanitarian relief in Somalia, the restoration of the democratically elected government of Haiti, and the deployment of the multinational Kosovo Force.

It is easy to forget that the UN was never meant to be a pacifist organisation. Its origins lie in the anti-Nazi wartime military alliance among Britain, the United States and the Soviet Union. The UN Security Council is the world's one duly sworn-in sheriff for enforcing international law and order. Under the impact of the Holocaust, the international community also progressively curtailed the right of sovereign states to use violence internally. The expansion of permissive norms for the international community to use force within sovereign jurisdictions paralleled the increasing fetters placed on the right of states to use force within and across borders. After the Cold War, the proliferation of complex humanitarian emergencies – and the inappropriateness of the classical tenets of UN peacekeeping for dealing with them – dramatised the uneven impact of the neutrality of traditional peacekeeping on perpetrators and victims. In highlighting this, the Brahimi Report was an important milestone on the road from humanitarian intervention to R2P.

The frequency and deadly consequences of armed conflict rise and fall on the ebb and tide of history and they have waned from a peak in the mid-1990s. But that statistical decline in the numbers and lethality per battle and per year is little solace to innocent civilians killed by intent or when caught in the crossfire, starved into submission or death, ethnically cleansed, displaced from their homes, villages and communities, and in other cruel fashion terrorised and brutalised. Moreover, unlike the non-linear movement on the number and lethality of wars, there seems to have been more or less a linear progression over the last two centuries in the increasing proportion of civilians being killed in conflict-related direct and structural violence.

'Humanitarian intervention' differs from traditional warfare, collective security, peacekeeping and peace-enforcement in that it refers to the use of military force by outsiders for the protection of victims of atrocities: us between perpetrators and victims, instead of us against them, one against all, or us between former belligerents.[19] The debate on 'humanitarian intervention'[20] was ignited in the closing years of the last century by humanitarian crises in Somalia, Rwanda, Srebrenica and East Timor which revealed a dangerous policy gap between the codified best practice of international behaviour as articulated in the UN Charter and actual state practice as it had evolved in the half century since the Charter was signed. The angry and bitter debate highlighted a triple policy dilemma – that is, a threefold protection gap – of complicity, paralysis or illegality:

1 To respect sovereignty all the time is to be complicit in humanitarian tragedies sometimes. If we have the means to stop mass killings underway or imminently threatened but choose to look the other way, we are not the moral equivalent of the perpetrators of the atrocities, but we are part-complicit through our deliberate act of omission. The Rwanda genocide in 1994 fits this description.
2 If we insist that any effective international action to protect populations at risk of mass atrocity must be formally authorised by the UN Security Council, the practical effect of this is to surrender the agenda to the obstructionist obduracy of any one of the five veto-wielding permanent members of the Council (P5), as has been the case in Syria in 2011–13, or indeed to the apathy and indifference of the Council as a whole: no draft resolution on Rwanda was submitted and vetoed in 1994.
3 But if we accept therefore that effective intervention by one power or a coalition of states is justified, as with the intervention by NATO in Kosovo in 1999, then we are endorsing action that under existing UN Charter law is illegal.

Since those conscience-shocking scenes from the 1990s, several efforts have been launched to strengthen the protection gaps in global governance. With respect to knowledge gaps: What are the causes of atrocity crimes and contributing factors behind them? Can we identify early warning signs? Who are the actors best placed to respond quickly and effectively to avert or halt atrocities? On normative gaps: How can old, out-dated and ineffectual norms be replaced by robust new powerful ones? Who are the norm entrepreneurs, brokers, champions, carriers and spoilers? On policy gaps: What policy remedies work best? By whom can they be adopted? On institutional gaps: Do we need new institutions or can existing ones be adapted, reformed and improved to be made fit for purpose? How can the division of labour between them be optimally allocated to avoid duplication and institutional infighting? Most crucially, what are the compliance gaps and how can they best be filled to ensure predictable, credible and reliable protection?

One answer to these series of questions came through ICISS which published its path-breaking report The Responsibility to Protect in 2001. In 2004, the Secretary-General's High-Level Panel reaffirmed the importance of changing the terminology from the deeply divisive 'humanitarian intervention' to 'the responsibility to protect' and endorsed the ICISS argument that 'the issue is not the "right to intervene" of any state, but the "responsibility to protect" of *every* State'.[21] Annan endorsed R2P as well.[22] The core elements of its ideas were adopted unanimously at the UN summit of world leaders in 2005. The 2005 Outcome Document with four atrocity crimes added clarity, rigor and specificity, limiting the triggering events to war crimes, genocide, crimes against humanity and ethnic cleansing. Norms frame identities and shape interpretations and behaviour. By realigning the emerging political norm of protection to the existing categories of international legal crimes, the 2005 formulation enhanced the prospect of the R2P principle becoming a norm robust enough to shape international behaviour.

A second triple policy gap

R2P represents a response also to a different triple policy gap. First, the typical form of armed conflict has changed from inter-state war to internal armed conflicts. But the UN Charter specifically prohibits the organisation from intervening in the internal affairs of member states. How can the UN abide by this injunction yet pursue its primary mandate of maintaining peace and security? Second, the Charter clauses on the promotion and defence of human rights have been reinforced by a growing number of human rights regimes and resolutions. But human rights are primarily, although by no means exclusively, claims by citizens against their own governments. This too raises troubling questions of UN competence with respect to two seemingly incompatible policy goals: the promotion of human rights and respect for state sovereignty. And third, human rights and international humanitarian law (IHL) originated in attempts to limit the use of armed violence by states against their own citizens and enemy soldiers. But the prevention and halt of atrocities inside sovereign borders may sometimes require the use of armed force by the international community across international borders against perpetrator regimes. How can this policy circle be squared?

R2P as the international cavalry

R2P can be discussed and analysed from any one or more of four distinct analytical perspectives: as a discursive conceptual advance; as a norm shift; as a policy template; or as a legal obligation. Its origins lie in the call to differentiate disinterested interventions authorised by the UN as the representative of the international community, from unilateral 'humanitarian intervention' by an individual or coalition of states pursuing a self-interested agenda. In today's world, the use of military force overseas is always highly controversial and fiercely contested. Sovereignty was enshrined in the Westphalian inter-state order as a means of controlling internal anarchy. In order to curb large-scale lawlessness, the state was granted a monopoly on the legitimate use of force. Similarly, in order to reduce inter-state violence caused by outside powers intervening on competing sides in internal power struggles, the external dimension of state sovereignty was held to proscribe intervention in the internal affairs of states. Thus, in both internal and external contexts, state sovereignty was viewed as the solution to the problem of violence and anarchy in domestic and international orders alike. The current controversy over R2P in the aftermath of the UN-authorised NATO operation in Libya brings to a head the question of whether the delegitimisation of internal atrocities comes with the ineluctable risk of relegitimising international force if used to stop internal atrocities: *a normative gap between delegitimising violence and using force to stop it.*

R2P does not address the distribution of jurisdiction and authority among states, but between states and international actors. Protective interventions do not wage war on a state in order to destroy it and eliminate its statehood. Rather, their motivation is to protect atrocity victims inside the state and to embed the protection in reconstituted institutions that will permit the intervention force to withdraw. While R2P preserves to states the responsibility to protect their own populations, it strengthens the UN's responsibility for the international community as a whole, and in doing so 'represents one of the most significant normative shifts in international relations since the creation of the UN in 1945'.[23] There had developed a widening gap between the practice of UN peace operations and their legal underpinnings in the UN Charter. Hammarskjöld had the skills but also the structural conditions to be able to exploit the margins and use equivocation 'in the service of virtue', as his aide Conor Cruise O'Brien put it.[24] In the more complex environment and challenges of the 1990s, this was no longer sustainable, and R2P steps into the breach to provide the necessary principled underpinnings. Orford concludes that R2P processed UN deeds since 1945 into words in 2001.[25] R2P is therefore an effort to integrate existing and evolving but dispersed practices of protection into a conceptually coherent account of international authority: to fill the gap between evolving practice and static formal authority.

The tensions inherent in his broadening conception and practice of UN executive action, kept dormant by the genius of Hammarskjöld's personality and diplomatic skills, could no longer be contained in the UN's expansive responses to the more complex humanitarian emergencies after the end of the Cold War. The only too public setbacks and flaws of UN actions in Somalia, Rwanda, the Balkans and East Timor raised questions about the organisation's authority, credibility and legitimacy with pressing urgency. According to Orford, ICISS stepped into the normative breach to provide the theoretical justification for the accumulated body of practices bequeathed by Hammarskjöld. Informed by a new global managerialism, international authority reaches deep into domestic jurisdictions to rearrange relations between the state, rulers and people with reference to external normative benchmarks.

Just as Hammarskjöld's notions of preventive diplomacy and peacekeeping were meant to avert great power intervention by inserting the UN as a neutral presence, so R2P came about in opposition to efforts to justify 'humanitarian interventions' by non-UN coalitions of the willing led by powerful states. It is a deliberate substitute for imperial visions and governance practices. Hammarskjöld's refusal to confront the reality of the collapse of state authority in Congo meant that he stubbornly resisted answering a fundamental question. If the UN was intervening with force, whose law and whose authority would it be upholding if not its own? The logic of Hammarskjöld's conception and legacy of practices with respect to UN executive action was to culminate at the turn of the twentieth century in international administrations in the Balkans and East Timor.

R2P and POC as sibling protection norms

As already noted, R2P and POC emerged as twin protection norms in the late 1990s.[26] Their parallel emergence and consolidation is no mere coincidence. The relationship between R2P and POC can seem confusing as there are many complexities and sensitivities involved. Both are concerned with the protection of civilians, have common normative foundations and have regularly been invoked together. The shared protection agenda can be undermined by a flawed grasp of the normative, institutional and operational relations between R2P and POC. Civilian populations can fall through gaps in protection, while R2P and POC actors can impair each other's work through a discrete pursuit of their separate objectives. Because POC is markedly less contentious, its advocates and practitioners fear contagion from the more politicised R2P.

On some points, the differences between them are straightforward. While POC, for example, applies to discrete acts of violence against individuals, R2P has a much narrower scope, applying to mass atrocity crimes only. Nevertheless, where mass atrocity crimes are occurring, the POC–R2P overlap is effectively complete. Contrary to common perception, moreover, POC is not restricted to armed conflict as defined by IHL. According to one classification,[27] 'narrow POC' refers to the obligations of parties to an armed conflict to distinguish between combatants and civilians, and to avoid attacking the latter or harming them beyond what is necessary to achieve military objectives. 'Broad POC', on the other hand, is a policy framework used by UN and other peacekeepers, the UN Security Council, the Secretariat and humanitarian agencies who aim to contribute positively to the protection of civilians in situations of widespread, grave and lawless violence that have not reached the threshold of armed conflict.

Another common mistake is claiming that protection of civilians is a legal concept, while R2P is political. The two reports by Ban Ki-moon in 2012 on POC and R2P, published two months apart, are internally inconsistent, if not in outright contradiction. 'The responsibility to protect is a concept based on fundamental principles of international law as set out, in particular, in international humanitarian, refugee and human rights law'.[28] By contrast, Ban's report on POC states that '*the protection of civilians is a legal concept based on international humanitarian, human rights and refugee law, while the responsibility to protect is a political concept*'.[29]

On the contrary, R2P and broad POC are both rooted in, but extend beyond, legal principles. The four R2P atrocity crimes – war crimes, crimes against humanity, genocide and ethnic cleansing – have legal definitions in the 1998 Rome Statute (which governs the ICC) and the 1948 Genocide Convention. Some R2P duties – for example those that prohibit complicity in genocide by such means as inciting communal hatred – are found in international law. By recourse to the UN Security Council, even military interventions are made consistent with international law, as distinct from Kosovo-style unilateralism, where NATO used military force against Serbia without UN Security Council authorisation.[30] Like R2P, broad POC draws on the law but extends beyond its strict requirements. The positive duties of peacekeepers to protect civilians are not dictated by international law. So, too, the UN Security Council has great discretion over the coercive measures it can take to protect civilians and the situations in which it may deploy troops. In 2011, Libya and Cote d'Ivoire, where the French military and UN peacekeepers ousted Laurent Gbagbo from the presidency, were cases in point.

R2P is comparatively more sensitive, as the presence of atrocities implies a perpetrator who may need to be identified and confronted. But it is a mistake to believe that protection of civilians, unlike R2P, is always impartial, neutral and apolitical. Broad POC used by humanitarian agencies is fully impartial and neutral. But peacekeeping protection of civilians requires the impartial pursuit of the *mandate* of the peacekeeping force. This may require rejecting neutrality in order to take decisive action against perpetrators, which occurred in Cote d'Ivoire. As the Brahimi Report emphasised, the UN, while striving to remain impartial, should subordinate its long-standing principle of neutrality between belligerents in favour of 'adherence to the principles of the Charter and to the objectives of [the] mandate'.[31] Where one side resorts to morally reprehensible conduct, the UN should no longer extend, directly or indirectly, a seal of moral equivalency in its relations with combatants.

The UN report criticising its own lack of action in Sri Lanka highlights the need for different protection players to be aware of one another's limits. Humanitarian protection workers can adopt highly apolitical stances to ensure access to those in need. But as the report said, 'The UN's reference to what was "political" seemed to encompass everything related to the root causes of the crisis and aspects of the conduct of the war'.[32] In this situation, it was vital to introduce protection actors with the authority and ability to challenge unacceptable behaviour by a UN member country, Sri Lanka. Humanitarian workers cannot do so. Only the Security Council can create and deploy strong protection forces.

Finally, many hold that peacekeepers, and humanitarian and human rights workers, may perform specific atrocity prevention work, but it is better not to refer to these as R2P activities. In some situations, needless controversy may indeed arise by referring to atrocity prevention as R2P. However, the systematic avoidance of R2P language by those engaged in protecting civilians would result in R2P being spoken about only as military intervention. This stance would neglect efforts to rebuild a country's institutions and provide international help to prevent atrocities. It would also produce a self-fulfilling collapse of R2P into coercive military intervention, ignoring its many major contributions to building a nation's capacity to exercise its sovereignty with responsibility.

Remaining protection gaps

Thus, both POC and R2P are important normative advances in the civilian protection agenda, filling some critical gaps in the twentieth century normative architecture. However, it is in the field with actual test cases where the rubber has already hit the road that the norm–implementation gap is most acute. Some are worth discussing for highlighting how limitations that are inherent in POC and R2P perpetuate protection gaps with respect to the situation of civilians caught in occupied territories, natural disasters, kin states, and armed civil wars and insurgencies.

The responsibility of occupying powers: Iraq 2003–13

Saddam Hussein's record of brutality in Iraq was a taunting reminder of the distance yet to be traversed before we reach the goal of eradicating domestic state criminality; his ouster and capture by unilateral force of arms in 2003 by a self-appointed international posse, led by Washington as the global sheriff, was a daunting setback to the effort to outlaw and criminalise wars of choice as an instrument of state policy.[33] Prior to the 2003 war, Britain and the US were the most insistent in keeping in place the comprehensive UN sanctions that caused large-scale deaths and inflicted considerable human misery on Iraqi civilians. The humanitarian toll of the 2003 war has been just as devastating. Nobel Peace Laureate Desmond Tutu, recalling the 'immorality' of the US and British invasion of Iraq, writes: 'in a consistent world, those responsible for this suffering and loss of life should be treading the same path as some of their African … peers who have been made to answer for their actions in the Hague'.[34]

By April 2013, the number of *US soldiers killed* totalled almost 4,500,[35] and the number of *combatants* of all nationalities killed was just short of 40,000.[36] According to the Iraq Body Count project, by mid-March 2013 (ten years after the war began), between 112,017 to 122,438 *civilians* had been killed in Iraq, with another 11,500 likely to be added to the total from the Iraq War Logs.[37] A US medical team, collaborating with Iraqi specialists, calculated the civilian casualty based on a scientific household survey and came up with the stunning figure of 650,000 'excess deaths' by June 2006.[38] Women and children made up more than half the total killed.[39] According to the Iraqi government, the death toll is almost a quarter million. The toll climbs to more than a million dead by August 2007 as estimated by the London-based polling organisation Opinion Research Business.[40] According to The Costs of War Project, finally, the distribution of deaths is as follows: US military, 4,488; US contractors, 3,418; Allied military and police, 10,819; opposition forces, 36,400; journalists and humanitarian workers, 293; civilians, 134,000. Importantly, however, the last study adds the caveat that its tally does not include indirect deaths, due to war-related hardship, which may total many hundreds of thousands more than this estimate.[41]

Epidemiologists use scientifically validated procedures to estimate the range of 'excess deaths': numbers dead who otherwise would have lived. The war badly degraded Iraq's health infrastructure and caused many doctors to flee, contributing indirectly but hugely to the death toll. Unless commentators are lazy, incompetent or intimidated, they should say 'between 174,000 and one million Iraqis have been killed or have died as a result of the 2003 war'. In addition, the war caused 'the largest human displacement in the Middle East since 1948'.[42] Two million fled abroad and another two million were displaced internally. Iraq's Christians in particular have left in large numbers.[43] Who should be held responsible for the protection of civilians in such circumstances?

It is not at all clear that the invocation of R2P would be the most relevant or helpful contribution to protecting civilians under foreign occupation. But if no other remedy is available, then by definition protection gaps remain.

Natural disasters

There is no morally significant difference between large numbers of people being killed by soldiers firing into crowds or the government blocking help being delivered to victims of natural disasters, as with Myanmar's deadly Cyclone Nargis in 2008. But the generals were in effective control of Myanmar. The only way to get aid quickly to where it was most needed was with the cooperation of the authorities. If they refused, the notion of fighting one's way through to the victims is ludicrous. The militarily overstretched Western powers had neither the capacity nor the will to start another war in the jungles of Southeast Asia; all the Asian powers were opposed in principle. If foreign soldiers are involved, it does not take long for a war of liberation or humanitarian assistance to morph into a war of foreign occupation in the eyes of the local populace. If the invocation of R2P does not help in the immediate emergency, may indeed cause even more determined opposition and intensify the backlash against R2P, then the painfully forged consensus on the R2P norm will fracture without any material help being provided to the displaced and distressed. But this is another way of acknowledging that R2P and POC norms are inadequate to cover the contingency of natural disasters in which the government lacks the capacity to render effective help to its affected population, but is not prepared to accept international assistance to fill the gap.

Cartographic lines of statehood versus bloodlines of nationhood

The map lines that delineate statehood can become blurred by the bloodlines of nationhood.[44] This happened with the conflict between Russia and Georgia over South Ossetia in 2008 and is of particular concern to many developing countries whose borders reflect the convenience of administrative boundaries of former colonial powers rather than territorial demarcations of different ethnonational groups. The general international opinion was that Russia invoked R2P to camouflage highly traditional geopolitical calculations in launching military action against Georgia in defence of its interests in South Ossetia. How can R2P be applied to the protection of persons belonging to national minorities who make up the majority in the neighbouring state (as with Tamils in Sri Lanka and India)? Whose responsibility is it to protect such persons? A sensible answer might come from the formula that France uses to describe its relationship with Quebec in Canada: *ni ingérence ni indifférence* (neither interference/intervention nor indifference). At the same time, the attempted but failed misappropriation attests to the power of the norm as an analogue to hypocrisy being the tribute that vice pays to virtue.[45]

Civil wars

In May 2009 there was fresh debate over the relevance and applicability of R2P to Sri Lanka in the closing stages of the government's successful military campaign against the Liberation Tigers of Tamil Eelam (LTTE). To what extent did R2P apply to the Tigers, the government and the international community for evacuating the civilians caught in the crossfire? At the Human Rights Council in Geneva, China, Cuba, Egypt and India were among 29 developing countries who supported a Sri Lanka-sponsored resolution that described the conflict as a domestic matter that did not warrant 'outside interference', praised the defeat of the Tigers, condemned the rebels for using civilians as human shields and accepted the government's argument that aid groups should be given access to the detainees only 'as may be appropriate'. While Colombo was jubilant, Western diplomats and human rights officials were shocked by the outcome at the end of the acrimonious two-day special session.[46]

In the Darfur crisis,[47] on the one hand, R2P was an influential mobilising pull on the world's conscience which triggered UN activism in addressing the plight of the affected populations and alleviating their humanitarian suffering, and led to the deployment of peacekeepers with more robust civilian protection mandates, the imposition of economic sanctions, and international criminal indictment. On the other hand, strangers in peril were not saved and Sudan's president is yet to be taken to The Hague. It is hard to see how coercive military measures against Sudan would have met the balance of consequences test in the context of the logistical and other practical difficulties. Among other things, humanitarian relief operations and the fragile peace process would have suffered collateral damage. The real failure therefore lay in the refusal to apply other measures rather than in 'the non-application of coercive force'. But Evans does concede that by failing to apply sustained diplomatic, legal and economic pressure, the international community 'has so far failed dismally in its responsibility to protect the people of Darfur from mass atrocity crimes'.[48]

By contrast, Libya in 2011 best showcased the mobilising power of the R2P norm that led to China and Russia abstaining from, instead of voting against, and thereby vetoing UN Security Council Resolution 1973. The initial response to the crisis was a textbook example of R2P Pillar Three military intervention. But the NATO operation very quickly showed up several critical gaps. First, there was a yawning gap between the UN Security Council mandated proclamation of a no-fly-zone, the prohibition of regime change and the effectiveness of civilian protection. Second, there was an unbridgeable gap between effective civilian protection with regime change and the maintenance of UN Security Council consensus. Third, there developed a significant gap between those who authorised Resolution 1973 to protect Libya's civilian population and those who implemented it to effect unauthorised regime change.

Conclusion

The protection of civilians is an outcome, not an activity. The growing numbers and types of POC actors include humanitarian, military and diplomatic personnel. While their numbers and activities might have grown, there does not seem to have been a commensurate increase in actual protection. POC and R2P norms impose moral obligations to act but do not by themselves indicate what courses of action to follow in order to achieve the best outcomes. Nor have satisfactory measures been devised to gauge impact and outcomes. But what does seem clear is that POC is a 'wicked problem' with no solutions, only better or worse outcomes. In keeping with the thesis of this chapter, it was noted at a Ditchley conference that the gap between the rhetoric of protection norms and their effective implementation in protecting civilians is widening.[49] Even so, it is important to emphasise that the primary responsibility for civilian protection is that of national authorities and conflict parties. The international community has only a fallback responsibility and the chief blame for atrocities should not be shifted to the UN or other regional or international actors.

R2P is no more self-guaranteeing than any other type of external intervention. It is not a magical formula by means of which good intentions can guarantee good policy outcomes in distant foreign lands. Hence the due diligence imperative: on an informed assessment, are we reasonably confident of doing more good than harm? That is, even with R2P, protection gaps remain in our normative architecture. Global governance understood as the filling of various discrete but inter-related gaps remains indeed an unfinished journey.

Notes

* Originally published in *South African Journal of International Affairs* 20:3 (December 2013), 321–33. Reprinted by permission of Taylor & Francis Ltd, www.tandfonline.com on behalf of the South African Institute of International Affairs.

1 Ban Ki-moon, *Implementing the Responsibility to Protect*, Report of the Secretary-General (New York: United Nations, document A/63/677, 12 January 2009), 26, paragraph 60.

2 The notion of 'excess state violence' has evolved to challenge the use of violence by any state in its internal and international behaviour beyond the level that international political actors consider to be legitimate. See Bruce Cronin, 'International Legal Consensus and the Control of Excess State Violence', *Global Governance* 11:3 (2005), 311–30.

3 Kofi Annan, 'A Progress Report on UN Renewal', Speech to the UN Association–UK, London, 31 January 2006, *New World* (journal of UNA–UK), April–June 2006, 8.

4 *Report of the Panel on United Nations Peace Operations* (New York: United Nations, document A/55/305-S/2000/809, 21 August 2000).

5 International Commission on Intervention and State Sovereignty, *The Responsibility to Protect* (Ottawa: International Development Research Centre, 2001). See also: Gareth Evans, *The Responsibility to Protect: Ending Mass Atrocities Once and For All* (Washington, DC: Brookings Institution Press, 2008); Alex. J. Bellamy, *Responsibility to Protect* (Cambridge: Polity, 2009); Ramesh Thakur, *The Responsibility to Protect: Norms, Laws and the Use of Force in International Politics* (London: Routledge, 2011); and Thomas G. Weiss, *Humanitarian Intervention: Ideas in Action*, 2nd ed. (Cambridge: Polity, 2011).

6 Security Council Resolution 1674, S/RES/1674 (28 April 2006) '4. *Reaffirms* the provisions of paragraphs 138 and 139 of the 2005 World Summit Outcome Document regarding the responsibility to protect populations from genocide, war crimes, ethnic cleansing and crimes against humanity'; Yemen S/RES/2014 (21 October 2011); South Sudan S/RES/1996 (8 July 2011); Presidential Statement S/PRST/2011/18 (22 September 2011).

7 S/RES/1970 (26 February 2011); S/RES/1973 (17 March 2011); and S/RES/1975 (30 March 2011).

8 See Ramesh Thakur, 'R2P after Libya and Syria: Engaging Emerging Powers', *The Washington Quarterly* 36:2 (2013), 61–76.

9 Mats Berdal and David Malone, eds., *Greed and Grievance: Economic Agendas in Civil Wars* (Boulder: Lynne Rienner, 2000).

10 Andrew Mack (director and editor-in-chief), *Human Security Report* (Oxford: Oxford University Press, 2005).

11 Jorge Heine and Ramesh Thakur, eds., *The Dark Side of Globalization* (Tokyo: United Nations University Press, 2011).

12 Jakkie Cilliers and Julia Schünemann, 'The Future of Intrastate Conflict in Africa: More Violence or Greater Peace?', *ISS Paper* 246 (Pretoria: Institute for Security Studies, May 2013), www.issafrica.org/publications/papers/the-future-of-intrastate-conflict-in-africa-more-violence-or-greater-peace.

13 Lester B. Pearson, 'Force for U. N.', *Foreign Affairs* 35 (April 1957), 401.

14 Ramesh Thakur, 'From Peacekeeping to Peace Enforcement: The UN Operation in Somalia', *Journal of Modern African Studies* 32:3 (1994), 387–410.

15 Major-General Lewis Mackenzie, the former Canadian head of UN forces in Sarajevo, made the memorable comment that a UN commander in the field should not get into trouble 'after 5 p.m. in New York, or Saturday and Sunday. There is no one to answer the phone'. Quoted in Adam Roberts, 'The United Nations and International Security', *Survival* 35:2 (1993), 17–18. In 1993 the UN established a 24-hour, seven days a week Situation Room that provides a direct link to its peacekeeping operations.

16 Alan James, 'Internal Peace-keeping: A Dead End for the UN?', *Security Dialogue* 24 (December 1993), 359–68; Roberts, 'The United Nations and International Security', 9–11.
17 Thomas G. Weiss and Ramesh Thakur, *Global Governance and the UN: An Unfinished Journey* (Bloomington: Indiana University Press, 2010).
18 Quoted in Mats Berdal, 'United Nations Peacekeeping and the Responsibility to Protect', in Thakur and Maley, eds., *Theorising the Responsibility to Protect*, 227.
19 See Ramesh Thakur, 'Humanitarian Intervention', in Thomas G. Weiss and Sam Daws, eds., *The Oxford Handbook on the United Nations* (Oxford: Oxford University Press, 2007), 387–403.
20 'If humanitarian intervention is, indeed, an unacceptable assault on sovereignty, how should we respond to a Rwanda, to a Srebrenica – to gross and systematic violations of human rights that offend every precept of our common humanity?'; Kofi A. Annan, *Report of the Secretary-General on the Work of the Organization* (New York: United Nations, document A/54/1, 1999), 48.
21 High-level Panel on Threats, Challenges and Change, *A More Secure World: Our Shared Responsibility* (New York: United Nations, document A/59/565, December 2004), paragraphs 201 and 207 (emphasis in original).
22 Kofi A. Annan, *In Larger Freedom: Towards Development, Security and Human Rights for All*. Report of the Secretary-General (New York: United Nations, document A/59/2005, 21 March 2005), paragraphs 122–35.
23 Anne Orford, *International Authority and the Responsibility to Protect* (Cambridge: Cambridge University Press, 2011), 41.
24 Quoted in Orford, *International Authority and the Responsibility to Protect*, 87–88.
25 Orford, *International Authority and the Responsibility to Protect*, 1.
26 The third sibling is international criminal justice. But because that involves punishment of perpetrators rather than protection of victims, it is not discussed here. See Ramesh Thakur and Vesselin Popovski, 'The Responsibility to Protect and Prosecute: The Parallel Erosion of Sovereignty and Impunity', in Giuliana Ziccardi Capaldo, ed., *The Global Community: Yearbook of International Law and Jurisprudence 2007*, Vol. 1 (New York: Oxford University Press, 2008), 39–61.
27 Hugh Breakey, Angus Francis, Vesselin Popovski, Charles Sampford, Michael G. Smith and Ramesh Thakur, *Enhancing Protection Capacity: A Policy Guide to the Responsibility to Protect and the Protection of Civilians in Armed Conflicts* (Brisbane: Institute for Ethics, Governance and Law, 2012), www.griffith.edu.au/criminology-law/institute-ethics-governance-law/research/responsibility-to-protect-protection-of-civilians-policy-guide.
28 Ban, *Responsibility to Protect: Timely and Decisive Response*, 3, paragraph 9. See also p. 16, paragraph 59 for a repetition of the claim that R2P is grounded in 'fundamental principles of international law'.
29 Ban Ki-moon, *Report of the Secretary-General on the Protection of Civilians in Armed Conflict* (New York: United Nations, document S/2012/376, 22 May 2102), 5–6, paragraph 21; emphasis added.
30 See Albrecht Schnabel and Ramesh Thakur, eds., *Kosovo and the Challenge of Humanitarian Intervention: Selective Indignation, Collective Action, and International Citizenship* (Tokyo: United Nations University Press, 2000).
31 *Report of the Panel on United Nations Peace Operations*, paragraph 50.
32 *Report of the Secretary-General's Internal Review Panel on United Nations Action in Sri Lanka* (New York: United Nations, November 2012), 19, paragraph 49, www.un.org/News/dh/infocus/Sri_Lanka/The_Internal_Review_Panel_report_on_Sri_Lanka.pdf.
33 Ramesh Thakur and Waheguru Pal Singh Sidhu, eds., *The Iraq Crisis and World Order: Structural, Institutional and Normative Challenges* (Tokyo: United Nations University Press, 2006).

34 Desmond Tutu, 'Why I Had No Choice but to Spurn Tony Blair', *The Observer* (London), 2 September 2012.
35 Costs of War Project, http://costsofwar.org/iraq-10-years-after-invasion.
36 Iraq Body Count, www.iraqbodycount.org/analysis/numbers/ten-years/.
37 Iraq Body Count, www.iraqbodycount.org/analysis/numbers/ten-years/.
38 Gilbert Burnham, Riyadh Lafta, Shannon Doocy, and Les Roberts, 'Mortality After the 2003 Invasion of Iraq: A Cross-sectional Cluster Sample Survey', *The Lancet* (11 October 2006); http://brusselstribunal.org/pdf/lancet111006.pdf.
39 Les Roberts, Riyadh Lafta, Richard Garfield, Jamal Khudhairi and Gilbert Burnham, 'Mortality Before and After the 2003 Invasion of Iraq: Cluster Sample Survey', *The Lancet* (30 October 2004). Experts consulted by *The Economist* – not one's average leftwing antiwar propaganda tract – confirmed that the study had been carried out to the standard professional level; 'Counting the Casualties', *Economist*, 6 November 2004, 80–81.
40 ORB, 'More Than 1,000,000 Iraqis Murdered Since 2003 Invasion', *Press Release*, 16 September 2007, www.zcommunications.org/more-than-1–000–000-iraqis-murdered-since-2003-invasion-by-orb.
41 Costs of War Project, http://costsofwar.org/iraq-10-years-after-invasion.
42 Alisa Roth and Hugh Eakin, 'They Fled from Our War', *New York Review of Books*, 13 May 2010, 26; Deborah Amos, *Eclipse of the Sunnis: Power, Exile, and Upheaval in the Middle East* (New York: Public Affairs, 2010).
43 William Dalrymple, 'Iraq's Disappearing Christians are Bush and Blair's Legacy', *Guardian*, 13 November 2010; Robert Fisk, 'Exodus: The Changing Map of the Middle East', *Independent*, 26 October 2010.
44 See Walter Kemp, Vesselin Popovski and Ramesh Thakur, eds., *Blood and Borders: The Responsibility to Protect and the Problem of the Kin-State* (Tokyo: United Nations University Press, 2011).
45 For an interesting argument on how even misuses and abuses of the R2P norm help to strengthen it, see Cristina G. Badescu and Thomas G. Weiss, 'Misrepresenting R2P and Advancing Norms: An Alternative Spiral' *International Studies Perspectives* 11:3 (2010), 354–74.
46 Catherine Philp, 'Sri Lanka Forces West to Retreat over "War Crimes" with Victory at UN', *The Times* (London), 28 May 2009.
47 See Roberto Belloni, 'The Tragedy in Darfur and the Limits of the "Responsibility to Protect"', *Ethnopolitics* 5:4 (2006), 327–46; Alex De Waal, 'Darfur and the Failure of the Responsibility to Protect', *International Affairs* 83:6 (2007), 1039–54; Nicholas J. Wheeler, 'A Victory for Common Humanity? The Responsibility to Protect After the 2005 World Summit', *Journal of International Law and International Relations* 2:1 (2005), 95–107; and Cristina G. Badescu and Linnea Bergholm, 'The Responsibility to Protect and the Conflict in Darfur: The Big Let-Down', *Security Dialogue* 40:3 (2009), 287–309.
48 Evans, *Responsibility to Protect*, 61.
49 Ditchley Foundation Director's Report, 'Protecting Civilians in Armed Conflict', Ditchley Foundation conference, 16–18 May 2013.

11 Atrocity crimes and global governance*

In this chapter, global governance is understood to mean the management of transnational issues by states, international institutions, social movements and other relevant public and private actors through norms, laws and policies. For the issue area covered in this chapter, the normative shifts have been the most significant changes in global governance, with flow-on implications for institutional and compliance elements. The focus of analysis therefore is primarily on the normative structure of the global governance of civilian atrocities.

The origins of the Westphalian sovereign state lie in the effort to limit uncontrolled domestic armed violence. Faced with internal anarchy and large-scale lawlessness, the state was granted a monopoly on the legitimate use of force as the solution to the problem of internal violence. In a matching vein, as competing outside powers intervened on opposite sides in internal power struggles, external state sovereignty and the doctrine of non-intervention as its logical corollary were seen as the solution to the problem of international violence and anarchy. This still leaves the question of what to do about the excessive use of force by states within their own borders.

This chapter first describes the new norms of international criminal justice and R2P as a two-part answer to the question. It then takes up the following key questions: What were the main sources of demand for the norms? Were the primary motivations normative, strategic, functional or a mixture of the three? Is there any evidence of agents from the global South being among the norm entrepreneurs? And what might be the way forward for the consolidation of the norms as part of the architecture of global governance? Because of space restrictions, I focus relatively more on R2P.[1]

Twin norms: duty to prosecute and responsibility to protect

Large numbers of civilians are killed in armed conflict from direct violence and through 'excess deaths' caused by conflict-related hunger and disease. Revulsion at the murder of large numbers of civilians killed in a range of atrocity crimes[2] has led to a softening of public and governmental support for the norms and institutions that prevent international assistance to protect the victims and shield the perpetrators from international criminal accountability. Two of the most significant recent normative advances are the establishment of the ICC in 1998 and the UN's adoption of R2P in 2005. The backdrop to both is the profound changes in the world since 1945, including the changing nature of armed conflict that has put civilians on the frontline of conflict-related casualties; the rise of an internationalised human conscience, a powerful human rights movement and the parallel growth of international humanitarian law; the emergence of a robust transnational civil society; and globalisation, which has shrunk distances, brought images of human suffering into living rooms and to breakfast tables in graphic detail in real time while simultaneously expanding the capacity to respond meaningfully.

R2P and the ICC alike spoke eloquently to the need to change the UN's normative framework in line with the changed reality of threats and victims. In the Feuerbachian reframing of state–citizen relations,[3] with the adoption of new standards of conduct under which individuals became subjects of international law as bearers of duties and holders of rights, R2P makes sovereign rights conditional upon the state delivering on the protection rights of people. Sovereignty was reconceived as a conditional right dependent upon respect for minimum standards of human rights. In pursuit of atrocity prevention, halting atrocities already in train and punishing policy and command-level perpetrators of such crimes, the relationship between sovereignty and mandated international actors is increasingly viewed as complementary. If states are manifestly unwilling or unable to protect citizens, the responsibility should be borne by the international community. Nevertheless, in both protection of victims and prosecution of perpetrators, the application of international mechanisms comes only after domestic authorities are unwilling or unable to do so.

The landscape of international criminal justice, with the ICC as its permanent institutional custodian, has changed dramatically over the last two decades. Starting with the Nuremberg and Tokyo tribunals after the Second World War and including ad hoc tribunals in former Yugoslavia and Rwanda as way stations, the world has made revolutionary advances in the criminalisation of domestic and international violence by states and in the individualisation of responsibility and criminal accountability for those acts. There have also been several 'people's tribunals', modelled on the Russell Tribunal (1966–67) that investigated the US war in Vietnam, dealing with Brazil, Chile, Eritrea, Western Sahara, the 2003 Iraq war, genocide against the Armenians in Turkey and Tamils in Sri Lanka, etc. It is difficult to judge how influential they have been beyond preaching to the converted. The ICC came into effect in 2002. It is located at The Hague but can conduct proceedings anywhere in the world. Its remit is to prosecute individuals for the crimes of genocide, crimes against humanity, war crimes and, since 17 July 2018 following activation in December 2017, the crime of aggression.[4]

While the still developing mechanisms at national, regional and global levels seek to apprehend and punish the perpetrators of atrocities, R2P aims to protect the victims. The cluster of norms inhibiting, if not prohibiting, 'humanitarian intervention' – the use of military force on the territory of a state without its consent with the goal of protecting innocent victims of large-scale atrocities – includes: state sovereignty, non-intervention, domestic jurisdiction, pacific settlement of disputes and non-use of force. Failure to act in the 1994 Rwanda genocide and non-UN-authorised humanitarian intervention in Kosovo in 1999 triggered deeply divisive recriminations around the world for acts of omission and commission.[5] In sharp conceptual contrast with humanitarian intervention, R2P does not address the distribution of jurisdiction and authority among states, but between states and citizens domestically, and states and international actors globally.[6]

The origins of R2P lie in the need to distinguish disinterested, legitimate, UN-authorised intervention of, by and for the international community from unilateral interventions by an individual or coalition of self-interested states pursuing their own narrow agenda. In the wake of the Kosovo controversy, the report of ICISS argued that the essential nature of sovereignty had changed from state privileges and immunities to the responsibility to protect people from atrocity crimes.[7] Where the state defaulted owing to incapacity, inability, or complicity, the responsibility to protect tripped upwards to the international community acting through the UN. The 2005 UN Outcome Document limited the triggering events to war crimes, genocide, crimes against humanity and ethnic cleansing. Since then actors engaged in referencing, clarifying and promoting the principle include Secretary-General Ban Ki-moon through annual reports from 2009 onwards, the General Assembly through annual debates, the Security Council through resolutions and presidential statements, and civil society organisations. Thus far Libya and Cote d'Ivoire in 2011[8] are the only two examples of coercive action being authorised by the UN under the rubric of R2P.

Sources of demand

An important explanation for the exceptionally rapid advance of R2P on the global policy agenda is that it was heavily demand driven in response to distressingly evident gaps in the existing normative architecture by the end of the last century. Doing nothing was no longer acceptable to a globally sensitised human conscience (Rwanda 1994), but doing something militarily when confronted with an impossible-to-obtain UN authorisation was not legally permissible either (Kosovo 1999). The existing normative consensus was no longer fit for purpose against the brutal facts of the real world. In attempting to answer where the demand comes from for effective action to prevent and stop atrocities and apprehend, prosecute and punish those responsible, the list of possible candidates includes Western allies, especially but not limited to the members of NATO; the progressive group of middle and small power Western countries, led by the Scandinavians but also including Australia, Canada and New Zealand; the victims of atrocities, concentrated in particular in Africa; civil society organisations advocating for them; and the United Nations.

NATO

The end of the Cold War was a triple triumph: of US and Western power, political pluralism and the market economy. The comprehensive victory risked a slide of the West into triumphalism that would simply brush aside objections from an impotent Russia and impose its priorities and value preferences around the world. The first Gulf War in 1991 confirmed to the rising crop of ambitious neoconservatives that US military power could be used in the Middle East – and by extension elsewhere – without fearing any counter-intervention by Russia.

In the unipolar post-Cold War world, the demand for undertaking effective protection was often directed at Washington. This first arose in the context of the instability in the Balkans following the death of Josip Tito and the collapse of the Soviet Union. Given the bloody history of the Balkans, the complexity of the conflict and the rugged topography, the initial US response was to treat it as a no-win quagmire and Europe's problem. As the scale of the atrocities became clear, Washington, sickened by Slobodan Milosevic's record of brutality, evasions and deceit, decided to intervene militarily through the multilateral framework of NATO without UN authorisation. The sharpest and most eloquent articulation of 'humanitarian intervention' as an emerging norm to justify the operation was a speech by British Prime Minister Tony Blair in Chicago on 22 April 1999: 'This is a just war, based not on any territorial ambitions but on values'.[9] Neither the UN Charter nor the corpus of modern international law incorporates the right to 'humanitarian intervention'. But NATO had asserted and acted on such a right and its members had the most economic, diplomatic and military weight in the world and included the world's leading democracies, promoters of the rule of law and ardent UN supporters.

United Nations and Secretary-General Kofi Annan

The old consensus on non-intervention, sacrosanct sovereignty and impunity had been shattered, perhaps irretrievably. Questions of validation, validator and process became the critical factors in determining the legality-cum-legitimacy of interventions. The UN was not set up as a pacifist organisation. Its origins lie in the anti-Nazi wartime military alliance among Britain, the United States, and the Soviet Union. The Cold War put paid to the Charter scheme of a collective security system and consent-based peacekeeping missions were used instead to keep local conflicts free of great power entanglements. In a prescient passage in 1960, Secretary-General Dag Hammarskjöld informed Katanga's secessionist leader, Moïse Tshombe, that the requirement for non-intervention in the domestic conflict did not void 'the duty of the United Nations Force to protect the civilian populations'.[10]

After the Cold War, the proliferation of complex humanitarian emergencies dramatised the uneven impact of the neutrality of traditional peacekeeping on perpetrators and victims.[11] In a number of cases in the 1990s – Bosnia, Somalia, Haiti – the Security Council endorsed the use of force with the primary goal of humanitarian protection and assistance. The 1994 Rwanda genocide and the massacre of Bosnian civilians sheltering in UN-protected safe areas in Srebrenica in 1995 were powerful stimuli to the normative shift from neutral, combat-averse and passive peacekeeping to the mandate to protect civilians under imminent threat. As a norm entrepreneur, the UN Secretary-General is a unique international actor with distinctive but limited characteristics and bases of authority and influence.[12] In a series of speeches and reports in 1998–99, Kofi Annan described the existing inadequacies and dilemmas and challenged member states to recreate a new normative consensus on this deeply bitter intervention debate.[13] The fact that he was the Under-Secretary-General for Peacekeeping in the 1994–95 Rwanda and Srebrenica tragedies is fundamental to his championing of new normative understandings and explains his comment after retirement as Secretary-General that R2P was one of his 'most precious of all' achievements.[14] In shepherding R2P through the delicate UN politics, Annan had an unmatched insider grasp of politics as they operated among member states and staff members.

The norm broker was ICISS, set up as an independent commission in response to Annan's challenge of humanitarian intervention.[15] R2P's state champion from start to finish was Canada, a country strongly committed to UN-centred multilateralism, with a history of close engagement with the world organisation, political credibility in both North and South, and a proud tradition of successful global initiatives. There were also several other like-minded countries like Norway and Switzerland, as well as major foundations like MacArthur and other actors like the International Committee of the Red Cross, which worked closely with ICISS in supportive advocacy. The Secretary-General's High-Level Panel on Threats, Challenges and Change, which included ICISS co-chair and then-President of the conflict resolution NGO International Crisis Group, Gareth Evans, reaffirmed its importance in 2004[16] and Annan himself endorsed R2P in 2005.[17]

Humanitarian community

The international humanitarian community was badly divided by the crises in the Balkans in the 1990s and Iraq in 2003. The central objective of traditional humanitarian policymaking has been to reduce the frequency and violence of war. In the 1990s, troubled by how the insistence on neutrality in conflicts had led to the well-fed dead of Bosnia for example, many humanitarians demanded the use of violence and war in order to advance their agenda. One of the most prominent voices associated with the debate on the side of the interveners, Samantha Power,[18] was the inaugural chair of the new US Atrocities Prevention Board and then the US Permanent Representative to the UN in Obama's second term.

Africa

Too many analysts neglect the role of countries from the global South in some major initiatives after the Second World War.[19] R2P is a distinctively African response that spoke to a distinctively African need, especially in the post-colonial violence. By the end of the last century, Africa was home to the overwhelming proportion of violent armed conflicts and associated civilian casualties.[20] Article 4(h) of the Constitutive Act of the new Africa Union (2000) explicitly spells out the 'right of the Union to intervene in a Member State' with respect to the commission of 'war crimes, genocide and crimes against humanity'.[21] During the ICISS outreach consultations in Maputo in March 2001 with a cross-section of governmental and civil society representatives from across sub-Saharan Africa, the tenor of the demands was for more outside intervention, but under the right motivations and conditions.[22] There are many possible explanations for the greater willingness of Africans to accept intervention. Their greatest fear is state failure leading to humanitarian crises, whereas the sensitivity to intervention is less. Far too many regimes – Haile Mariam Mengistu in Ethiopia, Idi Amin and Milton Obote in Uganda – had used the shield of sovereignty for their abusive records, treating Africans as objects rather than actors. Also, many weak African states lack empirical sovereignty, being subject instead to warlords, robber barons, gun and drug runners, etc. In response, civil society groups had concluded that, in the midst of egregious and massive atrocities and abuses, sovereignty should be subordinated to international concerns and humanitarian assistance. The real challenge was not to defend absolute sovereignty, but to ensure that interventions result from the explicit authority of a mandated multilateral organisation and to link them to a political strategy that allows for a strategic engagement with the country subject to intervention.

Mixed motives

International action to deal with atrocities – for example India, Vietnam and Australia in East Bengal, Cambodia and East Timor in 1971, 1978 and 1999 respectively – is typically based on mixed motives rather than just one. Moreover, international action is most successful when there is a confluence of the different motivations and least efficacious when they diverge. In addition, foreshadowing trends in the twenty-first century, much of the opposition to past interventions was also motivated by a mix of strategic and normative calculations.

Kosovo 1999

The debate on 'humanitarian intervention' was ignited in the closing years of the last century by humanitarian crises in Somalia, Rwanda, Srebrenica and East Timor. NATO intervention in Kosovo was an attempt to bridge the glaring normative gap between the doctrine of non-intervention and the urgent need for the protection of civilians at risk of being massacred. It was different from previous interventions of the twentieth century in postulating an alternative norm of 'humanitarian intervention' to displace non-intervention. The response from a largely sceptical third world was hostile. For most Westerners, NATO is an alliance of democracies and a standing validation of the democratic peace thesis. For former colonies, however, a notable feature of NATO is that every major European colonial power is a member (although not every NATO member was a colonial power). Efforts to legitimise and codify a new norm of 'humanitarian intervention' struck at the heart of the collective political identity of most developing countries and was an attempt, from their point of view, to renegotiate the essential terms of their engagement with the international community. Their unease and opposition were heightened by perceptions of bias, selectivity and strategic imperatives animating actual examples of intervention. Much of the 'selectivity stems from the strategic interests of the dominant North Atlantic Concert'.[23]

The Kosovo intervention also demonstrated incoherence with key norms in addition to non-intervention. Outside intervention on behalf of groups resisting state authority by force can encourage other recalcitrant groups to resort to violent challenges elsewhere as the trigger to internationalising their power struggle, as Annan subsequently acknowledged.[24] The war was a setback to the cause of outlawing the use of force in solving disputes except under UN authorisation. Alexei Arbatov argued that NATO's attack on Serbia removed a Russian taboo against the use of military force in Chechnya.[25] Sha Zukang, China's chief arms control negotiator, used it as the alibi for missiles exports.[26] Rebecca Johnson noted that 'though the Chinese were the only ones publicly to wonder if NATO would have bombed Belgrade if Yugoslavia had also been nuclear armed, there were many in the corridors who made the obvious connection'.[27] A former Indian foreign secretary concurred: 'If it is Iraq and Yugoslavia today, it could very well be India tomorrow. This demonstrates convincingly the importance of India's nuclear deterrent'.[28]

As well as problems with the normative justifications, power political calculations were inseparable from decisions on Kosovo. The collapse of the Soviet Union left a power vacuum throughout central and eastern Europe which the expansion of NATO tried to fill. The former Yugoslavia was the only significant military obstacle and the history of Europe in the 1990s is a history of cutting it down to size. Russia has been able to check NATO military action in Syria because it has recovered sufficiently not to be simply brushed aside as in 1999. (The Kosovo precedent was also invoked explicitly by Russia in defending its actions in detaching Crimea from Ukraine in 2014.) The justification resting on the need to preserve the credibility of NATO was also essentially strategic: 'It is difficult to imagine a legal justification based upon the need to support any organization's credibility'.[29]

Syria 2012–15

Both the calls for and resistance to international pressure and intervention in Syria show a similar mix of motives. By the end of 2011, the peaceful Arab Spring in Syria had mutated into a bloody armed uprising and then a full-fledged civil war in 2012–15 in which more than 250,000 people had been killed on all sides, including soldiers, rebel fighters and civilians, and several million displaced either internally or become refugees in neighbouring, European and other countries. Yet China and Russia remained firmly opposed to outside intervention in Syria, in part to protect geopolitical interests. Syria is a key Russian bulwark against US interests in the Middle East. The political importance of the Sunni–Shia domestic and regional divide across the Middle East is also important. The Saudi Arabia and Turkey-led Sunni crescent is firmly pro-Western and Moscow had little to lose in regional relations by backing Syria. But to say that Russia was partly motivated by strategic calculations in backing the Assad regime is to concede that the West would have made strategic gains through its preferred course of action.

In addition, however, Russia and China also deployed several principled arguments,[30] including: a 1973-type resolution would put Syria on the path to civil war; the Security Council should not dictate internal politics and succession; opposition groups must also receive condemnation for perpetrating violence and exhorted to engage constructively with the government; the draft Western resolutions would have inflamed, not calmed the situation; and the only solution to the Syrian crisis is through an inclusive, Syrian-led process to address the legitimate aspirations of the people in an environment free of violence and human rights abuses. In other words, while there are unquestionably strategic and economic imperatives behind Russia's policy in particular, the strength of the Sino-Russian opposition, backed by fellow-BRICS[31] also reflects a conflict of political approaches and rejects armed domestic confrontation backed by international enablers.

ICC

On first blush, the ICC might be thought of as resulting fundamentally from normative motivations. Yet in background, clauses and choice of indictees, international criminal justice can be shown to have been cross-infected by strategic calculations as well. There is little prospect of any political leader or military commander from a major power, its ally or client state finding himself in the dock at The Hague.

The Hague and Arusha ad hoc tribunals were set up as substitutes for effective action to halt the atrocities in the two regions:[32] they were alibis for no action, not indicators of toughening new standards of international judicial accountability. Their policy utility lay in the fact that indictments isolated the offending leaders diplomatically, strengthened rivals in the domestic power struggle and helped to pave the way for economic sanctions and even the use of military force.[33]

The tensions that can arise when normative, strategic and functional motivations work at tangents instead of in tandem is vividly seen in the operations of the ICC to date. If not resolved, these have the potential to cause serious, perhaps even fatal, damage to international criminal justice as a political project. The court's operations have created many complications and raised many questions in African and developing-country minds about the court, its prosecutor,[34] and the Security Council, demonstrating how international justice mechanisms can collide with regional norms and imperatives. The AU has issued several strongly worded communications to the ICC and the UN complaining that the court has singled out Africans for prosecution, and has advised member states not to cooperate with the ICC with respect to indictees from Sudan and Kenya. On 23 December 2010 Kenya's parliament urged Kenya's withdrawal from the court and five years later South African deputy minister Obed Bapela said the ICC had 'lost its direction' and the ruling African National Congress intended to withdraw from it.[35]

The third India–Africa Forum summit was held in New Delhi in October 2015, with 41 African heads attending, including Sudan's President Omar Hassan al Bashir who was under ICC indictment. South Africa's government defied its own courts in permitting him to leave peacefully after an AU conference in June 2015. The office of ICC Prosecutor Fatou Bensouda pointed to Security Council Resolution 1593 (2005) calling on all states – including those that have not joined the court – to cooperate fully with the ICC.[36] Human Rights Watch and Amnesty International were among 21 international and African NGOs calling on India to arrest Bashir.[37] India, which is not an ICC state party, said that Resolution 1593 is not binding on ICC non-signatories. India was happy to comply with its 'statutory international legal obligations' but not necessarily other directives.[38]

It is no more self-evident that Africans should subordinate AU norms to global than that Americans and Europeans should automatically and always privilege global norms and institutions over US/EU decision-making structures respectively. The Western powers, led by the US, effectively quashed any effort to hold Israel accountable following the recommendations of the 2009 Goldstone Report.[39] After the Iraq war, Prime Minister Blair and the UK defence and foreign ministers were accused of crimes against humanity by Greek lawyers who lodged a case with the ICC.[40] The doctrine of universal jurisdiction was employed also to threaten prosecution against President George W. Bush and General Tommy Franks (commander of the US forces in Iraq). Defense Secretary Donald Rumsfeld retaliated by warning that if US officials could no longer travel to Brussels without fear of prosecution, NATO headquarters would have to be relocated to another country.[41] In July 2003 Belgium amended its controversial law on universal jurisdiction and restricted trials in Belgian courts to crimes committed or suffered by its citizens or residents. In 2012, Nobel Peace Laureate Desmond Tutu refused to share the stage with Blair, believing that the former British prime minister deserved to be sharing the ICC dock with the Africans at The Hague.[42] Danilo Zolo concludes that international tribunals are little more than victors' police and a tool of Western imperialism.[43]

Functional

NATO's effort to implement R2P in Libya in 2011 ran into an incompatibility between the functional requirements to provide protection to civilians and the normative restrictions inherent to R2P. Because the functional logic coincided with strategic interests, many confused the two to conclude that NATO had acted primarily in pursuit of material self-interest. There was a critical gap between the Security Council-mandated proclamation of a no-fly-zone, the prohibition of regime change and the effectiveness of civilian protection. To ensure long-term civilian protection, the Gaddafi regime had to be changed. To maintain Security Council consensus, regime change had to be eschewed. Because NATO over-interpreted its mandate to pursue the former goal, there developed a significant gap in communications, expectations and accountability between those who authorised and those who implemented Resolution 1973. Parties go to war in order to settle on the battlefield the question that could not be resolved around the negotiating table, including who gets to control and rule over part or all of a territory. Limited impartial intervention is a delusion that merely stops decisive victory by either side, precludes mutual military exhaustion which can form the basis of a durable negotiated compromise, prolongs the military stalemate and perpetuates the underlying political power struggle.[44]

Most African and all the BRICS countries objected strongly to the shift from the politically neutral posture of civilian protection to the partial goal of assisting the rebels and pursuing regime change.[45] The sharply divergent North–South responses to the efficacy–legitimacy tension first flared up in a big way in Kosovo in 1999. NATO used the vocabulary of 'humanitarian intervention' to circumvent the UN Charter regime governing the use of international force. Faced with Chinese and Russian obstructionism in the Security Council, the only way they could protect the victims of ongoing Serbian atrocities was to launch military action through a coalition of the willing: function and mission determined the form. Serbia used the language of defence of sovereignty against armed external aggression. NATO governments succeeded in justifying their actions to one another because they already gave greater weight to popular sovereignty; Serbia's claim resonated among developing countries because, in their international moral order, they privilege national sovereignty over military intervention.

There are three sources of tension between efficacy and legitimacy in the search for effective global governance to provide international protection to victims of mass violence within states. With the nature of armed conflict having changed from predominantly inter-state to both inter- and intra-state, and a corresponding rise in the proportion of civilians as victims of armed conflict, the need for clarity, consistency and reliability in the use of armed force for civilian protection lies at the heart of the UN's credibility in the maintenance of peace and security. However, intervening in the internal affairs of member states is specifically forbidden in the UN Charter. This makes it challenging for the UN to implement its primary mandate of maintaining peace and security. Second, the Charter and a growing number of human rights regimes and resolutions enjoin the UN to promote human rights actively. But most human rights claims are directed by citizens at their own governments. Thus, here too the UN is tasked with pursuing two seemingly incompatible policy goals: the promotion of human rights and respect for state sovereignty. And third, the origins of human rights and international humanitarian law lie in attempts to limit the use of armed violence by states against their own citizens and enemy soldiers. Consistent with this normative inhibition to limit the recourse to coercion and violence by states, how can the UN sanction the use of armed force across international borders by outsiders for the preventing and halting atrocities inside sovereign borders?

The three structural impediments are a better explanation than indifference to the plight of the victims for the UN's difficulties in responding to the humanitarian crises in Darfur, Myanmar, Sri Lanka and Syria. On the last, the fluid and confused internal situation, question marks over the identity, intent and methods of the rebels, the risk of atrocities against minority groups if the regime collapses, relations with Iran, China, and Russia, the deepening Sunni–Shia divide, and the shrinking space for 'moderate' rebel groups as jihadists take control of anti-Assad movements, have made it impossible to assess the balance of consequences of outside intervention with any degree of confidence. They raise three critical questions in relation to civil wars: the right of the state to use force against armed challenges to its authority; the moral hazard of encouraging opposition groups to take up arms against governments all over the world, with the ensuing spread and escalation of humanitarian crises; and the means of protecting civilians when the balance of consequences test counsels caution in the use of military force by outsiders.

African agency

Following the Libya precedent, regional organisations may well acquire a critical 'gatekeeping role' in the global authorisation of R2P-type operations.[46] That role may not be as easily secured from the AU for any future operation in sub-Saharan Africa. Contrary to common belief and the appropriation of the discourse by Westerners, in many ways R2P is a distinctly *African* contribution to the global normative architecture, as argued by Mohamed Sahnoun, the often (unfairly) forgotten co-chair of ICISS.[47] Acharya develops this argument still further to make the strongest claim yet that R2P should be considered an African norm export that has been elevated to the global level. In addition to Sahnoun being a powerful and active ICISS co-chair, Acharya recalls the role of Francis Deng in reconceptualising sovereignty as responsibility and of Annan in calling for and then championing the resolution, in R2P, of the previous contradiction between sovereignty and 'humanitarian intervention'. As Acharya puts it: 'The fact that Deng and Annan were both from Africa should not be regarded as a mere or unimportant coincidence, but a central aspect of the genesis of R2P'.[48] From my own direct knowledge of the personalities, process and history of this normative shift, I would endorse his observation.

The way forward

There is a substantial body of knowledge that identifies predisposing or risk factors as well as precipitating or trigger factors. But knowledge is still patchy in trying to establish the pattern of events that culminate in atrocities, and similar patterns that can be arrested short of atrocities being committed; the permissive social, political and institutional environments that facilitate the commission of atrocities, and the institutional frameworks that can block or at least delay them; the optimal points of entry for local, national, regional and international actors, both governmental and civil society, with regard to timing, sequence, agency and tools; and the different compliance mechanisms on the mix of inducements-cum-incentives (payment of carrots) and penalties (sticks of coercion).

Nor is it clear that we possess detailed or complete knowledge on the national, regional, international and non-governmental capacity gaps in responding to atrocities. Following the adoption of R2P as the international community's default policy setting in 2005, there has been a marked institutional strengthening of national and international, public and non-governmental structures dedicated to atrocity prevention and response activities: national offices, focal points, early warning networks, international tribunals, R2P centres and coalitions, and the UN Joint Office of Special Advisers on Prevention of Genocide and R2P. Oftentimes, though, civil society organisations are at once more committed, nimble and effective at atrocity prevention than state bodies.[49]

On compliance gaps, it would be a mistake to believe that the menu of options is restricted to a stark either/or choice between doing nothing and intervening with military force. A range of political, economic and military sanctions can be instituted when the situation is not so dire as to warrant military intervention but grave enough to justify other forms of intervention. That said, military force cannot be taken off the table as the option of last resort if absolutely required.

The tension between efficacy and legitimacy remains an issue for the ICC. Its creation and operation was an important innovation in compliance mechanisms in international criminal justice. But over the past decade the African Union has taken an increasingly antagonistic position vis-à-vis the court. If the ICC as a political project is not to collapse under the weight of normative incoherence, it will have to become truly universal in reach and operations and also separate sharply the criminal justice process from the highly politicised Security Council, including countries not states parties to the ICC being able to vote on ICC referral and deferral.

Conclusion

R2P and the ICC have the potential to make a significant difference to the atrocity prevention and response agenda of global governance, but there are still many political, institutional and operational obstacles on the unfinished journey. The problem is the atrocities committed against innocent civilians. The interrelated twin tasks are to protect the victims and punish the perpetrators. Both R2P and the ICC require substantial derogations of sovereignty, the first with respect to the norm of non-intervention and the second with respect to sovereign impunity up to the level of heads of government and state. At the same time, both require sensitive judgement calls: the use of external military force to protect civilians inside sovereign jurisdiction must first satisfy legitimacy criteria rooted largely in just war theory, while the prosecution of alleged atrocity criminals must be balanced against the consequences for the prospects and process of peace, the need for post-conflict reconciliation and the fragility of international as well as domestic institutions. That said, although both R2P and the ICC are international standards, root cause, structural and operational measures most of the time are best implemented by most countries as part of the normal functioning of government.

Notes

* Originally published in Amitav Acharya, ed., *Why Govern: Rethinking Demand and Progress in Global Governance* (Cambridge: Cambridge University Press, 2016), 138–56. Reprinted by permission of Cambridge University Press.

1 My views on the ICC can be found in Ramesh Thakur, 'International Criminal Justice: At the Vortex of Power, Norms and a Shifting Global Order', in Charles Sampford and Ramesh Thakur, eds., *Institutional Supports for the International Rule of Law* (London: Routledge, 2015), 30–58.

2 Alex J. Bellamy, *Massacres and Morality: Mass Atrocities in an Age of Civilian Immunity* (Oxford: Oxford University Press, 2012).

3 Charles Sampford and Ramesh Thakur, 'From the Right to Persecute to the Responsibility to Protect: Feuerbachian Inversions of Rights and Responsibilities in State–citizen Relations', in Ramesh Thakur and William Maley, eds., *Theorising the Responsibility to Protect* (Cambridge: Cambridge University Press, 2015), 38–58.

4 ICC Press Release, 'Assembly Activates Court's Jurisdiction over Crime of Aggression', 15 December 2017, www.icc-cpi.int/Pages/item.aspx?name=pr1350.

5 See Ramesh Thakur, 'Rwanda, Kosovo and the International Commission on Intervention and State Sovereignty', in Alex J. Bellamy and Tim Dunne, eds., *The Oxford Handbook of the Responsibility to Protect* (Oxford University Press, 2016), 94–113.

6 Anne Orford, *International Authority and the Responsibility to Protect* (Cambridge: Cambridge University Press, 2011).

7 International Commission on Intervention and State Sovereignty, *The Responsibility to Protect* (Ottawa: International Development Research Centre, 2001).

8 S/RES/1970 (26 February 2011); S/RES/1973 (17 March 2011); and S/RES/1975 (30 March 2011).

9 Tony Blair, 'Doctrine of the International Community'; text available at: www.pbs.org/newshour/bb/international/jan-june99/blair_doctrine4-23.html.

10 Quoted in Mats Berdal, 'United Nations Peacekeeping and the Responsibility to Protect', in Thakur and Maley, eds., *Theorising the Responsibility to Protect*, 227.

11 See especially *Report of the Panel on United Nations Peace Operations* (Brahimi Report) (New York: United Nations, document A/55/305-S/2000/809, 21 August 2000).

12 See Simon Chesterman, ed., *Secretary or General? The UN Secretary-General in World Politics* (Cambridge: Cambridge University Press, 2007); Ramesh Thakur, *The United Nations, Peace and Security: From Collective Security to the Responsibility to Protect*, 2nd ed., (Cambridge: Cambridge University Press, 2017), Chapter 13.

13 These have been helpfully reprinted in Kofi Annan, *We the Peoples: A UN for the 21st Century*, edited by Edward Mortimer (London: Paradigm Publishers, 2014).

14 Kofi A. Annan, 'A Progress Report on UN Renewal', Speech to the UN Association–UK, London, 31 January 2006, *New World* (journal of UNA–UK), April–June 2006, 8.

15 For accounts of the role of international commissions in global governance, see Gareth Evans, 'Commission Diplomacy', in Andrew F. Cooper, Jorge Heine and Ramesh Thakur, eds., *The Oxford Handbook of Modern Diplomacy* (Oxford: Oxford University Press, 2013), 278–302, and Ramesh Thakur, 'High-level Panels', in Jacob Cogan, Ian Hurd and Ian Johnstone, eds., *The Oxford Handbook of International Organizations* (Oxford: Oxford University Press, 2016), 859–80.

16 High-level Panel on Threats, Challenges and Change, *A More Secure World: Our Shared Responsibility* (New York: United Nations document A/59/565, 2004), paragraph 201.

17 Kofi A. Annan, *In Larger Freedom: Towards Development, Security and Human Rights for All*. Report of the Secretary-General (New York: United Nations document A/59/2005, 21 March 2005), paragraphs 122–35.

18 See Samantha Power, *A Problem from Hell: America and the Age of Genocide* (New York: Basic Books, 2002).

19 Several chapters make this point in Acharya, ed., *Why Govern*.

20 Andrew Mack (director and editor-in-chief), *Human Security Report* (Oxford: Oxford University Press, 2005).

21 See Dan Kuwali and Frans Viljoen, eds., *Africa and the Responsibility to Protect: Article 4(h) of the African Union Constitutive Act* (London: Routledge, 2014).

22 This section draws on my own notes from the papers presented and ensuing discussions at that event.

23 Mohammed Ayoob, 'Humanitarian Intervention and International Society', *Global Governance* 7:3 (2001), 225.

24 Kofi A. Annan, *We the Peoples: The Role of the United Nations in the 21st Century* (New York: UN Department of Public Information, 2000), 48.

25 Alexei G. Arbatov, *The Transformation of Russian Military Doctrine: Lessons Learned from Kosovo and Chechnya* (Washington D.C.: The George C. Marshall Center Papers, No. 2, 20 July 2000), 'Executive Summary', v.

26 See Jim Mann, 'Quietly, U.S. and China Negotiate Arms Control', *International Herald Tribune*, 6 October 2000; and Michael R. Gordon, 'China Looks to Foil Missile Defense', *International Herald Tribune*, 30 April 2001.

27 Rebecca Johnson, 'NPT Report', *Disarmament Diplomacy* 37 (May 1999), 16.

28 Muchkund Dubey, 'The NATO Juggernaut: Logic of an Indian Defense Deterrent', *Times of India*, 8 April 1999. The sentiment was widely shared in India.

29 Hideaki Shinoda, 'The Politics of Legitimacy in International Relations: A Critical Examination of NATO's Intervention in Kosovo', *Alternatives* 25:4 (2000), 524.

30 See Ramesh Thakur, 'R2P after Libya and Syria: Engaging Emerging Powers', *Washington Quarterly* 36:2 (2013), 61–76.

31 See Ramesh Thakur, 'How Representative Are BRICS?' *Third World Quarterly* 35:10 (2014), 1791–1808.

32 Philippe Kirsch, John T. Holmes and Mora Johnson, 'International Tribunals and Courts', in David M. Malone, ed., *The UN Security Council: From the Cold War to the 21st Century* (Boulder: Lynne Rienner, 2004), 281.

33 Michael Scharf, 'Indicted for War Crimes, Then What?', *Washington Post*, 3 October 1999.

34 See especially Julie Flint and Alex de Waal, 'Case Closed: A Prosecutor Without Borders', *World Affairs* (Spring 2009), www.worldaffairsjournal.org/article/case-closed-prosecutor-without-borders.

35 Reuters, 'ANC Plans to Withdraw South Africa from International Criminal Court', *Guardian*, 11 October 2015, www.theguardian.com/world/2015/oct/11/anc-withdraw-south-africa-international-criminal-court.

36 Nita Bhalla, 'International Criminal Court says India Should Hand Over Sudan's Bashir', Reuters, 27 October 2015, http://af.reuters.com/article/topNews/idAFKCN0SL0ZW20151027?pageNumber=2&virtualBrandChannel=0&sp=true.

37 Human Rights Watch, 'India: Do Not Welcome Bashir', 19 October 2015, www.hrw.org/news/2015/10/19/india-do-not-welcome-bashir.
38 Express web desk, 'India-Africa Summit: Arrest Sudan President Omar al-Bashir, Demands Amnesty International', *Indian Express*, 26 October 2015, http://indianexpress.com/article/world/world-news/india-africa-summit-arrest-sudan-president-omar-al-bashir-demands-amnesty-international.
39 Richard Goldstone, Hina Jilani, Christine Chinkin and Desmond Travers, *Human Rights in Palestine and Other Occupied Arab Territories: Report of the United Nations Fact Finding Mission on the Gaza Conflict* (Geneva: United Nations Human Rights Council, A/HRC/12/48, 15 September 2009), www2.ohchr.org/english/bodies/hrcouncil/specialsession/9/docs/UNFFMGC_Report.pdf.
40 Helena Smith, 'Greeks Accuse Blair of War Crimes in Iraq', *Guardian* (London), 29 July 2003.
41 Noell Knox, 'Rumsfeld Warns Belgium about War-crimes Law', *USA Today*, 13 June 2003. Not for the first and probably not for the last time, US officials ignored the directly equivalent practice of US courts in subjecting foreign officials and officers to the jurisdiction of American courts. See Robert H. Bork, 'Judicial Imperialism', *Wall Street Journal Europe*, 18 June 2003.
42 Desmond Tutu, 'Why I Had No Choice but to Spurn Tony Blair', *The Observer* (London), 2 September 2012.
43 Danilo Zolo, *Victors' Justice: From Nuremberg to Baghdad*, tr. By M.M. Weir (London: Verso, originally published in Italian in 2006).
44 Richard K. Betts, 'The Delusion of Impartial Intervention', Chester A. Crocker and Fen Osler Hampson with Pamela Aall, eds., *Managing Global Chaos: Sources of and Responses to International Conflict* (Washington, DC: U.S. Institute of Peace, 1996), 333–41.
45 See the debates in UN Security Council, 66th session, 6528th meeting, S/PV.6528, Official Record, (New York: United Nations, 4 May 2011), 7–10. On BRICS, see Andrew F. Cooper and Ramesh Thakur, 'The BRICS in the New Global Economic Geography', in Thomas G. Weiss and Rorden Wilkinson, eds., *International Organizations and Global Governance* (London: Routledge, 2014), 265–78.
46 See Luke Glanville, 'Intervention in Libya: From Sovereign Consent to Regional Consent', *International Studies Perspectives* 14:3 (2013), 325–42.
47 Mohamed Sahnoun, 'Africa: Uphold Continent's Contribution to Human Rights, Urges Top Diplomat', *allAfrica.com*, 21 July 2009 (http://allafrica.com/stories/printable/200907210549.html). For another African perspective that also strongly supports R2P, see Samuel Atuobi, 'The Responsibility to Protect: The Time to Act is Now', *KAIPTC Policy Brief* No. 1 (Accra: Kofi Annan International Peacekeeping Training Centre, July 2009).
48 Amitav Acharya, 'R2P and a Theory of Norm Circulation', in Thakur and Maley, eds., *Theorising the Responsibility to Protect*, 65.
49 For an interesting confirmation of this in India, see Ashutosh Varshney, *Ethnic Conflict and Civic Life: Hindus and Muslims in India* (New Haven: Yale University Press, 2002).

12 Retrospect and prospect

International organisations are an integral part of contemporary world affairs, articulating norms; clarifying, developing and enforcing laws; and in myriad other ways establishing normative benchmarks for state conduct. This includes the circumstances in which – and the appropriate level thereof – a state may use force internally against its own citizens and internationally against other states. What happens then if some states want to use force internationally in order to protect victims of atrocities by a ruling regime within domestic jurisdictions? Like great powers, major international organisations too require organising principles for responding to critical challenges to peace and security. The innovative principle of R2P, first articulated by ICISS in 2001[1] and unanimously adopted by world leaders gathered at a UN summit in 2005,[2] is the organising principle for responding to mass atrocity crimes of genocide, crimes against humanity, war crimes and ethnic cleansing. By adopting R2P, the international community acknowledged that those who live in zones of safety have a duty of care towards those trapped in zones of danger.

In several previous chapters, I have highlighted distinctions between R2P as an analytic concept with a requirement for philosophical rigour and conceptual coherence, a normative enterprise seeking to entrench the principle as the new norm, and a political project operating in the messy and untidy real world of international politics. Gareth Evans, co-chair of ICISS and chair of the International Advisory Board of the Global Centre for the Responsibility to Protect, delivered a major stocktaking public lecture in Vancouver on 22 March 2017. Present in the audience and taking part in the private discussions over the next two days were most of the cast from the formation and workings of ICISS in 2000–01 and many of the key individuals involved in its development and promotion since 2005. In a characteristically elegant address, Evans outlined a useful framework for evaluating R2P and assessing its future potential and trajectory.[3]

Looking back

Looking back at achievements, Evans discussed the accomplishments, limitations and failures of R2P on four dimensions: as a normative force, with the UN system as the most authoritative voice of global norms continuing to cite R2P; as an institutional catalyst, for example with the appointment of national focal points; and as a framework for conflict prevention (for example in Kenya and Gambia). But its record is least satisfactory as a framework for effective reaction, with Syria being the most glaring but not the only example of its deficiencies and shortcomings.

Normative impact

Norms are understood differently by scholars of international law and international relations. Legal norms impose binding legal obligations. Political norms create moral obligations. But the latter can still be encased in a wider legal context and have legal effects. In regulating state conduct, both laws and norms serve enabling (licence) and restraining (leash) functions. The history of human rights movements (suffrage, anti-slavery, anti-apartheid) shows that while the social movements are motivated to enact moral norms into law, the moral authority of the norms by themselves exert a powerful 'compliance pull'.[4] In general, legal norms are more effective in regulating state behaviour. But in specific instances, a particular law may be breached while a political norm shapes a decision – on an act of commission or omission – through a calculation of reputational costs.

On mass atrocity crimes specifically, the 1948 Genocide Convention imposes legal obligations on states to act. By contrast, R2P is a global political norm that creates a moral responsibility but no legal duty on outside states to prevent and halt atrocities. However, even R2P has to be interpreted and applied in the broader context of binding obligations on states under national and international, humanitarian and human rights laws. For great powers in particular, R2P makes it more costly, on the one hand, to resort to self-interested unilateral interventions, including so-called 'humanitarian interventions' as the UK and US learnt in Iraq in 2003 and Russia discovered in South Ossetia in 2008. On the other hand, it also makes it more costly to resist disinterested UN-authorised calls to collective action to save strangers from mass atrocities. In 2011, for example, the power of the R2P norm overcame China's and Russia's instinctive opposition and they abstained rather than veto Security Council Resolution 1973 that authorised a human protection intervention in Libya. But the transformation of the NATO-led operation by stealth from civilian protection to regime change provoked a backlash that has allowed the two powers to veto successive efforts to manage the humanitarian crisis in Syria since 2011.

Thus, norms and laws are alternative mechanisms for regulating human and social behaviour. They do not just shape decisions; the language of norms and laws permits human beings to pursue goals, challenge assertions and justify actions.[5] For example, the Treaty of Versailles was widely perceived as unjust both by Germans and the allies, especially the British. The order established by the treaty therefore lacked legitimacy, which facilitated Hitler's challenge both to the Weimar Republic and the European order, on the one hand; and robbed people in the allied countries of conviction in defending the European order, on the other.

Norms are standards of appropriate behaviour; rules are specific applications of norms to particular situations, either prescribing or proscribing action to conform with the norm. Norms matter because people – politicians and officials as well as citizens – care about what others think of them. This is why approbation, and its logical corollary shaming, are so effective in regulating social behaviour. To be a member in good standing of a community is to subscribe to its moral framework and core values. And the behavioural prescription is not 'Do X in order to get Y' a la rules, but 'You should do X because good people do X' a la norms.

As norms become widely shared in any given in-group, they become embedded in the social institutions of that group. For a national group organised into a political entity, the resulting normative structure thereby influences the definition of state interests and so constrains the pursuit of short-term power or wealth maximisation. In constructivist theories, norms shape both the goals of states (the construction of state interests) and the means employed to achieve those goals. 'Shared ideas, expectations, and beliefs about appropriate behavior are what give the world structure, order, and stability'. Moreover, 'In an ideational international structure, idea shifts and norm shifts are the main vehicles for system transformation'.[6]

Collective norms constitute the social identity of actors while simultaneously constituting the rules of the game for regulating their social behaviour. The principle of sovereignty defines what a state is and underpins the entire system of states. The norm of non-intervention, a logical corollary of that principle, helps to regulate the interactions of states in international relations. Similarly, human rights norms increasingly constitute a 'civilised' state in contemporary international society, while regulating the matrix of citizen–state interaction. The human rights norm has also encroached increasingly on the non-intervention norm. Despite that, the definition of the state still entails a necessary reference to the notion of sovereignty.

As with laws, so with norms: violations in the particular do not invalidate the general. Specific transgressions of individual laws and norms can be compatible with the principle of a system of laws or norms. If an actor violates the norm of non-intervention, but insists that the action does not constitute non-intervention, or that there were extenuating pressures, then the actor is implicitly endorsing the validity of the norm in principle but rejecting its application or relevance in the specific instance. Alternatively, reaffirmations of an existing norm may suggest, by the very fact of their having to be proclaimed anew, that they are in the process or danger of being weakened.

Every year there are multiple references to R2P in Security Council resolutions, presidential statements and reports and statements by the Secretary-General covering conflict situations in multiple theatres. From 2006 to the end of July 2018, between them the Security Council, its presidents, the General Assembly and the Human Rights Council have referenced R2P a total of 144 times (Table 12.1). It is worth emphasising that 68 of the 75 Security Council

Table 12.1 R2P as a normative force: UN Security Council, General Assembly, Human Rights Council resolutions and presidential statements (as at 1 August 2018)

	Security Council resolutions	*Security Council presidential statements*	*General Assembly resolutions*	*Human Rights Council resolutions*	*Total*
2006	3	0	0	0	3
2007	0	0	0	0	0
2008	0	0	0	1	1
2009	1	0	1	0	2
2010	0	0	0	1	1
2011	6	2	0	3	11
2012	2	2	0	4	8
2013	7	4	1	4	16
2014	10	4	2	4	20
2015	14	4	3	2	23
2016	12	2	3	4	21
2017	12	2	2	7	23
31 July 2018	8	1	0	6	15
Total	75	21	12	36	144

Source: Global Centre for the Responsibility to Protect (www.globalr2p.org; www.globalr2p.org/media/files/unsc-resolutions-and-statements-with-r2p-table-as-of-31-july-2018-1.pdf; www.globalr2p.org/media/files/unga-resolutions-with-r2p-language-31-july-2018.pdf; www.globalr2p.org/media/files/hrc-resolutions-r2p-31-july-2018.pdf.).

resolutions referencing R2P until the end of July 2018 came after the NATO intervention in Libya in March 2011. As part of this trend, on 15 September 2017 the General Assembly voted (113–21) to include on its formal agenda, for the first time, a supplementary item on R2P and genocide prevention for the 72nd session starting in September 2019. This would offer the opportunity for a General Assembly resolution recognising and supporting R2P as an indispensable norm for protecting people from atrocity crimes.

Meanwhile the ninth General Assembly informal interactive dialogue on R2P was held on 6 September 2017.[7] It was addressed by 73 member states speaking on behalf of a total of 98 states, including a presentation from the Netherlands on behalf of the 50-strong Group of Friends of R2P. Five civil society organisations – the Asia Pacific Centre for R2P, the Auschwitz Institute for Peace and Reconciliation, the Canadian Centre for R2P, the Global Centre for R2P, and the International Coalition for RtoP – also delivered statements. The usual minority of Cuba, North Korea, Sudan, Syria and Venezuela criticised the principle, but the broad majority again showed strong conceptual agreement and reflected on the obstacles to consistent collective action to address the four R2P atrocity crimes. They reiterated their commitment to paragraphs 138 and 139 of the 2005 World Summit Outcome Document and underlined the importance of strengthening practical efforts for preventing the four crimes and protecting vulnerable populations.

In addition, dozens of civil society organisations, projects and programs, in every region of the world, are dedicated to the promotion and advocacy of R2P. There are hundreds of research projects, books and articles on it. Each year R2P is also tested and found wanting in real crises around the world. Regardless of whether it is a norm or not, there is general agreement that a normative shift has taken place from non-intervention, the dominant global norm in 1990 that shielded sovereign states from external intervention, to the Responsibility to Protect that seeks to qualify the norm of non-intervention in significant respects, albeit under narrow circumstances and tight procedural safeguards.

It seems incontestable therefore that R2P has continued to gain broad and wide acceptance as a principle or normative standard, both for individual states and for the international community. Today it is the normative instrument of choice for addressing atrocities inside sovereign borders. To those of us who remember the bitter divisiveness of 'humanitarian intervention' around the turn of the century, this is an astonishing advance in the primary purpose of ICISS, namely to identify a principle around which a normative consensus could be restored on the challenging question of when the use of force by outsiders to prevent and halt atrocities being committed inside sovereign borders can be both lawful and legitimate. There is a parallel debate, nonetheless, in both policy and academic circles on the precise status of R2P: does it have any legal force; should we describe it as a principle; has it attained the status of a global norm?

Consensus is most solid around Pillars One and Two of R2P, on the state's own responsibility to protect all peoples residing within its borders and on the international community's responsibility to provide all necessary assistance to build member states' capacity to discharge this responsibility. Disagreements creep in on the points at which Pillar Three become active and move across the continuum from consensual to increasingly coercive instruments in the international toolkit. That notwithstanding, from the point of view of the normative journey, the most remarkable feature is that serious dissent has almost totally subsided in the UN community about any element of the R2P principle as formulated in 2005. Taking into consideration the frequency with which R2P has been and continues to be referenced in General Assembly, Security Council and Human Rights Council resolutions and statements, Evans concludes that R2P has made the transition from an 'emerging' to a 'new' norm of state behaviour.[8] But it is not yet sufficiently embedded in international practice to constitute a new rule of customary international law.

Institutional impact

The roles that international institutions play include autonomous global actors, systemic modifiers of state behaviour and collective legitimators of national policy. Collective norms are inalienably embedded in the constitutive acts and constitutional clauses that establish the institutions and govern their policy and conduct. The adoption of a new norm like R2P, or a major reformulation of an existing one like sovereignty, will therefore have an impact on the bargaining outcomes reflected in institutional settings. For normative consolidation to translate into delivery of timely and effective protection in practice, institutional preparedness is necessary at the national, regional and global levels. In this, R2P has benefitted greatly from the increased sensitivity and attention to its sibling norm, POC. Several countries as well as regional organisations like the African Union and international organisations like the mandated UN entities and the World Bank have devoted much more systematic attention to the development of civilian response capability.

Abioudun Williams was head of the strategic planning unit in the executive office of Secretary-General Kofi Annan in 2005. He was actively engaged in the major reform effort ahead of and during the World Summit at the UN that fall. Responding to Evan's framework, Williams holds that:

> R2P has had an impact at the national, regional and global level as a normative standard and has served as an engine for the development of capacities to respond effectively to the threat or reality of mass atrocity crimes. The institutional reform initiatives undertaken by the Barack Obama administration aimed at improving the US government's capacity to prevent and respond to mass atrocities are emblematic of efforts at the national level. The Atrocities Prevention Board (APB) created in 2012 has provided a forum to examine crises through a mass atrocity lens, has elevated atrocity prevention in specific situations including in Libya in 2011 and northern Iraq in 2014, has enhanced overall early warning capability, and has improved interagency coordination.[9]

Between them, POC and R2P have been catalysts for institutional reconfiguration along four dimensions.

1 *National military forces* are rethinking force structures, doctrine, rules of engagement and training to be better prepared for responding to outbreaks of mass atrocity. As the original ICISS noted in Chapter seven of its report, R2P operations (us between perpetrators and victims of atrocities) fall somewhere between peacekeeping (us between former enemies) and full-scale war fighting (us against them). The evolution of peacekeeping doctrine and practice both by the UN and by the African Union has closely tracked the development of R2P policy.[10]
2 In September 2010, Ghana and Denmark launched a new initiative to create a global network of *national focal points*. As of July 2018, there were 60 such focal points from every region of the world.[11] The goal is to improve efforts within and among governments to prevent and halt mass atrocities with the designation of a senior official as the point person for promoting inter-agency R2P coordination within the country's bureaucracy and facilitating international cooperation through the Global Network of R2P focal points. The latter hold an annual meeting in different countries.
3 In some cases, the national focal points are buttressed by an *atrocity prevention board*, of which the most prominent has been the one set up by US President Obama, but whose existence and functioning is also under a cloud because his successor seems often to be motivated by a visceral hostility to any Obama initiative or legacy.
4 At *UN headquarters* itself, Secretary-General Ban Ki-moon helped to institutionalise R2P by elevating the rank of the Special Adviser on Genocide Prevention to Under-Secretary-General, appointing an additional Special Adviser on R2P specifically at the rank of Assistant Secretary-General, and co-locating both advisers in a joint office. However, the R2P adviser has remained an unpaid post and therefore lacking in real clout internally in the UN system; the joint office is seriously under-resourced; and there is scope for the two advisory positions to be rationalised, coordinated and strengthened.

Prevention

There is general agreement among policymakers and analysts alike that prevention before the outbreak of mass atrocities is more important than intervention after the fact. In addition, our understanding of the toolbox of preventive measures available at the different stages of the crisis and conflict cycle has also grown substantially. But the politics of investing more resources into the conflict prevention toolbox remains as challenging as ever: an armed conflict erupting today with accompanying civilian casualties will always command priority attention and resources over a potential conflict with mass atrocities tomorrow in an indeterminate location. A second problem is that successful conflict prevention stays behind the headlines and resources are always easier to garner for publicly demonstrable than behind-the-scenes successes: fire-fighting always makes for more spectacular media coverage than fire prevention.

Nevertheless, R2P-informed strategies and efforts have had their share of successes and need wider acknowledgement than they have received. Previous chapters have referred to Kofi Annan's R2P-driven efforts in Kenya after 2008. Evans also identified the cases of Sierra Leone after 2002, Liberia after 2003, Guinea and Kyrgyzstan after 2010, and Cote d'Ivoire after 2011. In addition, it could be argued that the R2P lens has also helped to contain the Burundi conflict from degenerating into a mass conflagration. Finally, UN peacekeeping operations now typically include POC and/or R2P mandates, not the least because all actors (the Security Council, the Secretary-General, the Special Representative of the Secretary-General who serves as the head of the peacekeeping mission, and the Force Commander) recognise that the failure to protect civilians within their area of operations will leave an indelible stain on all their reputations. Saying such protection was outside their mandate is no longer an acceptable alibi, in itself an indication of how far we have come since the gory days of the Rwanda genocide in 1994 and the Srebrenica massacre in 1995.

Probably the most crucial institutional need for the future is to create a culture of effective support for the ICC and the evolving machinery of international criminal justice, which machinery is designed to enable not only trial and punishment for some of the worst mass atrocity crimes of the past, but in doing so to provide an important new deterrent for the future. It is deeply regrettable that the ICC has come under so much recent fire from African states, including South Africa, although the threatened exodus of a number of them from accepting the Court's jurisdiction has not yet happened. Implementation of the ICC's mandate may not always have been perfect, but it is trying hard to fill what has far too long been a major institutional vacuum, and its processes should be respected.

Responding to atrocities

A norm can be defined ethically, to mean a pattern of behaviour that should be followed in accordance with a given value system; that is, to refer to the moral code of a society: *a generally accepted standard of proper behaviour*. Or it can be defined statistically to mean the pattern of behaviour that is most common or usual; that is, to refer to the 'normal curve': *a widely prevalent pattern of behaviour*. R2P has been accepted as a global norm on the ethical meaning but is yet to make the transition to becoming the empirical norm.

When it comes to translating R2P from an organising principle of the international community into national policy to take effective collective action, the policy of any country can range from affirming it but only for the affected national governments; accepting the second pillar responsibility of providing assistance to build institutional capacity and resilience of countries under stress; and/or accepting the collective responsibility to act decisively and in time under the third pillar of coercive measures, including military force as the last resort.

For example, the policy of most Asian governments, including China as a one of the five permanent members (P5) of the UN Security Council, is to endorse the first and second but not the third.

For most developing countries, the dominant policy is to support pillars one and two of R2P but for some Western powers, the default policy setting has already shifted to include pillar three military action as a discretionary (because of mixed motives) rather than mandatory option. That shared policy framework provided the rationale for convening a workshop 'of like-minded, politically influential, and operationally capable allies to develop and implement cooperative strategies' for mass atrocity prevention. Participants at the October 2014 conference examined 'existing policies, institutional capacities ... and shared interests related to' R2P and atrocity prevention in order 'to propose additional steps for supporting common security objectives'.[12] That is, to develop mutually reinforcing capacity to pursue the shared policy goal of giving effect to the norm of civilian protection.

That said, recent experience shows that often, the Western powers' penchant for regime change has proven to be a major impediment to investing in political dialogue between the local conflict parties as the primary tool of conflict resolution. In turn, this feeds the intransigence of rebel groups despite signs of flexibility from the regime in power that is under considerable domestic stress and international pressure. For countries like China and India, and indeed the BRICS generally, the policy is both to prioritise a political process over regime change by military means, and to respect and defend the principle of state sovereignty and the norm of non-intervention, albeit not absolutely (cf. India's intervention in East Pakistan in 1971, Russia's annexation of Crimea).

For most Western powers, the era of Westphalian sovereignty coincided with a history of interventions in contiguous, proximate and distant states. The most egregious example was colonisation, justified, in an analogue to slavery, by denying independent legal status to the conquered territories. But throughout this period even the Western powers did not challenge the norm per se of non-intervention. While affirming its continuing validity as the key organising principle of inter-state relations, all intervening powers justified their departures from the norm as an exceptional act due to special compelling circumstances (or, in the case of India in 1971, resting the legal defence in the language of self-defence against 'demographic aggression' in the form of ten million refugees).

In the NATO intervention in Kosovo 1999, by contrast, the North Atlantic powers challenged the validity and relevance of the norm of non-intervention itself and sough to replace it with the self-proclaimed emerging new norm of 'humanitarian intervention'. But the formerly colonised developing countries constituted the majority in the UN General Assembly and in that forum, as well as in others like the G77 and the Non-Aligned Movement, they emphatically rejected the self-interested claim of any so-called right of 'humanitarian intervention'. To the extent that the United Nations is the forum where raw power and collective values meet and are intermediated, Annan responded to the tension by issuing his famous 'challenge of humanitarian intervention' in 1999 and R2P was offered as the answer to that challenge.

R2P was from the start intended to be about deeds, not words; action, not verbiage. But this is the criterion on which it has fallen most short. That said, it is equally important to acknowledge that when R2P was first formulated, the weight of criticism directed at it was that it would legitimise great power interventions against the interests and preferences of the weaker majority of states, that it was merely the old wine of humanitarian intervention attractively repackaged in the new bottle of R2P, that it would militarise humanitarian crises, and so on. In other words, that it was a licence to intervene by the militarily powerful countries of the world. Those who criticised R2P from the opposite flank, that it had set the bar for intervention so high that it would fail to deliver on the core promise of human protection, were few and far between.

Yet in practice the leash function of R2P has been far more effective in restraining self-interested great power interventions dressed up in the language of humanitarian protection principles, than the licence function facilitating such interventions. That is, by the benchmark of expectations both of ICISS commissioners and of the international community, the empirical record shows there have been too few rather than too many interventions: 'on the critical challenge of stopping mass atrocity crimes that are under way, whether through diplomatic persuasion, stronger measures like sanctions or criminal prosecutions, or through military intervention, ... R2P's record has been mixed, at best'.[13]

Annan's successful R2P-framed mediation in Kenya in 2008 was followed by the successful R2P-based and UN-authorised interventions in Côte d'Ivoire and Libya in 2011. But as well as world opinion souring on the Libya intervention, other notable failures of R2P to be invoked in the global discourse include the brutal end of the Tamil Tiger insurgency in Sri Lanka in 2009; the unabated crises in Darfur, Sudan and South Sudan; the limitations of R2P in combating horrific atrocities by non-state actors like Boko Haram and Islamic State; and of course, Syria. As noted in the introduction to Part II, there are five sets of explanations altogether to explain the lack of effective action in Syria. In retrospect, the window of opportunity that existed for international intervention in Syria was in mid-2011 when the resort to mass violence was one-sided by the Assad regime. Fearing another slippery slope in Syria after Libya, a majority of Security Council members balked at a resolution to condemn the violence against unarmed civilians, the regime grasped its impunity, the situation deteriorated into a full-scale civil war, the rebellion was soon captured by extremists no less bloodthirsty than the regime and the moment for effective international intervention with a favourable balance of consequences passed.

Looking ahead

Thus, R2P has been mainstreamed in international diplomatic discourse, serves as a lens through which to evaluate events and frame responses and has sharpened calls to implement existing obligations and policies. But it is still some distance away from being a reliable catalyst for robust international action to save strangers in peril. For ICISS, the dual hope and expectation was that first, R2P would enhance the prospect of protective action by the Council without in any way guaranteeing such an outcome; and it would reduce but not eliminate the element of inconsistency in decision-making. The existence of R2P has become a factor in the construction of state interests and identities and conditions the politics of interaction in the Security Council. It has heightened awareness of the reality that the collective responsibility of the international community to protect populations at risk of serious harm means that identifiable actors have moral agency[14] and will be judged accordingly.

Earlier chapters have noted that while R2P and the sibling norms protection of civilians and international criminal justice represent important normative innovations, significant gaps remain in the normative architecture of world order for civilian protection. The normative advances came about because of growing unhappiness and frustrations at the inadequacies in the existing set of norms that prevented effective outside assistance to victims of atrocities inside state borders. The international community was determined to reposition the UN system to be empowered and capacitated to respond better on both the timeliness and effectiveness dimensions when confronted by repeat occurrences of humanitarian atrocities. Despite these valuable additions to the repertoire of the international community in dealing with atrocities perpetrated on civilians, there remain many gaps in the protection agenda's normative architecture.

Thus, R2P does not resolve all the dilemmas of how outsiders can provide timely, decisive and effective assistance to all groups in need of protection. It may be deep but remains so narrow that many areas beyond the four atrocity crimes fall outside its scope. It is subject to Security Council veto and paralysis and the French-origin initiative to agree on a code of conduct to abjure the veto in cases of humanitarian atrocities has not made much headway so far.[15] Explanations for the shortfall include unrealistic expectations raised by R2P, political limitations inherent in the R2P framework, moral dilemmas emerging from military action and tactical challenges operationally. In some cases, inaction reflected heightened scepticism about interventionism after the 2003 Iraq war and the 2011 Libya intervention. Many countries remain suspicious about strategic interests motivating Western interventions. But the most common explanation for the failure to take effective human protection action is the inability to satisfy the balance of consequences test, particularly against the logistical and other practical difficulties of using force in local conflict theatres and the likely damaging consequences for humanitarian relief operations and the fragile peace process. Often, disappointing results reflect the failure to utilise other measures in the prevention and response toolbox rather than a failure to use coercive force.

In sum, then, acceptance of the responsibility to protect norm no more guarantees 'humanitarian intervention' than its non-existence had foreclosed it as a tool of individual and collective statecraft. But, by shaping the calculation of the 'balance of interests', the norm makes it modestly more rather than less likely that victims will not be callously abandoned. The failure to guarantee reliable

UN protection of at-risk victims of atrocities ensures a continuing interest in unilateral humanitarian intervention. Many people and countries will continue to be attracted to humanitarian intervention as an alternative moral framework for responding to atrocities effectively and in time. But every such effort will provoke bitter global controversy immediately and also cause long-term damage to the principle of a global order governed by rule of law.

R2P is not a principle or norm looking for crisis that would validate its relevance. Instead it is the outgrowth of an attempt to find a broadly acceptable solution to a problem that is distressing but relatively infrequent, namely mass humanitarian atrocities. Under contemporary conditions of real time information and international standards of state conduct, mass atrocities are morally and politically unacceptable for a growing number of people and countries. True, R2P remains conceptually contested among scholars. In a useful essay, Noële Crossley disaggregates the critical scholarship into post-colonial, feminist, pacifist and pluralist camps but also notes a softening of the critiques over time.[16]

In any case R2P is no longer contested among policymakers at the level of principle. For them the controversies arise in relation to the manner of R2P implementation, not its status as a principle. The world of policymakers is typically untidy, messy and full of internal inconsistencies. Not for them the insistence on conceptual purity and analytical consistency demanded by scholars. Instead they are constantly compelled to weigh some interests against others, some values against others, and some interests against values. That is, the guiding motto for countries is not 'the national interest' but 'a balance of interests'.[17] Far from being a fatal flaw, therefore, policy inconsistency is the norm and it is most acutely manifested in the policies of the five permanent members of the UN Security Council. That said, it remains true that the most urgent task for R2P advocates is to rebuild consensus in the Security Council to take protective action no matter how challenging the circumstances.

Much attention has focussed on US President Donald Trump's retreat from the US-created and policed liberal international order after 1945, including the United Nations as the core of the rules-based global multilateral order. His 'America First' instincts are a far cry from the Obama administration's creation of the Atrocities Prevention Board. Meanwhile the sweeping expansion of China's comprehensive national power has seen an exponential increase in its weight in the global economy, in Asian and global power balances, and in regional and global governance institutions. In his address to the quinquennial party congress, President Xi Jinping affirmed that 'No country can retreat to their own island, we live in a shared world and face a shared destiny'.[18] China recognises that it has been a major beneficiary of the existing international order and it has proven to be a fast learner in operating as a responsible power within that order.[19]

China's primary goal therefore will not be to perturb the order, but to gain greater influence in writing the rules and running the institutions to develop and police the world order. Oliver Stuenkel argues that China has pursued the creation of parallel rather than alternative institutions.[20] Over 20 China-sponsored economic and political institutions underwrite infrastructure investment, trade, financial exchanges and security dialogues according to rules that are very similar to those of existing institutions and their members continue to participate in the older institutions as well. That said, as China's self-confidence grows, it is becoming emboldened in rejecting inconvenient global rules and norms, not unlike numerous precedents set by the US. Of all the actors, China and the US are likely to have the biggest role in shaping the form and determining the fate of R2P in the foreseeable future.

There is also an important role to be played by other emerging powers, as argued in Chapter 7. Yet, for all its vibrant democratic ethos and global aspirations, India remains a 'hesitant' rule-shaper.[21] Sandra Destradi conceptualises 'reluctance' as encompassing both 'hesitation' rooted in shared antipathy to the problem at hand but ambivalence about the strategy on offer to deal with it; and recalcitrance leading to the lack of responsiveness to the problem.[22] In other words, the emerging powers' reluctance reflects the normative tension between their abhorrence of atrocity crimes and the desire to protect civilians, on the one hand, and commitment to the long cherished norms of sovereignty and non-intervention.

As emphasised in several previous chapters, R2P is not a Western attempt to interfere in other people's problems. Rather, it is a global attempt to deal with a Western problem at the heart of the Westphalian system, namely how the community of states can deal with the universal vice of mass atrocities. Nevertheless, efforts are being made within the global South and among other emerging powers also to try and find ways to move forward on how best to prevent and halt atrocities. Of course, it could be argued that the southern democracies have a particular role to play.[23] But of the three democracies in BRICS, only Brazil, which has its own tradition of normative activism,[24] has offered a constructive paper on 'Responsibility while Protecting' (RwP).[25] In many ways this picked up on the precautionary principles in the original ICISS report in 2001 that was reformulated as the legitimacy criteria by the High-Level Panel in 2004. It proposed that an agreed set of criteria or principles should guide Security Council deliberations before any authorisation of an R2P military intervention; and that a monitoring or review mechanism should be created in order to maintain the Security Council's oversight role over the operation during implementation.[26] The first requirement would help to achieve a broad consensus and the second would help to sustain that consensus.

Secretary-General Ban acknowledged that the Brazilian initiative would help to ensure that R2P implementation was 'consistent with the purposes, principles and provisions of the Charter and with the intent of the Heads of State and Government expressed at the 2005 World Summit'.[27] Similarly, as noted in Chapter 7, the Chinese and Russian foreign ministries and foreign policy analysts have also been grappling with the reality of R2P and how the new global principle might be refined to accommodate their interests and values.

India's Permanent Representative on the Council during the tumultuous years of 2011–2012, Hardeep Singh Puri, does not believe that the Libyan experience is sufficient justification for the world to walk away from R2P:

> The international community needs to act if a mass atrocity seems likely to take place. In my view, if the concept of R2P is to survive and form the basis of action by the Security Council, it must be anchored in the concept of RwP [Responsibility while Protecting].[28]

Conclusion

In sum, R2P is part of the current international diplomatic mainstream. It is the international community's default lens to evaluate humanitarian crises, demand the implementation of existing obligations by states and frame global responses and policies. Taking everything into consideration, the assessment by Gareth Evans seems the most balanced that despite the setbacks, disappointments and failures, R2P's overall impact has been largely positive.[29] Following Evans, I have measured the R2P record of accomplishments and shortfalls against four benchmarks: as a normative force, a catalyst for institutional change, a framework for preventive action to avert humanitarian atrocities, and a framework for effective reactive action to halt atrocities already being committed.

On the one hand, interventions were common before 2001 when R2P was introduced. On the other hand, interventions are subject to too many variables to offer certainty to victims even since R2P's unanimous adoption in 2005. Indeed, the Iraq war in 2003 confirmed that the real choice is not if intervention, but whether the intervention will be ad hoc or rules based, unilateral or multilateral, and divisive or consensual. R2P has been accepted as the central organising principle for the international community to respond to humanitarian atrocities being committed inside sovereign jurisdictions. Controversies notwithstanding, R2P has an assured future because it was essentially demand driven in origin, not supply driven and, unhappily, the demand for it is unlikely to disappear anytime soon. As noted in Chapter 5, the tyrants who rule by terror are not the monopoly of any particular civilisation, race, religion or gender. Rather, a tyrant is an equal opportunity offender and that is why mass atrocities need a universal norm to prohibit and end them.

As long as the international order rests on sovereign states as its basic unit, some thug-rulers will exhibit the worst of human nature and commit atrocities and the international community will struggle to respond in time and effectively. Other states and peoples will want to respond based on their better angels to help innocent victims. By its very nature, including unpredictability, unintended-cum-perverse consequences and the risk to innocent civilians caught in the crossfire, warfare is inherently brutal: there is nothing humanitarian about the means. The risks of perverse consequences are only too real. The use of military force must always – *always* – be the option of *last resort* (conceptually, not sequentially), not the tool of choice for dealing with threatened or occurring atrocities. Equally, however, it *must* be the option of last resort; it cannot be taken off the table. R2P, especially when backed by legitimacy criteria that have been agreed in advance, will help to shift the balance towards interventions that are rules based, multilateral and consensual. This is critical to ensure that the international community is normatively, organisationally and operationally prepared to tackle humanitarian atrocities wherever and whenever they occur.

However, being better prepared in advance is still no guarantee of good outcomes being achieved in any particular crisis. Success can never be guaranteed by *any* principle or formula for international interventions and R2P is no more self-guaranteeing than any other type of external intervention. Good intentions are not a magical formula by which to shape good outcomes in foreign lands. But the chances of success can be enhanced and the controversy surrounding interventions can be muted if they are based on an agreed normative framework with regard to triggering threshold, authorising agent and implementation guidelines. One way or other, R2P speaks to these concerns and needs. Inevitably it will be adjusted and recalibrated in line with evolving circumstances and priorities, but it is not likely to be discarded anytime soon.

Notes

1 International Commission on Intervention and State Sovereignty, *The Responsibility to Protect* (Ottawa: International Development Research Centre, 2001).
2 *2005 World Summit Outcome*, resolution adopted by the UN General Assembly A/RES/60/1 (New York: United Nations, 24 October 2005), paragraphs 138–40.
3 Gareth Evans, 'Taking Stock of The Responsibility to Protect: Achievements and Challenges'. Public Lecture under the auspices of the Simons Foundation of Canada, Vancouver, 22 March 2017. The text of the lecture and the report of the meeting can be accessed at: www.thesimonsfoundation.ca/projects/responsibility-protect-re-energizing-key-players: 67–73.
4 Thomas M. Franck, *The Power of Legitimacy Among Nations* (Oxford: Oxford University Press, 1990).
5 Friedrich V. Kratochwil, *Rules, Norms, and Decisions: On the Conditions of Practical and Legal Reasoning in International Relations and Domestic Affairs* (Cambridge: Cambridge University Press, 1989), 10–11.
6 Martha Finnemore and Kathryn Sikkink, 'International Norm Dynamics and Political Change', *International Organization* 52:4 (1998), 894.
7 Global Centre for R2P, 'Summary of the Informal Interactive Dialogue of the UN General Assembly on the Responsibility to Protect, 6 September 2017', (October 2017), www.globalr2p.org/publications/568.
8 Evans, 'Taking Stock of The Responsibility to Protect', 69.
9 Abioudun Williams, 'The Responsibility to Protect and Institutional Change', *Global Governance* 23:4 (2017), 540.
10 See Kwesi Aning and Frank Okyere, 'The African Union', in Alex J. Bellamy and Tim Dunne, eds., *The Oxford Handbook of the Responsibility to Protect* (Oxford: Oxford University Press, 2016), 355–72.
11 Global Centre for the Responsibility to Protect, 'Global Network of R2P Focal Points', www.globalr2p.org/our_work/global_network_of_r2p_focal_points.
12 Stanley Foundation, 'Advancing Transatlantic Linkages on Responsibility to Protect and Mass Atrocity Prevention', *Policy Dialogue Brief* (Muscatine, IA: Stanley Foundation, November 2014), 1, www.stanleyfoundation.org/publications/pdb/R2PSPC2014PDB1114.pdf.
13 Evans, 'Taking Stock of The Responsibility to Protect', 71.
14 See Toni Erskine, 'Moral Agents of Protection and Supplementary Responsibilities to Protect', in Bellamy and Dunne, eds., *The Oxford Handbook of the Responsibility to Protect*, 167–85.

15 See Jean-Baptiste Jeangène Vilmer, 'The Responsibility Not to Veto: A Genealogy', *Global Governance* 24:3 (2018), 331–49.
16 Noële Crossley, 'Is R2P Still Controversial? Continuity and Change in the Debate on "Humanitarian Intervention"', *Cambridge Review of International Affairs* (forthcoming).
17 Ramesh Thakur, 'A Balance of Interests', in Andrew F. Cooper, Jorge Heine and Ramesh Thakur, eds., *The Oxford Handbook of Modern Diplomacy* (Oxford: Oxford University Press, 2013), 70–87.
18 Benjamin Haas, 'Xi Jinping Speech: Five Things You Need to Know', *Guardian*, 18 October 2017, www.theguardian.com/world/2017/oct/18/xi-jinping-speech-five-things-you-need-to-know.
19 Gregory Chin and Ramesh Thakur, 'Will China Change the Rules of Global Order?', *The Washington Quarterly* 33:4 (2010), 119–38.
20 Oliver Stuenkel, *Post-Western World: How Emerging Powers Are Remaking Global Order* (Cambridge: Polity, 2016).
21 Waheguru Pal Singh Sidhu, Pratap Bhanu Mehta and Bruce Jones, eds., *Shaping the Emerging World: India and the Multilateral Order* (Washington, DC: Brookings Institution Press, 2013).
22 Sandra Destradi, 'Reluctance in International Politics: A Conceptualization', *European Journal of International Relations* 23:2 (2017), 315–40.
23 See Daniel Peters and Dan Krause, eds., *Southern Democracies and the Responsibility to Protect* (Baden-Baden: Nomos, 2017).
24 See especially Philip Cunliffe and Kai Michael Kenkel, eds., *Brazil as a Rising Power: Intervention Norms and the Contestation of Global Order* (London: Routledge, 2016).
25 Permanent Mission of Brazil to the United Nations, 'Responsibility while Protecting: Elements for the Development and Promotion of a Concept' (New York: United Nations, document A/66/551, S/2011/701, 11 November 2011).
26 See Oliver Stuenkel, 'Responsibility While Protecting', in Bellamy and Dunne, eds., *The Oxford Handbook of the Responsibility to Protect*, 620–37.
27 Ban Ki-moon, *Responsibility to Protect: Timely and Decisive Response* (New York: United Nations, document A/66/874-S/2012/578, 25 July 2012), 13–15.
28 Hardeep Singh Puri, *Perilous Interventions: The Security Council and the Politics of Chaos* (Noida: HarperCollins India, 2016), 208.
29 Evans, 'Taking Stock of The Responsibility to Protect'.

Index